The Practice of Ethics

For Eva, who has been so much a part of my life

The Practice of Ethics

Hugh LaFollette

Blackwell
Publishing

© 2007 by Hugh LaFollette

BLACKWELL PUBLISHING
350 Main Street, Malden, MA 02148-5020, USA
9600 Garsington Road, Oxford OX4 2DQ, UK
550 Swanston Street, Carlton, Victoria 3053, Australia

First published 2007 by Blackwell Publishing Ltd

1   2007

Library of Congress Cataloging-in-Publication Data

LaFollette, Hugh, 1948–
    The practice of ethics / Hugh LaFollette.
        p.   cm.
    Includes bibliographical references and index.

    ISBN-13: 978-0-631-21945-3

    1. Applied ethics.   2. Ethical problems.   I. Title.
BJ1031.L34 2007
170—dc22

                                2006007480

A catalogue record for this title is available from the British Library.

Set in 11.5 on 13.5 pt Perpetua
by SNP Best-set Typesetter Ltd, Hong Kong

For further information on
Blackwell Publishing, visit our website:
www.blackwellpublishing.com

Contents

Acknowledgments

I would like to thank those people who made comments on one or more chapters of the book: David Archard, Charles Mills, Brook Sadler, Todd Lekan, David Copp, John Hardwig, Michael Pritchard, Hillel Steiner, Antony Duff, Nicholas Dixon, Lester H. Hunt, Michael Menlowe, James Spence, Paul Tudico, Christopher Hookway, Joel Feinberg, Robert Evans, Ray Frey, and Thomas W. Pogge.

Special thanks are due to Kit Wellman for his careful reading and astute comments on the entire manuscript. He saved me from many an error. Unfortunately for me, I probably took less of his advice than I should have.

Finally, thanks to my wife, Eva, to whom this book is dedicated, who has served as companion, friend, copy-editor, and philosophical conversationalist.

Text Credits

Some sections of the following chapters appeared in, or were inspired by, my previous essays and book sections. I thank the various publishers for permission to reproduce copyright material and to borrow from the ideas.

Chapter 2: "A Tale of Two Theories," from "Theorizing about Ethics," in H. LaFollette (ed.), *Ethics in Practice*, 3rd edn. (Oxford: Blackwell, 2007).

Chapter 4: "Relativism," from "The Truth in Ethical Relativism," in *Journal of Social Philosophy*, 20 (1991): 146–54.

Chapter 5: "Racism," from "Pragmatic Ethics," pp. 400–19, in H. LaFollette (ed.), *The Blackwell Guide to Ethical Theory* (Oxford: Blackwell, 2000).

Chapter 9: "Slippery Slope Arguments," from "Living on a Slippery Slope," in *The Journal of Ethics* (2005): 475–99.

Chapter 10: "Autonomy, Children, and Paternalism," from "Two Forms of Paternalism," pp. 188–94, in A. Peczenik and M. Karlsson (eds.), *Law, Justice, Rights, and the State* (Stuttgart: Franz Steiner Verlag, 1995); and "Circumscribed Autonomy:

Children, Care, and Custody," pp. 212–37, in J. Bartkowiak and U. Narayan (eds.), *Having and Raising Children* (State College, PA: Penn State University Press, 1999).

Chapter 12: "Gun Control," from "Gun Control," in *Ethics* 110(2) (2000): 263–81; and "Controlling Guns," in *Criminal Justice Ethics* 20(1) (2001): 34–9.

Chapter 15: "Animals," from "Animal Rights and Human Wrongs," pp. 79–90, in N. Dower (ed.), *Ethics and the Environment* (Edinburgh: Gower Press, 1989); and (with N. Shanks), *Brute Science: Dilemmas of Animal Experimentation* (New York: Routledge, 1996).

Chapter 16: "World Hunger," from "World Hunger," pp. 283–53, in R. Frey and C. H. Wellman (eds.), *A Companion to Applied Ethics* (Oxford: Blackwell, 2002).

Chapter 18: "Egoism: Psychological and Moral," from "The Truth in Psychological Egoism," in J. Feinberg (ed.), *Reason and Responsibility: Readings in Some Basic Problems of Philosophy*, 4th edn. (Belmont, CA: Wadsworth, 1988).

Every effort has been made to trace copyright holders and to obtain their permission for the use of copyright material. The publisher apologizes for any errors or omissions in the above list and would be grateful if notified of any corrections that should be incorporated in future reprints or editions of this book.

Introduction

Practice is primary in medicine. Medicine's ultimate aim is not to intellectually understand the body and its workings, but to improve people's health. Medicine that only increased understanding would not be medicine. Of course medicine cannot promote human health by focusing narrowly on diagnosis and cure. It can achieve its ends only by becoming an integrated practice informed by clinical and epidemiological evidence, structured by the theoretical insights of biology, chemistry, physics, and the theory of evolution (Nesse and Williams 1994).

Practice is also primary in ethics. The ultimate aim of ethics is not to enhance ethical understanding but to improve how people live. Ethics that only heightened understanding, without generally helping people live morally better lives, would not be ethics. However, ethics cannot help us live better lives by focusing narrowly on individual moral behavior or decisions. It can achieve its aims only by becoming an integrated practice informed by relevant insights from history, psychology, sociology, and biology, and structured by normative theorizing and meta-theoretical reflection.

The overarching aim of this book is to defend this claim: to argue – and, most especially, to show – that in this respect, ethics is akin to medicine – and indeed, most forms of human inquiry. The best overall moral practice is one in which normative questions arise from our attempts to wrestle with concrete moral issues; in which meta-ethical questions emerge from our attempts to grapple constructively with both practical issues and normative theories; and in which careful reflection on each inquiry illuminates, and is illuminated by, the other two.

Although many philosophers practice ethics as if practical, normative, and meta-theoretical issues are wholly distinct, the idea that these elements are intertwined is far from new. Its roots trace back to the ancient Greeks; its current incarnation was made popular by John Rawls (Rawls 1999/1971: 19–21, 46–51). Many contemporary philosophers have extolled this approach, yet few have explicitly used the methodology, no doubt in part because it is such a monumental task. There are a few exceptions, but most of these focus on a subset of ethical issues, most especially, issues in biomedical ethics (Buchanan et al. 2002; Daniels 1996). I want to employ this methodology more broadly.

Although this methodology is, in one sense, quite ordinary, we often do not notice the constant interplay between theory and practice. So let me offer a non-moral example to illustrate it. Suppose an ordinary citizen wants to know why George W. Bush led the United States into invading Iraq. How might she decide? One thing is clear: No theoretical consideration or single piece of evidence will ground an adequate answer. It won't do to say that: "We can answer that question if we know Bush's stated reasons. If he says he invaded Iraq to protect us from terrorism, then that is why he did it." Doubtless his claims are one bit of evidence – but not suffi-cient. After all, people may lie about their motives (sometimes for good reasons); they may misdescribe their motives; or they may not know why they do what they do. We can exclude these options only if we have important background knowledge which informs our interpretation of his self-reports.

It will also not do to say: "He invaded Iraq to secure our supply of oil; after all, he is a former oilman." Perhaps this is an option we should consider. But it is far from decisive. Not everyone (and perhaps not most people) would lead a country into war simply for financial gain. To evaluate this claim we also need more background knowl-edge that informs our interpretation of his actions.

Answers that depend upon a single piece of evidence will always be inadequate. Few actions are done for a single motive. Moreover, our interpretations of another's motives always rest upon more general claims about (a) the normal motivations of the person in question, as well as (b) more general claims about what motivates most people in power. For instance, those who think money usually distorts people's judg-ments will be more inclined to think that the quest for oil was an important (even if not exclusive) motive, and those who think that presidents (or self-proclaimed Christians) are trustworthy will be more inclined to believe Bush's self-report. These more general beliefs themselves rest upon any number of factors, including our knowledge of history (what have presidents done in the past?), other beliefs about human motivation (are most people selfish?) and human knowledge (how do we know if people are trustworthy, and so on?). And, to complete the circle, these more general beliefs rest, at least in part, on our particular experiences, including our interactions with others.

These judgments are especially difficult since most of our evidence is mediated by journalists, historians, etc. Therefore our judgments will be shaped by our beliefs that some newspaper or journalist is informed, careful, and trustworthy. And how do we decide if they are informed . . . or careful . . . or trustworthy?

What this shows is that even when thinking about something relatively simple – deciding someone's motivation – our beliefs are never driven simply by what we immediately see or experience, nor are they ever driven simply by theoretical con-siderations. Rather they are the product of an intricate interplay between immedi-ate experience (what we see or hear), some middle-level or second-order beliefs about how to interpret those particular experiences, and some higher-level beliefs about how we make any decision. Reasonable beliefs always emerge from the interplay of practice and theory, between experience and theorizing about that experience.

There is nothing special about ethics in this regard. All inquiry proceeds in the same way. Biology is not just a list of observed "biological facts," nor is it simply a recitation of going biological theories. Biology strives to provide a coherent account of living organisms, which is built from observations, our current best theoretical attempts to explain and interpret the phenomena, and some higher-order reflection (e.g., the philosophy of science) about the nature of science and scientific inquiry.

Ethics should proceed in the same way. As a practice it is a marriage of practice and theory. My particular strategy is to begin as each of us might begin to think about morality: by making initial, and clearly incomplete, attempts to deal with several practical issues, and then seeing how these inquiries prompt us to ask more general, more theoretical questions. These first moves will be somewhat superficial – but superficial in just the way all initial inquiry is. Thinking about these practical issues will help us isolate important theoretical considerations (Daniels 1996: 10, 12). The resulting theoretical developments will give us some (still rough) conceptual tools to think more carefully about those practical problems, and to prompt further normative and meta-theoretical reflection.

Put differently, my overarching aim is to construct a web of ethical belief. The metaphor of the web – which inspired Rawls's view of reflective equilibrium – was first proposed by W. V. Quine (Quine and Ullian 1978). According to Quine, our knowledge of the world is holistic (1961/1951: 41). The only way we can reasonably think that our beliefs are true is if they fit together coherently, that particular details and theoretical claims form a strong web of belief (ibid. 42–3). That is my aim: to weave a strong, coherent ethical web from strands of arguments about practical issues, normative theories, and meta-ethical reflection.

It might seem that this approach is incompatible with many approaches to ethics. Perhaps it is incompatible with some of them – but not as many as one might think. For even heavily intuitionistic and foundationalist accounts depend on showing, by means of some coherent picture, why we need foundational principles which themselves do not depend on further evidence. Even divine command theories of ethics require providing a coherent picture in which god plays a special role.

I will do little to explicitly argue for this approach; I assume its virtues have been defended by many others. I simply show how one might seek wide reflective equilibrium. I am convinced that the best way to defend this idea is to show that it refines ethical understanding and improves ethical behavior.

REFERENCES

Buchanan, A., Brock, D. W., Daniels, N., and Wikler, D. (2002) *From Chance to Choice: Genetics and Justice*. Cambridge: Cambridge University Press.

Daniels, N. (1996) *Justice and Justification: Reflective Equilibrium in Theory and Practice*. Cambridge: Cambridge University Press.

Nesse, R. M. and Williams, G. C. (1994) *Why We Get Sick: The New Science of Darwinian Medicine*. New York: Times Books.

Quine, W. V. (1961/1951) "Two Dogmas of Empiricism." In W. V. Quine (ed.), *From a Logical Point of View*. Cambridge, MA: Harvard University Press, 20–46.

Quine, W. V. and Ullian, J. S. (1978) *The Web of Belief*, 2nd edn. New York: Random House.

Rawls, J. (1999/1971) *A Theory of Justice*, 2nd edn. Cambridge, MA: Harvard University Press.

PART ONE

Learning to Theorize

ONE

The Ethical Impulse

All of us must make ethical choices. Sometimes those choices seem so easy that we do not even see them as choices. We don't consciously decide to comfort a close friend whose son was just killed; we just do. At other times the ethical choices we face baffle us. We may not know whether to have an abortion or to object to a pending war. Or, we may know what we should do but do not know how to do it: we feel obligated to support that friend whose son was killed but not know how best to do that. Still other times all available options appear objectionable: none of the choices is good, and we do not want to live with the consequences of making any of them. A gut-wrenching example is "Sophie's choice," as described in the novel and movie by that name: a Nazi officer forces a Polish woman to choose which of her children will be killed. He tells her that if she does not choose, then he will kill them both. She *had* to choose and live with the consequences of having made that choice – even if she chose not to choose.

Doubtless some people are oblivious to moral questions: they just blindly pursue their own interests, never caring how their actions affect others. We can be glad that such people do not dominate the world, for soon there might be no world to dominate. Fortunately, most people are aware of the moral dimensions of their lives. Unfortunately, many of us fail to fully appreciate their precise nature and significance. We all have restricted moral vision; many of us have vast moral blind spots. Most of us are ignorant of historical, political, economic, sociological, and psychological insights that can inform moral action. To make better choices, we must become aware of our options and the relevant background information; we should identify the consequences of our actions for others, for ourselves, and for the people we will become. With effort and practice we can learn to make more informed moral decisions.

This is also true of purely self-interested actions. We may fail to understand the importance of self-regarding virtues like self-control. Or we may know that we should be more disciplined, persistent, or insightful, yet not know how to inculcate these traits. We may also lack the relevant empirical information we need to make wise personal choices. With effort and practice we can obtain that information and learn to make more prudential decisions. Of course, even if we know precisely what is in our self-interest, we may fail to act accordingly. We may eat that extra serving of pizza knowing that we shouldn't. We may likewise fail to do what is right even if we know it. I may know that I should visit a depressed friend, but watch a movie instead.

How do we sharpen our moral vision? How can we make better moral choices? How do we learn to do what we think we should do, what we are obligated to do? A comprehensive answer to these questions is beyond the scope of this book. However, I am convinced that careful philosophical reflection will help. We should critically evaluate what we do and why we do it. We should think carefully about ethical quandaries we have not yet faced. If we do when we are not under pressure to make a quick and potentially momentous decision, we will be better equipped to make good decisions when we must act.

When we start thinking systematically about practical ethical issues, we begin to theorize morally. Too often we see moral theorizing as a quaint intellectual practice of bearded, pipe-smoking, briefcase-toting philosophers. Moral theorizing is not an activity of the few and the weird; it grows out of, informs, and is informed by, everyday moral choices by everyday people. Formal ethical theories are simply more organized, more structured attempts to morally theorize. Since they are more systematic, familiarity with them can help us place our ethical choices within a broader context, to see how each choice is related to other practical ethical issues, and to think about the logical consequences of positions we hold, actions we undertake, and views we endorse. It can also give us a rich normative and meta-theoretical vocabulary for describing, understanding, and discussing our actions, choices, and character.

However, I am getting ahead of myself. Let me begin where I think most of us do – indeed must – begin thinking about ethics: by wrestling with concrete moral questions. We face a problem and we are uncertain how to act; we may be morally pulled in multiple directions. Wrestling with specific practical decisions will prompt and inform theorizing: it will give theorizing the appropriate richness, seriousness, and texture. To illustrate how we might have begun morally theorizing, I briefly discuss three types of moral choices we all make. Some concern wholly personal interactions; others, our roles as employers (or employees); and still others arise from our position within a social/political system. I will not resolve them here. Moreover, the initial discussion will be overly simplified, in part because it lacks the depth theorizing brings. Still, discussing the cases will help show why we cannot resolve them without thinking more abstractly – without theorizing about them. We will return to discuss these cases later with the benefit of some newly acquired theoretical tools.

Three Cases

To tell the truth?

We regularly face situations in which we must decide whether to tell the truth. Sometimes we choose to lie; sometimes we choose to tell the truth; often we do not even notice the choice. We just do one or the other spontaneously. Occasionally these choices seem insignificant. A friend, Jack, wants to know whether we like his new haircut. We think it is unbecoming or even repulsive. What should we do? Should we be completely candid and tell him that we think his haircut (with which he must live for at least the next month) is repugnant? Or should we soft-pedal our evaluation and tell him we slightly preferred his hair the other way? Or should we avoid the issue with some vague remark: "Why are you asking me? It's your hair. You should wear it the way you like." Or should we seek to boost his ego by telling him that we find the new cut becoming? These choices seem far from earth-shattering. Perhaps appearances are deceiving.

Sometimes the decision to lie is serious. Soon after my father had major heart surgery, my cousin called to say that my Dad's eldest sister had died. Should I tell him? Should I just carefully avoid any reference to his sister? What if he explicitly asked me how she was doing? The issue here is arguably more important than the first. It is information he would have wanted, yet the information might have harmed him. There are other cases where even more is at stake. Your cousin June is in a bad automobile accident in which her 14-year-old son David is killed. She is in a serious condition but momentarily awakens from her drug-induced stupor and asks you if David is okay. Should you tell her he is dead (and perhaps be "totally honest" by telling her that he died a slow and painful death)? Or should you tell her that he is in a critical condition? Or should you tell her he is just fine, knowing that you must later (after she has recovered) tell her the truth – including the truth that you lied?

Each of us must decide whether to lie at work. Suppose you sell stereo equipment in the local electronics store. A patron, Jody, enters the store hell bent on buying an expensive but unreliable sound system. You will receive a healthy commission if you sell the system. Should you disabuse Jody of her ill-informed belief that this system is the best she can buy? Suppose you try to be honest and quietly mention your misgivings; she bristles at the suggestion that the system is defective. You fear she will take her business elsewhere. Should you now persist in pressing your concerns? Or should you ignore your qualms and extol the virtues of the system? ("I'm glad you really want this system, Jody. I voiced the concerns because I did not want you to spend your hard-earned money unless you wanted. Now that I see that you want the best, and are prepared to pay for it, I can be honest with you. This is, without a doubt, the best system you can buy.")

Or suppose you work in the federal health department. Your boss, at the behest of the President (Prime Minister) or Congress (Parliament), directs you to develop a health program that you think is inefficient, ineffective, and seriously unjust. Should you do it? Suppose you think you should. Having done it you are then asked to defend the program before the relevant regulative or legislative body. You agree. A Representative (or Member of Parliament) asks you point blank whether you think the program is defensible. Should you hold your tongue? Should you openly lambast the program, knowing that it will likely cost you your job? Should you advocate the plan to protect your livelihood? Or should you advocate the measure because you feel obliged to carry out the express wishes of the duly elected members of government?

Or, to take a recent real-life example, if you are a member of the Central Intelligence Agency, how should you respond to the Vice-President's pressure to say that you have firm evidence that Iraq has weapons of mass destruction (Pincus and Priest 2003)?

How can we resolve these practical issues? If we focus on each example in isolation, we may attend to vivid but morally irrelevant factors. To find an adequate solution we should step back and think about the issues more abstractly. We see that each has two distinct dimensions: the relevant details and the underlying values. To resolve each case we must identify both.

We must first know the relevant details of the case. Is Jack emotionally fragile after coming off a bitter divorce? Is June's medical condition critical? Just what will happen if the government puts this health care program in place? These details will help us understand our options and enable us to predict what will happen if we lie. If we are candid with Jack about his haircut, will he be angry with us? If we tell June that David is dead, will the shock kill her or hamper her recovery? If we tell Jody that the Super-X Stereo System is vastly overpriced, will we lose our commission? If we offer the Representative our candid assessment of the health plan, will it pass nonetheless?

Predicting these outcomes is sometimes, though not always, difficult. This difficulty sometimes explains our inability to know how we should act; it is sometimes the source of disagreements about what is morally appropriate. If we were certain about the consequences of our actions, we might be confident which one is morally appropriate. If we knew that telling Jack that we find his haircut tacky won't bother him at all, then virtually everyone will agree that lying to him would be bad.

Even if we completely agree on the facts, we may still disagree about what we should do if we disagree about the relevant values. Some people might claim that although Jack will be upset by our reaction to his haircut, we *ought* to tell him the truth nonetheless. Some of these people would claim that we err in focusing only on the immediate effects on Jack. There are important long-term consequences of lying. In being dishonest to Jack I might make him less capable of accepting personal criticism or I might develop a habit of lying that will have detrimental consequences later. That is why I ought to tell Jack the truth. Others contend that I ought to tell him the truth, consequences be damned. The moral rules require me to do so.

I wonder, though, if this latter position is defensible in this wholly unqualified form. Is it plausible to think the morally upright person never considers consequences in any form? I do not see how. If they are not relevant *at all*, then we have no way to distinguish lying to Jack about his hair from lying to June about her son. Yet even those who think we should be truthful to both would think there are important differences between these cases. The likelihood that June might die is an important – even if not singularly compelling – reason why lying to her is more defensible.

On the other hand, even those who think consequences count morally do not think all consequences are morally relevant. Nor do they think all consequences are equally relevant (Singer 1993). Most think some consequences (a five-cent increase in the cost of Tabasco Sauce or the decline in the popularity of *Friends*) are morally irrelevant. Most will also think that among those consequences that are relevant, some (the death of 10,000 innocent people) are morally more important than others (maintaining one's personal purity). Of course, there will be cases about which people disagree. Can I lie to Jody so that I can get my plump commission? Presumably not. But why not? It cannot plausibly be because self-interest never justifies lying. After all, most people think I could justifiably lie to save my life from a crazed killer (for another view, see Kant 1993/1785). The proper action is less clear if the personal cost is less than my life but more than my commission. Can I lie if telling the truth costs me my job or a needed promotion? In summary, even if consequences are morally relevant, we may be unsure about which consequences are relevant and just how relevant they are. This is something theorizing about ethics can help us resolve. It gives us a broader perspective from which to identify the factors we should consider and the choices we should make. Before theorizing further, let us turn to our second category of examples.

Sexual harassment

Women in the workplace were once regularly subject to blatant sexual harassment. In those days few men (and not even all women) would have noticed it – and fewer still would have openly objected to it. Times have changed. If I demand that an employee sleep with me each week to retain her job, then everyone will recognize my behavior is sexual harassment and beyond the moral pale. Even if I do not explicitly demand that she sleep with me, but unmistakably imply that by my behavior, then virtually no one will deny that I have sexually harassed her, that my behavior is morally outrageous.

Here, as elsewhere, we find many people agree about paradigm instances of morally wrong acts. Unfortunately, when cases stray from the paradigms, people are more likely to disagree about whether an action is morally wrong. They are even more likely to disagree about why it is wrong. Our disagreements can be either *interpretive* or *evaluative*. The disagreement is *interpretive* if we disagree about how to categorize someone's behavior. Was I really implying that an employee must sleep with me to keep her job, or was I "just" joking? The disagreement is *evaluative* if we disagree whether someone's behavior, so interpreted, constitutes sexual harassment. Is telling ribald jokes at work or asking an employee for a date sexual harassment?

Although it is helpful to initially distinguish these, they often bleed into one another. Both disagreements emerged in the confirmation hearings for Supreme Court nominee Clarence Thomas. While heading the Equal Employment Opportunity Commission (EEOC), Thomas repeatedly asked female employees for dates. Employees said he told off-color jokes around the office, that he made public comments about the size of his penis, and that he told female employees about his sexual conquests. Committee members considering his nomination had to determine how to interpret and how to evaluate his words and actions. (And, of course, they also had to determine if Thomas said and did what others attributed to him – although, for the most part, that was not in question.) In Thomas's case all these determinations were further complicated by three considerations. One, since his was a politically loaded nomination, there was a tendency for political allies to downplay the significance of his actions and for political opponents to highlight them. Two, since Thomas was black, the charges bolstered stereotypes about black male sexual aggression. That made some people more likely to believe the charges and others less likely. Three, since the events in question took place during his tenure at the EEOC – which is the main governmental body responsible for enforcing laws against sexual harassment – acknowledging his guilt would taint the image of the agency under the direction of Presidents Reagan and Bush Sr.

Although these factors surely complicate the discussion, they do not make it impossible to think clearly about his nomination. After all, some moral questions – and especially those we find most perplexing – are complicated. That is not a reason to cease thinking about them, but rather a reason to think hard. That requires, among other things, that we ask whether our stated reasons are ones we think applicable to other cases as well. That is why we must theorize about ethics. It helps us decide which factors are morally relevant and why.

Here, as with the earlier examples about truth telling, we see the tension between concern for consequences and the belief that we should follow some moral rules or principles no matter what the consequences. Among those who think we should consider consequences, some supported Thomas simply because they wanted another black member of the Supreme Court (he was to replace Thurgood Marshall, the first black member of the Court). Others supported Thomas because he opposed abortion and they wanted, above all else, a member of the court who would limit, or at least not expand, the legal right to an abortion. Those who took both positions may have thought that Thomas's nomination was unfortunate but, under the circumstances, a worthy tradeoff.

As with the previous cases, some people would be appalled at this tradeoff, although their reasons may vary. Some hold that moral tradeoffs are always impermissible. For them, morality is a matter of strictly following clearly defined rules or principles. Even if we can consider consequences, we should never use immoral means, no matter how minimal, to achieve moral ends, no matter how laudable. For people holding this theoretical position, if Thomas's behavior were sufficiently immoral so that he did not "deserve" the seat, then he should have been rejected no matter how beneficial the consequences. Or, if he "deserved" a seat on the Court, then he should have been approved, never mind the detrimental consequences.

Likely most who thought this was a bad tradeoff were not categorically opposed to considering consequences or making moral tradeoffs. Rather they thought this was a bad tradeoff. They either rejected their opponents' judgments about (a) the seriousness of Thomas's offense, or (b) the relevance of the predicted consequences. They may have thought sexual harassment is so objectionable and a permanent post on the Supreme Court so important, that Thomas should have been rejected no matter what his other purported virtues (e.g., being black or being anti-abortion). These people might hold that had Thomas been guilty of a less serious moral offense, then he should have been ratified. Those who reason this way think we ought to consider

consequences when making moral decisions. Sometimes, though, some consequences are so important that they usually tip the moral scales. People may disagree
about exactly which consequences are important and about exactly how important
they are. We will discuss these issues later. First we turn to the third case.

The death penalty and personal responsibility

In 2001, 36-year-old Andrea Yates called the Texas police to tell them that she had
just killed her five children. One by one she drowned her children – all under the
age of eight – in the bathtub. Then she carefully laid them side-by-side in her bed.
She told the police that she had been a bad mother, had failed to raise them right-
eously, and therefore was compelled to kill them to protect them from Satan's
torment. It was the only loving thing she could do.

Such a crime is as horrendous as they come. We cannot fathom a sane mother
killing her children, let alone killing them one by one in such a painful way. That is
precisely what the defense argued: that she was not sane and, therefore, was not
legally responsible for their deaths. Therefore, she should not be incarcerated but
rather hospitalized until she was cured. The grounds for claiming she was insane were
clear: in the previous three years she had been hospitalized four times for mental
illness, had twice tried to commit suicide, and was currently being treated for post-
partum depression.

What should the state do? Should they execute her for this heinous crime, as the
prosecution demanded? Should they consign her to a mental hospital for treatment,
as her attorneys argued? Or should they incarcerate her rather than execute her, as
the jury eventually decided?

There are, of course, a host of other issues concerning the death penalty: does it
deter potential murderers? Even if it does, should a civilized state execute anyone?
These more general questions we confront in Chapters 3 and 11. Here I focus on
this one aspect of this case: was Yates morally and legally responsible for what she
did? Or did her mental state excuse or at least attenuate her responsibility? Was she
legally insane, and, even if she were, does that excuse or mitigate her responsibility?

Most Americans are leery of – or completely opposed to – the use of the insanity plea. They think it is often used successfully to avoid deserved punishment. Many
also do not understand why insanity, even if it were established, would show that
the person was not responsible for her actions. The first worry is easily dealt with
since the defense is rarely tried, and it is successful only a fraction of those times
(McGinley and Pasewark 1989). That is not to say that it is never misused, only that
it is rare.

The second issue goes to the heart of the idea of criminal responsibility. Law has
long held that a person is criminally responsible for an action only if she did the
illegal action *and* had the requisite mental state. The rationale for this latter requirement (*mens rea*) is simple. We recognize that in some circumstances *I* might not
be responsible for harm my body causes. Suppose a tornado throws my body into
Joe, killing him. We would all agree that I did not kill Joe, even if my body was the

immediate physical cause of his death. After all, I had no control over what happened; I lacked the appropriate mental state. To be legally or morally responsible, I – and not just my body – must cause the harm. In some relevant sense I must have been the source of the harm.

This possibility makes room for the insanity plea. For if something outside me can propel my body to cause harm, then it seems plausible to think that something "inside" me – some inner compulsion, mental illness, brain lesion, or mental deficiency – might do the same. We already recognize that some internal deficiencies can eliminate responsibility. If a three-year-old kills his brother while playing with a loaded gun he found lying around, we would not hold him legally or morally responsible (although we might hold the parents responsible); we would think the child temporarily lacks the appropriate knowledge, understanding, and control required to hold him responsible. He would not be punished, although we might offer him counseling. If the child's incapacity can exculpate, then it seems reasonable to think temporary mental incapacity could do the same. Under such conditions I am arguably not responsible for what my body did (Feinberg 1970/1968).

Everyone acknowledges that even when environmental and mental factors are insufficient to eliminate responsibility, they can lessen or mitigate it. We often forgive people for what they do when acting under duress (extreme economic distress, the loss of a child, or even a severe headache). Even if we may not forgive them for their inappropriate actions, we think they are less responsible than they would have been had they not been under duress. That is why, however horrible Andrea Yates's behavior was, most people do not think her behavior was *as* horrible as it would have been had she killed them to collect life insurance. That is doubtless why the jury decided she should not die.

Here is an indirect way of understanding the importance of mental factors. Most people say that people should get equal punishment for equal crimes. What, though, makes two crimes equal or two punishments equal? Is every murder the same? Is Andrea Yates's murder of her children morally the same as Ted Bundy's murder of several dozen young women or John Wayne Gacy's murder of several dozen young men? Should everyone who commits the same crime (e.g., murder) receive precisely the same punishment? Can we sometimes (always? often?) legitimately consider the criminal's background, environment, or mental condition? We make such exceptions in ordinary life. We are less upset at someone who is rude to us after their house burned down. It seems plausible to think mental condition (and especially mental illness) can affect whether and how much someone is responsible for her actions.

If most people thought these mental and environmental factors were not relevant, it would be silly to recount their details in the press and to permit their being offered as evidence in court. It would make no more sense for Andrea Yates's attorneys to mention her condition than it would be for them to trot out her dental records, samples of her handwriting, or her prom pictures. Barring special argument demonstrating the legal relevance of these documents, they would be inadmissible in court. To that extent, despite the common misgivings about the insanity plea, it seems courts – as well as most people – do think a person's mental state is relevant to her guilt and eventual punishment. Of course, that does not eliminate disagreement about whether such facts can eliminate or merely mitigate responsibility, and, if the latter, just how much they lessen responsibility. Nor does it eliminate disagreement about exactly which factors mitigate or exculpate.

Finally, even if we settle these value issues, we must still settle factual issues in particular cases. We would still need to know whether someone charged with a crime really was insane, in some way incapacitated, or whether they were just using this plea as an attempt to evade punishment. We would want to know, for example, whether Yates's problems were of the kind and severity that would render her not responsible for the murders. Although these questions are beyond the reach of this book, they are critical for any final determination about her case. Once again, we see that concrete moral judgments importantly depend not only on judgment of value, but also on empirical details.

What These Examples Show

We can now articulate some tentative findings from our discussion of these practical ethical issues.

Morality concerns the interests of others

Each example shows that morality primarily concerns behavior that affects others. However, there are many ways that our actions may affect others. Which ones should we evaluate morally? Everyone agrees that if my behavior harms others, then it is subject to moral evaluation. However, people disagree about behavior that (a) harms others only indirectly, (b) that "merely" creates a risk of harm, (c) that fails to prevent harm, or (d) that benefits (or fails to benefit) others. By driving near your cornfield, the pollution from my car might kill some insects pollinating your crops. Am I therefore forbidden from driving near your cornfield because it might slightly and indirectly harm your livelihood? By driving 70 mph in a 50 mph zone I may not harm anyone, but I do increase the probability that I will (I engage in risky behavior). Should that be prohibited? You are drowning; I can save you without endangering myself. If I fail to save you have I harmed you? I am your boss and you desperately want a job I have. Do I harm you if I give it to someone else? In short, people often disagree about what counts as harm and about which harms are morally weightier (Scheffler 2004). Despite these disagreements, most people will acknowledge that if someone's action clearly and substantially affects others (either benefits or harms them), then even if we do not yet know whether those actions are right or wrong, we can agree that they should be evaluated morally.

The central role of reasons

When someone asks us why we made a decision or why we support some position, we offer, or should be prepared to offer, reasons for our actions, decisions, or conclusions. Those who think Yates should have been executed may claim that she deserves to die, that her insanity plea is just a ruse, or that we need to kill her to deter other murderers, while those who think Yates should not be executed might claim that she is truly insane or that capital punishment does not deter. Those who want to censor pornography may argue that pornography degrades women, while supporters might claim it is a form of free speech that should be protected by law.

To evaluate these arguments we need to know both whether the purported facts are true (that capital punishment deters, that Yates was insane, that Thomas told ribald jokes in front of female workers, etc.) *and* whether those facts, if true, would support their respective moral conclusions. The former questions require serious empirical investigation: that is why practical ethics must look at the "facts." The latter questions require ethical theorizing.

The claim that we should have reasons for our beliefs is not confined to moral deliberation. It is true of science (why is evolutionary theory plausible?), most prudential decisions (why should I take this job, marry this woman, exercise three times a week?), and non-moral value judgments (why do I judge this book, painting, or movie to be excellent or deeply flawed?). We (should) defend our judgments by citing some features of the action or thing, features we think justify our evaluation. Our claims are plausible inasmuch as (a) the action or thing has these features and (b) its having those features are reasons supporting our evaluation. I might justify my claim that "*Return of the King* is a good movie" by claiming that "it has well-defined characters, a gripping plot, and the appropriate dramatic tension." I identify features of the movie that I think justify my evaluation. However, the features I cite are not unique to this movie. If they were, then they would not be reasons for my evaluation. In giving these reasons, I imply that "having well-defined characters" or "having a gripping plot" or "having the appropriate dramatic tension" are criteria of good movies. That is not to say these are the only or the most important criteria. It is to say that if a movie satisfies any of them, then we have *a* reason to think it is good.

There are three ways you can challenge my evaluation of the movie: you can challenge my criteria, the weight I give them, or my claim that the movie satisfies those criteria. For instance, you might argue that having well-defined characters is not a relevant criterion, that I have given that criterion too much weight, or that *Return of the King* does not have well-defined characters. In defense, I could explain why I think it is a relevant criterion, why I have given that criterion the appropriate weight, and why I think the movie's characters are well developed. In defending my claims about *Return of the King*, I must cite specific facts about the movie and defend more theoretical claims about the appropriate criteria of good movies.

Constraints on reasons

In offering a reason I may not give a real reason, that is, I may not justify my conclusion. I might merely be excusing or rationalizing my views or action. To identify some ways in which my purported reasons may fail to support my moral view, let us think about three different ways that my grading of students' work can go awry.

1. I might grade their work inconsistently, that is, I might not employ the same criteria for all students. Priscilla gets an A because she has a pleasant smile; Waldo because he works hard; Abigail, because she agrees with my views. Of course knowing that I should use consistent criteria does not tell me what criteria I should employ or what grades the students should receive. Perhaps on sound academic grounds they all deserved the As they received. However, it is not enough that I accidentally gave them the grades they deserved. I should give them As because they deserved them.
2. I might use improper grading criteria. It is not enough that I have consistent criteria. After all, I might adhere unwaveringly to wholly inappropriate criteria. For instance, I consistently give high grades to students I like or who mouth my views. If so, I grade the papers inappropriately, even if consistently.
3. I might apply the criteria inappropriately. I might have appropriate and consistent grading criteria, yet misapply them because I am imperceptive, inattentive, ignorant, close-minded, exhausted, preoccupied, ill-motivated, or just stupid.

I can make parallel "mistakes" in moral deliberations.

1. I might apply moral considerations inconsistently.
2. I might use inappropriate moral criteria.
3. I might apply moral standards inappropriately.

Let us look at each in more detail.

Consistency

We expect others to act consistently. If I lie to you to promote my interest, but get incensed if you lie to me to promote your interests, then you rightly criticize me for being inconsistent. I also expect you to be consistent. This idea has often been described as the principle of universalizability: that we should treat two creatures the same unless they are relevantly different, different in ways that justify treating them differently. Just as students expect teachers to grade consistently, we expect others and ourselves to choose and act consistently. This expectation pervades our thinking about ethics. It undergirds common strategies for defending our moral views and criticizing others. We often defend our views by claiming that we are being consistent. We often criticize others' views by charging that they are inconsistent.

Unfortunately, although most of us abstractly recognize the importance of consistency, many of us fail to be consistent in the concrete. Some who supported Clarence Thomas's nomination to the Court did so simply because they thought it was vitally important to have a strong opponent of abortion on the Court. They judged that this consequence outweighed any costs of appointing him. Yet some of those people would be appalled at someone who, in a different case, so blatantly appealed to consequences. Conversely, some who condemned this consequentialist justification for supporting Thomas would, in other circumstances, openly make moral tradeoffs. Or, those who argued that Andrea Yates should be executed for murder, no matter what her mental condition, would, in other circumstances, be more than willing to excuse their own, their kin's, or their friends' inappropriate behavior for far less compelling reasons. This tendency to be inconsistent is instructive. We regularly make exceptions for ourselves and for views we endorse. Sometimes we do it consciously; more commonly we do so subconsciously. We do not like to admit that we are inconsistent. If pressed, we usually claim that the presumably inconsistent cases are, despite appearances, morally quite different. Some of these explanations are plausible. If you explain to me why your lying to June about her son's death is morally different from my lying to Jody about the stereo, I will (or should) quickly see that the cases are relevantly different. However, we should not tolerate ad hoc explanations. Explanations of why two cases are different should identify some general and relevant difference between them. Thus, if I justify lying to you because the lie promotes my financial interests, then, unless I am willing to countenance your lies to promote your financial interests (even when those lies harm me), then my supposed justification, being ad hoc, is no justification at all. It is just my attempt to rationalize my behavior, to deflect others' criticism of me.

Of course, we cannot always easily distinguish an ad hoc justification from a legitimate one. Someone may appear to act inconsistently, but only because we do not understand the complexity of her moral reasoning or because we are ignorant of relevant details. As we will see, determining what is and is not morally relevant is often at the center of moral debate. Nonetheless, although it is often difficult to decide whether someone – including ourselves – is inconsistent, what everyone would acknowledge is that if someone is being inconsistent, then that is a compelling reason to reject her argument.

Correct criteria

It is not enough for us to act consistently. We must also employ the appropriate criteria – whether these are understood as guidelines, standards, rules, or principles of relevance. One central aim of theorizing about ethics is to identify the most defensible criteria – those criteria we should consider when making moral decisions. If I think deterrence is an appropriate goal of punishment, I should be able to defend that claim. I should be able to rebut the claims of someone who thinks it is not a morally relevant consideration. I must defend my view with reasons that might appeal to someone who does not already agree with me.

Correct "application"

Even when we "know" what is morally relevant, and even when we act consistently, we still make moral mistakes. The same flaws that may hinder my ability to identify the appropriate criteria can also interfere with my "application" of them. Consider the ways I might misapply the "rules" prohibiting lying or harming another's feelings. To use an earlier example, Jack asks me if I like his haircut. There are any number of ways I might act inappropriately. (1) *I may not see the alternatives*: I may assume that I must baldly lie or substantially hurt his feelings. (2) *I may be insufficiently attentive to his needs and interests*: I may over- or underestimate how much he will be hurt by my honesty (or lack of it). (3) *I may be unduly influenced by self-interest or personal bias*: I may lie not to protect his feelings but because I do not want him to be angry with me. (4) *I may be unduly swayed by my upbringing*: I may lie to him simply because my parents would have. (5) *I may know precisely what I should do, but be insufficiently motivated to do it*: I may lie because I just do not want the hassle. (6) Or, *I may be motivated to act as I should, but lack the talent or skill to do it*: I may want to be honest but lack the verbal and personal skills to be honest in a way that won't harm him.

These are all failings with practical significance. A comprehensive ethical theory should not only identify the appropriate criteria for moral deliberation but also give us a robust moral psychology explaining how people best learn what is moral, and how they learn to act on what they know to be best. These are questions I address (albeit briefly) later in the book. Now I want to isolate the criteria that seem to play an important role in thinking morally – criteria that emerged from our discussion of these cases.

Important criteria

Consequences

Most people think the consequences of their actions are morally relevant. In deciding whether to tell the truth, we often ask ourselves what will happen (or likely happen) if we tell the truth (or lie). To use the earlier example, will telling June that her son has been killed hamper her recovery or even kill her? If so, most people believe that that is *a* reason – and likely a compelling reason – to lie. By acknowledging that this consequence is *a* reason, we show that we are committed to the claim that consequences of our actions are morally relevant. They are one reason for acting, although we may disagree profoundly about which consequences are relevant, exactly how weighty they are, and whether they are sometimes trumped by different moral considerations. However, if we think these consequences justify lying to Jody, then, since we think lying is generally wrong, then consequences must not only be morally relevant, but sometimes quite weighty.

Likewise, in deciding whether we should have capital punishment, one reason that many people support the practice is that they think it deters some people from committing the punishable offense. Some who reject capital punishment do so because they think it does not deter potential murderers. Other critics may think there are substantial social or personal costs of having state-sanctioned executions – costs that outweigh any gains from deterrence. Still others may think that although consequences are morally relevant, they are insufficiently weighty to justify capital punishment. That is, they would be opposed to the practice even if there were some evidence that it deterred. However, what if there were unequivocal evidence (as Ehrlich 1975 claimed) that each execution saved the lives of several innocent civilians who would be killed if we did not have capital punishment? Would that give the opponent of capital punishment a reason to now support the practice? Suppose we had evidence that it would definitely save the lives of 50 innocent civilians? Perhaps the opponent will hold her moral ground, although most people would contend this moral ground is not worth holding.

Here is another reason to think that consequences are morally relevant. If consequences were not relevant, then we would not need to know many factual details of the case in question. We would need to know only enough to know how to categorize the case (as an instance of murder, or robbery, or embezzlement, or dishonesty). However, when we reason about moral issues we frequently find that even seemingly minor details are relevant to our moral assessment. To use an earlier example, although we may be quite clear that something is a lie, we think the details matter in deciding whether the lie is morally permissible. If so, then consequences do matter morally. Still, that does not make consequences the whole moral story; it need not even mean that they play the leading role.

Principles

After all, we also sometimes think it is important to "stick by our moral guns," even if the likely consequences of doing so are detrimental. Most of us think we should not hide the truth from prospective customers so we can get a hefty commission. We think it would be wrong of us to kill an innocent person to use his organs to save four other people.

Those who think consequences are morally important may think they can explain these beliefs without having to rely on consequence-independent principles. However, those who think morality includes (or is even constituted by) rules will find all consequentialist explanations wanting. Even if they don't give us poor moral guidance, they cannot explain our obligations. We should lie to Jody about her son, this person might claim, not because it promotes the best consequences, but because in this case one moral principle (to tell the truth) is trumped by a more stringent one (to protect innocent life). On this view my lie is justified because that is what the appropriate moral rule tells me to do.

Using all the considerations

The preceding discussion might suggest that there are two different types of ethical considerations – consequences and rules – and that these inevitably conflict. Stated in this stark way, it appears we may consider consequences *or* we may consider rules, but that we cannot legitimately consider both. Yet most people find themselves citing both consequences and rules to justify their actions and their evaluations of others' actions. Most of us assume we can legitimately employ both sorts of considerations. It is not, someone might claim, that in building a house we must use a hammer or we must use a saw. We use both depending on the task to be done. All we need is a theory that explains how we successfully employ both moral tools.

Many philosophers think there are plausible combined theories. If there are, that would be gratifying. Unfortunately, one thing that happens when we begin to theorize about ethics is that we find we may not be able to rationally do what we might, pre-theoretically, want to do. At least some philosophers think this is one of those cases. They think we must choose between one of these theories. Seeing why is not difficult. Suppose we say that I can legitimately lie to Joan about her son's tragic death, at least until she recovers. How can I justify that lie? Our impulse is that say that there is a rule against lying, and that the rule, in this case, is trumped by the significant consequences to Joan. However, it is difficult to know precisely what that means. It suggests that sometimes the rule is supreme and sometimes it is not. If so, how do we decide when we can lie and when we cannot? How can we merge consequentialist and non-consequentialist considerations into a single theory? We appear to have only three options: (1) there is some rule which explains when to follow rules and when to appeal to consequences; (2) there is some consequentialist consideration which tells us when to follow rules and when to abandon them; or (3) there is no decision procedure which specifies which rule or principle is paramount.

The first option appears to imply that, at base, morality is simply a matter of rules, though occasionally rules tell us to consider consequences; the second implies that, at base, morality is a matter of promoting the appropriate consequences, although consequentialist considerations may occasionally require that we follow certain rules. Put differently, the first two options suggest that the "combined" theory is still fundamentally either consequentialist or rule-based. The third option permits appeals to both rules and consequences, but it seems that it exacts a substantial cost. If no rule tells me when to follow which rules and when to heed consequences, and if no consequentialist consideration tells me which rules to follow when, then it appears I can give no definitive reason why I should act one way rather than another. Many people have thought that wholly abandons the rational moral assessment of action. That is why many have assumed that they must (regrettably) choose rules or consequences. Looking at these two familiar theories is where our theoretical inquiry must begin.

REFERENCES

Ehrlich, I. (1975) "The Deterrent Effect of Capital Punishment: A Question of Life and Death," *American Economic Review* 65: 397–417.

Feinberg, J. (1970/1968) "What's So Special about Mental Illness." In J. Feinberg (ed.), *Doing and Deserving: Essays on Responsibility*. Princeton, NJ: Princeton University Press, 272–92.

Kant, I. (1993/1785) "On a Supposed Right to Lie Because of Philanthropic Concerns." In *Grounding for the Metaphysics of Morals*, 3rd edn. Indianapolis, IN: Hackett, 63–8.

McGinley, H. and Pasewark, R. A. (1989) "National Survey of the Frequency and Success of the Insanity Plea and Alternate Pleas," *Journal of Psychiatry and Law* 17 (2): 205–21.

Pincus, W. and Priest, D. (2003) "Some Iraq Analysts Felt Pressure from Cheney Visits," *Washington Post* (June 5).

Scheffler, S. (2004) "Doing and Allowing," *Ethics* 114 (2): 215–39.

Singer, P. (1993) *Practical Ethics*, 2nd edn. Cambridge: Cambridge University Press.

TWO

A Tale of Two Theories

While wrestling with several practical ethical issues in the last chapter, we often employed two styles of reasoning. One focused on the consequences of our actions; the other on rules or principles we should follow independently of consequences. We should not be surprised to find that many people thought (and still think) about practical ethical issues in similar ways. On my account of the origins of moral theorizing, that is precisely what we would expect. In people's quest to resolve practical ethical issues, they are impelled to think more abstractly, and most people's moral thinking proceeds in roughly similar tracks. We find that most people share enough moral beliefs to make rational discussion of particular ethical issues possible, even when they deeply disagree over them.

These two types of reasons are embodied in two categories of ethical theory that have shaped the contemporary understanding of ethics. Consequentialism states that we should choose the available action with the best overall consequences, while deontology states that we should act in ways circumscribed by moral rules or rights, and that these rules or rights are at least partly independent of consequences. There are other styles. I will discuss some later in the book. However, since these are commonly employed in everyday moral discussion, it is the sensible place to begin. My initial descriptions of these theories will be oversimplified. After we understand why and how these initial descriptions are flawed, we can better see how they can be made more sophisticated, more plausible. This should not be surprising since this is just how we first theorized about ethics. As we began to think about real problems, we were forced to theorize, and our first attempts at theorizing were inevitably simplistic.

One caution before we begin. It is tempting to assume that people who embrace the same theory will make the same judgments about practical ethical issues, and to assume that those who make the same practical ethical judgments embrace the same theory. Not so. It is easy to see why, if we think about disagreements in non-moral evaluations. Two people with the same criteria for "a good movie" may nonetheless differently evaluate *Return of the King*, while two people who evaluate *Return of the King* similarly may have different criteria for "a good movie." We can see the same divergence in ethical judgments. Some deontologists and some utilitarians will agree that abortion is morally permitted (or grossly immoral), while two deontologists (or two consequentialists) may disagree whether abortion is permissible. Knowing someone's theoretical commitments does not tell us which actions she thinks are right or wrong. It tells us only how she reasons about moral issues – although, as we shall see, that tells us a lot. For although moral theories do not dictate how we should act in all situations, they do specify whether and why certain features of actions (e.g., the consequences, the fact that we made a promise, etc.) are morally relevant. Different theories identify different criteria of moral relevance (different considerations we should use in moral reasoning), and even those that employ the same criteria may weigh them differently.

A Brief Description

Consequentialism

Consequentialists claim that we are morally obligated to act in ways that produce the best consequences. It is not difficult to see why this is an appealing theory. It employs the same style of reasoning we use in making purely prudential (wise, self-interested) decisions. If you are trying to prudently select a major, you will consider the available options, predict which one will likely lead to the best overall outcome, and then choose that major. If you are trying to decide to keep your present job or take a new one, you will consider the consequences of taking each job (working conditions, location, salary, chance of advancement, how the change might alter your personal and family relations, etc.), and then choose the one with the best overall consequences.

There is one critical difference between prudence and morality. Although both employ a similar reasoning style, they include different factors in their "calculations." Whereas prudence requires us to advance only our own personal interests, consequentialism requires us to consider the interests of all affected. When facing a moral decision, we should consider available actions, trace the likely consequences of each for all affected, and then select the one with the best overall consequences.

Of course, a consequentialist need not consider every consequence of an action, nor must she consider them all equally. Two consequences of my typing these words are that I am strengthening the muscles in my hands and increasing my eye–hand coordination. However, barring unusual circumstances, these are not morally relevant: they are neither a means to nor a constituent of my or anyone else's welfare, happiness, or well-being. That is why they play no role in moral deliberation. Although everyone would agree about this example, consequentialists profoundly disagree whether and how relevant other consequences are. That is why any adequate consequentialist theory must specify (a) which consequences are morally relevant (i.e., which we should consider when morally deliberating); (b) how much weight we should give them; and (c) how, precisely, we should use them in moral reasoning.

Deontology

Most of us grew up thinking morality was primarily negative – a list of "don'ts," a series of actions we should avoid. We thought that if we avoided the "don'ts" (and occasionally did the "dos"), then we were moral. There are clear benefits of this understanding of morality. It is easy to teach. We can also be confident that we know how we should act and how to morally evaluate ours and others' actions. For those who like to neatly divide the world between the good guys and the bad guys, this is a sterling advantage.

However, we must say more to distinguish deontology from consequentialism. Many consequentialists think their theory also permits – or even requires – moral rules: it is generally better if everyone follows the same rules than if they decide for themselves what is moral. Nonetheless, the theories disagree about the basis and status of rules. The consequentialist thinks the "rules" are derivative. They are defensible only if following them will bring about the best consequences. In contrast, deontologists claim that our moral obligations – whatever they are – are defined by the rules, partly independently of consequences. Even when following moral rules does not have the best consequences, we should adhere to them. Most people accept this idea in some form. We are offended if someone lies to or about us, even if it produces significant benefits for others. We are appalled at researchers who conduct non-consensual medical experiments on people – experiments like those by the Nazis on Jews (Lipton 2000), or by American physicians on rural blacks (Tuskegee Syphilis Study Legacy Committee 1996), even though such experiments presumably benefited other humans.

The sophisticated consequentialist would agree that the cost of conducting non-consensual experiments on humans normally *vastly* outweighs any purported benefits. They also know (or should know) that most of us tend to bend the rules for our own benefit and that most of us have trouble accurately judging risk. Therefore we should be extraordinarily careful before ignoring normal moral prohibitions. Still, it seems a consequentialist would say that if violating these moral norms were the *only* way to save a *much* larger number of humans, and there were no other adverse moral effects, then experimentation (or killing non-aggressors) would be morally permissible, and perhaps even morally obligatory.

Deontologists contend there are strict moral limits on what we can do to others. Consequentialists do not. That is the source of the most common objection to consequentialism: that if we consider only consequences, then we will eventually – and perhaps often – act immorally. Deontologists also contend that even when consequentialists offer the right moral prescription, they give the wrong reasons. This is significant since the deontologist thinks that it is important not only that we do the right thing, but that we do it for the right reasons.

Although deontologists think rules or principles are important independently of consequences, they disagree about which actions are right (or wrong) and just how right (or wrong) they are. They may disagree, for instance, about the status of the fetus or the right of the woman to choose to have an abortion (Marquis 2002/1997;

Thomson 2002/1971). They are also likely to disagree about how we determine which actions are right. Some claim we need only abstract reason (Kant 1999/1785: 1); others claim we must use intuition (McNaughton 2000); while still others say the proper rules emerge from explicit or hypothetical agreements (Gauthier 1986; Sayre-McCord 2000).

This quick glance reveals that both deontology and consequentialism come in widely divergent forms. Nonetheless, the distinction between these theories marks two important ways of thinking about ethics, ways that shape our moral deliberations in particular cases. I will now explore these theories in more detail. I will then explain how each is formulated by one important historical advocate.

A Closer Look

Consequentialism

As I noted above, consequentialists must explain (a) *which* consequences we should count, (b) how much *weight* or consideration we should give those that do count, and (c) *how* we should use these considerations when deliberating. Although these elements are deeply intertwined, it is important to distinguish between them. I briefly discuss each and explain how it shapes deliberations about practical moral issues.

Three dimensions

Which consequences?

This question arose in several issues discussed in the previous chapter. In deciding whether to tell my father that his sister had died, exactly which consequences should I have considered? Some, it seems, I need not consider at all: to tell my sister about our aunt's death, I would have to walk into the hospital hallway out of hearing of my father – and thereby slightly wear the soles of my shoes. Or to lessen the chance he might ask me how she was doing, I would have to choose a different salad dressing that evening since my favorite dressing ("Marie's") has the same name as his sister. These are morally insignificant consequences, and therefore should play no role in my deliberation. Other consequences mattered morally. I assumed the knowledge would depress him and might diminish his meager chances for recovery. I thought these consequences were important, and, indeed, decisive. I also predicted that his knowing about his sister's death lacked any clear beneficial consequences. In his current condition, he could not have done anything to comfort his nieces and nephews or to express his grief concretely. That is why a consequentialist would claim that the former actions (which affected his significant interests) matter morally, while trivial interests (slightly wearing the soles of my shoes and choosing a different salad dressing) do not.

How much do they count?

The consequentialist needs to know not only which consequences count, but also *how much* each counts. A consequence's *weight* is the product of the nature of the interests it affects, the number of interests affected, and their respective probabilities.

The factors that determine whether a consequence counts also determine its nature: does it advance or set back someone's significant interests? The more significant the interest affected, the more weight it has. Of course, we might disagree about the importance of a particular interest. We normally think freedom is valuable. Is it valuable to be able to ride in one's car without a seat belt? Many states have laws forbidding people from driving without a seat belt. Few people object to them. These same people, though, might think that laws forbidding freedom of speech, freedom of press, or freedom of assembly are wholly objectionable. Perhaps they are just being inconsistent; perhaps they should judge both cases the same. However, many people think these cases are relevantly different. We needn't resolve this issue here. We need note only that the consequentialist should explain how we properly determine a consequence's nature.

Suppose we determine that some action affects a significant interest. By itself, that is not enough to tell us what we should do. We also need to know how many such interests it affects. Setting back many people's significant interests is morally more weighty than setting back one person's comparable interest. Finally, to determine a consequence's weight we must also know the probability of its occurring. An effect's probability in a circumstance will raise or lower its moral weight and thereby influence our judgment about what we take to be the morally appropriate action. If a consequence is highly improbable, then the factor is less weighty *in that circumstance*. If telling my father would have led him to rebound, then that would have been morally significant. However, that result was so improbable that it was not only not weighty, I needn't have considered it at all.

How they count

Even if we know which factors are morally relevant and how weighty they are, we must also know *how* they enter into moral deliberation. For each action do we decide which alternative has the best overall consequences? Or do we decide how to act based on our judgment about which rule or pattern of behavior will have the best consequences? To see why this question is important, let us discuss the dominant form of consequentialism – utilitarianism. Utilitarianism holds that the sole consequence we need consider is happiness. The best action is the one that promotes the greatest happiness of the greatest number. In its simple form, it is often the target of philosophical potshots.

Simple utilitarianism: the philosopher's foil

Some ethics texts begin with a simplistic account of utilitarianism. When facing a moral choice, a practicing utilitarian dons her utilitarian blinkers, and asks herself, from her current perspective and condition, which alternative will likely have the best overall consequences. She should not be shackled by rules, authorities, or codified ethical wisdom. She should calculate based only on the evidence currently to hand. If her deliberations lead her to deceive others, to kill others, or to engage in other acts normally thought to be immoral, so much the worse for normal thought. She is simply doing what morality requires.

It is not surprising that utilitarianism, so defined, is easy prey. However, no sane utilitarian has ever held this view. The fact that it can be shown to be defective shows nothing. As John Stuart Mill put it: "There is no difficulty in proving any ethical standard whatsoever to work ill, if we assume universal idiocy to be conjoined with it" (1998/1863: 70). We should instead examine more plausible accounts. These differ from simple utilitarianism in two important respects. One, they empha- size the need to see all likely moral consequences, not only a subset of them. The second concerns *how* morally relevant consequences should enter deliberation. We have seen these – and especially the first – in our earlier discussion of practical ethical issues.

Consequences viewed broadly

Many objectors say or imply that utilitarians may consider only a few consequences, and may consider those narrowly. Given these assumptions, a utilitarian might coun- tenance a doctor's forcefully taking a healthy person off the street, carving out her organs, and transplanting them into five dying patients. Although one utilitarian has argued that we should have a "survival lottery" that would occasionally allow people to be used for their organs (Harris 1994/1975), the lottery must be formal, public, specific, and democratically supported. He holds that it would be morally intolerable to let single doctors make these decisions unilaterally.

Still, the fear that utilitarians would be prone to construe consequences narrowly is plausible. After all, even the most morally cautious person often considers only a small subset of relevant consequences. We do the same thing when judging our own interests. We want the extra helping of food, the extra beer, and are willing to miss two hours of sleep. The following morning we remember all too well what we had conveniently forgotten the night before. The tendency to see consequences narrowly, especially when our own interests are at stake, is a factor any clear-thinking conse- quentialist must acknowledge and seek to counter. There are several strategies con- sequentialists employ to limit bias by constraining the way we evaluate consequences. Most are forms of indirect consequentialism.

Direct / indirect consequentialism

To explain this idea, let us trace some parallels between consequentialism and pru- dence. Jane wants to be a successful student. She knows that students who read their assignments, think about the issues outside class, and begin working on their essays well before they are due, generally learn more and perform better than students who procrastinate or are lazy. However, this does not mean that she will be a good student only if she carefully reads *every* assignment and begins *every* essay weeks before it is due. If she misses the odd assignment and writes the occasional paper a few days before it is due, she can still be a stellar student.

What, then, should Jane do? Should she stop before working on each assignment to consciously decide if *this* is one she needs to do or if *this* is one she can safely put off? No. First, she would likely spend so much time deliberating that she loses valuable studying time. Second, she will occasionally misjudge which assignments she really should do and which she can safely delay. Third, and perhaps most important, by regularly deliberating she likely undermines the study habits that would make her a good student. Therefore, she should arguably not deliberate about each assignment, but simply carefully study for all and resist the urge to procrastinate. If she occasionally fails to do an assignment or occasionally procrastinates, it will likely not harm her overall performance. That is why she can best pursue the goal of being a good student indirectly: by developing good study habits. To whatever extent she does deliberate, she should deliberate about where and why these habits fail, and how to cultivate and strengthen them.

Consequentialists often make similar moves when reasoning morally. There are two different strategies they may take. The *act utilitarian* does not think that we should decide, in each case, which alternative will be more likely to promote the greatest happiness of the greatest number. That would be futile. Some would propose adopting "rules of thumb" we should follow unless we have compelling reasons to abandon them (Smart 1973: 42–3). That is the best way to maximize the greatest happiness of the greatest number.

Rule utilitarians take this strategy a step further. They deny not only that we should make moral decisions case by case; they also deny that moral rules are merely "rules of thumb." They contend that rules specify what we should do morally. It is just that the rules are justified by utilitarian principles. We determine which rules, if followed by most people, would promote the greatest happiness of the greatest number. Having justified these consequentialistically, we then follow them unwaveringly, as if they had independent status. Well, not quite. Most rule utilitarians recognize that these rules, so derived, can sometimes conflict. To resolve conflicts we employ judgment and sensitivity; we should not blindly adhere to another rule (Hooker 2000: 1, 90–2).

Thus, while an act utilitarian might decide that lying in some cases is justified because it maximizes the happiness of all those concerned, the rule utilitarian will not (often) permit such exceptions. Since a rule permitting lying would diminish happiness, it is better to have a blanket rule against lying even if, in some cases, lying might plausibly better promote the greatest happiness of the greatest number. Other rule utilitarians might defend rules with explicit exceptions permitting lying in select cases. If we face a choice covered by the exception, then lying would be acceptable. If not, then it would not be permitted even if the evidence to hand suggests it might be beneficial. To illuminate these ideas, I want to describe a form of utilitarianism forwarded by a historically significant defender of the theory.

John Stuart Mill

Mill's *Utilitarianism* is the classic statement of the theory. It remains one of the best. There are places where Mill is unclear and flirts with inconsistency. His theory is certainly incomplete. But he is neither as unclear, inconsistent, or incomplete as many critics are wont to claim.

Utilitarianism is so appealing, Mill claims, because it gives us a way to resolve moral disagreements. People widely disagree about how we should act in particular cases; they also disagree about the appropriate moral criteria. Utilitarianism resolves these problems by giving us a usable moral decision procedure. That procedure can be usable, though, only if it rests on a single principle. Suppose he is right. What would that principle be? He thinks the answer is clear. When most of us decide how we should act, we typically consider our actions' effects; we expect others to do likewise. We would be perplexed by someone oblivious to the consequences of her actions, especially to the effects on others' happiness. No "school of thought . . . refuses to admit that the influence of actions on happiness is a most material and even predominant consideration in many of the details of morals" (1998/1863: 51).

It is not enough, though, to say that we should consider people's happiness; we must know its precise role in moral deliberation. Mill's answer is this: "Actions are right in proportion as they tend to promote happiness; wrong as they tend to produce the reverse of happiness" (1998/1863: 55). And whose happiness does Mill think we should promote? "The happiness which forms the utilitarian standard of what is right in conduct is not the agent's own happiness but that of all concerned. As between his own happiness and that of others, utilitarianism requires him to be as strictly impartial as a disinterested and benevolent spectator" (1998/1863: 64). A conscientious utilitarian must be disinterested: she should not let personal interests distort her moral judgment. She must also be benevolent: she must care about others' interests.

Mill's proposal answers the first two questions consequentialists must answer. What counts? Happiness. How much? To the degree that it increases or decreases happiness. These answers are helpful, though, only inasmuch as we know what happiness is. Humans may enjoy episodic euphoria and rushes of physical pleasure. However, although these may be part of human happiness, they do not exhaust it. Humans also need higher pleasures of thought, sensibility, art, love, politics, and community. These distinctly human pleasures are qualitatively superior to swinely pleasures. That is why "it is better to be a human being dissatisfied than a pig satisfied" (1998/1863: 57).

The happiness of which humans are capable is neither sentimental nor unrealistic: "The happiness which is meant is not a life of rapture, but moments of such, in an existence made up of few and transitory pains, many and various pleasures, with a decided predominance of the active over the passive, and having as the foundation of the whole not to expect more from life than it is capable of bestowing" (1998/1863: 60). On his view, (1) whatever happiness is, it is not merely a matter of internal feeling. Nonetheless, (2) feeling is an important element of it. People constantly racked with pain or wholly devoid of simple pleasures are unlikely to be happy. However, (3) no matter how much pleasure and how little pain people experience, they will be unhappy if they are primarily passive. They should have interests they wish to pursue, ends they want to realize. However, (4) that won't be enough if they (a) misunderstand the nature of happiness and (b) have wholly unrealistic expectations for their own happiness. If people expect life to be constant bliss – wholly absent of pain, frustration, suffering, and disappointment – then they will surely be miserable. Things happen over which we have no (or painfully little) control, and these factors occasionally frustrate us, they disrupt our plans. We will find these painful, especially if we think our lives should always go exactly as we wish.

The chief impediments to happiness are either external or internal. The most common external impediments are flawed social institutions. These impoverish some people, deny them basic health care or education, and deprive them of basic liberties. Defective institutions will not guarantee that citizens are unhappy; however, they make that more likely. Conversely, sound institutions will not guarantee that citizens are happy, but they make that more likely. Each society, barring bad luck or external intervention, has the ability to create and sustain sound institutions. These are largely within a society's control.

Internal obstacles are, barring bad luck or external intervention, largely within each individual's control. Those who are miserable even when there are no external obstacles to happiness are usually so because they (a) care for no one but themselves or they (b) lack mental cultivation. If we care for others and can indulge in the higher pleasures, then we will have limitless sources of pleasure (Mill 1998/1863: 61–2).

Once we have identified the external and internal obstacles to happiness, we can determine how to best promote the greatest happiness of the greatest number. Minimally we will see why we cannot simply implore people to consciously maximize the greatest happiness of the greatest number. Since external impediments to happiness are so important, we must also pursue utilitarian ends indirectly by creating the appropriate economic, social, and political institutions.

> We must ensure that laws and social arrangements should . . . place the . . . interest of every individual as nearly as possible in harmony with the interest of the whole; and . . . that education . . . should so use (its) power to establish in the mind of every individual an indissoluble association between his own happiness and the good of the whole (Mill 1998/1863: 64).

Specifically, our economic, social, and political systems are not obstacles to human happiness. For instance, we should not encourage forms of competition in which some people "win" only by trampling on the interests of others (Wilkinson 1996). We also need positive institutions that provide the economic opportunities, the education, and the liberty people need to pursue a good life. Finally, we need institutions that enable people to develop the appropriate moral dispositions and character (Driver 2001; Frey 2000: 178).

Clearly this account of utilitarianism is not subject to the blithe dismissals oft tendered in introductory texts. That is not to say that the theory is ultimately satisfactory. It is to say, however, that the theory is more sophisticated and more defensible than its critics suggest. Nonetheless, deontologists think even sophisticated versions of consequentialism are deeply flawed.

Deontology

Deontology has two marks in its favor. One, it reflects the way most of us acquired and developed our moral beliefs; two, its main competitor is subject to seemingly serious criticisms. Let me explain each. Most of us were taught morality as a set of rules. Typically those rules were negative – a list of things we should not do. As children we were told: "Don't be mean to your sister," "Don't lie to me," "Don't take Kenneth's toys." Those moral rules were taught alongside social conventions and rules of etiquette ("Don't chew with your mouth open," "Don't disrespect your elders," etc.). This approach to morality remained the norm as we grew older. We were told "Don't have sex before marriage," "Don't be rude to your teachers," or "Don't use that kind of language." As we became adults, the centrality of rules still shaped most people's view of morality. Through their laws, governments told us: "Don't steal," "Don't lie on your tax return," or "Don't speed." Given this, it is not surprising that most people assume morality is a list of rules and that many think the rules are normally (if not exclusively) negative.

Deontology is also appealing because many people think consequentialism – its main rival – is flawed. Consequentialists hold that rules play no *fundamental* role in morality (although rules may be justified derivatively). Most people, though, think there are things we morally ought not to do, regardless of the consequences. Moreover, even when consequentialists reach the proper moral conclusion (e.g., that I shouldn't break my promise to Joan), they arguably give the wrong explanation for why the action is wrong. They say I shouldn't break my promise *because of the consequences*; deontologists say I shouldn't *because I should keep my promises*.

Despite these advantages, deontology faces its own problems. Even if most people think consequences don't count for everything, they think consequences count for something morally. So deontologists must either give consequences the appropriate moral weight or else they must show that, contrary to ordinary opinion, consequences really don't matter. Most deontologists try the former approach. Some claim that moral rules explicitly enjoin me to promote the happiness of others (Ross 1988/1930), although I should not follow this rule if I thereby violate some stronger or more important rule.

This captures the structure of many deontological theories. Morality is a set of moral rules, some of which are weightier than others. The problem is knowing which is weightier and by how much. We need to know that to know what to do when two or more conflict. There are four deontological strategies. Some claim that appearances are deceiving: moral rules do not really conflict. A few, like Kant, whom I discuss in detail later, claim there are no conflicts because there is really only one rule. Most who take this tack acknowledge there are multiple rules; it is just that these never conflict. On their view the rules we first learned are approximations of more complex rules, simplified to aid moral instruction. Consider the following analogy. In American football, two players on the offensive line are identified as tackles. Each tackle is two positions to the right of the center (the person who gives the ball to the quarterback). Under most circumstances, the tackle is not eligible to catch a forward pass from the quarterback. Hence, one might, when teaching a youngster the rules of the game, tell her that the tackle is not an eligible pass receiver. This is a sound approximation of the correct rule – but only an approximation. There is one condition, the details of which I needn't explain here, where the tackle is eligible. Because this circumstance is rare, teams may use this as a trick play. Deontologists often treat moral rules as if they were similarly complex – too complex to be taught to young children. We begin by first teaching them approximations of the rules; after they mature, we can make the rules suitably complex. We might tell them to "Never lie," only to later mention complicating factors. Young children couldn't appreciate the exceptions until they first grasp the simplified rule.

Other deontologists cope with apparent conflicts by saying that the rules themselves specify what to do when they conflict. In most games some rules take precedence over others. Let's call them "primary rules." They define the game's basic moves. If a player violates a primary rule, then they are no longer playing that game. Chess is not chess if one moves one's rook diagonally, soccer is not soccer if a player picks up the ball and runs with it, and tennis is not tennis if players grab the ball and throw it across the court. If a primary rule clashes with another rule, the primary rule always takes precedence. Perhaps morality also has some such rules. For instance, rules protecting human life might always take precedence over conflicting considerations.

On the third approach, deontologists seek to accommodate apparent conflicts between rules by claiming that there is always some meta-rule that explains what we should do when rules conflict. These might be analogous to some rules in sporting competitions. Most sporting events have more than one umpire or referee. There is a rule that explains what you do when the judgments of the two referees clash. This meta-rule does not specify how to play the game or how to make judgments. It simply specifies what to do when two referees disagree. Some deontologists suggest that that is how we handle conflicts between moral rules. For instance, some meta-rule may specify that it is always worse to violate a right than to (merely) fail to fulfill one's obligations, if those obligations are not correlative to someone else's rights.

There is also a fourth strategy. On this view we lack a clear mechanism for resolving conflicts. Some thinkers who advocate this option are not concerned. We can still resolve moral claims, just not via a decision procedure. Instead, morally sensitive people can discern the moral truth in particular cases via intuition or cultivated judgment (appropriately called "moral particularism"; see McNaughton 2000). Others go further: they claim some conflicts are rationally irresolvable: we may be forced to choose although none of the available choices is right (Gaita 1991; Williams 1985).

This final strategy is arguably dangerous: it means that there is no correct way we should act. In some cases that is not grounds for worry. There may be diverse ways friends can support each other. In other cases, however, failure to find a best way to act may be highly undesirable; it may be, to use the earlier analogy, that the moral game ends. However, whether that is a flaw of this final maneuver, or simply represents an accurate rendering of the boundaries of morality, is an issue we will set aside until Chapter 17.

Immanuel Kant

To give this discussion of deontology the appropriate historical dimension, I will briefly explain the seminal views of Immanuel Kant (1956/1788; 1991/1785; 1999/1785). Although Kant employs the first (and least popular) strategy I mentioned, many aspects of his theory remain central to deontological thought. To understand his theory you must first understand the importance he places on "the good will."

The good will

Kant wonders what things might be good without qualification. Most of us are inclined to think any number of things are good: happiness, health, intelligence, generosity, etc. Kant does not deny the obvious: these are often good. However, they are not good without qualification. For each we can envision circumstances in which the condition or trait works for ill. Some people are happy at the misery of others; intelligent and healthy assassins are more effective; misplaced generosity can encourage recipients to become dependent, etc. That is why none of them is good without qualification. The only thing that is good without qualification is "the good will."

Before we can understand why he thinks "the good will" is uniquely valuable, we must know what he thinks it is. Some people might think Kant is claiming that anyone who thinks they act correctly has a good will. He is not. Kant recognizes that many of the world's worst evils were perpetrated by people who thought they were right. So the "good will" must be more than thinking we are right. It is. It is doing one's duty because it is one's duty (Kant 2002/1785: 196). These are the only circumstances in which a person's action has any moral worth. If our actions are to have any moral worth, we must know how to identify our duty. We can do so only by examining "the *principle of volition* in accordance with which the action was done . . ." (201). However, not just any principle of violation will do.

> The only thing that could be an object of respect (and thus a commandment) for me is something that is conjoined with my will purely as a ground and never as a consequence. . . . Nothing remains that could determine the will except objectively *the law* and subjectively *pure respect* for this practical law (202).

In acting on the law we do our duty; in doing our duty we do what is uniquely valuable.

Categorical imperative

Kant thinks only one principle could satisfy this requirement: the *categorical impera-tive*. The categorical imperative is not the name for a rule like "Be kind to animals." It describes a way of determining what is moral. Before explaining the role of the categorical imperative, I must first explain why he calls it this imperative *categorical*. An imperative is a statement or command specifying what a person should do. We may say (or are told) that we should pay our taxes, tell the truth, exercise three times a week, keep our promises, care for our children, avoid using alcohol and barbitu-rates at the same time, and do our homework. These are all imperatives inasmuch as they tell us what we should do. Still, they differ in critical ways. Most tell us what we should do *if* we wish to achieve some goal. Someone who tells us that we should study is really telling us, Kant would say, that "If you want to do well in school, you should study." Even if they do not state the "if" phrase – the hypothetical – it is still a hypothetical.

These imperatives are conditional on the "if" phrase (the antecedent); they are binding only on those who want to achieve the goal specified by that phrase. If the consequent (the "then" phrase) of the hypothetical is the best means to that end, then the hypothetical imperative is binding on that person. If someone doesn't care about the specified end, then the imperative does not tell them what they should do. Con-sider the children portrayed in *Searching for Bobby Fischer*, a movie about aspiring chess players. Doubtless these children's parents implored them to practice and study the game. Although this was sage advice to them, it would be inappropriate for children who wanted instead to be concert violinists.

Kant thought morality was different. Moral requirements are not hypothetical imperatives. It is not that people ought to be moral *if they want to* or *if they think it will gain them eternal life* or *if they think it will make them upstanding citizens* or *if they think it will make their parents and friends accept them*. No, says Kant. People ought to be moral, period – no matter what their desires or interests or beliefs. If it is wrong for me to kill an innocent person, then it is wrong for me to kill an innocent person. I need not have any other interests or beliefs or desires for that imperative to bind me. The imperative binds me because I am a rational creature.

Why does Kant identify the categorical imperative in this way? Remember that for Kant the only good thing is a good will. A will is good *simply* because of its willing. Inclinations, desires, and consequences do not matter morally. Since we cannot con-sider these factors when determining what is moral, we must look only at the form of the moral law. Whenever I act, Kant says, there is always a maxim of my action, a principle that describes – and is usually thought to justify – my action. If I give Susan an A *because* the quality of her coursework merits an A, then my rationale for giving Susan the A is that *students should receive grades based on the quality of their course-work*. That is the maxim of my action. Can I will that that maxim should become a universal law? If I can, then I have done what the moral law demands. If not, then my action is not in conformity with duty, and is certainly not done because it is my duty. To decide whether I could will the maxim of my action to be a universal law, I need not know whether following such a law would advantage me or others. I needn't have any experience of the world. I need know only that the "principle is the universal conformity of actions to law as such" (202).

This sounds heady and convoluted. Kant thinks his claim is down-to-earth: he thinks he has captured ordinary moral understanding. "Common human reason, when engaged in making practical judgements, also agrees with this completely and has that principle constantly in view" (203). He is right in part: something like this is an important strain in ordinary moral reasoning. In deciding how to act, we often ask ourselves whether we want others to act in the same way we did.

To explain, let's fill out one of Kant's own examples. Suppose I borrow $1,000 from you knowing that tomorrow I will file for bankruptcy and, therefore, not repay the loan. I have promised you that I intended to repay you, but when I made the promise I knew I wouldn't. Repaying the loan is not part of the maxim of my action. Rather I am guided by the maxim that I can make a pretend promise if that serves my interest. Kant would ask – philosophical tongue firmly in cheek – "Would I be willing to make it a universal law that people can make false promises whenever it is to their advantage?" The answer is an emphatic "No." I would not want others to break their promises to me for similar reasons. Nor would I want to be part of a society in which such "promises" were common. Hence, I should not make false promises.

This way of speaking has a decidedly consequentialist ring: it sounds as if I decide what to do based on judgments about the consequences of my acting. Appearances are misleading – in two ways. When asking whether I would be willing to make the maxim of my action a universal law, I am not asking about the *projected* consequences of my false promise. I might have perfectly good reason to think that no detrimental effects will follow from it in this case. Neither is the maxim morally unacceptable because acting on it *will* have unseemly consequences. Kant claims it is rationally impossible for me to make such a promise. I could not rationally will that people make false promises whenever it is to their advantage since "with such a law, there would actually be no promising at all. . . . As soon as it became a universal law, ⟨it⟩ would necessarily subvert itself" (204).

Kant's point is not as mysterious as it sounds. Think for a moment. When I promise you that I will do something, I give you my assurance that I will do it, and that I will do it even at some personal cost to me. If I were merely promising you that I will do it *if* I am later so inclined, then there is no reason why I should have made – or you would have wanted – the promise.

Suppose I promise Judy that will take her to her appointment with the eye doctor. She assumes the doctor will dilate her eyes during the exam, and hence, that it would be unsafe for her to drive home. My promise enables Judy to keep her appointment. However, when I make the promise I know that I will be out of town on a business trip. I don't tell Judy that because I don't want anyone to know about the trip; I assume that would be to my advantage.

Would it be legitimate for me to give a false promise in these circumstances? Kant says "No." The reason he says "No" is not that the fake promise will have bad consequences, although it normally will – normally, but not always. This day it might be beneficial: Judy cancels her appointment, and the building housing her eye doctor explodes at the very time that she would have been in the office. My false promise saved her life. So, the false promise cannot be wrong because of its consequences. The reason the "promise" is wrong, Kant claims, is that my action is self-contradictory. I make a promise (to fulfill some action even if it is at some disadvantage to me), yet the maxim of my action (that I can make false promises) nullifies the promise. My action is self-defeating. A promise a person has no intention of keeping is not a promise.

Other formulations of the imperative

According to Kant the categorical imperative can also be formulated in other ways. One provides arguably the most appealing element of his theory. In reasoning morally, we see that the categorical imperative binds all rational creatures, and binds us equally. I should not merely use you for my purposes; nor should you merely use me. "[E]very rational being does exist as an end in himself, not merely as a means to be used by this or that will as it pleases. In all his actions, whether they are directed to himself or to other rational beings, a human being must always be viewed at the same time as an end" (Kant 2002/1785: 229). We all occasionally use others for our own satisfaction. I expect my auto mechanic to fix my car, my realtor to sell my house, and my accountant to accurately fill out my taxes. That is fine. However, in so doing I must also treat these people as ends in themselves, as rational creatures. They are not inanimate objects (like pencils and computers) whose sole purpose is to enable me to achieve my ends. They are ends in themselves.

Elsewhere Kant expresses this idea differently when he says that humans have dignity and not merely a price. An object with a price "can be replaced by something else that is its equivalent" (2002/1785: 235). People can trade a $100 bill for an object worth $100; both will be satisfied. Humans, though, are not objects to be bartered (or simply used). They are ends in themselves; they have dignity. What is it that gives them dignity? Autonomy: the ability to rationally choose, and then act upon their choices. That is an idea we explore further in Chapter 10.

Kant captures significant elements of most people's moral understanding. However, his view also has problems. The idea that inappropriate maxims are self-contradictory seems to work well for promises and lies. It is doubtful that this could explain all moral judgments. Moreover, although his view captures the common idea that we must be leery of inclinations – since they often lead us to make exceptions in our own case – it is unclear why acting from inclinations is always devoid of moral worth.

However, before pursuing our theoretical inquiry further, I return to see if our theorizing will help us think a bit more clearly, more productively, about the problems first discussed in Chapter 1.

REFERENCES

Driver, J. (2001) *Uneasy Virtue*. Cambridge: Cambridge University Press.

Frey, R. G. (2000) "Act-Utilitarianism." In H. LaFollette (ed.), *The Blackwell Guide to Ethical Theory*. Oxford: Blackwell Publishers, 165–82.

Gaita, R. (1991) *Good and Evil: An Absolute Conception*. New York: St. Martin's Press.

Gauthier, D. P. (1986) *Morals by Agreement*. Oxford: Oxford University Press.

Harris, J. (1994/1975) "The Survival Lottery." In B. Steinbock and A. Norcross (eds.), *Killing and Letting Die*, 2nd edn. New York: Fordham University Press, 257–65.

Hooker, B. (2000) *Ideal Code, Real World: A Rule Consequentialist Theory of Morality*. Oxford: Clarendon Press.

Kant, I. (1956/1788) *Critique of Practical Reason*. New York: Liberal Arts Press.

Kant, I. (1991/1785) *The Metaphysics of Morals*. Cambridge: Cambridge University Press.

Kant, I. (1999/1785) *Grounding for the Metaphysics of Morals*, 3rd edn. Indianapolis: Hackett.

Kant, I. (2002/1785) *Groundwork for the Metaphysics of Morals*. Oxford: Oxford University Press.

Lipton, R. J. (2000) *Nazi Doctors: Medical Killing and the Psychology of Genocide*. New York: Perseus Publishing.

Marquis, D. (2002/1997) "An Argument that Abortion is Wrong." In H. LaFollette (ed.), *Ethics in Practice: An Anthology*, 2nd edn. Oxford: Blackwell Publishers, 83–92.

McNaughton, D. (2000) "Intuitionism." In H. LaFollette (ed.), *The Blackwell Guide to Ethical Theory*. Oxford: Blackwell Publishers, 268–87.

Mill, J. S. (1998/1863) *Utilitarianism*. New York: Oxford University Press.

Ross, W. D. (1988/1930) *The Right and the Good*. Indianapolis: Hackett.

Sayre-McCord, G. (2000) "Contractarianism." In H. LaFollette (ed.), *The Blackwell Guide to Ethical Theory*. Oxford: Blackwell Publishers, 247–67.

Smart, J. J. C. (1973) "An Outline of a System of Utilitarian Ethics." In J. J. C. Smart and B. Williams (eds.), *Utilitarianism: For and Against*. Cambridge: Cambridge University Press, 3–74.

Thomson, J. J. (2002/1971) "A Defense of Abortion." In H. LaFollette (ed.), *Ethics in Practice: An Anthology*, 2nd edn. Oxford: Blackwell Publishers, 63–71.

Tuskegee Syphilis Study Legacy Committee (1996) "A Request for Redress of the Wrongs of Tuskegee." (Online) Available at: http://hsc.virginia.edu/hs-library/historical/apology/report.html. (Accessed May 15, 2003.)

Wilkinson, R. G. (1996) *Unhealthy Societies: The Afflictions of Inequality*. London: Routledge.

Williams, B. (1985) *Ethics and the Limits of Philosophy*. Cambridge, MA: Harvard University Press.

THREE

Using and Sharpening the Theoretical Tools

In the first chapter I discussed three practical ethical issues and used them to isolate ways we theorize about ethics. In the second, I outlined two dominant types of ethical theory that embody these ways of theorizing. Here we explore ways these theoretical considerations help us better understand these practical issues. Although this discussion will not resolve them, it should eliminate some inappropriate solutions. Discussing these practical issues will also further isolate problems for and gaps in these theories – problems we address in later chapters, gaps we will try to close. We will also use insights gleaned here to inform discussion of other practical issues.

Telling the Truth

We all claim to prize honesty. We are angry when others lie to us. Yet in many respects our society encourages personal, professional, and political dishonesty (Bok 1978). Perhaps the most common are "white lies."

White lies

Most of us occasionally tell "white lies" – lies which, to all outward appearances, are relatively minor. We lie to others about their appearance, clothes, or cars; we lie about our reactions to what they say or do. If we try to justify these lies at all, we usually say that we lied to protect the other person's feelings. If I lie to Jack about his hair, I might think that the truth will cause him unnecessary hurt; besides, the lie is about something trivial.

This justification is spurious. I say that the lie is trivial, yet my stated justification for lying is that the truth will cause him unnecessary upset. If the truth will hurt him, then the choice between lying and telling the truth is not trivial, while if it won't, then my reason for lying is undercut. Finally, it is hard to imagine that any ordinary person will be hurt by the knowledge that I dislike his hair. He is far more likely to be hurt if he discovers I deceived him because I thought he could not handle honesty. Suppose, though, that Jack is incredibly sensitive and would be hurt by my comments. How should we treat him (and people like him)? There is at least one reason to think I should be honest: by pandering I reinforce this propensity. I make him (them) less able to deal with honest disagreements.

This again illustrates the oft forgotten point about consequentialism: we should consider all relevant consequences. When people try to justify lying, they typically focus on one consequence to the exclusion of others. Yet no consequentialist worth her moral salt would resolve important moral decisions by considering a single consequence. Sometimes it might appear they do. When it does, it is likely that one consequence is so weighty that it determines the appropriate behavior – as, perhaps, it was in the case of deciding not to tell my ailing father about the death of his sister. However, those cases are not the norm, and even in these cases we should still consider other factors. It is clear that some consequences are so momentous that they dominate the landscape of ethical deliberation.

What this suggests is that proffered justifications for white lies are typically rationalizations. They may be a way to avoid conflict or they may indicate our indifference to or lack of respect for the person to whom we lie. We should be leery of such rationalizations. The "reasons" we offer for white lies are rarely ones we would tolerate from others. Doubtless we abstractly recognize our tendency to rationalize what we do. Unfortunately, we take few active measures to counteract it. This is akin to our propensity to discount our fallibility. Although we all recognize our tendency to make mistakes.

> the fact of their fallibility is far from carrying the weight in their practical judgement which is always allowed to it in theory; for while everyone well knows himself to be fallible, few think it necessary to take any precautions against their own fallibility, or admit the supposition that any opinion of which they feel very certain may be one of the examples of the error to which they acknowledge themselves to be liable (Mill 1978: 17).

It is not enough to admit that we rationalize our behavior (or that we are biased or insensitive or unduly self-interested). We should protect ourselves from moral error; we should actively root out our rationalizations, biases, and insensitivity. When telling white lies we should consider that our "justifications" are usually a subterfuge. We rarely, if ever, trace the likely effects of the lie and then decide that lying has the best overall consequences. Rather, we respond habitually; we assume there is a justification lurking in the background. Perhaps we don't think these lies require justification. When someone asks us what we think about their clothes or their hair, etc., our first inclination is to tell them what we think they want to hear. Full stop.

The power of society and the importance of habit

The previous discussion now permits us to identify two important factors we should consider when theorizing about ethics: (1) our beliefs, attitudes, and habits – moral or otherwise – are significantly shaped by our parents, teachers, and society, often in ways we do not realize; (2) we are largely habitual creatures. We see both at play here.

In our society, white lies are taken for granted. Most of us have just absorbed this "teaching" and continue to be guided by it, especially since it typically coincides with our perceived self-interest. Here, as elsewhere, we are blind to (or indifferent to) the ways that social forces shape our views; we deceive ourselves about why we think what we think and do what we do. We usually feel justified in believing and acting as we do, even when we just mouth or mimic what we heard or saw from our parents, teachers, preachers. Instead, we should critically examine our views. Only then can we justify our beliefs. Only then can they become *our* beliefs.

None of this implies that parents or society err by morally instructing their children – far from it. Parental and societal instruction aids moral education: it provides us content against which to react, it gives us the sense that ideas matter. Nor does it imply that society's instruction is always or even usually wrong. What it does show, however, is that as we become adults we should critically scrutinize what we were explicitly and implicitly taught so that we accept what we think reasonable, and refine or reject what is dubious. We certainly expect others to scrutinize *their* beliefs.

The second, and closely related, element is that humans are largely habitual creatures. Humans do not consciously deliberate about each, let alone most action(s). In our youth we acquired patterns of action. These shape what we tend to do "instinctively." That is clear with lying. Liars – people who regularly and consistently lie – don't decide to lie on each occasion; they just do. Honest people do not normally consciously decide to be honest. They just are honest; that is what comes "naturally" to them. Of course liars sometimes consciously decide to lie (or even to be honest) while honest folks sometimes consciously decide to be honest (or even to lie). However, what defines them as liars and honest folk is not what they do consciously on individual occasions, but what they do habitually – normally, regularly, as part of a predictable pattern.

These habits are initially formed by social forces. They can be reinforced by blind repetition, and reformed or abandoned by our choices. This isolates an important negative consequence of lying, even about something as insignificant as Jack's hair. Whenever I perform an action regularly, I develop a tendency to respond similarly in the future. This tendency is not inevitably good or inevitably bad; but it is inevitable. We call it "learning"; what we learn becomes part of who we are. When I first learned to drive, I was a little better than dreadful. Now I am a competent driver. Practice at driving may not make perfect, but it usually makes better. I had to drive badly before I could drive well. Early on I had to consciously remember to apply the brake and the accelerator, to use the clutch. Each move was wholly deliberate and, partly for that reason, stiff, jerky. As I practiced, I *learned* to drive, and what was once done consciously was then done without conscious thought. Of course, there are occasions where I should be consciously aware of what is happening: the flow of the traffic, water pooling on the road, the erratic driver to my left, etc. However, I can profitably attend to these conditions because I no longer have to consciously attend to shifting, clutching, braking, or turning the wheel. I may also reflect on my driving after the fact, and, in so doing, discover patterns I can profitably change: to watch the road more carefully, to drive within the speed limit, etc.

The same is true of all learning, including moral learning. If I consciously choose to regularly lie about things trivial, I will develop and sustain a habit of lying, even about things important. I will later lie without consciously choosing to do so. What is true of individuals is equally true for a culture. Cultures that uncritically accept white lies create a social climate that makes lies more common (Gehring 2003: 19). These are reasons why any careful consequentialist must consider the effect of our actions on individuals and on the culture (Bok 1978).

Some consequentialists might claim that concerns about the cultural effects of lying are overblown, the idle speculations of moral neurotics. They correctly note that such consequences are difficult to predict. I agree. That is why we should not prohibit an action simply because it *might* have deleterious consequences. In political and moral debate people often make grand and highly speculative predictions about the long-term consequences of actions, and, based on those predictions, make unqualified assertions about what we as a society ought to do. That is the familiar mechanism of "slippery slope" arguments – a familiar style of argument we will examine in considerable detail in Chapter 10.

However, I am not claiming there is a *serpentine* and *obscure* causal link between regularly lying and creating in oneself and in one's society an increased likelihood of lying. My argument is based straightforwardly on the knowledge that we are habitual creatures and knowledge of the general ways that habits are established and perpetuated. This is not information that has been uncovered by science in the past 50 years. This is a truth of human behavior on which we have relied for eons. It is the basis of all education and training: we practice certain behaviors so we can do them better. We should, of course, try to identify the precise nature of habits and the ways that they are formed (Doris and Stich 2004; Doris 2002). However, a failure to know their precise mechanisms does not hamper our ability to comfortably predict that certain actions will form, change, or strengthen our traits, our habits, our propensities to action.

I will say more later about what habits are, how they are formed, and what role they play in moral behavior. However, we can set those details aside for a while and simply rely on a rough and ready view of which behaviors will create which habits. If I claim that playing the piano makes people better typists, then that claim, although plausible, is debatable and should be tested empirically. If I claim that handwriting increases typing skills, that claim would be contentious and in need of firm empirical evidence. Were I to claim that typing would make me a better philosopher, others would be rightly dubious since that claim does not fit with anything we know about learning. However, the claim that people can generally improve their handwriting by practice is uncontroversial.

Acknowledging that we are habitual creatures spells trouble for Kant's view as commonly understood.

One worry for Kant

Kant's theory has been enormously influential; most people embrace significant ele-ments of it. However, his theory can neither explain nor accommodate the habitual nature of human beings. Here's why. As you may recall, Kant claims there is an unbridgeable moral gulf between human inclination and reasoned choice. No action, no matter how beneficial, has moral worth if motivated only by inclinations, no matter how good (e.g., benevolence). "The universal wish of every rational being ⟨is⟩ to be wholly free of them" (Kant 2002/1785: 229). Actions have moral worth only if done because they are our duty. Kant's misgiving about the role of inclination isolates one critical insight about morality. It also leads to a serious problem for his theory.

Here's the problem: we are psychologically so constituted that by doing an action regularly – even if initially chosen consciously (say, from duty) – that we will even-tually come to do it habitually, without conscious choice. That is the kind of crea-tures we are. Thank goodness. Habitual action is more reliable. Even the most diligent person cannot always triumph over inclination. It is also usually more effective. If your friend is depressed and you help her instinctively – without consciously decid-ing to do so – you will likely be less stilted, more genuine, and more effective than if you decide to help her consciously. Most of us would think that the former action, inasmuch as it better responds to your friend's need, has more moral worth. Not Kant. That is where he has a problem. He does not understand that habits are inevitable and desirable – inevitable, because of the kinds of creatures we are, desir-able, because they are a critical part of morality. When people successfully inculcate good habits, they generally act from inclinations shaped by those habits. That seems highly valuable. As we shall see in Chapter 14, virtue ethicists agree. However, Kant thinks such acts are devoid of moral worth. His theory cannot give habit any legiti-mate role.

Here's the insight: sometimes, we do not want to do what we morally ought. To do what is right in these cases we must battle our current inclinations. More generally, we must constrain inclination while inculcating good habits. That is, although habits are important elements of the moral life, we must sometimes resist current habits and create new ones. What Kant ignores is the psychological fact that if we succeed in establishing good habits, we no longer need fight inclination (Herman 1981).

Joan's tragic loss

Of the cases mentioned earlier, this is the most compelling one for lying. If there is good reason to think that the shock of telling Joan the truth might kill her, then we would have a powerful reason to lie to her. A lie, even if bad, is not as bad as her death. Even so, there is something to be said for telling Joan the truth. Some deon-tologists, e.g., Kant, think we should always tell the truth no matter what the cir-cumstances. There are also consequentialist reasons for thinking we should not lie to Joan. If she knows that friends (and hospitals) are inclined to lie to people in her condition, then she will not believe a lie. She will not only not believe a lie, she will be disinclined to believe the truth! She suspects you will tell her that David is all right *even if he isn't*. It does not matter if you are very sincere ("Yes, Joan, I would have lied to you had David been dead, but I really, really swear to you that he is just fine"). Why? If the original rationale for lying has moral weight, then one should defend the lie to the hilt, even if it requires giving such assurances. Joan knows that. Therefore, she will likely infer, or at least fear, that David is not all right, no matter what you tell her, no matter what his condition. If the knowledge that David is dead will likely harm her health, then the suspicion that he is dead will likely have the same effect. The lie serves no purpose.

Such an argument, in the end, may not withstand scrutiny. But it is plausible. Two additional factors might undercut this argument. One is special to this case; the other, more general. First, the above scenario could occur only if Joan is alert enough to think that you might be lying to her even if you aren't. Suppose, though, that Joan drifts in and out of consciousness. During a brief moment she awakes and asks you about David. She is unlikely to be alert enough to judge that you are lying to her and may well not even remember asking you the question. So lying would not have the aforementioned negative consequences.

Second, these consequences are likely only if she knows, or has some reason to think, that you will lie to her if David is dead or seriously hurt. If she thinks you will tell her the truth no matter how dreadful, then she will believe you even if you are lying (unless, of course, you are an inept liar). This is crucial. Lies offered by known liars, or even people who are known to lie *in certain kinds of circumstances*, will not be believed, at least in those circumstances. Therefore, if someone intends to lie in such circumstances, and wants the lie to have the desired effect, then she should work to be *known* to be someone who regularly tells the truth, come what may. Of course, it is likely she can form that reputation only if she does regularly tell the truth come what may. Consider the nun in *Les Miserables* who lies to Inspector Javert to protect M. The inspector believes her precisely because she is known to be steadfastly honest.

This is connected to the claim we shall see several times in this book: the claim that moral rules must be public (Fuller 1977/1964; Raz 1980). If we do not know what morality requires, then we cannot know what to do. We cannot properly be blamed for failing to do what we did not know we should do. This leads to a problem. If exceptions to a moral rule against lying are publicly promulgated, then the exception cannot achieve its desired result (in this case, protecting Joan from the shock of learning that her son is dead). If the exception cannot achieve that result, then it won't be justified. Hence it seems we must reject explicit exceptions to moral rules against lying or we must abandon the requirement of publicity. Neither option is attractive.

Lying in one's professional capacity

Consider the bureaucrat who is asked to develop a health policy she finds objectionable. During a hearing before Congress (or Parliament), a representative asks her personal opinion of the policy. She could try to sidestep the question. But either her maneuver will be obvious, and thus not effective – at least not if she is trying to hide her view. Or it will be very subtle, in which case she has *effectively* lied by stating her views in ways she knows will mislead. Could either theorist justify her lying? Kant couldn't. But some deontologists could. They could claim that bureaucrats in a democracy should advance the policies of their elected governments, even if they personally think the government is mistaken. Some deontologists might even argue that refusing to tell the truth here is not even a lie. Consider the following analogy. Poker players do not lie when they bluff. Everyone who plays the game knows players sometimes bluff. Asking a player if she is bluffing wouldn't be a real question and therefore wouldn't warrant an accurate answer. Likewise, everyone knows (or should know) that the bureaucrat's job is to support the administration's position. Hence, asking her if she agrees is not a *real* question and does not warrant an accurate answer. By refusing to divulge her personal view, she has not thereby lied.

A consequentialist might offer a seemingly parallel argument for why the bureau- crat not only may hide her view, but why she should do so. A utilitarian might claim that the best way to promote the greatest happiness of the greatest number is to unwaveringly carry out the "people's will" as expressed by the people's elected rep- resentatives. The problem is that this theorist is unlikely to be able to defend this specific prediction with any confidence. Still, she might offer an indirect argument, one akin to John Stuart Mill's argument in *On Liberty*. Mill argues that the best way to find the truth (moral and otherwise) is by allowing, encouraging, and engaging in open discussion. On his view, a good society permits the majority to make mistakes and learn by them, at least if the mistakes are not too harmful and are reversible. These considerations would give bureaucrats good reason to generally support demo- cratically reached conclusions. However, it would not warrant the categorical claim that the majority's will should always be honored. Moreover, it would not support the claim that the best way for bureaucrats to honor the people's will is to always support the administration. In some cases, at least, by speaking their minds the bureaucrats needn't undermine democracy; they might enhance it by giving the public a new perspective.

This helps us isolate a significant difference between consequentialism and deon- tology – even between a consequentialism that gives rules some role and a deontol- ogy that includes rules directing us to care about the consequences of action. For reasons like those outlined earlier, a consequentialist is likely to think that a gov- ernment cannot work unless bureaucrats generally do what they are told by elected officials, even when those bureaucrats individually judge that the elected officials err. Moreover, both deontologists and consequentialists are likely to think that if the con- sequences of the policy were sufficiently bad, then a morally responsible person should tell the truth, especially if she thinks that, by so doing, she has some chance to stop it from being implemented (Kamm 2000: 218–19). What differentiates these thinkers is that the deontologist will be more reticent to override the moral rules; she will demand more and stronger evidence of the negative consequences of following the rules. And, of course, these theorists will describe and justify any exceptions differently.

Sexual Harassment

Once we understand that humans are habitual creatures we can also better understand and evaluate sexual harassment. A male boss who regularly harasses his employees likely does not consciously decide to harass them. Rather, he just "sees" women in a certain way and responds accordingly. Few of them will think they are harassing these women. The offenders rarely understand that – let alone why – their behavior is wrong.

Yet it is important to know why it is wrong; otherwise, we will have trouble identifying the proper moral response. A consequentialist would claim it is because harassment has negative consequences. To defend this claim she must specify those consequences. In paradigm cases of sexual harassment that is easy. If (a) I tell you that you cannot keep your job unless you do something (sleep with me), (b) you do not want to do what I want you to do, and (c) this is the only job you can find that will allow you to adequately support your children, then I have coerced you. You must sleep with me or your children will be hurt.

It is not clear, however, that these three factors by themselves can explain why this harassment is so wrong. To see why, consider a different case. I am an employer with the only job in your town. The job is distasteful (cleaning out septic systems), and requires that you work 50 hours a week for minimum wage. Although this job wouldn't pay enough for you to support your family well, it is better than nothing. My offer is not only less objectionable than the paradigm instance of harassment, but most people will think that I do nothing wrong by offering you this job. Many would think I have done you a favor. How, precisely, is this different from paradigm cases of harassment? In each you find the job distasteful, but you need it. In each I take advantage of your need. There are, of course, some important differences. You will find it much worse to sleep with me under these circumstances than to clean septic systems. However, I do not think that explains why harassment is very wrong, while taking advantage of your need to get you to clean septic systems is not wrong at all.

To help us better understand why harassment is so objectionable, let us contrast these cases with less dramatic cases of sexual harassment – those where I create a "hostile work environment." I am Jennifer's boss. I constantly brag about my sexual prowess, stare at and take pictures of my female employees, post nude pictures around the office, etc. This makes her very uncomfortable. Does that, by itself, make my actions immoral? After all, although we could all agree that it would be nice if people worked in congenial environments, many people cannot. Brian may be highly religious and be offended at having to work in an environment in which his boss curses. Or he may be uncomfortable knowing two of his co-workers are gay. Nonetheless, he is (or feels) compelled to tolerate these conditions to keep his job.

Are Jennifer's and Brian's cases morally different? According to the principle of universalizability, which we saw in the previous chapter, we must evaluate "the same situation" in the same way unless we can find some general and relevant difference between them that justifies a different evaluation. If consequentialists wish to distinguish Jennifer's case from Brian's (and surely they should), they have to specify which consequences befell Jennifer and only Jennifer, and then show how those consequences are worse than the consequences to Brian. It is doubtful that they could succeed.

It should be apparent why. The wrong to Jennifer, which is considerable, can be understood fully only in historical context. Jennifer is not some single individual who is harmed. She is being harmed *because she is a woman*, and the degree to which it is wrong requires understanding the history of mistreatment of women, in particular, their being seen as sexual objects upon which harassers can prey with impunity. That is why harassment is a wrong against all women, and not just the specific woman I harass (Superson 2002/1997). To further elucidate this claim, consider two other cases. In both I do no obvious or direct harm to the women, although I have surely harassed them. In the first, I demand that Courtney sleep with me to receive and retain her job. It so happens that Courtney finds me attractive, and likes (or thinks she likes) demanding men. She accedes to my demands – indeed, is excited by them. However, since I did not know she would be receptive, I still harassed her. In the second, two of my employees, Barbara and Bertha, have developed exceptionally thick skins. They have learned to endure sexual boasts, ribald stories, and nude pictures. Now they do not even notice my offensive behavior. If so, there are no negative consequences *for them*, certainly none that is serious. If moral wrongs are always against specifiable individuals – as many people suppose – then I did not harm them. If harm is a necessary element of harassment, then neither did I harass them. However, I think it is implausible to think my behavior was somehow less objectionable – or less an instance of harassment – than the behavior of a boss who made the same demand of a female employee who did not want to sleep with him, or said and did the same things around female employees not psychologically immune to predatory behavior.

If my behavior toward Courtney, Barbara, and Bertha are instances of harassment, then we must abandon the belief that wrongs are wholly explained by the reactions of women who are their specific targets. Harassment is also – and perhaps primarily – an attack against women as a group (ibid.). When bosses demand sex or create a hostile work environment, all women are belittled and abused.

Although controversial, this position is plausible. Even if it cannot fully explain sexual harassment, it suggests that we cannot understand or evaluate it without understanding the behavior's effects on women as a whole. The underlying idea here is not unusual. There are contexts in which we hold groups responsible for actions. We hold corporations (Exxon, for the Valdez disaster) or associations (Ku Klux Klan, for some violence) legally and morally responsible for their collective action. We also hold countries (Nazi Germany or Japan) collectively responsible for their aggression. If groups can be sufficiently cohesive to be held morally responsible for their actions, then it is reasonable to think they are sufficiently cohesive that they can also be collectively benefited or burdened. This is common in law. Policies are judged to variously harm (or help) the poor, the family, children, minorities, whites, Native Americans, immigrants, Anglo-Saxons, African-Americans, etc. We will discuss this issue in more detail later.

Death Penalty

We see both consequentialism and deontology at work in ordinary thinking about the death penalty. On the one hand, most people are concerned about its consequences, especially whether the death penalty deters others from committing similar crimes. Most are also concerned about seemingly non-consequentialist considerations, especially whether the criminal deserves to die for her crime. In the previous chapter we focused on the second issue, although we will say a bit more about it here and still more in Chapter 11. Here I primarily discuss deterrence. Both issues are important, not only for their relevance to capital punishment, but to punishment more generally. Exploring them will also help us see strengths and weaknesses of familiar ways of reasoning morally.

Deterrence

There are both empirical and moral questions about deterrence. The central empirical question is: does capital punishment, in fact, deter potential murderers? The moral question is: if it does deter, is that a reason – or even a sufficient reason – for employing capital punishment?

Does it deter?

The debate over deterrence typically begins with armchair psychologizing. Many people play the lottery in the hopes of getting the big payoff. Suppose that, in addition to a slight chance of winning several million dollars, participants had the same chance that they would be killed (officials auction their body parts to finance the lottery). I am confident that would dampen most people's enthusiasm for the lottery. The price, however improbable, is just too high. Likewise, many drivers speed even though they know that if they are caught they could pay a hefty fine. Suppose some states began executing randomly selected speeders. Surely fewer drivers would speed.

The explanation is simple. We assume most people are moderately rational, that they will decide what to do based on judgments about the probable outcomes of their actions. If the cost for breaking the law is minimal, then those who do not see the wisdom of the law will be more inclined to break it. When the cost for breaking the law increases, rational people will be increasingly disinclined to break the law, even if they think the law is misguided, unjust, or against their self-interest. That is why using the death penalty to punish the most horrendous crimes will make most people less likely to commit them. So the death penalty does deter.

This is a plausible argument. A wholly rational person who thinks she will likely be apprehended, convicted, and executed will be deterred by a threat of death. Unfortunately there are also strong armchair arguments suggesting that the death penalty does not deter many potential murderers. First, most murderers do not decide, after hours of cool reflection, to kill someone. Most murderers kill relatively spontaneously, usually after an interpersonal squabble (Bureau of Justice Statistics 2003a). When people are angry, or in some other way under stress, they have trouble making careful calculations about the likely consequences of their actions. They are unlikely to give possible negative consequences due weight; hence they are unlikely to be deterred. Those wholly devoid of rationality – even if only temporarily – won't be deterred at all.

Second, some people could be deterred by the threat of the death penalty if they thought they would be apprehended. However, few criminals think they will be caught. Perhaps they think the police are incompetent or grossly overworked. Maybe they think they can commit the perfect crime. Whatever the explanation, only a small percentage of criminals are caught (Bureau of Justice Statistics 2003b). For those confident they will not be caught, even the threat of death is unlikely to seriously deter them.

We do not need to rest on armchair psychologizing. Social scientists have conducted studies on the deterrent effect of capital punishment. I shall mention two. The first, by Otto Zimring, claims that the death penalty does not deter (Zimring and Hawkins 1973). The latter, by Ehrich, not only argues that it deters, but claims that every execution saves seven potential victims (Van den Haag and Conrad 1983; Van den Haag 1991).

How do we choose between competing studies? Assuming we lack the knowledge, skill, or money to conduct such studies ourselves, we should look to see if there is a general agreement among authorities. There is. When criminal justice scholars evaluated the collective evidence, they concluded, in their 1987 annual meeting, that "social science research has found no consistent evidence of crime deterrence through execution" (American Society of Criminology 1987). Although they may be mistaken, it is sensible to bow to their judgment unless we have good reason to think they are wrong.

For the moment, though, let's set aside this consensus; after all, experts are sometimes mistaken. What should we do when we do not have first-hand evidence about the deterrent effect of punishment and experts disagree? There are four common responses (which are not always incompatible). (1) Some continue to debate the issue based wholly on armchair arguments. That approach, as we have seen, yields opposing conclusions. (2) Some claim that in the face of uncertainty, we should assume that it does deter (the "Best Bet" argument). Since we don't know if capital punishment deters, we can assume that there is an equally good chance that it does and that it does not. If we try capital punishment and it does deter, we save innocent lives (potential victims), while if we are wrong, we execute some murderers unnecessarily. If we revoke capital punishment and it does not deter, we save some murderers who would have been executed, while if we are wrong, we lose the lives of additional innocent people who will be victims. Given these options, it is better to bet that it does deter (Pojman 2002: 497–8).

Third, others (for example, the Society of Criminologists, cited above) conclude the opposite. They hold that since capital punishment would be murder if not justified, in the absence of evidence that it deters, we have compelling reason to abandon it. Especially since the penalty is applied unjustly. Perhaps the single most telling statistic supporting this latter assertion is that in the 25 years since capital punishment was reinstated, 12 whites were executed for murdering blacks, while 178 blacks were executed for murdering whites (Death Penalty Information Center 2003). Those figures are *wildly* out of proportion to the percentage of blacks in our society (Bureau of Justice Statistics 2003c).

Fourth, some claim uncertainty demands that we shift the focus of the debate. Some on both sides use this strategy. Supporters may claim that the deciding factor should be the cost of incarcerating a murderer over a lifetime. Given the severity of the crime, we should neither release murderers from prison nor expect the public to support them for their entire lives. It takes $20,000 a year to keep a criminal incarcerated in the USA. If we imprison them for an average of 30 years, the taxpayers must pay $6 million per murderer. That is money we could use to educate children or provide health care for the elderly, etc. Therefore, they conclude, the death penalty is justified.

Opponents of the death penalty respond that although we might think it is cheaper to execute a prisoner than to incarcerate them for life, in fact, the reverse is true. Both countrywide and jurisdiction-specific studies show that when we consider the additional costs of housing criminals on death row, and the additional legal costs involved in lengthy appeals, it is cheaper to simply incarcerate the person for life (Dieter 1994).

Some supporters of the death penalty acknowledge that these figures are correct, but claim that the cost of executions is so high only because we permit lengthy appeals that increase legal costs and extend time spent on death row. That can be remedied by eliminating most appeals. They are right. However, that makes one frequent objection to capital punishment – namely the danger of executing the innocent – all the more potent. However, before we look at that issue, we need to ask whether it would be morally relevant if capital punishment did deter.

Is deterrence morally relevant?

A consequentialist would have to say that if a policy saves innocent lives then we would have *a* reason for implementing it. Some might contend other considerations usually trump it. Even so, saving innocent lives is a morally relevant consideration. Still, we should not forget that the consequentialist is concerned not only about deterrence, but about consequences broadly. Even if punishments deter, that is not all they do. Suppose capital punishment also made the average citizen more suspicious and hateful, less sympathetic, and generally less concerned with their fellow humans. These consequences would also be highly relevant. Whether these are likely, and whether they are weighty, I cannot decide here. The consequentialist, though, will insist that we examine all relevant consequences, that we widen our moral scope. But just how wide? For instance, we would all like to ease the victims' families' pain. Suppose executing convicted murderers eased their pain. Would that give us a reason to execute the perpetrator? It seems a consistent act consequentialist will have to say "Yes." Whether this factor has much weight is another matter.

Suppose, though, that the families would feel even better if we slowly tortured the murderer. Does that give us any reason to torture them? Or suppose the family would be delighted if we slowly tortured the murderer's family. Does that give us any reason to do that? Most people will want to say "No" to both proposals – and certainly to the second. Why? Why is it legitimate to kill the murderer, but not to torture her or her family? Most deontologists – at least those of a Kantian bent – will presumably claim that torture is categorically wrong, that we shouldn't torture people, no matter what the consequences. What about an act consequentialist? Can she hold that torture is categorically wrong? I don't see how. I assume act consequentialism would not hold that any action is always wrong, no matter what the circumstances. However, she can certainly claim that such consequences could justify torture only in the rarest of rare circumstances. Indeed, she would have one explanation for thinking it is almost categorically wrong. Since utilitarianism's aim is to promote the greatest happiness of the greatest number, then any action which brings some people happiness only by making others miserable works against the theory's very aim. Therefore, such behavior should not be countenanced, counted, or encouraged (Narveson 1967). On this view, seemingly non-consequentialistic considerations can be captured by a deeper consequentialist analysis. Whether this argument is finally convincing we cannot decide here. Still, this does indicate why and how it is difficult to be a consistent consequentialist. This is one reason deontologists thought consequentialism was easy philosophical prey.

Executing the innocent

Although the United States permits numerous appeals of a death sentence, since 1950 at least 24 innocent people have been executed (Bedau 1997). Moreover, since the reintroduction of the death penalty in 1973, 119 people have been sentenced to death but later cleared (Death Penalty Information Center 2005) (the details of one case are carefully chronicled in Adams et al. 1991). These people were saved from death only by a lengthy appeal process. It is also likely that there are, and were, other death row inmates whose innocence we have not (or did not) discover.

It is bad for an innocent person to even be charged for a crime she did not commit. It is even worse to convict and incarcerate her. It is still worse to execute her. Of course *any* system will make mistakes, even a system with significant checks and balances. However, if we limit opportunities for appeal, either as a way of lowering the costs of executions or speeding the time to punishment, we can only increase the number of innocent people who will be executed. Is that morally acceptable, especially if we lack clear evidence that capital punishment deters?

This question helps isolate some critical differences between (some) consequentialists and deontologists. At least some deontologists will want to say that the state's executing an innocent person, even by accident, is so morally intolerable that no gain in consequences could justify it. Some consequentialists will also say that those

consequences are so bad that only clear and unequivocal evidence that capital punishment deters a substantial number of potential murderers could possibly justify
establishing a practice that we know will lead us to occasionally take the lives of innocent persons.

This discussion does not pretend to resolve the issues, although we return to
discuss them a bit more in Chapter 11. However, it does isolate important practical
factors we must consider. It also helps us better understand the workings of standard ethical theories.

Responsibility for our actions

The system of criminal punishment assumes people have some control over, and are
thus responsible for, their behavior. If people had no control – if they were like trees
or amoebae – then we would be no reason to legally constrain unwanted behavior
or to punish those who break the law. This is an issue we discussed in the previous
chapter and will discuss more generally in Chapter 11. Here I want to say just a bit
about its connection with the issue of capital punishment. For if we are going to use
the "ultimate punishment" for some subclass of criminals, then we must be confident
that those criminals are responsible for their crimes.

Andrea Yates's attorneys argued that when she committed the murders, she was
not rational, and therefore could not control her behavior. The jury did not accept
her defense, although it is unclear whether they rejected the factual claims about
her psychological condition, or whether they doubted whether such a condition
would eliminate her responsibility. What would have eliminated or mitigated her
responsibility?

Consider the case of Charles Whitman, a Vietnam veteran, who, in the summer
of 1967, climbed the tower at the University of Texas with a small arsenal, and
began shooting students walking across the campus. He was killed by police
who stormed the tower. During his autopsy, the medical examiner discovered he
had a large brain tumor in the hypothalamic region of the brain, an area known
to control aggression and violence. Suppose he had not been killed by police, and
they had discovered the presence of the tumor. It is highly plausible to think that
the tumor affected Whitman's sense of reality and his ability to control himself.
Moreover, he had gone to a therapist for help when he first began thinking about
doing what he ultimately did. Would that have mitigated or even eliminated his
responsibility?

The same issues come up elsewhere in slightly different guise. Should we execute
retarded murderers? Recently the US Supreme Court ruled in *Adkins v. Virginia* that
we should not (536 US 304 (2002)). I find it intriguing, though, that the courts asked
only whether Adkins's retardation was sufficient to disqualify him from execution.
They did not ask whether it also undercut his legal responsibility for the crime. Did
they judge that he was retarded enough to mitigate his responsibility, yet "normal"
enough so that he was still somewhat responsible for his actions? Would they have
ruled differently had he been a bit more retarded?

What if the murderer is a juvenile? The Supreme Court has ruled that the state cannot execute someone who committed the crime before he reached the age of 16 (*Thompson v. Oklahoma*, 487 US 815 (1988)) . It subsequently ruled (summary judgment) that those committing crimes when they were 17 years old *could* be executed (*Stanford v. Kentucky*, 492 US 361 (1989)). Given that we do not let people vote until they are 18 – presumably because we think them incapable of making responsible judgments – how can we find them sufficiently responsible for their actions to execute them? Clearly debates about the conditions for ascribing personal responsibility are important for determining whether it is legitimate to execute some subset of murderers. They also have wider implications for our understanding of personal choice, personal responsibility, as well as autonomy – issues we discuss in Chapter 10.

Some Theoretical Reflections

This discussion helped us better understand the different ways consequentialists and deontologists reason about practical ethical issues. It isolates and explains some key differences between these theories. Let me focus on one difference.

Key theoretical differences between the theories

When discussing several practical issues we noticed that people often employ a distinction between actions and omissions. Within the philosophical literature that distinction is now more commonly described as the distinction between doing and allowing (Foot 1978, 1994; McMahan 1993, 1998; Quinn 1989). Most people suppose – and many philosophers agree – that it is morally worse to do an evil than to allow an evil to occur. For instance, they think that, barring special circumstances, killing Robert is much worse than failing to save Robert's life; and killing Indian children is not only much worse than refusing to provide these same children with food, the failure to provide food is not even immoral.

This distinction often tracks the difference between deontological and consequentialist moral theories. Since consequentialists are more concerned with the results of people's choices, they are not inclined to think that doings are *fundamentally* more important than allowings. Sure, it often appears that these are morally different. However, if we look carefully, we will see that other factors explain the difference in moral evaluation. For instance, we usually have more control over what we do than what we allow to happen. Since morality is largely concerned with what we can control, then we can assume that, in general, it is worse to do an evil than to allow an evil to occur. However, it is worse not because the doing/allowing distinction isolates a fundamental moral difference (a difference that is relevant in itself) but because, given certain truths about human psychology and the causal structure of the world, the distinction is usually associated with other morally relevant differences.

Deontologists, on the other hand, are more likely to think the doing/allowing distinction is fundamentally significant. It is significant in itself, not because it is often related to factors that are significant. They think the consequences of our actions are either morally irrelevant, or at most only a small portion of the moral story. That is why they emphasize what we do rather than what we allow. Most deontologists not only think the doing/allowing distinction is morally relevant, they think it marks a crucial moral divide such that doings are sometimes categorically worse, and standardly *much* worse, than allowings.

This has interesting implications for the debate over capital punishment. If this distinction is morally fundamental, we should have misgivings about capital punishment given the prospects, however slight, of executing the innocent. If killing an innocent person is *much* worse than allowing an innocent person to die, then establishing an institution that we know leads to the death of innocent people would be much worse than failing to establish an institution which would save some innocent victims. Furthermore, if the distinction is morally fundamental, there is something *prima facie* wrong with using capital punishment to deter potential murderers. When we execute people, we are doing something that, if not justified, would be grossly immoral, while, even if deterrence unquestionably worked, the failure to execute murderers would "only" allow innocent people to be killed. We cannot justify executions (doings) as a means of preventing others from being victims (allowings). Conversely, if deterrence is morally relevant, then the doing/allowing distinction would not mark a fundamental moral difference.

Supplementing the traditional theories

Both consequentialism and deontology are appealing, yet both have weaknesses. Some weaknesses have led some thinkers to reject one or both theories. Perhaps the theories can be patched in ways that make them more plausible. If they can be, our discussion suggests they should incorporate at least two ideas. Let me reiterate each.

The importance of habits and character

To understand and resolve moral questions about lying and sexual harassment we needed to attend to the habitual nature of humans. Yet standard theories imply that morality is primarily a matter of conscious choice. Certainly it sometimes is – but not always, and probably not even normally. Most moral behavior is habitual: regular and subconscious patterns of behavior that we often describe as a person's character. All the morally significant character traits – honesty, benevolence, kindness, sensitivity, empathy, humility, etc. – are not, for the most part reflected in consciously chosen actions. Empathic people do not have to decide to feel the pain of others: they just do. Humble people aren't those who regularly want to be haughty but choose to be circumspect. They simply have an appropriate sense of their worth relative to others.

Any adequate moral theory must accommodate these facts and employ them in describing how we should act and how we can best promote moral behavior. We have to ask whether the actions we expect of ourselves and others are reasonable; we must determine how best to instill good habits. Yet far too often we assume that the job of morality is merely to pass down moral prescriptions.

The moral status of groups

The discussion of sexual harassment suggests that morality concerns not only individuals but also groups. We should understand how groups act collectively and institutionally. We must see how individuals' and institutional actions may affect groups in ways that must be evaluated morally. Whether this is a plausible shift – and how the shift might be incorporated into existing theories – is something I explore in detail in Chapters 5 and 6.

Reiterating Our Initial Findings

The previous chapters should have demonstrated the importance of reasons in moral debate. When trying to convince someone of our position we must give (or be prepared to give) reasons for our moral actions and conclusions. We must be willing to explain why we think our reasons are true, relevant to, and sufficient for the conclusions we reach. If I support capital punishment because it deters, then I must be willing to defend the empirical claim that it deters, the moral claim that deterring potential murderers is *relevant*, and the moral claim that these benefits are sufficient to offset all costs of using capital punishment. It is not only that I must be able to defend these points to others. More importantly, as a responsible human being I must be able to defend them to myself. The purpose of studying moral philosophy is not to have an argumentative club I can use to bash those who disagree with me. It is to help me identify the best ways to behave, and to give me some guidance about how to inculcate the habits to make moral behavior more likely.

Second, morality primarily concerns the ways our actions affect others. Therefore, in reasoning morally, we must consider and give due weight to the interests of others. And, since we know our own proclivities to let bias cloud our judgment, we must make active efforts to counteract bias.

Third, in making an informed moral judgment about a particular action, we need a firm grasp of the relevant empirical evidence. That evidence is important, whether one is a deontologist or a consequentialist. Even a diehard deontologist needs to know the relevant evidence so she can determine whether a particular moral rule or principle is applicable. The consequentialist will need that evidence to accurately assess the likely consequences of her actions. Without such knowledge, she simply cannot determine the best action.

All these theoretical observations are firmer than they were before. But they are still tentative. These insights arose from our reflection on three practical moral issues.

Further reflection on other problems should help us refine these theoretical observations. They might even lead us to reject some of them. Finally, as we further refine
them, they will help us think more carefully about other practical moral issues. After
discussing moral relativism, we will discuss several practical issues.

REFERENCES

Adams, R. D., Hoffer, W., and Hoffer, M. M. (1991) *Adams v. Texas*. New York: St. Martin's
Press.

American Society of Criminology (1987) "Resolution on the Death Penalty." (Online) Available at: http://sun.soci.niu.edu/~critcrim/dp/dp.html. (Accessed June 2, 2003.)

Bedau, H. A. (1997) *The Death Penalty in America: Current Controversies*. New York: Oxford
University Press.

Bok, S. (1978) *Lying: Moral Choice in Public and Private Life*. New York: Pantheon Books.

Bureau of Justice Statistics (2003a) "Homicide by Circumstance." US Department of Justice.
(Online) Available at: http://www.ojp.usdoj.gov/bjs/homicide/circumst.htm#reasons.

Bureau of Justice Statistics (2003b) "Homicide Trends in the United States." US Department
of Justice. (Online) Available at: http://www.ojp.usdoj.gov/bjs/homicide/homtrnd.
htm#contents.

Bureau of Justice Statistics (2003c) "Homicide Trends in the US: Trends by Race." US Department of Justice. (Online) Available at: http://www.ojp.usdoj.gov/bjs/homicide/
race.htm.

Death Penalty Information Center (2003) "Race of Death Row Inmates Executed since
1976." (Online) Available at: http://www.deathpenaltyinfo.org/article.php?scid=
5&did=184. (Accessed June 5, 2003.)

Death Penalty Information Center (2005) "Innocence and the Death Penalty." (Online) Available at: http://www.deathpenaltyinfo.org/article.php?did=412&scid=6. (Accessed June
25, 2003.)

Dieter, R. C. (1994) *Millions Misspent: What Politicians Don't Say about the High Cost of the Death
Penalty*, 2nd edn. Washington, DC: Death Penalty Information Center.

Doris, J. M. (2002) *Lack of Character: Personality and Moral Behavior*. Cambridge: Cambridge
University Press.

Doris, J. M. and Stich, S. P. (2004) "As a Matter of Fact: Empirical Perspectives on Ethics."
In F. Jackson and M. Smith (eds.), *Oxford Handbook of Contemporary Analytic Philosophy*.
Oxford: Oxford University Press.

Foot, P. (1978) "The Problem of Abortion and the Doctrine of Double Effect." In *Virtues and
Vices and Other Essays in Moral Philosophy*. Berkeley: University of California Press, 19–32.

Foot, P. (1994) "Killing and Letting Die." In B. Steinbock and A. Norcross (eds.), *Killing and
Letting Die*. New York: Fordham University Press, 280–9.

Fuller, L. L. (1977/1964) *The Morality of Law*, 2nd edn. New Haven, CT: Yale University
Press.

Gehring, V. V. (2003) "Phonies, Fakes, and Frauds – and the Social Harms They Cause,"
Philosophy and Public Policy Quarterly 23 (1/2): 14–20.

Herman, B. (1981) "On the Value of Acting from the Motive of Duty," *The Philosophical Review*
90: 359–92.

Kamm, F. M. (2000) "Nonconsequentialism." In H. LaFollette (ed.), *The Blackwell Guide to
Ethical Theory*. Oxford: Blackwell Publishers, 205–26.

Kant, I. (2002/1785) *Groundwork for the Metaphysics of Morals*. Oxford: Oxford University Press.

McMahan, J. (1993) "Killing, Letting Die, and Withdrawing Aid," *Ethics* 103 (2): 250–79.

McMahan, J. (1998) "A Challenge to Common Sense Morality (a Review Essay of *The Act Itself*)," *Ethics* 108: 394–418.

Mill, J. S. (1978) *On Liberty*. Indianapolis, IN: Hackett.

Narveson, J. (1967) *Morality and Utility*. Baltimore, MD: Johns Hopkins University Press.

Pojman, L. P. (2002) "In Defense of the Death Penalty." In H. LaFollette (ed.), *Ethics in Practice: An Anthology*, 2nd edn. Oxford: Blackwell Publishers, 493–502.

Quinn, W. (1989) "Actions, Intentions, and Consequences: The Doctrine of Doing and Allowing," *The Philosophical Review* 98 (3): 287–312.

Raz, J. (1980) *The Concept of a Legal System: An Introduction to the Theory of Legal System*, 2nd edn. Oxford: Clarendon Press.

Superson, A. (2002/1997) "Sexual Harassment." In H. LaFollette (ed.), *Ethics in Practice: An Anthology*, 2nd edn. Oxford: Blackwell Publishers, 400–09.

Van den Haag, E. (1991) *Punishing Criminals: Concerning a Very Old and Painful Question*. Lanham, MD: University Press of America.

Van den Haag, E. and Conrad, J. P. (1983) *The Death Penalty: A Debate*. New York: Plenum Press.

Zimring, F. E. and Hawkins, G. (1973) *Deterrence: The Legal Threat in Crime Control*. Chicago, IL: University of Chicago Press.

FOUR

Relativism

We have discussed practical ethical issues as if there were objectively better and worse solutions. The discussion might even be thought to imply that in all situations there is one uniquely correct action. Many people will think this latter claim is mistaken. Some think the former is dubious as well. They think someone's beliefs about moral matters simply reflect her cultural mores or personal preferences. As these thinkers see it, moral judgments are not objective in any important sense; they are *relative* to the individual or culture.

It is easy to see why moral relativism is appealing. Sometimes we are uncertain about what we morally ought to do. Other times we feel confident about our moral judgments until we notice that bright and sincere people advocate opposing positions. Moreover, in studying history we are struck by the dramatic ways that moral beliefs diverge between and within cultures and over time. These considerations may lead us to have doubts about even those moral beliefs of which we are most confident. We might wonder if any moral belief can be justified, if every moral claim is just as good as another.

The problem is that although some people claim to think this, I have yet to meet anyone who really embraces *strong relativism*. I have never met anyone who thought there was no moral difference between Adolph Hitler and Mother Teresa, or thought that killing another person for fun is morally acceptable. I have never met a student who thought it would be morally acceptable for me to give her a failing grade just because I disliked her. Strong relativism is not a position anyone could knowingly embrace.

Yet some feel driven to embrace it because they think we should be tolerant of others, and they assume that only relativists are tolerant. This is a serious mistake. Surely some relativists are tolerant. However, if they are, that is, according to the strong relativist, just a reflection of their personal preferences. Others will have different preferences: some will relish condemning those who disagree with them; some will want to compel others to do as they prescribe. If strong relativism were correct, there is nothing whatsoever wrong with these latter people's preferences, or with their acting on those preferences. How could there be? On this theory there are no moral truths; every view is equally good.

This is not what most people mean when they say that we should be tolerant. They think tolerance is not just one preference among many. They think intolerance is wrong. I agree. People *should* be tolerant even when they are not inclined to be. However, if that is true, then there is at least one moral claim that is true. Moral beliefs are not all equally good.

Although strong relativism is indefensible, there are weaker versions that are plausible. Unfortunately, many philosophers, in their quest to reject strong relativism, tend to overlook or downplay significant but non-pernicious ways in which ethics is relative. Conversely, those who embrace relativism note salient respects in which ethics *is* relative, but erroneously infer that ethical values are just matters of opinion. Understanding the ways that ethics is (and is not) relative is theoretically desirable; it also helps us intelligently discuss particular practical ethical issues.

In this chapter I identify ways that ethical principles and behavior legitimately vary from culture to culture and from individual to individual, without embracing an insidious relativism that denies that we can profitably reason about ethics. I advocate an ethic that (a) emphasizes the importance of reason in moral deliberation, (b) holds that some behaviors are demonstrably preferable to others, yet (c) recognizes our mutual fallibility, and (d) contends that some moral diversity in belief and action is not only tolerable but desirable. Such an idea is both commonplace and radical. It is commonplace in that there are many evaluative contexts in which we take this view for granted. It is radical in that many people resist applying this view to morality.

Situation Sensitivity

Most if not all ethicists recognize that ethical principles are situation sensitive. When as children we first learned moral rules like "Don't lie," we assumed these rules dictated how we should always act. As we became older, we began to recognize that different situations required exceptions to this (and other) moral rule(s). We found ourselves in situations in which following a rule led to morally objectionable consequences or in which two or more moral rules conflicted. We subsequently came to think of moral rules not as absolute prescriptions to be unwaveringly followed, but as either (a) *rules of thumb*, or (b) *abridgements* of complex moral principles. On the former view *rules of thumb* do not tell us what to do, but are rather tools for good moral reasoning. On the latter view, rules like "Don't lie" are abridgements of more complex rules with specific qualifications or *ceteris paribus* clauses. Some options might be: "Don't lie unless one must do so to avert great moral harm," or, even more vaguely, "Don't lie, other things being equal." These rules of thumb and abridged principles are presumably general (i.e., relatively context-free) and exceptionless (applicable to all cases) (Schneewind 1993). They apply to all cases, even if what they prescribe or proscribe varies with the relevant features of the situation.

Both options are ways of capturing the idea that morality is relative to circumstances. When situations are relevantly different, we should be sensitive to those differences. This does not make morality relative in any objectionable sense. We need not abandon our ability to reason about ethics; nor need we claim that we cannot distinguish between better and worse ways of acting morally. Just the opposite. It is by reasoning about ethics that we see that and how situations vary in morally significant ways. Here's a parallel: objects on earth weigh more than they do on the moon. However, that does not make the law of gravity relative. The law is equally applicable on both planets. It is just that the gravitational force on earth is much greater than on the moon. Reason shows us that the same physical law has different effects in different environments. Ethics is similarly situation sensitive.

Of course different theorists understand and describe these relativities differently. Many deontologists seek to formulate complex rules and principles with significant qualifications specifying which circumstances are different, and how these differences determine our obligations. Consequentialists argue that their theory does not need such qualifications. Different circumstances lead to different consequences; what is moral depends on the consequences of one's actions. Thus, the theory is automatically sensitive to different situations.

Despite disagreements about how to describe and accommodate situation sensitivity, these theorists agree that some behaviors and choices are better and worse than others, and that we can rationally determine which is which. This assumption is common to all normative ethical theories. It guides ethical thinking. If we thought all actions were equally good or equally bad, we would have no reason to choose one action over others. However, no one can live as if all behaviors are morally equivalent. When others are mean or inconsiderate to us or dishonest with us, we are quite convinced that they act inappropriately. Even philosophers who claim that ethics is relative, standardly argue that some ways of living really are preferable to others – although they may cloak their position in relativistic garb (Mackie 1977).

Collectively this explains why we recognize that moral judgment can be rationally evaluated: that by reasoning we can see that some actions really are better than others. Of course we sometimes have trouble discerning which is which, and even when we are confident, we may be wrong. After all, we are fallible. Moreover, we need not deny that sometimes two or more actions are morally acceptable. Indeed, as I shall argue, we shouldn't deny this, for sometimes – and arguably often – it is morally better if not everyone acts the same, even in the same situation. Moral diversity is not only permissible, it is valuable. People with different personalities, experiences, histories, and relationships can sometimes act morally, even if acting differently.

Two Relativities

Advantages of moral diversity

Many disagreements about how we should act morally are disagreements over moral means. People may agree that we should help those in need, respect others' autonomy, and not cause people needless harm, yet disagree about precisely what these morally require. Sheryl and Shirley may both think it is important to promote freedom, but while Sheryl thinks that means we should require motorists to wear seat belts and that we should militarily overthrow corrupt regimes, Shirley does not. Both may think it is important to encourage individual responsibility, but while Sheryl thinks that primarily requires instituting harsh criminal punishments, Shirley thinks it primarily requires improving state-supported education and giving teenagers more autonomy.

In such cases they seemingly agree about moral ends but disagree about the appropriate means. Must a non-relativist hold that at least one of them is wrong? Certainly not in all cases. Both might have defensible moral positions. That is relativistic in one sense: it holds that sometimes people may act morally even when they act differently. However, this does not abandon reasoning about ethics – quite the contrary. It is in reasoning about ethics that we see that differences in moral means are not only sometimes acceptable but even desirable. Consider the following non-moral analogy. Philosophy professors typically have roughly similar teaching goals. However, even when our goals are identical, we often choose somewhat different means to them. Two teachers who claim their overarching aim is to teach their students how to think critically may use different readings and requirements to achieve this pedagogical end. One may use classic philosophical texts; the other, contemporary texts. One may use exams to evaluate students; the other, essays. One may emphasize getting the students to understand other philosophers' ideas; the other, getting them to state and defend their own ideas.

Do these differences show that one teacher is pedagogically flawed? No. Perhaps one or both are mistaken about the best way to reach the agreed-upon pedagogical end. Perhaps, though, each professor's approach is wholly defensible. Philosophy departments are almost always better if different teachers embody different styles than if they all are pedagogical clones. Different students learn better from teachers with different styles. And the same student may learn better from different teachers at different stages in her college career. Finally, students should acquire many skills, and they cannot learn them all at once or at the same pace. Teachers emphasizing different skills thus benefit different students at different stages of their careers. To serve students well, universities should not only allow but encourage teachers to develop unique styles. This does not make us pedagogical relativists in any pernicious sense.

Some professors also disagree about pedagogical ends. A philosophy teacher who exclusively uses classical texts may think that the principal goal of philosophy is to introduce students to the great thinkers, full stop. These teachers doubtless think that doing so will enhance students' critical skills and expand their knowledge of important practical issues. Still, these are either subsidiary goals or not goals at all – just welcomed side effects of pursuing what these professors see as the main goal of teaching philosophy.

Other professors think the principal goal of philosophy is to inculcate critical thinking skills. Some think that goal is best achieved by introducing students to the philosophical classics. However, for these professors exposure to the classics is either a subsidiary goal or not a goal at all; it is just a welcomed side effect of their way of achieving the main goal of teaching philosophy.

Although professors often have divergent pedagogical means and ends, these rarely diverge wildly. Most endorse broadly similar ends even when they disagree about the specific weight given to each end. The most common ends are also inter-related, and the most common means usually promote several ends. This broad con-sensus on pedagogical ends and means is precisely what we should expect. Reasonable, bright, and well-intentioned people, each seeking to teach as best they can, will usually choose pedagogical cousins, even if they categorize (and theorize) about them differently. On those rare occasions where professors' pedagogical goals and means are wholly incompatible, a non-relativist about pedagogy would conclude that one must be mistaken. Except when facing these rare dramatic disagreements, we will accept and even applaud pedagogical diversity. The point is not that we do not know the best way to teach, and, since we are ignorant it is better to permit diversity – although that is surely true. The point is that pedagogical diversity directly contributes to students' education.

The same is true for ethics. Mill persuasively argues in *On Liberty* that society ben-efits from not only permitting, but encouraging, people to embrace and advocate different beliefs and to engage in experiments in living. This diversity is not evil; it is an essential factor in our quest for truth and moral excellence. Only by being exposed to different ideas do we have any hope of finding the truth. That is why we should not merely tolerate it but embrace it. Such diversity has inherent benefits, not unlike the benefits of diverse teaching styles (Mill 1978).

Of course there are limits on what we should accept in teaching and in ethics. Some purported pedagogical ends (e.g., making intellectual mannequins) are intol-erable. Nor need we tolerate teachers who do nothing in class but read their yel-lowed, outdated notes. Some purported moral ends (e.g., "purifying the Aryan race") are likewise intolerable. Nor need we accept murder, rape, and torture simply because some people think they are acceptable. However, although not just anything goes, we should not infer that only one thing goes.

Let me offer a historical example that illustrates the benefits of moral diversity. The Civil Rights Movement included people with conflicting ideologies. They dis-agreed about the appropriate aims of the movement and, even when they agreed on aims, they sometimes disagreed about the best way of achieving them. Some were separatists; others, integrationists. Some advocated open rebellion; others rejected rebellion but made it clear they would use violence to protect themselves; still others renounced violence and employed Gandhian pacifistic resistance. Advocates of each stance doubtless thought others were mistaken, perhaps even insincere or malicious. Depending on their perspective, "opponents" were deemed "revolutionaries," "hot-heads," "chickens," or "Toms." Many assumed that only their approach was correct. At the time this response was understandable. Much was at stake, and it was im-portant that people vigorously embraced and advocated their respective positions. However, when we, at some distance, evaluate the historical record, we may con-clude that although some approaches were surely wrong, not all were; even some wrong behaviors may have still advanced the cause.

I understand why some philosophers are wary of permitting, let alone endorsing, such moral diversity. They fear that in so doing they are opening the door to relativism. However, we need fear that only if we are limited to two options: only one action is morally acceptable or all actions are morally acceptable. These are not our only options. We don't think that is true of teaching. Although some teaching styles are wholly unacceptable, many are pedagogically appropriate. Likewise for morality. We needn't insist that only one action is morally defensible before we can plausibly judge that some behaviors are morally unacceptable.

To see why, think again about the Civil Rights Movement. Some historical approaches were surely inappropriate, or at least overstated. Yet when I observe the movement historically, I am convinced that without some mix of these, the movement would not have made the progress it has, however inadequate. The "hotheads" demonstrated to recalcitrant whites just how serious they were, thereby forcing whites to acknowledge the systematic mistreatment of blacks. If all had been hotheads, however, the movement would have been crushed as a rebellion. Cooler, more temperate members made the movement less threatening, more palatable, to the white majority. Yet if all had been moderates, whites might not have taken the movement seriously. In short, I suspect that if a preponderance of members had been at either extreme, the movement would have faltered, if not collapsed. It is not just that participants were ignorant of the best approach, and given this ignorance it was best to permit each to act as they thought appropriate – although that is also true. Diversity in both ends and means was critical for the movement's success.

Before proceeding, I want to block two inferences some might draw from what I said. First, someone might think that if we tolerate and encourage others' views, then we belittle, abandon, or become less committed to our own. Far from it. We should advocate our views, criticize opposing ones, and live according to the results of our moral inquiry. The best way to find the truth and promote moral excellence is if each of us strongly advocates and lives by our respective views, and is open to the ideas, experiences, and perspectives of others.

Second, I argued that without moral diversity we would not have made some important moral advances. However, that does not mean that every behavior that contributes to a worthy moral goal is morally legitimate. Bull Conner's decision to set the dogs on demonstrators incensed the American public and arguably helped speed Civil Rights legislation. However, this is an example where we brought a good result from a bad action. It does not show that his actions were moral. I claim only that the movement would have faltered had everyone acted identically. I have no algorithm for specifying which contributory features are moral, but then, that tells us that moral behavior cannot simply be straightforward adherence to pre-established and unambiguous moral rules. It requires judgment and insight.

Ethical relevance of personality traits

Many ethicists suggest that individuals' personality differences are irrelevant for determining how we should act. I understand the concern: recognizing their relevance seems to justify making exceptions in one's own case. However, it need not have this consequence. To say that some personality traits can be relevant does not imply that all are. Nor does it mean that those that are relevant in some contexts are always relevant. Acknowledging their relevance is also critical for a satisfactory rendering of ethics. To illustrate, let me borrow an example I developed in an earlier paper (1983). Suppose I have a recently divorced friend who is very depressed. How should I relate to her? Should I let her cry on my shoulder and bolster her diminished self-esteem? Should I offer advice, even if she does not request it? Or should I ignore or at least downplay her pain to urge her to get on with her life? Doubtless she may not want a friend to point out her errors or to urge her to move on. Yet that may be precisely what she needs, and precisely what a loving friend would provide. Moreover, what seems clear is no one reaction is always best. If different friends react differently she is more likely to come to terms with the divorce and to learn from her (and his) mistake(s). If all her friends were sensitive listeners, she might become mired in her pain and ignore her contributions to the breakup. If all her friends offered spontaneous advice, she might lose some self-respect. If all her friends urged her to move on, she may be unable to come to terms with her pain.

Realizing that, how should I relate to my friend? I cannot simply consult some list of rules. I must decide what I, with my particular temperament and abilities, can best do to sensitively respond to her. If I am reserved, likely I should just be a supportive listener. If I am more assertive perhaps I should point out ways she contributed to the marriage's failure and then urge her to move on. That is as it should be. She may need both responses. However, a timid friend is unlikely to be good at confronting her: the confrontation may appear shrill. An assertive person is unlikely to provide a quiet shoulder to cry on; the caring may seem artificial. In similar ways, different personality traits play a critical role in determining a person's "best" teaching style. Shy and gregarious people could not teach in precisely the same ways.

Someone might contend that this case does not support my claim since we do not have an obligation to help friends; helping them is supererogatory: it goes beyond what is morally required. Although there are reasons for distinguishing duty from supererogation, any way we do so will not characterize *all* interpersonal interactions as supererogatory. At least some interpersonal interactions are governed by moral considerations, and differences between personalities, experiences, and the history of the relationship can alter how friends should behave (Pincoffs 1993/1971).

The Nature of Language

We can better understand the ways ethics is relative if we compare it with a familiar practice that is similarly relativistic, albeit − like ethics − not in objectionable ways: language. We have general rules of grammar, standards for proper prose. Sentences should have a noun and verb; the subject and verb should agree in number; a pronoun should refer univocally to its antecedent; prose should be clear and concise. These express sage wisdom to the novice, continued guidance to the veteran.

Although these principles distinguish powerful prose from ineffectual scribbling, they are not algorithms nor can they tell us which, of all the possible sentences or phrases in some context, is most appropriate. To use E.B. White's example, no rules explain why Thomas Paine's "These are the times that try men's souls" is stylistically preferable to grammatically acceptable alternatives (Strunk and White 1959). What is clear, however, is that although knowledge of the rules of grammar and principles of style do not automatically enable someone to pen such a gem, someone without such knowledge could not.

Rules of grammar and style not only fail to distinguish minimally acceptable prose from masterful style, they occasionally proscribe stylish writing. The best writers occasionally use grammatically incomplete sentences or seemingly awkward or circuitous prose, all to good effect. There are no precepts specifying when these deviant forms are appropriate. However, the overriding aim of effective communication legitimizes them. This is not to make "effective communication" a rule that adjudicates between competing grammatical rules. To say we wish to communicate effectively merely states our aspirations; it does not prescribe a procedure for realizing those aspirations. We have no precise account of "effective communication." The stylist helps determine, albeit tentatively, what effective communication is, and thus, what good grammar and forceful style are.

All this seems obvious once we recall how grammar evolved. No one emerged from the caves imploring us to be clear or warning us about misplaced modifiers. It was millennia after our ancestors began speaking that they even knew what a modifier or clarity was. These ideas emerged from their attempts to communicate (Dewey 1988/1922: 54–9). Doubtless something like this happened: astute speakers realized communication was hampered by inappropriately placed modifiers (though if language had developed differently we might not have had modifiers, let alone misplaced ones). They informed other speakers of their "discovery." When enough people discerned the wisdom of these speakers' observations, a convention outlawing misplaced modifiers emerged. Nothing mysterious.

Rules arose because people thought they served important communicative functions; sometimes they were later discarded or modified if speakers discovered otherwise or if circumstances changed in ways that altered the shape of communication. Grammarians once forbad writers to split infinitives. No longer. The strict rule was abandoned once many people realized that blind adherence to it was unnecessary.

In summary, (1) language developed to enhance communication. (2) Although there are limits on how language could have evolved, no language is privileged. (3) No set of linguistic rules covers all cases; nonetheless (4) knowing those rules is vital for effective communication. Finally (5) we can debate the wisdom of rules of grammar: we can determine when it is reasonable to ignore those rules; we can decide if the rules no longer serve their original purposes and therefore ought to be discarded. This explains how different people use language differently yet manage to effectively communicate. This does not mean that language usage is subjective or a matter of personal whim. If we are going to communicate we cannot write just any way we wish. There are better and worse ways of writing. Of course, if language had evolved differently, what we consider good grammar and eloquent prose would differ. However, that is not relativistic either, at least not noxiously so. It merely recognizes the mundane truth that a different array of rules could also enable us to communicate effectively. No natural language is indisputably superior to all contenders.

These are just the senses in which ethics is relative without being subjective. Once we understand that, we no longer feel compelled to deny the rather ordinary ways in which both forms of inquiry are relative, nor need we conclude that either is noxiously subjective. Both ethics and language usage face "questions" with patently obvious answers. For ethics those might be: "Should I beat my children for exercise?" Or: "Should I yell at my neighbor to boost my ego?" For language usage it could be: "Is the sentence, 'My teeths bad hurted yesterday,' grammatically proper?" Or, "Is the sentence, 'The really very good story was nice and rather interesting,' either engaging or illuminating?" Other questions about prose and ethics are seemingly intractable. Some are so complex that they elude pre-established categories. Even when we are moderately certain which grammatical or stylistic rules or considerations are relevant, we may be unable to determine a uniquely preferable sentence. That is why different writers "follow" different rules and follow them differently. That is why some diversity in communication is not only appropriate but desirable. Analogously, relevant features of a moral decision do not fall neatly under the scope of extant rules, and we may be incapable of predicting the consequences of our actions. Different people "follow" different moral rules or focus on different considerations, yet all may act morally. However, in embracing this diversity and in acknowledging our fallibility, we do not commit ourselves to a pernicious relativism. Our fear of relativism should not drive us to embrace a rigid set of grammatical rules . . . or a simplistic morality.

A Rational Relativistic Ethic

The debate over relativism has been badly framed. Too many people assume we have only two options: a rigid moral absolutism or complete relativism. Those who embrace absolutism claim that ethics can be rational only if we have a deductive model yielding clear and unchanging moral principles. Relativists argue that there is no such method and conclude that ethics is therefore not subject to rational evaluation.

We should reject this false dichotomy and think about ethics in the same way we think about language usage. Language usage is relative in ordinary but non-pernicious ways. But not just anything goes. People's speaking and writing can be elegant or clumsy, precise or vague, engaging or boring. Ethics is similarly relative in ordinary but non-pernicious ways. Sometimes more than a single act is morally permissible. However, not just anything goes. Some actions are wrong; others are demonstrably worse than alternatives.

That is precisely what we should expect. All intellectual pursuits are relativistic in these senses. Political science, psychology, chemistry, biology, and physics are neither certain nor subjective. As Shapere puts it, science "involves no unalterable assumptions whatever, whether in the form of substantive beliefs, methods, rules or concepts." Everything is up for grabs, including the notions of "discovery" and "understanding" (Shapere 1984).

As I have suggested from the first chapter, ethical inquiry is broadly similar to other forms of inquiry. We begin with the ideas taught us by others – in the case of morality, principles taught by parents, teachers, preachers, and society. Then, as we acquire new information and hone our reasoning skills, we evaluate our beliefs. In the case of morality, we may also find ourselves inexplicably making certain valuations, possibly because of inherited altruistic tendencies. We also learn from experience that some actions generate unacceptable consequences. Or we may reflect upon our own and others' "theories" or patterns of behavior and decide they are inconsistent or incoherent or incomplete. We reform our views and then test them by considering the consequences of those actions on ourselves and on others. We correct our mistakes through reflection, thought, and experience (Wilson 1978, 1975).

Of course, we may not like such a ragtag process. We may yearn for the "good ole days" when we thought our ethical principles were absolute, that they bore the stamp of certainty. However, moral certainty is not – nor ever was – on the menu (Dewey 1984/1929; Rorty 1972). This is not cause for worry. If certainty is not on the menu neither is full-blown relativism (Blackburn 2000; Davidson 1973). We are left within the real world where none of us has all the moral answers. However, neither do we possess an algorithm for determining correct language usage but that does not make us throw up our hands in despair, claiming that, without linguistic certainly, we can no longer communicate.

If we understand ethics in this way, we can see the profound value of ethical theorizing. Theorizing is important. It does not provide abstract solutions we can apply straightforwardly to all practical issues, although I doubt that most ethical theorists ever thought it did. Ethical theorizing is important because it helps us notice salient features of moral problems and it helps us understand those problems in context. Theorizing helps us see problems we had not seen, to understand problems we had not understood, and thereby empowers us to make informed moral judgments, judgments we could not have made without an appreciation of moral theorizing. In that respect ethical theories and grammar serve similar functions: good grammarians may not be effective communicators; however, a grasp of grammar empowers us to communicate effectively. Ethical theory does not guarantee moral behavior; however, a grasp of theory empowers us to act morally and responsibly.

We should instruct each other in the basic principles inherited from the past (respect for persons, reverence for human life, etc.) and act upon those as circumstances warrant. Then, we must listen to others' evaluations of our actions and non-condemnatorily offer reactions to theirs – all the while acknowledging our and their fallibility. We must carefully reflect on what we say, do, and think. When we agree that some actions are especially horrendous (e.g., murder) we should legally prohibit them. We should leave less harmful acts to the arena of ideas. This puts a burden on each of us to carefully and critically evaluate inherited moral wisdom, as well as our own actions. And it demands that we govern our behavior by what we find.

REFERENCES

Altman, A. (1983) "Pragmatism and Applied Ethics," *American Philosophical Quarterly* 20: 227–35.

Blackburn, S. (2000) "Relativism." In H. LaFollette (ed.), *The Blackwell Guide to Ethical Theory*. Oxford: Blackwell Publishers, 38–52.

Davidson, D. (1973) "On the Very Idea of a Conceptual Scheme," *Proceedings of the American Philosophical Association* 17.

Dewey, J. (1984/1929) *The Quest for Certainty*, vol. 4. Carbondale, IL: Southern Illinois University Press.

Dewey, J. (1988/1922) *Human Nature and Conduct*. Carbondale, IL: Southern Illinois University Press.

Kant, I. (2002/1785) *Groundwork for the Metaphysics of Morals*. Oxford: Oxford University Press.

LaFollette, H. (1983) "Applied Philosophy Misapplied." In N. Rescher (ed.), *The Applied Turn in Contemporary Philosophy*. Bowling Green, OH: Bowling Green State University Press, 88–96.

Mackie, J. L. (1977) *Ethics: Inventing Right and Wrong*. New York: Penguin.

Mill, J. S. (1978) *On Liberty*. Indianapolis, IN: Hackett.

Mill, J. S. (1998) *Utilitarianism*. New York: Oxford University Press.

Pincoffs, E. (1993/1971) "Quandary Ethics." In S. Hauerwaus and A. MacIntyre (eds.), *Revisions*. Notre Dame, IN: University of Notre Dame Press, 92–112.

Rorty, R. (1972) "The World Well Lost," *Journal of Philosophy* 69: 649–65.

Schneewind, J. (1993) "Moral Knowledge and Moral Principles." In S. Hauerwaus and A. MacIntyre (eds.), *Revisions*. Notre Dame, IN: University of Notre Dame Press.

Shapere, D. (1984) *Reason and the Search for Knowledge: Investigations in the Philosophy of Science*. Dordrecht: D. Reidel.

Singer, M.G. (1971) *Generalization in Ethics: An Essay in the Logic of Ethics, with the Rudiments of a System of Moral Philosophy*. New York: Russell & Russell.

Strunk, W. and White, E.B. (1959) *Elements of Style*. New York: Macmillan.

Wilson, E.O. (1975) *Sociobiology: The New Synthesis*. Cambridge, MA: Belknap Press of Harvard University Press.

Wilson, E.O. (1978) *On Human Nature*. Cambridge, MA: Harvard University Press.

PART TWO

The Moral Status of Groups

FIVE

Racism

To hear most white people talk, racism died with Lester Maddux and Bull Conner. Today few people call blacks "nigger" or "boy"; they do not proudly proclaim that they are segregationists; they do not (openly) assert that blacks are stupid, lazy, and stink. There is the odd old-fashioned racist around. But such racism is unfashionable – like Amos 'n' Andy and Blackface. Its adherents are dismissed as uneducated rednecks, throwbacks to the time when George Wallace was king (Arsenault 2004).

We assume things have changed. After all, we passed civil rights legislation; we created Martin Luther King Day; Colin Powell served as the US Secretary of State. These are promising developments; however, they do not show that racism is dead. It is alive, albeit in different forms. These forms are not as blatant as the old ones. In some respects they are less virulent – certainly blacks are less likely to be lynched on the courthouse lawn. Still, they are virulent enough. They shape our responses to people and events. They shape economic, political, and social institutions in ways that disadvantage African-Americans. Unfortunately these forms are tougher to spot. We cannot eradicate what we do not see. But before we can isolate and remedy current forms of racism, we must first understand the old-fashioned form.

Old-fashioned Racism

What is old-fashioned racism? Most people think it is a mix of the following inter-related elements: (1) it is discriminatory: people are disadvantaged simply because of their racial heritage (typically identified by their skin color); (2) it is individual: those harmed (and those doing the harm) are always particular people; and (3) it is primarily an attitude. This common view, although vaguely accurate, is misleading. Understanding why will help us better understand racism, both past and present.

Discrimination

The idea that racism is (inappropriate) discrimination is accurate as far as it goes. However, if stated unqualifiedly it masks morally relevant considerations. It implies that there is no moral difference between discriminating against blacks and against whites. Yet there are differences. Four are arguably morally relevant.

1. An isolated act of discrimination is not as harmful as the "same" act that is part of a network of discrimination. It is bad if one person refuses to hire Martin because of his race; it is worse if most employers won't hire him. It is bad if Martin is barred from living in one area of town because of his race. It is worse if he is permitted to live in only one area of town. Blacks have been subject to systematic discrimination over centuries; whites have not been.

2. Discrimination against a wide range of behaviors is more detrimental than discrimination against a few. It is bad to limit where people can live; it is worse to also forbid them from eating in many restaurants, to bar them from gainful employment, and to inappropriately turn them down – or charge them exorbitant rates – for home mortgages (Association of Community Organizations for Reform Now 2002). Blacks have faced all these forms of discrimination. Whites have not.

3. Multiple acts of discrimination are not as harmful if the perpetrators are relatively weak. The "same" act is more harmful when the perpetrators are powerful. The rich can harm the poor in a way and to a degree that the poor cannot harm the rich. Whites in the Western industrialized world have long held most political, social, and economic power. This is one more reason why blacks are more pervasively harmed by discrimination than are similarly treated whites.

4. Acts of discrimination occurring over a short time are not as detrimental as are patterns of discrimination occurring over a longer time. Sustained patterns of discrimination are not only especially harmful, they also create self-perpetuating social, cultural, and political institutions. These prolong the effects of discrimination long after overt discrimination has ceased. Blacks have been subject to systematic discrimination in the United States for hundreds of years.

These differences show why the context in which discrimination occurs matters morally. They explain why seemingly "similar" acts of discrimination harm blacks more than they harm whites. We could have a world in which the tables were turned: where blacks had systematically enslaved and mistreated whites for hundreds of years, where whites had been systematically excluded from power and wealth. In that world discrimination against whites would be worse than discrimination against blacks. However, that is not our world, and knowing the nature of this world is critical to knowing how to behave. Sound moral judgments depend critically on knowledge of the relevant context, including knowledge of history, politics, economics, and psychology.

This might seem so obvious as to not require stating. Unfortunately, it is too easily forgotten, and forgetting it leads to bizarre conclusions. David Benatar recently argued that men are victims of sexism since they (a) have to go to war while women do not, and they (b) are pressured to succeed in ways women are not (Benatar 2003: 178, 194). His claim is to some degree true. True, but horribly misleading. Males *are* expected to do things females are not expected to do and they may be subject to some negative consequences women do not face. What should we infer from this? That males are discriminated against? No, at least not in any way that requires comment. For it was also true that, having colonized Africa and confiscated residents' land, whites then had "the burden" to care for the people they had colonized.

It is also true that the seventeenth-century duke and a twenty-first-century CEO will expect their children to succeed in ways that a serf and a garbage collector will not. However, it is odd to call succeeding an expectation, at least when "expectation" is portrayed pejoratively. The children of the serf and the garbage collector would gladly trade places with the children of the duke and the CEO. That is why this "burden" is usually not onerous and is never unjust. It is a "burden" they prefer to the burden of poorer, less privileged citizens. I doubt any would relinquish this burden if it meant working long hours at minimal wages, having no real chance for financial well-being, no ability to educate their children, etc. The fact is, everyone faces expectations, and one's expectations are structured by our parents, community, and society. However, to infer that all expectations are discriminatory so weakens the notion of discrimination as to make it empty. Finally, whatever burdens the well-off have, they have *because* of the discrimination against the less powerful group. If they wish to be rid of these burdens they can. The people on the bottom do not have this power.

Do I deny that some males are burdened by their privileged position? Of course not. Do I deny that some individual males are sometimes disadvantaged? Of course not. Do I deny that some British and South African whites felt encumbered by the "White Man's Burden"? Of course not. Nonetheless, these disadvantages and burdens are the doings of white males and the system mostly works to their advantage. Doubtless we should regret burdening an individual white male who loathes his advantages and the "expectations" placed upon him. However, that should not blind us to the real wrongs.

It is a wrong against individuals

Understanding the context in which racism occurred helps explain why we should reject the common view that racism is a wrong against individuals. Racist acts are not directed at specific individuals because of who they as individuals are. They are directed at people *because* of their race. A minority citizen who witnesses but is not herself victim of those acts is nonetheless harmed by them. She will see the acts as an attack on the entire race. Racist institutions are likewise attacks on blacks *as a group*. Consider the following analogs. Some Northerners claim that Southerners are ignorant. If you are a Southerner and you hear Northerners complain about "stupid Southerners," you will feel attacked even if the comments are not directed at you. It wouldn't help if you were treated as an exception ("Don't worry; *you're* a smart Southerner"). You would likely have this reaction even though our society does not define people by their geographical location. However, as I explain in detail later, our society does define people by their race (and gender). Negative comments about and harmful actions toward someone who is black *because she is black* are attacks on all blacks. For the four reasons given earlier, these words and actions are more harmful to blacks than are "equivalent" comments about or actions towards whites.

Racism is an attitude

The third element of the common view is that racism is fundamentally an attitude. This defective attitude causes people to mistreat blacks, to restrict their liberty, or to say derogatory things to and about them. This view has several important implications. First, each of us can know if we are racists simply by looking "inside" to see if we have the requisite attitude. Second, the only way to eliminate racism is to eliminate the attitude. Limiting racist actions may curb some of racism's objectionable effects. However, these changes are superficial; they leave racism untouched.

Although I understand the appeal of this way of thinking, it is mistaken. There are two seemingly different, but effectively equivalent, objections to it. One, we can accept the common view of attitudes as mental states differentiated by how they feel to the agent, and then argue that racism is not an attitude. Two, we can reject the common view of attitudes, and then argue that racism is an attitude *if* attitudes are identified by what people are disposed to do. Let me discuss the second approach first.

Many people think attitudes are internal states to which the agent is normally, if not invariantly, directly acquainted. On this view each of us is standardly the best judge of our attitudes. If I sincerely think that I am kind or honest or non-racist, then I am. Such a view makes self-knowledge easy. However, self-knowledge is not easy and it is never complete. If we are at all self-reflective we realize that we are sometimes (and perhaps often) mistaken about our attitudes. We thought we were not jealous, but get upset when our partner talks to a colleague. We thought we were humble, but get puffed up when we win an insignificant award. We thought we were not elitist, but are appalled at the prospects of letting the majority rule. Attitudes, in any rich and interesting sense, are not merely internal mental states defined by how they feel; they are primarily propensities to behave (LaFollette 1996: 28–31). That is why we can know ourselves only if we observe how we behave in a variety of circumstances (Dewey 1985/1932: 174).

Thinking otherwise leads to moral error. By focusing exclusively on an inner mental state we encourage "men to neglect the purpose and bearing of their actions, and ⟨we encourage them⟩ to justify what they feel inclined to do on the ground that their feelings when doing it were innocent and amiable . . ." (ibid.). Nowhere is this more apparent than with racism. If we think racism is an attitude – and that an attitude is an internally accessible mental state – then if we do not detect that attitude we will infer that we are not racists. Yet most of us were reared in racist homes in a racist state, shaped by a racist history. We are thus likely, despite our best intentions, to be disposed to see events though racist eyes. Before we say more about this aspect of racism, I should first say more about why racism is especially immoral.

Why Racism is Wrong

We can begin to understand why racism is wrong by using the notion of universalizability, which was mentioned in several early chapters.

Universalizability and morally relevant differences

In some form the principle of universalizability is a tenet of all ethical theories. We also employ it in thinking about practical ethical issues – as we saw in our discussions of honesty, sexual harassment, and capital punishment. The principle states that we should treat like cases alike, or, to put it differently, that we should treat all people the same unless there is some general and relevant difference between them that justifies a difference in treatment.

Why should differences be general and relevant? Despite the appearance of this wording, generality is not an independent criterion; rather it is a necessary condition of relevance. In specifying that moral features be general, theorists exclude any consideration that explicitly favors particular individuals. *Being me* (or you or Jo) is not morally relevant. However, although all relevant features are general, not all general features are relevant. After all, race and gender are not morally relevant features, but they are general. So we must decide how to identify the relevant ones. Many people seem to think we can just look and see if a feature is relevant. We cannot. Moral relevance is not a distinctive feature of acts or persons; it is a theoretical notion. Relevant features are those linked to central elements of a justified moral theory. For instance, the classical utilitarian holds that happiness is the only morally relevant characteristic. Other characteristics are relevant indirectly to the degree that they lead to the promotion or diminution of happiness. In contrast, deontologists identify morally relevant characteristics via some moral principle. For instance, actions or people are morally relevant if they protect or set back individual autonomy, if they deserve reward or punishment, if they cause others harm or benefit, etc.

This discussion might imply that most people generally agree about what is relevant. To some degree they do. Without some agreement we cannot even discuss moral issues. Still, the agreement is far from a consensus. Many disagreements about particular moral issues arise because people disagree about whether (and how much) some characteristic is morally relevant. Opposing sides of the capital punishment debate often disagree whether deterrence is relevant (or, if so, how relevant); those who disagree whether (and when) lying is justified may disagree about the importance of individual autonomy; while those who disagree whether, when, and why sexual harassment is wrong may disagree about the moral status of groups. Despite these disagreements, people now widely recognize that bare race is not morally relevant.

It was not always so. For much of Western civilization, only propertied white males were given full legal rights. Less than 100 years ago, women could not vote in the United States. And it was not until 50 years ago that racial segregation was deemed unconstitutional. It took at least another 15 years before the last legal remnants of overt racism were eliminated. When we examine the development of moral thought we see that the circle of people given full moral consideration has been expanding. We can describe these changes in two ways. One, we could say that the criteria of moral relevance remained constant; we just became more enlightened about the number of people who satisfied those criteria. Two, we could say that our criteria evolved; we now see that we were mistaken when we thought race and gender were relevant features. I am inclined to say that it is primarily the second, with a whiff of the first. Here's why. Those who think some difference (say, race, gender, or species) is morally relevant are inclined to see differences that are not there, and are inclined to construe any differences they do see as showing that group members are relevantly different from the dominant group. When racism and sexism became unfashionable, then most of these racists and sexists changed their tune. They now claim that they are not really opposed to blacks per se. Rather they claim that blacks (or women or animals) have some trait(s) disqualifying them from full moral consideration. They deny that they are racists. They claim, for example, that blacks are intellectually inferior (Herrnstein and Murray 1996).

Why do I say this is a subterfuge? A variety of reasons. One, folks who are thoroughgoing racists (or sexists) will not change their views in the face of evidence. If others argue that the victims are relevantly similar to the dominant group, these people will find some way to ignore or reinterpret the evidence. Two, even if they eventually acknowledge the evidence, they will just change the arguments they use to justify discrimination. Three, they claim they are not discriminating against members of that group since group members have some detrimental trait or lack some positive trait. However, if they really believe that, then they should not spurn a member of the group who demonstrably has the same traits as the dominant group. That does not happen. Racists demean, mistreat, or harm blacks simply because they are black. That explains why racism is wrong – at least in part. However, this view, although accurate in part, is also misleading. To see why, we should specify the detrimental effects of racism.

The effects of racism

Racism profoundly affects blacks' self-perception, others' perceptions of them, and their opportunities. To understand the nature and extent of these effects, let's begin by thinking about the most egregious forms of racism: (a) slavery and (b) Jim Crow laws which were in effect until the passage of civil rights legislation during the 1960s. If we can understand why these virulent forms were morally outrageous, we will be better able to understand the continuing effects of racism, and, relatedly, the precise contours of racism's new face.

There is a temptation to offer a limp explanation for why slavery is so terrible. Many people will say or imply that slavery was objectionable because it denied slaves their freedom. No doubt extensive restrictions on autonomy are evil, all things considered; in later chapters I will have more to say about what autonomy is and why limitations on it are morally odious. However, to suggest that slavery is just or even primarily a restriction of freedom grossly understates why it is evil. It overlooks the pervasive and significant ways blacks were mistreated, ways that go far beyond mere "restrictions on freedom." They were subjected to grueling working conditions, unsanitary and inadequate housing. They were verbally demeaned, families were forcibly and permanently separated, and slaves had to be ever vigilant to not say or do anything that would catch the attention of the overseer and make it more likely that they would be beaten, raped, mutilated, or killed (Berlin 1998).

Things were not much better after "emancipation." Free blacks were still poor, uneducated, lacked political and social power, and had to fear for their bodies, their lives, and their property. As a group, blacks were still systematically disadvantaged, verbally abused, had few legal protections, and, in many jurisdictions, were explicitly disadvantaged by the law. Even blacks who attained a level of relative affluence had to be on guard to insure they did not say or do something that might upset whites.

The claim that old-fashioned racism was bad because it was a restriction on freedom belittles what happened to blacks; it also misleads us about how to eradicate current racism. If we assume that racism is "merely" a restriction of freedom and further construe freedom negatively – as the absence of overt limitations on people's choices – then we can completely and instantaneously eradicate racism simply by ending those restrictions. However, racism was and is much more than a limitation of freedom. It is a systematic and ongoing attack on all blacks, as blacks.

The Shape of Current Racism

I have explained why the common view of racism is unable to explain what it is or why it is wrong. A more complete account requires understanding the roles of *individual habits* and *social institutions* in defining and perpetuating racism. Let me talk about both. Each element is important for understanding not only racism but much moral behavior.

Habits

For the most part even vehement old-fashioned racists do not consciously choose to be racists. They simply see the world as racists and respond to people and events as racists. This fact about racism verifies my earlier suggestion that habits play an important role in understanding why we act and in prescribing how we ought to act. It is now time to explain more fully what I mean by "habits" and to identify habit's role in morality. There is an immediate payoff in doing so: it will illuminate racism and give us a better sense of how we might eliminate it.

The nature of habits

Many people might be leery of all this talk of habits, because they think habits are behavioral repetitions, largely beyond our control, and often negative. On this view habits can force us to bite our nails, compel us to drink, and lead us to be lazy, etc. Habits, however, are not mere repetitions, they are not necessarily bad, and they are not forces compelling us against our wills (LaFollette 2000). What we learn becomes embodied in our habits, which transport the past into the present and future. Habits have four principal elements: (1) They are created, shaped, and sustained by our interactions with the physical and social environment. (2) They are not single actions but organized collections of smaller actions. (3) They are typically exhibited in overt behavior in a variety of circumstances, and (4) even when they are not exhibited in standard ways, they are still operative.

Consider a mundane action: walking. (1) Infants learn to walk by interacting with their environment; it takes practice to walk, and more practice to walk well. (2) Walking is not a single action, but an organized collection of smaller actions: moving our feet and arms, looking ahead, varying our paths to avoid obstacles, etc. (3) The walking habit is present in overt behavior: in the appropriate circumstances, we walk in ways we learned. Finally, (4) this habit operates even when not immediately guiding behavior. What makes us walkers is not merely what we do when we walk, but what we do when we do not. Walkers think, remember, and imagine differently than non-walkers. This is obviously true when comparing a sprinter to someone who is wheelchair bound. It is equally (but differently) true of those who are able to walk but rarely do. A "walker" might think of her office as "a twenty-minute walk" from home, while a sedentary person considers it a five-minute drive. Walkers also imagine the future differently than do those who normally travel by auto. Walkers' thoughts about and plans for an Alpine trip will differ substantially from those who rarely walk.

Thinking is also habitual. (1) It is learned by prior activity; it takes practice to think, and considerably more practice to think well. If we could think effortlessly, we would not need to be educated. Yet, we do need to be educated, and there is ample evidence that some types of education encourage more and better thinking. (2) Thinking is a coordination of distinct intellectual actions. To think well, we must discern the relevant point, have relevant background information, remember crucial details, trace the implications of our views, and evaluate those implications. (3) Thinking exhibits itself in overt behavior: when appropriately trained, we question what we have been told, will engage in spirited conversations, etc. Finally (4) thinking is operative, even if not immediately guiding behavior. Thinkers will consider options, entertain ideas, and imagine possibilities, even if there is no one with whom to converse, even if there is no way that their thoughts can lead to immediate action.

Habits empower and restrict

Habits are two-edged swords: they both empower and restrict us. They empower us by carrying our previous decisions, actions, learning, and experiences into the present and future. They constrain us by narrowing what we notice, by restricting what we consider options. A chemist is a scientist because of her habits. Her habits embody her education, experiences, and previous research. These shape what she studies and how she studies it. Yet by narrowing her focus, those same habits may also lead her to overlook significant chemical phenomena. Likewise, language empowers us, since we need it to speak (and even to think), while constraining us since we can say only what we can say in that language.

As habitual creatures we must walk the fine line between (a) acting blindly on our habits and (b) constantly re-evaluating them. Neither option is good. We should not just plod through life, mindlessly absorbing the habits of our culture without ever evaluating them. Nor should we become so enthralled by "the delights of reflection [that] we become afraid of assuming the responsibilities of decisive choice and action . . ." (Dewey 1988/1922: 137). We must benefit from our past experiences without letting them close off important possibilities. Knowing how to do that is itself a more complex, higher-order habit, refined by practice, over time.

Social nature of habits

Talking about an individual's habits of walking, talking, or thinking might suggest that habits are purely personal possessions. They are not. Since habits arise from experience, our cultures play a central role in forming them. Culture shapes how we eat and talk, what we read and believe, and how we think. The social transmission of habits began in the instruction (either formal or by example) we received growing up. We inherit (and then refine) habits from our ancestors, who inherited (and refined) habits from their ancestors, and so on. We live in cities rather than caves not because we are cleverer than our distant kin, but because we had better ancestors. Ours gave us universities and the Internet; theirs gave them cave paintings and fire. Recognizing this fundamental debt to others, Dewey claims, is the root of all virtue. "It is of grace and not ourselves that we lead civilized lives" (ibid. 20). Once we recognize that we are who we are and live the lives we live because of our predecessors, then we must recognize that the habits we give our progeny and our peers will likewise shape *their* worlds, them, and their institutions.

Habits and will

The fact that social forces shape habits might suggest that individuals cannot choose, and are thus not responsible for, what they do. Far from it. Habits – including our traits, abilities, and character – carry the marks of our environment. That is the sense in which our habits are social. They also embody our previous choices, including our choices to strengthen or alter our habits. That is the sense in which the habits are of our own making. Habits are the primary vehicles for transmitting our personal choices and social history into present action. That is why habits "constitute the self; they are will" (Dewey 1988/1922: 21).

Seeing that habits unite social influences and individual choice helps explain human action that would otherwise be mysterious. Why do some people become writers while others become accountants and still others, clerks? Why are some people honest while others are dishonest? Why do some people work hard, while others piddle away their lives? These are explained by habits that embody individual choices and social instruction. The alternative is to assume that each choice is made by a brute will, free from environing forces and previous personal decisions. However, that is nothing more than "belief in magic . . . ⟨whereby we hope⟩ to get results without intelligent control of means" (ibid. 22). If we take that approach, we abandon control over our lives; control comes primarily by instilling and refining habits of thought and action.

Changing habits

Although our environments shape our habits, the resulting habits are not beyond our control. We can change them. However, we cannot change them directly and immediately. To believe we can is another form of mental magic. Too often we think we can close our eyes, tell ourselves to become more honest, more caring, more hard-working, and that, if we just wish hard enough, our dreams will come true. Believing this makes personal change at least difficult and probably impossible. Real change requires hard work, attention to detail, and perseverance. Habits are changed not by private willing, but (a) by identifying and (b) then altering the conditions that make and sustain our habits, and finally, (c) by substituting and sustaining a more productive habit for the old detrimental one.

Unfortunately, many of us think (or hope) that we can shape our desires and frame our intentions in the recesses of a private mind. We do not. Genuine intentions are themselves habits acquired, developed, and enhanced over time. As a child, I daydreamed of being Superman, of being an astronaut, and of being a soldier. I envisioned myself zipping though the sky "faster than a speeding bullet," rocketing to the moon, and single-handedly besting an enemy squad. Nonetheless, it would be silly to say that I intended to become an astronaut or soldier, or that I desired to be Superman. Daydreams are neither intentions nor desires. They are mental magic. Humans cannot fly unaided. Moreover, although some people are astronauts and others are soldiers, the belief that I could be either merely by dreaming is no less magical than the belief that I could be Superman.

Yet we continue to confuse daydreams with intentions. We assume that if we pleasantly contemplate some goal, then we desire to achieve that goal, and that if we contemplate it often, then we intend to achieve it. I might assume that I want to quit smoking if I daydream about quitting. I might assume that I desire to be calm, patient, and less judgmental if I envision myself as an American Gandhi. However, passing thoughts are neither desires nor intentions. They are adult daydreams. Daydreams are not necessarily bad; they can provide grist for the intention mill. However, unless we use daydreams to prompt specific plans, then we are reveling in fantasies, not forming desires or intentions.

How, then, do we turn daydreams into realities? How do we reshape our habits? None of us designed our initial environments; neither did any of us wholly design our current environments. To that degree, we cannot completely control our habits (Nussbaum 1986). However, we do have some control, and that control depends on our understanding, and then deliberately altering, the conditions that make and sustain habits. "Social engineers" alter the environment to prompt changes in others.

We can also each engineer our own environments. We can employ both mechanisms to remake ourselves: we can change the social environment to help us change our habits – for instance, by placing high taxes on tobacco or supporting tough laws against drunk driving. Both mechanisms rely on the intervening hand of delibera-tion: purposefully adjusting the environment to diminish, eliminate, or strengthen our (or others') habits. However, deliberation is no occult property. It is also an intel-lectual habit developed and refined by education, experience, and deliberation. "The deliberative and the moral, like the muscular powers, are improved only by being used" (Mill 1985/1885).

Multiple habits

If we have few habits, we will have difficulty modifying faulty ones. We are thus unlikely to find satisfactory ways to act in new situations. We would be like a chess player who knows only one opening or a musician who plays only one tune. If our opponent makes a different first move, or if the only musical composition we know ("Bad Moon Rising") is inappropriate in the circumstances (a wedding), then we do not know how to act. Good chess players know different openings and employ dif-ferent strategies. That knowledge and those strategies are habits that pave the intel-lectual roads along which chess-playing deliberation travels. This is essential for being a good chess-player. These habits empower the player to respond appropriately to their opponents' moves, even moves they have never seen. Multiple habits empower us to be sensitive to varieties of situations, thereby making us more responsive to the relevant features of problems. Habits are the creative engines of chess playing and of life.

The presence of multiple habits also explains people's uncharacteristic behavior. Ron is a kindly fellow: generally he responds sympathetically to others in pain. One day he snaps at Belinda, who has asked him for help. "Why," he says, "are you always bugging me? Go pester someone else." Everyone, even Belinda, recognizes Ron is "out of character." But what does that mean? Does than mean someone other than Ron was snappish with her? No. It just means that being snappish is one of Ron's habits that is normally constrained by his more powerful and benevolently inclined habits. As Ron develops a unified character, his tendency to be brusque diminishes; acting rudely becomes even more uncharacteristic. But it does not disappear.

Morality is a habit

It should now be clear that morality is best understood as a sophisticated habit. It is not normally the immediate product of conscious deliberation. If we always (or even often) had to rely on wholly conscious decisions to be moral, we would be even less moral than we are. John trips on the sidewalk; Susan reaches down to help him up while Robin walks by. That afternoon, Susan has to adjudicate a dispute between two employees; she is sensitive, yet direct and candid. Robin faces a similar problem; he is cold and ineffective. What distinguishes Susan from Robin? In the first case, Susan saw John and immediately reached out to him. Robin never seriously considered helping; probably he did not even "see" John. In the second case, Susan understood the problem and the interests of those involved; Robin did not recognize or seriously consider the employees' interests. The core difference between them is not explained by their conscious decisions – although those may have differed as well. Rather they differ because of what each is habitually disposed to (a) see, (b) consider relevant, (c) think about, and (d) use in guiding their actions. Moral people do not standardly decide to consider the interests of others; they are the kind of people who just do. When they do deliberate, those deliberations are also shaped by habits (just as the deliberations of philosophers and engineers and lawyers and accountants are shaped by their professional habits).

Like other habits, moral habits both empower and restrict. They empower us because, in embodying previous learning, we can respond quickly and appropriately in morally serious situations. Yet they also restrict, since, when operating, we overlook aspects of our action that may be morally relevant. That is why we need multiple habits: first-order habits to make us sensitive to others' interests, and second-order habits to evaluate our first-order habits to insure that they are appropriate, especially in changing circumstances.

Racism is a habit

We can now wrap up this long discussion of habit by showing how it elucidates the nature of racism and explains why it is so difficult to eradicate. Like all habits, racism is shaped by our early beliefs and experiences. The resulting patterns of reaction and response maintain themselves over time. Deeply ingrained racism is, to use Amélie Rorty's language, a magnetizing disposition that forms "our emotional dispositions, habits of thought, as well as habits of action and response" (1980: 106). Habits have motivational inertia. Simply removing the cognitive elements that shape them will not eliminate visceral and reactive elements. Consider the following analogy: many reared in strict religious backgrounds were taught to feel guilty about sex and about not attending church. If these individuals become agnostics or atheists, they may still feel guilt about these actions even if they lack the cognitive beliefs grounding that guilt. Likewise for racism. Given our history, racism is embodied in our individual and social habits. Its remnants influence whites' beliefs about, experiences of, and expectations for blacks in ways that will be difficult to identify, and thus, difficult to counter or eradicate. Our racist habits insure that we will not notice when shop clerks scrutinize blacks, when blacks are denied raises, or when local realtors redline.

The institutional nature of modern racism

The habitual basis of racism is created, shaped, supported, and sustained by social, political, and economic institutions. These institutions, like our habits, may not have been assumed or designed with the aim of mistreating blacks (although some were). Nonetheless, once established, habitual and institutional inertia carry the effects of racism past into the present and future. Let me illustrate.

Blacks were legally or effectively barred from accumulating significant wealth until at least the 1960s. Even after the legal barriers to full membership in the society were lifted, blacks' incomes continued to be much less than that of whites. In short, they began with less wealth, and were able to accumulate less; therefore, it is not surprising that they are far less wealthy than whites. Whites average 12 times the net wealth of blacks (Oliver and Shapiro 1995: 86). Race alone accounts for two-thirds of the difference in wealth, even between blacks and whites in similar jobs (ibid. 135). It is a predictable result of centuries of second-class citizenship. Well, at least it is predictable if we don't take positive steps to ensure that it doesn't happen.

We haven't. In fact, these historical differences in wealth are guarded by social, political, and economic institutions. To take one example, the US tax code permits substantial tax breaks for a home mortgage, education expenses for and gifts to one's children; it also permits passing on vast accumulated wealth, usually to one's children. From the whites' vantage these institutions are eminently reasonable. The privileged can maintain or expand their wealth and can significantly benefit their children, who are then better positioned to forward their interests and the interests of *their* children (Johnson and Shapiro 2003: 174). This also substantially affects the chance that their children will attend college, or excel there (US Department of Education 2005).

This unquestionably affects people's life chances. Few middle-aged blacks inherited more than a pittance from their parents. Therefore they typically had to settle for a weaker education, and, even then, often had to go further into debt. Few blacks received significant assistance from their parents when they purchased their first home. Thus many have had to delay, if not forego, home ownership. Those that did purchase a house typically had to buy a smaller one on which they assumed loans with higher mortgage rates (Association of Community Organizations for Reform Now 2002). Thus, they were less likely to build any equity. These factors insure that the racial gap in wealth will not soon be closed, let alone eliminated. Indeed, the disparity has expanded. "Between 1999 and 2001, the net worth of Hispanic and Black households fell by 27 percent each. The net worth of White households increased by 2 percent" (Kochhar 2004: 4).

In sum, these institutions perpetuate racism's effects, and they do so in ways that few people notice and for which no one appears to be at fault. Just as we do not normally notice the air that we breathe, most whites do not notice the presence, let alone the workings, of these institutions. We take them for granted; we do not notice the ways they constrain and harm blacks. Even if we did, we are loathe to change them since we are their beneficiaries.

The moral importance of groups

Racism plays a central role in US history. That indicates one way that group membership can be morally significant. Racism is not just, or even primarily, a wrong by a particular white against a particular black. Victims are selected not because of who they uniquely are, but simply because their race. We would thus expect that racial membership profoundly shapes how Americans understand themselves and how they understand and relate to others. Our expectation would be right. Think, for a moment, about your teachers, colleagues, friends, and acquaintances. You know their race and gender. You know it immediately without having to remember ("Gee, is Sean black or white?"). However, if I ask you about Sean's hair color, eye color, height, or weight, you may not know. Even if you do, you will likely have to consciously think about it. Not so with race (or gender). Race is part of our understanding of others.

Why do we know people's race and gender in a way and to a degree that we do not know their other characteristics? Simple: race and gender are not ways of describing people; they are categories we use to classify them, ways to lump people with others of "their kind." These categories reflect not just or primarily what people look like, but what we expect of them and how we assume we should relate to them. Since race and gender play these important conceptual roles, we immediately classify those we meet. If for some reason we cannot, e.g. if someone is androgynous or has slightly dark skin, we look at them more carefully. Most of us are uncomfortable when we cannot classify someone by her race or gender (Wasserstrom 1977).

Here's an illustration of this phenomenon. A newsman reports that a black male has robbed the local convenience store or that the female Senator from California has sponsored a new gun control bill. Why does the newsman mention the criminal's race or the Senator's gender? Is the newsman offering a physical description so we can spot them on the street? Of course not. We may not know precisely why he used these "descriptions." The newsman probably doesn't know either. Still, we can safely infer that these adjectives serve some purpose, even if we don't know what purpose. What is clear is that race and gender play a pivotal role in people's description of themselves and others in ways that other physical characteristics do not. A newsman would not report that a blue-eyed person had robbed the store, that a blonde Senator had introduced a bill, that a tall person was chosen CEO of a local corporation, or that a fat DA presented her case to the grand jury.

Since race (and gender) are fundamental classifications in our society, it is easy to see why and how people's race importantly shapes their interests, desires, beliefs, reactions, self-perceptions, expectations, and opportunities. In extreme cases, this is indisputable. Being the son of a seventeenth-century king or a twenty-first-century billionaire makes failure a singular accomplishment and success the expectation (at least where success is judged by money, power, and status). In contrast, the children of early nineteenth-century American slaves had no chance of achieving anything beyond bare survival.

Even in less extreme cases, the power of group membership is profound – although if we are members of a privileged class, we may fail to notice, let alone acknowledge, that. After all, we do not want to treat our successes as anything other than the fruits of our intelligence, perseverance, and efficiency. However, as a white I was never told that I could not use a public bathroom available to others; I was never told that I was inferior simply in virtue of my race; I never feared that I might be singled out as a shoplifter or stopped and frisked by police because of my race.

Present and Future of Racism

Habits and institutions conspire to make it difficult for blacks to escape their relatively constrained positions. Racist habits still shape most whites' attitudes no matter how progressive they are. And social, political, economic, and legal institutions would constrain blacks even if all of us individually had banished our racist habits.

So what is modern racism? *It is an inability or unwillingness to acknowledge the role that habits and institutions play in perpetuating racism, and it is an unwillingness to do anything about it.* These engines of contemporary racism are not as easy to spot as old-fashioned racism, but that does not make them less potent. Unfortunately, few whites acknowledge their own racism or see the racist effects of our institutions. They assume (or act as if) racism is (almost) gone (Bonilla-Silva 2003). Blacks who continue to talk about racism are then thought to be "playing the victim." Whites are thus less likely to take black claims seriously, and more likely to act in ways that sustain racism.

REFERENCES

Arsenault, R. (2004) *Freedom Riders: 1961 and the Struggle for Racial Justice.* New York: Oxford University Press.

Association of Community Organizations for Reform Now (2002) "Separate and Unequal: Predatory Lending in America." (Online) Available at: http://www.acorn.org/acorn10/ predatorylending/plreports/SU2002/main.htm. (Accessed June 23, 2003.)

Benatar, D. (2003) "The Second Sexism," *Social Theory and Practice* 29 (2): 177–210.

Berlin, I. (1998) *Many Thousands Gone: The First Two Centuries of Slavery in North America.* Cambridge, MA: Harvard University Press.

Bonilla-Silva, E. (2003) " 'New Racism,' Color-Blind Racism, and the Future of Whiteness in America." In A. W. Doane and E. Bonilla-Silva (eds.), *White Out: The Continuing Significance of Race.* New York: Routledge, 271–84.

Dewey, J. (1985/1932) *Ethics*, vol. 7. Carbondale, IL: Southern Illinois University Press.

Dewey, J. (1988/1922) *Human Nature and Conduct.* Carbondale, IL: Southern Illinois University Press.

Gadamer, H. G. (1975) *Truth and Method.* New York: Seabury Press.

Herrnstein, R. J. and Murray, C. (1996) *Bell Curve: Intelligence and Class Structure in American Life.* New York: Free Press.

Johnson, H. B. and Shapiro, T. M. (2003) "Good Neighborhoods, Good Schools: Race and the 'Good Choices' of White Families." In A. W. Doane and E. Bonilla-Silva (eds.), *White Out: The Continuing Significance of Race.* New York: Routledge, 173–87.

Kochhar, R. (2004) "The Wealth of Hispanic Households: 1996 to 2002." Pew Research Center, Washington, DC. (Online) Available at: http://pewhispanic.org/files/ reports/34.pdf.

LaFollette, H. (1996) *Personal Relationships: Love, Identity, and Morality.* Oxford: Blackwell Publishers.

LaFollette, H. (2000) "Pragmatic Ethics." In H. LaFollette (ed.), *The Blackwell Guide to Ethical Theory.* Oxford: Blackwell Publishers, 400–19.

Mill, J. S. (1985/1885) *On Liberty*. Indianapolis, IN: Hackett.

Nussbaum, M.C. (1986) *The Fragility of Goodness: Luck and Ethics in Greek Tragedy and Philosophy*. Cambridge: Cambridge University Press.

Oliver, M. and Shapiro, T. (1995) *Black Wealth / White Wealth: A New Perspective on Racial Inequality*. New York: Routledge.

Rorty, A. (1980) "Explaining Emotion." In A. Rorty (ed.), *Explaining Emotion*. Berkeley: University of California Press, 103–26.

US Department of Education (2005) "First Generation Students in Postsecondary Education: A Look at Their College Transcripts." US Department of Education, Washington, DC. (Online) Available at: http://nces.ed.gov/pubsearch/pubsinfo.asp?pubid=2005171.

Wasserstrom, R. (1977) "Racism, Sexism, and Preferential Treatment: An Approach to the Topic," *UCLA Law Review* 24 (3): 581–622.

SIX

Affirmative Action

Affirmative action – the practice of giving special consideration to minorities and women in hiring and school placement – once enjoyed widespread support in the United States. No more. Although the US Supreme Court recently (2003) declared that some affirmative action programs are legally permissible (*Grutter v. Bollinger et al.*), many Americans now reject the practice. In the 1996 general election, Californians overwhelmingly supported a proposal forbidding governmental agencies from practicing affirmative action. What explains this decline in support for affirmative action? Doubtless sociological factors may play some role. However, the change also occurred because opponents offered seemingly more persuasive arguments than supporters. I will first explore arguments against affirmative action for African-Americans. If affirmative action can be justified, blacks would be the most deserving recipients. Therefore, if the arguments against affirmative action for them are cogent, we can infer that no such programs are justified. Conversely, if we find that affirmative action for African-Americans is justified, we have some reason to think affirmative action for women and other select minorities might also be justified.

Most objectors to affirmative action employ several of the following interrelated arguments: (1) affirmative action is merely reverse discrimination. The practice (2) hurts white applicants who are in no way responsible for past harms to blacks, and (3) who are often more qualified. It also (4) stigmatizes blacks. Finally, some people argue that (5) these programs deprive employers of the right to hire whom they want. Let us look at each argument in turn.

The Arguments against Affirmative Action

Reverse discrimination

Everyone except diehard racists now admits that systematic discrimination against blacks is wrong. It was wrong to deprive people of jobs, housing, health, public benefits, and legal and civil rights merely because of their race. Affirmative action, they claim, is wrong for the same reason: these programs discriminate against whites simply because of *their* race. Two wrongs do not make a right.

This argument looks persuasive. According to the principle of universalizability we should treat cases the same unless there are general and relevant differences between them that can justify a difference in treatment. If both old-fashioned discrimination and affirmative action are simply "discrimination based on race," then we must judge both the same. That is the nub of truth in this objection. Unless these cases are relevantly different, then affirmative action is just old-fashioned discrimination in new guise. However, as I argued in the previous chapter, there are four important differences between these cases. Whites have subjected blacks to decades of systematic and widespread discrimination. In contrast, affirmative action is not part of a network of discrimination against whites. Whites are not thought to be inferior to blacks. Indeed, whites' interests have been – and continue to be – well protected by political, legal, economic, and social institutions. That is why even after years of affirmative action programs whites maintain disproportionate political, economic, and social power.

These morally relevant differences show why this objection is not telling, why it is a mistake to say blacks receive affirmative action simply *because of their race*. We have affirmative action for blacks because they are *members of a pervasively, systematically, and continuously victimized race*. If affirmative action is wrong, it is not for the same reasons that discrimination against blacks is wrong (Wasserstrom 1977).

Consider the following analogy. Should we favor people simply because they have a high IQ? Of course not. IQ does not intrinsically merit favored treatment. However, that does not mean IQ plays no legitimate role in distributing professional jobs. Since we need especially talented people in these jobs, having a high IQ will be indirectly relevant to applicants' qualifications. An intelligent person may deserve the job, but not simply because she is intelligent. She deserves it because she is most qualified – although she is most qualified, in part, because of her IQ.

Defenders of affirmative action offer a parallel argument. They say that these programs favor blacks, but not because they are black. It favors them because they are members of a systematically victimized group. This history of discrimination explains why the reverse discrimination argument against affirmative action, at least in its simple formulation, will not do. That does not yet tell us if the practice is morally justified. It tells us only that this argument against it is not decisive.

We have seen these ideas at play before when we discussed the pivotal role of consistency in moral reasoning. We should act consistently. To know if we are being consistent we must compare two or more actions to see if they are relevantly similar. The problem is that the same action can invariably be described in multiple ways. Not all descriptions are equally appropriate. For example, here are two descriptions of the same event: (1) Mohammad Atta boarded an airplane in Boston; (2) Mohammad Atta flew an airplane into the World Trade Center. Although both descriptions are accurate, they do not prompt the same moral judgment. The second is preferable since it *accurately reflects all empirically and morally relevant features of the action*. The first is seriously incomplete. In the same way, simply dubbing affirmative action "reverse discrimination" is incomplete since it ignores relevant historical and moral facts.

There is a more plausible modified version of this argument: although we can conceptually distinguish between these cases, many, if not most, people will be psychologically inclined to slide between them. Given our psychological natures we cannot achieve racial color-blindness unless we cease using race in making public policy.

This is an empirical claim about human psychology. It could be right. However, those who make this claim tend not to base it on any empirical evidence. They offer it as if it were a truism. A truism it is not. After all, in other contexts most people can psychologically, as well as cognitively, distinguish two broadly similar behaviors. For instance, most people have no trouble distinguishing paternalism toward adults from paternalism toward children. They can see that while paternalism toward children may be frequently justified, paternalism toward adults rarely is.

Hurts those who have done no wrong

Compensatory justice requires that people pay for damage they cause others. After a blow-out, my car veers to the right and hits your car. I must compensate you for the damage even though I did not intend to hit you. Since someone has to pay for the damage, it is only reasonable that I do. If I rammed your car intentionally, or were grossly negligent, I will normally be expected to pay punitive, as well as compensatory, damages.

These widely accepted principles give us reason to think whites should compensate blacks for the substantial and ongoing harm to them (Schuchter 1970). Since the harm was intentional, there is reason to think whites also owe blacks punitive damages. Affirmative action is a plausible form of compensation, since one of the best ways for blacks to improve their status, wealth, and power is if they obtain higher-paying, more prestigious, and more powerful jobs (Feinberg 2003: 289).

Opponents of affirmative action disagree. People should be judged by what they do now, not by what their grandparents did. Taking someone's land or money would be akin to imprisoning them for murder or theft committed by their grandparents. The grandchildren did not harm blacks. They should not have to pay for the sins of their parents and grandparents. That is why affirmative action is morally inappropriate.

It is true that the grandchildren did not perpetrate the worst harms to blacks – true, but, by itself, not wholly relevant. Affirmative action does not punish sons for the sins of their fathers. Rather it holds that the children and grandchildren of those who wronged blacks should not continue to benefit from those ancient wrongs, and that the progeny of wronged blacks should not continue to suffer effects of those wrongs. That is why many supporters of affirmative action think that contemporary whites should compensate blacks, even though the central perpetrators and victims are dead.

Suppose Andrew and Bob were business partners during the Great Depression. Andrew steals the business; Bob goes broke. Most people would agree that if the wrong were demonstrated, say, five years later, that Andrew should compensate Bob. However, suppose the wrong was not uncovered until five decades later. Before Andrew died, he had become wealthy and powerful; Bob had committed suicide. Andrew's children were well educated and had every chance to succeed. Bob's children grew up poor, relatively uneducated, and generally disadvantaged.

Now Andrew III is CEO of a multinational corporation; Bob III is a welder in the local Ford plant. Does Andrew III have any reason to compensate Bob III? Since everyone agrees that Andrew should have compensated Bob had the wrong been uncovered after five years, does the passage of 45 more years change things? People who advocate affirmative action likely think it doesn't. That's not quite right. They would probably claim that the passage of time arguably lessens Andrew III's responsibilities to Bob III; it just does not obliterate them. They likewise think that the passage of time does not eliminate the need for whites to make recompense to blacks.

Opponents of affirmative action disagree. They claim that although blacks may "deserve" compensation in some cosmic sense, there are empirical and moral reasons why the passage of time dissipates any reason for whites to compensate blacks. First, the effects of ancient evils diminish with time: blacks have had sufficient opportunity to overcome any lingering effects of slavery and Jim Crow. Second, people are not morally accountable for their predecessors' wrongs. Those who suffered and those who perpetrated the most egregious harms (slavery) are long since dead. Victims and victimizers of later wrongs – lynchings, Jim Crow laws, etc. – are either dead or soon will be. Given this lapse of time, it would be wrong to expect whites to compensate blacks.

Advocates of affirmative action reject both arguments. First, serious wrongs usually have significant effects rippling into the distant future. They do not die when the perpetrators and victims die. In our scenario, Andrew's actions significantly limited Bob III's life prospects: they made it more likely that he would be poor, less educated, and less healthy. Andrew's actions also enhanced Andrew III's life prospects: they made it more likely that he would be better-educated, healthy, and wealthy. If this is true of an interaction between two individuals, it is even more obviously true of blacks, who were victims of two centuries of systematic and widespread discrimination. One cannot plausibly think that the history of discrimination against blacks does not affect the wealth, status, and opportunities of contemporary blacks. The claim that this systematic mistreatment did not benefit whites is equally dubious. Although some blacks may have escaped relative poverty and some whites may have squandered their fortunes, these are the exception, not the rule. A person's life chances are heavily shaped by the economic and social standing, as well as the educational attainment, of their parents.

Let me give an example. My parents were two of the brightest, hardest-working, most efficient people I have ever known. Both grew up in relatively impoverished families. One of them graduated from high school; the other finished the eighth grade. Despite their diligence, talents, and fiscal conservatism, they could ascend only to the (lower) middle class. Indeed, that they could ascend that far is testimony to their brightness and unrivaled work ethic. Why did my parents end up where they did, while other people their age who were less bright and energetic became wealthy and powerful? They were not lazy or untalented – anything but. The answer must be found in the social, economic, and educational status of their respective families. As Dearing, McCartney, and Taylor put it: "One of the most consistent findings in the development literature concerns the association between childhood poverty and negative development outcomes" (Dearing et al. 2001). People's history shapes their opportunities. Since the history of blacks in America is one in which they have been systematically harmed, then their opportunities have been, and continue to be, limited.

In saying this, the advocates of affirmative action need not think or claim that whites' actions *determined* blacks' life prospects. Actions with long-term effects do not fix the future. That is why we have reason to think the need for compensation diminishes with time. Although it may diminish, it does not automatically disappear. Whether these effects are lessened, virtually eliminated, or continue unabated depends on the social, political, and economic institutions in place. A society (a) that permits accumulation of massive wealth, (b) that lets parents pass their wealth to their progeny, and (c) in which the parents' wealth, social status, and education heavily influence the life prospects of their children, is one in which significant ancient wrongs endure.

American society contains such institutions. Under current inheritance laws, a single person can bequeath $1 million tax free; a couple, $2 million. Most give this money to their children. Congress, at the urging of President Bush, has even tried to make all inheritance exempt from taxation. Why do people support such laws (and proposals)? For two reasons: (1) They think parental bequests improve their children's lives – that is precisely why they support them; (2) they think that is morally appropriate.

If parental bequests standardly improve children's lives, then their absence will standardly limit them. And if it is appropriate for children's lives to be enhanced by their parents' actions, it must also be appropriate for children's lives to be limited by those actions.

This creates two related problems for critics of affirmative action. One, these institutions sustain or magnify the effects of discrimination. In a world with these institutions, discrimination does not die with the perpetrators and victims. It has continuing effects to their children and grandchildren. If we are going to maintain these institutions, then we need others that counteract their ill effects. Affirmative action is just such a policy.

Two, the very reasons given for supporting strong inheritance laws undermine several objections to affirmative action. Supporters of these inheritance laws think that the successes and failures of one generation should be transmitted to successive generations. If so, then the grandparents' children and grandchildren should not only reap the benefits of their legitimate successes, but their progeny should also incur their grandparents' obligations, including the obligation to compensate those they have wronged.

Objectors might respond by reformulating their objection: blacks who benefit from affirmative action policies are not the ones who suffer the continuing effects of systematic discrimination, while whites disadvantaged by affirmative action policies are normally not those who most benefited from those effects. There is truth to this objection. It would be preferable if the people who suffered and benefited from affirmative action did so in precise proportion as they benefited and suffered from discrimination past. However, our inability to provide perfect justice is no reason to abandon affirmative action. After all, all blacks have suffered some effects of discrimination, while almost all whites have benefited from it. One cannot imagine how any black could live in a historically racist culture and not suffer the continuing effects of racism. Many blacks more than 40 years old grew up in wholly segregated communities and had inferior educations and opportunities. They were likely victims of open discrimination in employment and housing. Younger blacks may not have suffered such open and egregious wrongs; but they were reared by those who did. Doubtless, too, they suffered their share of indirect and subtle discrimination.

Likewise, although I suppose a few whites have not benefited from discrimination against blacks, most have. If nothing else, they (and their parents – whose income, wealth, and social status affected *their* life prospects) faced less competition for jobs than they would have faced in a wholly non-discriminatory society. Finally, whereas blacks knew many whites abhorred them, whites have not experienced such deep and widespread hatred – not even white ethnic groups (Irish, Italian, and Polish) who were themselves victims of discrimination when they first immigrated (Kraut 2001).

What we see here is the convergence of two ideas we have been exploring since early chapters. First is the claim that our respective histories shape our abilities, interests, desires, and life prospects. Second is the claim that some group memberships matter morally. These factors are intermingled when discussing racism, sexism, and affirmative action. In US society race and gender play especially central historical roles. Who we are, what we want, and what we can do are significantly influenced by our race and gender. That is why this particular argument against affirmative action does not work. Blacks have been historically disadvantaged; the nature of US institutions perpetuates that disadvantage. Affirmative action is one weapon in the battle to overcome that disadvantage.

The qualification argument

Others object to affirmative action because they claim it deprives more deserving applicants of jobs and university placement. Just as we normally think the most deserving students should receive the best grades, persons with "the best qualifications" should always receive jobs and school positions. This argument is plausible – plausible, but not compelling. It rests on a misguided view of what it means to be the "best qualified" candidate, and it ignores ways in which we temper – or explicitly reject – the principle that the best qualified person should always get the job, promotion, position, etc. Let me explain each.

As commonly stated, this objection assumes that "being best qualified" is a characteristic of applicants we can identify independently of the context within which we hire people, give them promotions, or admit them to professional schools. However, whether an applicant is most deserving always depends on context. If I have high grades and sterling scores on standardized tests, should I automatically be admitted to medical or law school? No. First, we must know who applied. Otherwise we cannot know if I deserve admission relative to the competition. Second, we must know the needs of the business for which we are hiring or the profession for which the applicants will be training. Since these needs may change, what counts as "the best qualified" candidate may change from year to year.

In one way this is relatively uncontroversial. The purpose of a medical school is not to divvy up awards according to merit. It is to prepare doctors to serve the public. So when medical school officials set qualifications for admission, they must first determine the kinds of doctors they want to produce. They then set admissions criteria to increase the chance that the school will admit applicants likely to become those kinds of doctors. Once, medical schools thought doctors needed single-minded knowledge of the basic sciences. They subsequently made knowledge of these sciences the primary criterion for admission. Now, most schools recognize that doctors also need interpersonal skills and general cultural knowledge. Medical schools have changed their selection criteria to reflect this new understanding. When medical schools subsequently pass over the narrowly focused science students, they have no grounds to complain. They do not deserve a place in these schools simply because their biology and chemistry scores are stellar. The most "deserving" students are those who will best meet society's needs, as identified by the medical school admissions committee.

This is directly and indirectly relevant to the assessment of affirmative action. It is indirectly relevant because it undercuts the suggestion that some applicants, simply in virtue of their personal characteristics, merit a seat in professional schools. It is directly relevant since it may specifically justify a narrow range of affirmative action programs. Evidence shows that blacks, as a group, receive substantially inferior medical care to whites. Many lack money for medical care and even those with money often have trouble finding physicians located nearby. Evidence further shows that blacks are more likely than whites to become physicians serving black communities. Therefore, one way of elevating health care for blacks is to ensure that more blacks graduate from medical school.

Of course, the government could seek to improve health care for blacks by inducing white doctors to locate in largely black communities. However, this is not obviously a satisfactory solution. First, we do not want to police white physicians to ensure they live up to their pledges, especially if, after working in the black community for several years, they do not like it. Coerced physicians are not good physicians. Second, we have evidence that in this racially tense environment, some blacks are more comfortable being treated by another black, even if white physicians are geographically closer (Coffman et al. 2001: 1). This suggests that race is a qualification for medical school, at least in the current milieu.

However, this argument would justify only limited affirmative action programs. Perhaps blacks may get better legal counsel from black lawyers, blacks learn better from black teachers, etc. Nevertheless, even if all such arguments were successful – and that is dubious – it would still justify only some portion of current affirmative action programs.

Affirmative action stigmatizes blacks

A black woman lands a job in the government treasury office, which has an affirmative action policy. People in that office may assume she got the job simply because of her race. They infer that she is not the best qualified candidate and perhaps not qualified at all. That is why affirmative action stigmatizes all blacks who get jobs, even those who get them entirely on their qualifications.

There is some truth to this objection. Many people do assume that blacks who get jobs are not qualified. However, this is an odd assumption for someone who claims not to be a racist; there is no reason to think that all or even most blacks who are hired do not deserve these jobs, even in agencies with strong affirmative action programs. Why, then, do so many people believe this, and believe it strongly? I can think of two explanations. One, they are old-fashioned racists who think blacks are inferior – so of course they think blacks are not qualified for competitive posts. Two, although they do not think that blacks are naturally inferior, they think that given the history of discrimination, most blacks are insufficiently qualified for highly competitive jobs. Defenders of affirmative action have plausible responses to both objections. To the first they would say that the state should not pander to racists. To the second they would say: if the history of racism makes most blacks unqualified for many jobs and professional school positions, then that gives us powerful reason to establish some affirmative action programs to ensure more blacks become qualified and are subsequently employed. Perhaps this argument would not justify the very programs we have; but it would provide reasons for some programs.

Perhaps, though, there is something relevant lurking in this objection. Although many successful black candidates are eminently qualified, many co-workers, given the presence of affirmative action programs, may not know if a specific black worker really is qualified. White workers will therefore be prone to relate to black co-workers *as if* they were not qualified. Moreover, successful blacks will think or fear that they received the jobs simply because of their skin color.

This response misunderstands the aim and practice of affirmative action. These programs are not supposed to hire or admit just any black. Successful black candidates should be qualified for the post, even if they are not the most qualified. Under these circumstances, deserving blacks have no reason to feel or be stigmatized. Certainly they should be and feel stigmatized if they did not deserve a job or school position at all. That may sometimes happen. Affirmative action programs, like any hiring or placement process, may misfire. However, if successful blacks are qualified, they need not be stigmatized by the thought that another applicant might have been better qualified. After all, in a buyer's market, where there are many highly qualified applicants, any successful applicant has reason to think that she was not the most qualified applicant. Yet we do not think all successful applicants should feel or be stigmatized.

I am further skeptical about the claim that most blacks feel stigmatized by affirmative action, for, if they did, it is difficult to imagine why they overwhelmingly support such programs. Deeply racist folk who think blacks are seriously incompetent, might believe blacks are willing to take jobs they know they cannot do, attend schools at which they cannot succeed. However, short of such patently racist assumptions, we must conclude that most blacks do not feel stigmatized by affirmative action policies. Moreover, it does seem odd to complain that affirmative action is deficient because it stigmatizes blacks, especially since the nature of the social system affirmative action is trying to change has unquestionably stigmatized blacks for centuries. Why will giving them jobs likely stigmatize them at all? Even if it did, we can be confident that the stigma is less than what they have historically faced (Schmidt 2005).

Finally, this objection ignores the fact that we now distribute many jobs and school positions on grounds other than merit. Businesses regularly hire close family members, distant relatives, friends, and friends of friends. Schools regularly give extra consideration to the children of alumni. Many institutions favor veterans. If the people hired or placed are wholly incompetent, then the business owners or schools will come to regret their decision. However, as long as those hired or placed are competent, then the business, school, and the public are not upset. We take these policies and practices for granted, without comment. Yet volumes have been written condemning the practice of affirmative action, even if some of the people hired are only marginally less competent than the best white applicants. That suggests we are not meritocrats who object to affirmative action because it occasionally denies a job to the most deserving applicant. Perhaps we are racists after all.

The rights of employers

Most opponents of affirmative action will be sympathetic with the preceding arguments. A few will also advance a fifth. Employers, they say, have the right to hire whomever they want. Affirmative action policies limit whom employers can hire. Thus, affirmative action policies infringe employers' rights.

People advocating this view contend that employers have property rights barring others from interfering with how they run their businesses as long as they do not directly harm others. They do not harm others by hiring whom they want. Therefore, the government should not tell them whom to hire. It is important to notice that this non-consequentialist argument is incompatible with all earlier arguments against affirmative action. Someone embracing this fifth argument cannot claim, for example, that affirmative action is wrong because it denies jobs to the most deserving applicants. If employers can legitimately hire whomever they want, then employers are free to hire anyone, even someone who is demonstrably unqualified. The employer could, of course, adopt an affirmative action program. But they could also choose to hire only whites. That is the central reason many people will not find this argument convincing: it is the same position that overt racists used for decades to exclude blacks. Moreover, this argument, even if telling, would be applicable only to private employers. It would not categorically rule out affirmative action by governmental agencies. Since "the people" are the employers, then "they" could hire whomever they want. Therefore this argument cannot be grounds for rejecting all such programs.

An Argument for Affirmative Action

These objections to affirmative action are not as potent as they might first appear. Still, they are sufficiently potent to raise doubts about the practice unless we can find a compelling argument for it. I think there is an argument, one that employs a mix of considerations, including several I offered in response to arguments against affirmative action.

Continuing racism: veiled and indirect

If racism were a relic of the past, then some arguments for affirmative action would be out of place. However, as I argued here and in the previous chapter, racism is not dead. It is alive and thriving in the United States. However, its shape has transformed. Current racism is less flagrant. It does not wear a sheet or burn crosses. Now it lurks in the boardroom, the courtroom, and the classroom, embodied in our habits and enforced by our institutions. Since it is veiled, today's racist would never acknowledge that she is a racist. She will likewise deny that past racism has significant effects on contemporary blacks. That is precisely what makes her a racist. She lets racism continue, and rejects all attempts to remedy it.

Consider the following analogy. I am chair of an academic department in which the previous chair systematically discriminated against female faculty: they received fewer raises, taught more (and more labor-intensive) courses, were given heavy service assignments, and never received sabbaticals. During my first year as chair, one female faculty member applies for promotion, another applies for a sabbatical, and both want merit raises. The administration has a strict quota: I can recommend only one person for promotion, one for sabbatical, and two for merit raises.

I would never mistreat women in ways my predecessor did. Indeed, I openly opposed his sexist behavior. I want people to be judged solely on their merits. I assume that means I should only examine their respective paper credentials. I carefully examine all applications for promotion, sabbatical, and merit raises. The women's applications are worthy, just not quite as worthy as some male applicants. What do I do? I give the promotion, the sabbatical, and both raises to male faculty.

Under these circumstances I would be guilty of sexism. By choosing to ignore the systematic mistreatment of these faculty, I allow its effects to continue. It is not merely that the former chair gave the women poor assignments; those assignments affected their credentials and thus their ability to compete now. Joe may have a sterling publication record, a promising sabbatical proposal and superb letters of recommendation from significant players in the discipline – each slightly better than Joan's. If I stop there, I err. I should recognize that she achieved her record while teaching twice as much as Joe, and without any administrative support for her research. If I ignore this history and the way it shapes their respective credentials, I allow past immoral actions to continue into the future. I am thus complicit in my former chair's sexism.

Equality of opportunity

Against the background of veiled and institutional racism, a central function of affirmative action is to promote equality of opportunity for blacks. We cannot counter racism simply by imploring people to be non-racist. We must undercut racist habits, and corral racist institutions. Affirmative action is a reasonable and effective way to do both. These programs are especially apt at promoting equality of opportunity. They do so in four ways.

First, affirmative action programs constrain blatant racism. If left unchecked, overtly racist employers and school officials will openly discriminate against blacks. Affirmative action demands that hiring and school placement be open to inspection. That makes overt discrimination difficult. Two, these programs require employers and school personnel to inform black applicants about openings and to encourage them to apply. This insures a larger pool of quality black applicants. Three, these programs require employers and school admissions officers to think more carefully about how they choose whom to hire or admit – and why. If employers and school officials are more conscious of race – and conscious of the ways it shapes their perceptions of applicants' skills, experience, and collegiality – then they are better able to constrain subconscious racism. Finally, these programs encourage employers and admissions officials to ask how black applicants would have competed in a fair market, in a fair world. This will not require them to hire someone who is incompetent. However, it does force them to recognize that paper credentials do not exhaustively reveal an applicant's qualifications.

So how do we assess qualifications? We have to determine, among other things, how jobs and school positions would have been distributed if we had wholly fair competition. Let me explain. Slightly more than 12 percent of the US population is black. It is thus reasonable to infer that in a world without a history of discrimination, in a world of equal opportunity and fair competition, blacks would hold roughly 12 percent of professional jobs. However, they hold half that number, and that number is as high as it is only because of affirmative action (Coffman et al. 2001: 6). Why do only 6 percent of these jobs go to blacks? The most plausible answer is: because of the history of discrimination against them.

To simplify the example, let us assume that a medical school has 100 openings in its first-year class. In a fair world, we would expect 12 percent of the class to be black, and, to simplify the discussion, that 88 percent would be white. In the current

world at least 94 whites and fewer than 6 blacks will be admitted. Suppose we established a strong affirmative action program that required that 12 percent of the class
be black. That means that six whites who would have been admitted under the system
without affirmative action would not be admitted once the program is in place.
Doubtless these white applicants will think they are being discriminated against, that
they are having to pay for earlier generations' mistreatment of blacks.

However, if we judge this from the vantage point of a fair world rather than the
current world, things look very different. In a fair world, the weakest six white candidates would not have been admitted anyway – more qualified blacks would have.
Therefore, these white applicants are not paying for the sins of their fathers or grand-
fathers. The program simply does not allow them to continue to benefit from the
ongoing effects of historical discrimination. So even if the burden of affirmative
action falls squarely on them, they have no grounds to complain. The distribution
that would result from affirmative action is precisely the result we would expect in
a fair world.

Of course, that oversimplifies the case. Although we can plausibly assume that
blacks would have received those six additional positions in a fair world, we cannot
know which blacks would have been admitted or which six whites would have been
the least qualified. That is not an insurmountable problem. For although we cannot
be certain that the same six whites would be rejected in the ideal world and the
world with affirmative action, we could reasonably expect that many of them would
be. We have less reason to think that the blacks admitted under affirmative action
would be the same blacks admitted in the fair world. Still, it is better that some
blacks be admitted than to scrap the program because we cannot determine the
precise people who would have made it in a fair world. Affirmative action programs
do not pretend to be a perfect remedy.

No legal regulation, no matter how valuable, is perfect. All rules and regulations
governing job hiring and admissions to professional schools are far from perfect.
Some extremely deserving people fail to get the job or the school position. Some
demonstrably undeserving people are hired or admitted because of flaws in the
system. If the system for admitting people regularly misfires, then we have grounds
for concern. However, if the system usually gets it right, that is enough. Likewise, if
affirmative action programs usually benefit deserving blacks and rarely hinder mer-
itorious and relatively disadvantaged whites, then that also ought to be enough –
especially considering the extent to which blacks have been systematically deprived
of the full benefits of American society for so long.

What we must remember is that since blacks were wronged *because of their race*,
then any scheme for promoting equality of opportunity – or for providing recompense – *must* make reference to their race. How else could we rectify this ancient
wrong? Taken together, these provide reasons for thinking that affirmative action is
an important tool for battling racism. At least we cannot assume, as many people do,
that the idea is morally bankrupt.

Conclusion

This discussion of affirmative action employed both deontological and consequentialist considerations. Nothing in this discussion showed that there is anything fundamentally flawed with either theory – although both need to be tweaked so that they can better take account of the moral status of groups. What is important to note is although these theories clearly played a role in our discussions, their roles were in the background. We did not just consult an ethical theory so we could know what to do. That is not the way theories work. Nonetheless, they are still very important. They help us isolate relevant features of moral choices, and thereby help us decide on the best way to act. In later discussions of practical issues, we will see that the theories function in similar ways.

REFERENCES

Coffman, J., Levin, R., Colburn, L., and Grumbach, K. (2001) "Holding onto Our Own: Migration Patterns of Underrepresented Minority Californians in Medicine." California Policy Research Center: Oakland, CA. (Online) Available at: http://www.ucop.edu/cprc/medmigration.pdf.

Dearing, E., McCartney, K., and Taylor, B. A. (2001) "Change in Family Income-to-Needs Matters More for Children with Less," *Child Development* 72 (6): 1779–93.

Feinberg, W. (2003) "Affirmative Action." In H. LaFollette (ed.), *Oxford Handbook of Practical Ethics*. Oxford: Oxford University Press, 272–99.

Kraut, A. (2001) *The Huddled Masses: The Immigrant in American Society, 1880–1921*, 2nd edn. Arlington Heights, IL: Harlan Davidson.

May, L. (1987) *The Morality of Groups: Collective Responsibility, Group-Based Harm, and Corporate Rights*. Notre Dame, IN: University of Notre Dame Press.

May, L. and Hoffman, S. (1991) *Collective Responsibility: Five Decades of Debate in Theoretical and Applied Ethics*. Savage, MD: Rowman & Littlefield.

Schmidt, P. (2005) "Studies Offer Mixed Assessments of Race-Conscious Admissions Policies and Texas' 10% Plan," *Chronicle of Higher Education*, A25. (Online) Available at: http://chronicle.com/prm/weekly/v51/i26/26a02501.htm.

Schuchter, A. (1970) *Reparations: The Black Manifesto and Its Challenge to White America*. Philadelphia, PA: J. P. Lippincott.

Wasserstrom, R. (1977) "Racism, Sexism, and Preferential Treatment: An Approach to the Topic," *UCLA Law Review* 24 (3): 581–622.

PART THREE

Life and Death

SEVEN

Religion and Morality

Some readers will think my emphasis on arguments, my stress on moral relevance, rules, principles, and theories are diversions from the truth that morality typically or invariably depends upon religion. The claim that morality is somehow connected to religion is highly plausible – but also ambiguous. It might mean (a) that many people's moral beliefs developed from their religious upbringing, (b) that religion motivates many people to be moral, or (c) that morality logically depends on the existence of a specific type of god (Adams 1973, 1996; Lewis 2001/1952, especially chapter 1; Quinn 1978, 1990, 2000). The first claim is almost certainly true, the second, plausible; and the third, almost certainly false. Let us look at each in turn.

The Origins of Morality

Historical and sociological explanations

Most people were reared in religious environments and most religions promulgate moral beliefs. That is why we should be astonished if religion played no role in the origins and contours of most people's moral views. This claim is sufficiently obvious to grant it without further discussion. Although true, it is far less significant than many people suppose.

Authority and rational belief

The fact that most people's moral beliefs arose from their religious upbringing is just one instance of a general truth about the origins of humans' beliefs, a truth we first discussed in Chapter 3. We all acquired our initial beliefs from the testimony of our parents, and later from our teachers, preachers, siblings, and peers. (If this seems at all dubious, imagine what would happen to a child who grows up with no human influence – see Masson 1997.) From our parents and teachers we learned what motivates us and others; we learned about the nature of the world. We also acquired our initial non-moral values (what tastes good, what goals we should pursue, what is beautiful) as well as our moral beliefs. We understandably assumed that what they said was true and that what they did was appropriate.

Most of us continue to hold variations of our initial beliefs with little critical thought. We each assume that of all possible sets of beliefs, ours must be (mostly) right. Apparently we think that while others' parents and teachers failed to instruct them correctly, ours were excellent teachers. Of course, others think the same thing about their parents, teachers, etc. This explains why and how people can hold widely disparate views and each be convinced that their views are correct. We forget or ignore the truth stated by John Stuart Mill nearly a century and a half ago, that "mere accident has decided which of these numerous worlds is the object of his reliance, and that the same causes which make him a churchman in London would have made him a Buddhist or a Confucian in Peking" (1985/1885: 17).

If we stop and think about it for a minute, most of us see that Mill was right. Why do most people in the United States tend to be Christians while most people in Baghdad are Muslims? Did all of us scrutinize competing religions and just happen to settle on the ones we were first taught? No one could plausibly think so. Yet while we tend to adopt some variation of whatever we were first taught, we may become irritated when others uncritically mouth what they were taught – at least when their views clash with ours. For instance, most Americans just cannot imagine why many Arabs hate us. Somehow we expect them to see the error of their ways. In short, although we acknowledge our fallibility in the abstract, that knowledge does not carry

> the weight in . . . practical judgement which is always allowed to it in theory; for while everyone well knows himself to be fallible, few think it necessary to take any precautions against their own fallibility, or admit the supposition that any opinion of which they feel very certain may be one of the examples of the error to which they acknowledge themselves to be liable (ibid.).

That is a common source of moral error. This propensity explains how basically decent people can perpetrate horrible evils: slavery, genocide, racism, sexism, etc. (Arendt 1994/1963; Sabini and Silver 1982: 55–88; Staub 1989: 79–88). If their parents or society say that blacks are inferior, that women are incapable of making wise decisions, that Arabs hate Americans because of our freedom, then most people will believe what they have been told, and they will act accordingly. We can avoid these errors – and the moral evils they bring – only by rationally evaluating our views, and then by guiding our actions by what we find.

The implications of this for the current discussion are clear: we are not justified in believing god is the author of morality simply because our parents told us so. One, they might be mistaken. This acknowledgment does not demean our parents or their beliefs. Even the smartest people in the world are sometimes mistaken. Two, perhaps what they taught us is true, e.g., that god *is* the author of morality. Nonetheless, they may be mistaken about what god commands. After all, different religions advance disparate – even wholly incompatible – views about what god is and what she expects. They cannot all be right. So we must rationally evaluate their competing claims. Three, they may be justified in their beliefs – that is, they may have the good evidence for their belief – yet still be wrong. Scientists who adopted Newton's laws were acting on the best available evidence; but we now know that Newton's theories are at least incomplete, and in some sense, wrong. Four, perhaps our parents are both correct and wholly justified in their beliefs. However, we cannot transfer justifications the way we transfer money. If we could, education would be simply a matter of giving people true beliefs, along with their accompanying justifications. It is not. To be educated is to acquire the knowledge and skills to assess evidence ourselves. Although I think each of these claims is relatively uncontentious, we can better understand why if we first become clearer about how to evaluate testimony. This will illuminate not only this current issue, but also several topics we discuss later in the book.

Evaluating testimony

Although we must decide which testimony to believe, we cannot do without it. We cannot have first-hand evidence for everything we know. We cannot draw our own maps, develop our technology, devise our own scientific theories, or determine the contents of canned goods at the grocery before we purchase them. Nor can we directly obtain the empirical information necessary for making moral decisions. Did Clarence Thomas make lewd comments to his employees? Does capital punishment deter? What are the effects of lying? Our answers must rely partly on the reports of others. We were not there when Thomas interacted with his employees. We do not conduct our own studies of the deterrent effects of crime.

That is why testimony is essential. We depend on others for information. At the same time we must recognize that "people disguise the truth in certain situations, whether out of deviousness, self-deception, ignorance, or fear. They also, of course, misremember, misjudge, or misreason" (Quine and Ullian 1978: 55–6). So our choice is not between always believing or always rejecting testimony. We must decide which testimony to believe. I cannot provide a complete explanation of how to best do that; however, I can offer some general observations (ibid. 51–9). When someone introduces herself, I believe she is who she says she is. When someone tells me that she traveled to Venice, I generally believe her. Why? Two reasons. One, they are matters about which each person should be knowledgeable, about which each is normally an authority. Second, barring special information, I have no reason to doubt them.

Sometimes, though, I do have specific reason to doubt people's claims, especially if (a) someone's claims clash with other things I know, or if (b) something important hangs on my believing them. If I am attending a party and someone introduces herself as Laura Bush, I will rightly be dubious. I cannot fathom that she would attend any party I would attend, and, if she were, she would be surrounded by secret service agents. That background information shows that this partygoer's claim is almost certainly false. Or suppose another partygoer wants me to invest $20,000 in a company she is starting, or someone dressed in a police officer's uniform announces that she is going to arrest me. I would want more evidence that they are who they say they are before I invest my hard-earned money or voluntarily leave the party with them. Too much is at stake to believe these claims without question.

Assessing testimony is more difficult if the claims are complex and require special training or study to evaluate; they are still more difficult to assess if they concern issues about which experts disagree. Since I know that not all experts can be right, I must decide whom to believe. There are five things I can do. First, I should assess a purported authority's "credentials." Does she have the requisite training, experience, or professional standing? Is she an authority *about the issues or facts in question*. Joan may be a brilliant physicist, but that doesn't make her an authority on your name, medicine, law, or politics. Second, if genuine authorities disagree, I should find out which ones are more widely cited and respected. Do a preponderance of these embrace the same view? Third, if the issue is especially important, I may directly assess some of the authority's arguments. For instance, although I am not a social scientist, I have some ability to judge if a study was well designed and well executed. Fourth, I can examine the inferences authorities draw from their data. Fifth, I can compare what they say with other things I (think I) know. The better established my other (background) beliefs, the better able I am to assess testimony. If a purported authority tells me that the sun is made of butter, I am confident she is wrong. That claim clashes with a nest of strong beliefs about the heat of the sun and my knowledge that butter melts at temperatures above 40 degrees Fahrenheit. To believe this testimony about the composition of the sun would require abandoning many well-established beliefs.

This last strategy, although essential, is dangerous. It is deadly if our background beliefs are wrong. Given our propensity to seek or concoct evidence supporting our current views, and to quickly dismiss evidence clashing with them, we can easily err. We may use ill-informed beliefs as grounds to reject reasonable ones. To prevent such mistakes, we must vigilantly protect ourselves from error. We need a repository of well-founded beliefs and the critical skills that allow us to reasonably assess testimony.

Implications for the current issue

We inherit physical traits and behavioral tendencies from our parents. Our upbringing and our personal choices shape how those traits and tendencies develop. We also "inherit" our initial beliefs from our parents. But experience, the reactions of others, and self-reflection often lead us to modify – and sometimes reject – those beliefs. All people, even those reared in restrictive environments, change at least some "inherited" beliefs: adults' beliefs are never bare copies of their parents'.

That is why religion will not be the only influence on a person's moral beliefs. And, if John Stuart Mill is correct, it is also not the dominant influence for most of us. In discussing the average Christian, Mill says:

The standard to which he does refer is the custom of his nation, his class, or his religious profession. He has thus, on the one hand, a collection of ethical maxims, which he believes to have been vouchsafed to him by infallible wisdom as rules for his government; and on the other, a set of every-day judgments and practices, which go a certain length with some of those maxims, not so great a length with others, stand in direct opposition to some, and are, on the whole, a compromise between the Christian creed and the interests and suggestions of worldly life. To the first of these standards he gives his homage; to the other his real allegiance (Mill 1985/1885: 39).

Many Christians will surely reject his assessment. Yet I think there is more than a mite of truth in it. Let me explain. Read the "Sermon on the Mount" – the longest presentation attributed to Jesus. In it, he claims that "the meek shall inherit the earth," that "whosoever smites you on the right cheek, turn to him the other also," and that you should "take no thought for the morrow." Later in those chapters he demands that the faithful feed the hungry, heal the sick, and visit the imprisoned. The content and tone of these passages dramatically clash with the average layperson's understanding of Christianity. It is not that the average layperson thinks the previous statements describe a moral ideal to which they aspire, but fall short; rather, most believers never seriously consider that these principles correctly describe how they should live. Most believers despise meekness, enthusiastically support their country's going to war, condemn those not concerned about money, spend considerable energy planning for the future, and want even harsher punishments for those in prison. When the demands of morality, as specified in the New Testament, butt up against going social norms, so much the worse for the religiously based demands.

These social norms also distort other biblical maxims. Many conservative Christians consider homosexuality an especially heinous sin. That view cannot be sustained by a careful reading of the Bible. Jesus never explicitly mentions it, there are *relatively* few biblical verses that do, and many of these, according to some biblical scholars, are not best read as condemnations of homosexuality (Martin 1995). However, even if every verse that these people cite as condemning homosexuality were such, the Bible condemns homosexuality infrequently relative to other sins – greed, indifference, hypocrisy, and self-righteousness. Yet these others sins, which are roundly condemned in the Bible, are infrequently condemned by Christians, and certainly not with the intensity that they direct toward those who are gay. It would never occur to these believers to advocate a constitutional ban on greed, hypocrisy, war, or self-righteousness, yet some have pushed for a constitutional amendment banning gay marriage. What makes the difference? As Mill would say: not their belief in god but the beliefs of their nation, social class, or particular religious denomination.

I realize this argument is truncated. Some will surely disagree. However, in rejecting Mill's claims they indirectly verify the point he is making. They contend that although *their* moral views are based upon their religion, that is not so for many Christians. They think that Christians who do not condemn homosexuality or who support the right to an abortion do not practice *real* Christianity. *Their* views must be the product of non-religious factors. To that extent they agree that religion is not the primary determinant of many people's moral beliefs. Finally, even if religion were the primary determinant of people's moral beliefs, it would still not justify those beliefs. I discuss that issue in the last section of this chapter after first exploring another way that religion is arguably connected to morality.

Moral Motivation

Morality sometimes demands that we act in ways that seem to inhibit, or at least not promote, our personal interests. It may require us to be honest or altruistic when we would prefer to be dishonest or selfish. In these circumstances, we might wonder: "Why should I do what morality requires?" We will explore this general question in Chapter 18. Here we look at three ways religion has been thought to motivate morality.

Three ways

Morality pays

People who are generally moral are more likely to be trusted than those who are shysters. They are also more likely to establish and maintain close personal relationships and sound professional and business relationships. If they are honest, then they do not have to remember which lie they told to whom (in an effort to avoid being discovered). To that extent morality pays off for most people in most circumstances. Even so, it is doubtful that morality always pays off to the agent, at least in any direct, immediate, and obvious way.

Even these benefits do not necessarily fall to those who *are* moral; rather they fall to those who are thought to be moral. Someone who successfully pretends to be moral while surreptitiously being crooked, may, at least for a time, gain these benefits. Conversely, someone who is moral may not gain these benefits if others think she is immoral.

The former option is relatively rare. As Abe Lincoln reportedly said: "You can fool some of the people all of the time, and all of the people some of the time, but you can not fool all of the people all of the time." If a community shares similar moral standards and is free of massive propaganda, then most observant people will know whether others *generally* meet or *generally* ignore moral standards. Generally – but not enough to give someone purely prudential reasons for being moral.

Some religions claim god can fill this gap: that she provides people reason to be moral by rewarding good behavior and punishing bad behavior. Some contend that god rewards believers now, by making them peaceful or happy or rich, and punishes immorality now by making non-believers miserable and alone. Others think religion pays off primarily in the long run, via eternal rewards and punishments.

Although this seems to be a benefit of some religious views, it is a benefit some religions could not have. Many Protestants think salvation is solely through the grace of god: good works are neither necessary nor sufficient for gaining eternal life. A morally wicked person might be saved and gain eternal life, while a morally upright person might be banished to hell. These religions could not provide any direct motive for acting morally.

It is also important to note that many people – including many religious people – will find these "appeals" morally objectionable. They think it is inappropriate – indeed irreligious – for people to be motivated merely by promise of reward and threat of punishment. That is old-fashioned selfishness in religious dress. Religion, properly understood, should not encourage selfishness, let alone make it a central motive for religion.

Religion makes believers altruistic

Religion can also indirectly motivate people to be moral. On this view, truly religious people are motivated not by the promise of reward or punishment – either now or in an afterlife – but by their love of god. God loves humans. When believers recognize the depth of her love, they will normally respond by doing as god commands (Quinn 2000: 57–60). Although this idea is plausible, whether it is an entirely plausible explanation of people's motivation to act morally depends, in important measure, on whether there is a god and whether we think god is good. If she is not, then we would have no reason to think that the best way of reciprocating her love is to be moral.

In a later chapter, I explicitly discuss whether people are motivated only by self-interest. In the last major section of this chapter, I will discuss what it means to say that god is good. Before I discuss that issue I must first mention one last way religion likely motivates people to be moral.

Religion provides moral support

Believers may also claim that religion motivates us to be moral by providing a supportive community. Most of us find it difficult to do what we think is right, at least if what we think is right differs from others. Our reticence might reflect uncertainty about our beliefs; perhaps it is just an unwillingness to oppose the majority (Cohen 2001: 147–9). Whatever the explanation, knowing that other people agree with and support our decisions and actions empowers us to do what we think is right (even if it is not), especially in difficult circumstances.

This claim, like several previous ones, explains why and how religion could motivate people to be moral. That is to be expected in a society in which many people believe that religion is a necessary motivation for being moral. However, it is important to note that religion could play these motivational roles even if there were no god, or if there were a god but she was not the author of morality. It is also important to note that this belief has a worrisome corollary. If someone who holds this belief ceases to believe that god exists, then she will lose her motive for being moral. Whether there is a god is not an issue I address in this book. We will, for purposes of discussion, assume that there is. Assuming there is, we must still ask if god is, or could be, the author of morality.

God is Necessary for Morality

The Divine Command Theory

The Divine Command Theory claims that god is the author of morality: that right and wrong are determined by god's commands or intentions. Without a god we might still develop some requirements that faintly resemble morality, that is, requirements derived from judgments of enlightened self-interest. I might be nice to others because I think that by so doing others will be more likely to be nice to me. I might have also noticed that people who generally consider others' interests often have more and better friends, and are more likely to succeed in their businesses and professions. This might stop me from taking advantage of others. However, most people think this is insufficient to justify a robust morality. They think morality usually clashes with our "natural" inclinations. As the Apostle Paul put it,

> For I know that nothing good lodges in me – in my unspiritual nature, I mean – for though the will to do good is there, the deed is not. The good which I want to do, I fail to do; but what I do is the wrong . . . I perceive that there is in my bodily members a different law . . . the law of sin (Rom. 7:18–20 New English Bible).

For some Christians this gap between self-interest and morality is immense. "Loving everyone as we love ourselves is, I think, obligatory in Christian ethics, and it has that status, as the Gospels showed us, because of god" (Quinn 2000). The idea that we morally ought to love everyone makes no sense, Quinn claims, unless there is some divine lawgiver who requires us to so love. It is not just that people who are not religious will lack the motivation to do what is moral, which is true enough. Without a divine lawgiver we could not make sense of our having such stringent obligations.

There are two distinct issues here. The broader one concerns just how demanding morality is. I address that issue in Chapter 17. The second, uniquely religious issue, I address here. The Divine Command Theorist claims that a god is necessary for morality: without god people could not be moral since, without god, morality (and not just enlightened self-interest) could not exist. Just as human laws require a lawgiver, so do moral laws.

Author or authority?

On the standard interpretation of this view, god is the *author* of morality in the same sense that John Steinbeck is the author of *Of Mice and Men*. God's commands fix what is right and wrong. In saying that Steinbeck was the author of *Of Mice and Men* we imply that he could have chosen not to write that novel or that he could have written the novel differently. He could have changed the names of a central character ("Laurence" rather than "Lennie"), introduced a new character (Lennie's twin brother), changed the traits of a central character (so that Lennie is mean-spirited and vicious), or changed a central character's behavior (Lennie rapes and tortures Curley's wife). Steinbeck was not forced to write the novel precisely as he did. He could have written anything he wanted, or he could have written nothing at all. If he had written a different novel, we might have loved it. We might have hated it: we might have thought the plot was thin, the characters unbelievable, and the prose stiff. However, it would make no sense to say that it was the *wrong* novel, at least not in the sense that we would say that "2 + 2 = 5" is wrong. Similarly, if god were the *author* of morality, she could have written a different morality, passed down different rules. We might not have liked the rules. However, we could not meaningfully say that the rules are wrong since god, on this view, determines what is moral.

There is an alternative account of the relationship between god and good – what I will call the *authority* view. On this view god is not the author of morality. Morality is independent of god. However, god – being good – always correctly tells us what morality requires. This may sound like verbal sleight of hand. It is not. Let me use an analogy to explain. Consider the following two sentences:

(1) "Hugh says X is a triangle, because it is."
(2) "X is a triangle because Hugh says it is."

Although these sentences contain the same words, they mean very different things. The *authority* view implies there is a standard of a triangle that is independent of me. Therefore, if (1) is true, it is true because I correctly state that X meets that standard (that X really is a triangle). In contrast, (2) encapsulates the *authorship* view which holds that my proclaiming "X is a triangle" *makes* X a triangle. My proclamation sets the standard. These views are profoundly different.

If there is an independent standard, we know what it would mean for me to make an error, *even if I never erred*. Were I to say (even if I never said), "This is a square," while pointing to a triangle, then, on the authority view, I would be mistaken. In contrast, on the authority view, it is not merely that I am never mistaken, but that we cannot understand what it would mean to say that I am mistaken. Since I determine what a triangle is, my proclamation makes it a triangle.

This has one further significant implication: it would be meaningless to say that I am good at recognizing triangles. It makes sense to say I am good at a task only if we could understand what it would mean for me to do it badly or in a mediocre way. Let me explain. Suppose I developed a game called "Chesskers." Chesskers uses the same board and pieces as chess but has only one rule: "Whatever move Hugh makes wins." Whereas the claim that I am a good chess player would be sensible (even if false), the claim that I am a good chesskers player would be nonsense. Although I always win (in a peculiar sense) that says nothing about me, my skills, or my character. Nothing.

In sum, the *authority* and *authorship* views differ substantially. If the *authority* view were true, then (a) we could understand what it would mean to say that god made a mistake, *even if we thought she would never do so*, and, therefore, (b) we could sensibly say that god is good. After all, god not only always recognizes what is right, she correctly communicates those expectations to humans. In contrast, if the *authorship* view were true, (a) the idea that god could be mistaken would be senseless since anything god says is right *is* right; therefore, (b) it would be nonsense to say that god is good. This last consequence would be most unwelcome by many believers (especially Christians), who claim that one reason for believing in *their* god is that she is good.

Possible responses

There are three responses the advocate of the *authorship* view might make. First, she might claim that although god could have chosen different standards, she gave us the standard we have and promised us that it would not change. However, this response is untenable since on this view "being true to one's promises" is moral only inasmuch and as long as god says it is. Therefore, there could be nothing wrong if god began promulgating different commands. The new commands – e.g., that we hate our neighbors and torture little children for fun – would then be right. Such a view is untenable.

The second (and related response) is that god sets standards for any world she creates and then, having set the standard, cannot change it. That, defenders say, is precisely what we should expect on the authorship view. Although Steinbeck could have written many different novels, having written them, he could not unwrite them – that would be logically impossible (like god's making a rock bigger than she can lift).

There is something right about this response. Nonetheless, an omnipotent creature could still *effectively* unwrite a story by, for instance, making everyone forget the original story. Finally, even if she could not unwrite her previous standards of morality, she should issue new standards, and these new standards, being her commands, would now fix right and wrong. The old standards would be akin to a previous novel. "Yes," someone might say, "god once said that murder is wrong, but now she says it a virtue." If this seems odd, it is because it is. We are not quite sure what to make of the claim that murder might be good and malevolence a virtue.

Third, a defender of Divine Command Ethics might respond that I have ignored the fact that god is "essentially just" (Quinn 2000: 70). This claim is not merely a claim that god never acts immorally nor commands us to be immoral. After all, believers who think right is independent of god believe *that*. To claim that god is essentially good is to claim that it is *impossible* for her to command what is immoral.

I fail to see how this avoids the previous problems, and it also creates new ones. If it were *impossible* for god to do anything but what is right, it would have to be for either of two reasons. One, a good god would not give us incorrect commands. However, that is equivalent to the authority view I discussed earlier. God's disposition is to command only what is right. This view is quite sensible, but sensible precisely because god is not morality's author. Two, god is the author of morality – so that her saying it is right makes it right. If so, this is just the authorship view in different guise. On this view it doesn't make sense to say god is good.

We can now see two further worries with the authorship view. The first is peculiar to Christianity. If god were the author of morality, then the story of Jesus' temptation is a ruse. Since on this view Jesus is God, whatever Jesus did would be right. However, being tempted assumes that at least some of his choices would have been wrong. Yet, by definition, any of his choices would have been right. The idea that Jesus could be really tempted makes sense only on the authority view.

Second, if whatever god says is good is good, what makes it so? It cannot be god's omniscience. Since there is no good independent of god, there is nothing for god to know. And we cannot say that the goodness comes from his goodness. That is circular; besides, as I have argued, to say that god is good requires that we can at least understand what it would mean to say that god is not good. Therefore rightness must derive straightforwardly from god's power. How could this be? My saying something is good does not make it so. Why would god's saying it be any different? The only answer I can imagine is that it is because god is omnipotent. That, though, assumes, to use common parlance, that might makes right. Surely that is false. The school bully who steals lunches from his classmates – and gets away with it – does not thereby define morality. Had Hitler won World War II, he could have doubtless have had enormous power (as if he did not already). But no matter how much power he had, that would not make his actions define the moral. How could omnipotence make power a more plausible determinant of good? If being the toughest kid on the block or the toughest dictator in the world does not make one's actions thereby moral, how would being the most powerful creature in the universe do so? Of course selfish people, knowing that there were such a creature, would likely do what she says. However, that stance, no matter how prudent, does not show that god is good; indeed, it is at odds with it.

The plausibility of the authority view

All this suggests that if most believers understood the *authority* view, they would find it preferable to the *authorship* view. Although god is not the author of morality, she could be good since she always does – and commands – what is right. She would also be a helpful (and perhaps the best) source of our knowledge about what is moral. Finally, she might also motivate many of us to be moral. Many believers – even those who thought they endorsed the *authorship* view – will see these as advantages of the *authority* view, especially since this view is compatible with the historical, sociological, and psychological claims with which we began the chapter. Many people's moral insights were initially developed and later refined by their religious beliefs, their reading of sacred texts, and the support of other like-minded people.

Of course, the authority view does not avoid the need to rationally justify our beliefs. It just changes it in either of two ways. One, a believer might think that the principal source of information about morality comes from divine commands as recorded in scripture and revealed directly by god. Or, she might think that god provides a way for all people – believers and non-believers alike – to see the moral truth, for instance, via conscience or reason (although believers have an advantage since they have additional religious ways of acquiring moral truths). Both options give reason a critical role in determining what we morally ought to do. The first option requires that we must know which god to heed, which scripture to read, how that scripture is to be interpreted, and which purported revelations to believe. After all, there are many major world religions, each of which claims, to various degrees, to be true. Each religion has its own scripture that is presumably authoritative. Each sect of each religion has its own preferred interpretations of that scripture. How can we know which is the right god, the right religion, the right scripture, and the right interpretation? For similar reasons we would also need to use reason to determine the moral truths even on the authorship view. We cannot just accept the purported testimony of the scriptures since there are competing scriptures each claiming to be authoritative.

The second option holds that a good god would make the demands of morality accessible to all people, even those who are not believers (as well as those who are not "the right" believers). A good god would not deceive her people; she would make moral expectations readily accessible. Christianity seems to depend on just such a prereligious understanding of morality. It assumes we know what is good. That is how we decide that the Christian god is a good god.

This discussion still leaves open two significant theoretical issues we will see again. First, what does and can motivate people to be moral? It is not enough that people know what is good; they must also act in ways to achieve the good. And the need to account for moral motivation is something any adequate theory must explain. Second, just how much can morality demand? Can morality require us to make significant personal sacrifices? We will address the first issue in Chapter 17, and the second in Chapter 18.

In the next chapter we discuss one issue where religious beliefs have played an especially pivotal role.

REFERENCES

Adams, R. M. (1973) "A Modified Divine Command Theory of Ethical Wrongness." In G. Outka and J. P. Reeder, Jr. (eds.), *Religion and Morality*. Garden City, NY: Anchor, 318–47.

Adams, R. M. (1996) "The Concept of a Divine Command." In D. Z. Phillips (ed.), *Religion and Morality*. London: Macmillan, 59–80.

Arendt, H. (1994/1963) *Eichmann in Jerusalem: A Report on the Banality of Evil*. New York: Penguin Books.

Cohen, S. (2001) *States of Denial: Knowing about Atrocities and Suffering*. Cambridge: Polity Press.

Lewis, C. S. (2001/1952) *Mere Christianity*. San Francisco: Harper.

Martin, D. B. (1995) *The Corinthian Body*. New Haven, CT: Yale University Press.

Masson, J. M. (1997) *The Wild Child: The Unsolved Mystery of Kaspar Hauser*. New York: Touchstone.

Mill, J. S. (1985/1885) *On Liberty*. Indianapolis, IN: Hackett.

Quine, W. V. and Ullian, J. S. (1978) *The Web of Belief*, 2nd edn. New York: Random House.

Quinn, P. L. (1978) *Divine Commands and Moral Requirements*. Oxford: Clarendon Press.

Quinn, P. L. (1990) "The Recent Revival of Divine Command Ethics," *Philosophy and Phenomenological Research* 50: 345–65.

Quinn, P. L. (2000) "Divine Command Theory." In H. LaFollette (ed.), *The Blackwell Guide to Ethical Theory*. Oxford: Blackwell Publishers, 53–73.

Sabini, J. and Silver, M. (1982) *Moralities of Everyday Life*. New York: Oxford University Press.

Staub, E. (1989) *The Roots of Evil: The Origins of Genocide and Other Group Violence*. Cambridge: Cambridge University Press.

EIGHT

Death, Dying, and Physician-assisted Suicide

In 1997 the state of Oregon passed a law making it legal for a terminally ill patient to have her doctor's assistance in ending her life. Attempts to pass similar laws in several other American states (e.g., California, Maine, and Michigan) have failed, but by only small margins. It is likely such laws will pass elsewhere soon. Polls show a significant number of Americans support physician-assisted suicide (hereafter, PAS). Some are working to reverse this trend. In 2004, the US Attorney General filed suit in federal court seeking to invalidate the Oregon law (*State of Oregon v. John Ashcroft*). The following year, Congress and the White House tried to override the decision of Florida courts to let Terri Schiavo die.

Advocates on both sides of this issue think the debate is clear-cut. Defenders think physician-assisted suicide is obviously morally acceptable and should be legally permissible: that people who are dying have the moral autonomy, and should have the legal right, to quickly end their own lives, and, if they wish, to have the assistance of a physician in doing so. Opponents think such practices obviously ought to be legally prohibited; most also think they are immoral. Both sides cannot be right. To become clearer on the issues, we must clear the conceptual undergrowth. Then we will address three central questions.

1. Are there reasons for thinking it is (almost?) always wrong for a person to voluntarily end her own life, with or without the assistance of others?
2. Do dying adults have a moral right to end their own lives, at least in some circumstances?
3. Are there sufficient dangers of permitting physician-assisted suicide so that we should legally forbid the practice, even if it is sometimes morally justified?

Although these questions capture the debate as it now stands, it was not always so. Understanding the historical context of the issue can inform the current debate.

The Historical Context

When I began teaching this issue 30 years ago, few students openly endorsed physician-assisted suicide. Most held one of two positions. A significant number claimed or implied that people have a positive obligation to stay alive, to use every available means to sustain their lives. They thought that refusing any medical treatment, when doing so would speed death, is categorically wrong, just as wrong as suicide. Over the years the number of students who voiced that view steadily declined, so that now few advocate it. That does not mean that the view has disappeared. During the recent controversy over Terri Schiavo, most of those condemning the courts were deeply committed to that – or some closely related – position. That strong position is usually grounded in the belief, discussed later in this chapter, that life is sacred.

The second common position was that although seriously ill people could legitimately refuse medical treatment, once they started a treatment they could not legitimately stop it (by "pulling the plug"). Today most people would find this view quite odd. However, it played a critical role in the pivotal case of Karen Anne Quinlan. Doctors would not permit Ms. Quinlan's parents to remove her from a ventilator, even though everyone agreed she was in a persistent vegetative state. The parents had to sue before they could remove her (in re Quinlan, 70 N.J. 10, 355 A. 2d 647). After that decision, I didn't hear many people advocating that position. Perhaps one important reason is that it forced people to make treatment decisions before they had all the evidence. Many people would try treatments if they knew they could stop them if they wished, but would be reluctant to try them if they knew they could not discontinue treatment they no longer desired.

A clear majority of Americans now reject both these positions (Harris Poll 2005). That indicates just how dramatically the debate has changed. One way of seeing this change is to track the legal evolution of the living will. In the 1960s the Euthanasia Society of America proposed that states permit citizens to have living wills, specifying their preferences for end-of-life decisions. California became the first state to permit their use in 1976. Within 16 years every state legally recognized them. It is now standard practice for hospitals to ask – even require – all patients to have a "living will" and "durable power of attorney" on file. Even the American Medical Association officially recognizes the patient's right to refuse or cease treatment at any time, for any reason (2002).

Despite these changes, all states continued to prohibit assisted suicide. Some individuals have ignored the law and helped loved ones end their own lives (Rollin 1985). Some who did were prosecuted by the state. In 1985, a 76-year-old Florida man, Roswell Gilbert, was convicted for killing his ailing wife who begged him to kill her. By the time he had served five years of his sentence, public support for PAS had dramatically increased. The governor granted him clemency. Shortly thereafter Oregon passed its "Death with Dignity" act that permits PAS. Although the idea that dying people should be able to actively end their own lives is contentious, a sizeable number of Americans think it should be legalized. So that is where we will focus our debate. I will begin somewhat circuitously by discussing death. Then I return to look at the arguments for and against PAS.

Death

Westerners are not good at dealing with death. We generally do not think – let alone think carefully and honestly – about death and about the choices we must make when we, or those we love, face death. Relatively few people have talked about death with their spouses, children, or parents, although in the aftermath of the Schiavo affair that has changed somewhat. When we do mention death, we often employ euphemisms to soften or mask death's reality. We talk about "losing" someone or about their "passing away." Our reluctance to squarely face, think about, candidly discuss, or prepare for death does not make it disappear. Although we might escape taxes, we will not escape our own deaths or the deaths of those we love.

How death affects value

Death profoundly shapes our lives and our values. Understanding why and how helps isolate both misgivings about and reasons for physician-assisted suicide (PAS).

Consider how different our lives and our values would be if we were immortal. Much (all?) that we now do would be unnecessary; much (all?) that we now value would be less (or in-) valuable. A few differences seem beneficial: we would no longer need to worry (as much) about what we eat, whether we exercise, how fast or carelessly we drive, etc. Most differences seem detrimental: we could never retire since no one or no pension plan could support us forever. A central rationale for having families would disappear since we could no longer have children after the society attained a manageable population. We could go on. Mortality profoundly shapes our lives and our values.

After all, we generally value things to the degree that they are vulnerable: to the degree that they are easily lost and costly (or impossible) to replace. That does not mean that we value everything that is vulnerable. But we do not value things that are (or we think are) invulnerable. Compare the prospects of losing the following objects: (1) your deceased father's pocket watch and the only picture of your entire family; (2) your uninsured car or house; (3) a box of matches and two safety pins. You would react differently to the loss, or threatened loss, of each, and the differences in reactions are explained by the objects' relative vulnerability. You would be devastated by the loss of the watch or the picture since, although their monetary value is slight, they cannot be replaced. You would be upset by the loss of your car or house. Although you could, in principle, replace them, the cost of doing so would be significant in the first case and likely prohibitive in the second. You will be indifferent to the loss of matches and safety pins since these things, although easily lost, are also easily replaced.

That largely explains why the loss or threatened loss of our lives and the lives of those we love is ordinarily so devastating. Lives are irreplaceable. It is not just that we forever lose the person we love, we usually feel some guilt: we remember something hateful we said to or about the deceased, we recall the times we were inattentive to them. We wish we could retract our words and undo the pain we caused them. Somehow we assumed we would always have another opportunity to make up for our indifference, callousness, or selfishness. Sometimes we do; sometimes we don't. The problem is: we don't know in advance. Something similar happens if we face our own mortality. People who learn they are about to die may radically alter their behavior. They change their priorities to reflect what they now take to be important, to reflect their understanding of what is most vulnerable.

In short, acknowledging our and our loved ones' vulnerability can (and often does) make us reassess our lives, rethink our values. That is usually so even for those who believe in an afterlife. Even if people think they will meet their spouses, parents, children, and friends after they die (at least those in the same "place" as they are), they will not meet them again *here*. That is still an irreplaceable loss. For those who live much longer than those they love, the loss can be devastating. Were my wife to die 30 years before I do, it would not be much (if any) consolation to learn I would see her 30 years hence. I would have still irretrievably lost those 30 years with her.

Life is deathlike

In revealing our vulnerability, death makes us more aware of what is valuable in life. Coming to see that everyday life is also vulnerable will further enhance our understanding of what is valuable in life. Our actions always "die" in one significant sense: we cannot redo them (although the hope that we could has inspired its fair share of science fiction). In acting we close off options and make some futures less likely. If I eat that hot fudge sundae, I will not lose the weight I wanted, or else I must run an extra two miles to burn off the excess calories. If I cheat on an exam, the exam is no longer really *mine*. If I lie to a good friend, I can never again say or think that I have always been honest with her.

To better grasp why understanding this is so important, let's duplicate the thought experiment we used earlier. What would happen if our actions (and failures to act) were "immortal" – if they did not foreclose any options or change any probabilities for the future? We could always and painlessly undo every mistake we make. If we fail to do our job today, we can always do it tomorrow. If our relationships founder, we can always rebuild them without any untoward effects. Any opportunity we miss will present itself again.

This could happen only if our actions had no consequences. At first that would seem wonderful: we could no longer make mistakes in any interesting sense. But neither could we succeed. Yet we can. Reading, practicing the piano, assisting a stranger in need, and loving our spouses and children have consequences: they increase our knowledge, develop and refine our skills, help strangers, enhance our relationships, and encourage our children to develop strong character. Our actions shape the world in which we live and the people we, and those around us, will become.

Yet we seem to think we are impotent. We are not. If I deceive a good friend, I may destroy our relationship. If I miss a class assignment, I may be unable to make it up. If I fail to sustain a friendship, it will likely die. Even if I can help the person later, even if I can ask my friend to forgive me for lying, even if I can make up the lost assignment, and even if I can partially resurrect the friendship, I cannot do any of these without some cost to me, to my relationships, and to my future. These facts about the nature of value help us better understand what it means to have a good or a bad death. They also help us decide whether or when PAS might be appropriate. But they do not exhaust what we might mean by a "good" or a "bad" death. I must say more.

A good death

Given that we all will die, we think there are better and worse ways and times of doing so. Some deaths are especially horrible – either in their manner or timing – while others are relatively good; most people will vastly prefer them to others. We distinguish a good from a bad death along five dimensions: (1) its *manner* (is it especially painful or debilitating?); (2) its *circumstances* (what promoted it?); (3) its *environment* (e.g., is person near those she loves?); (4) the *age* of the dying person; and (5) the dying person's (and others') *perspective* on her life. Let me say a bit about each.

Manner. Many people are as worried about the nature of the illness, condition, or situation that leads to death as they are about the death itself. They do not want to suffer (or have their loved ones suffer), especially for a long time. Nor do they want to die having lost their mental faculties e.g., from Alzheimer's or in a persistent vegetative state. Recent polls suggest this may be most people's biggest fear.

Circumstances. We are especially upset by deaths caused by other humans – murders or deaths caused by others' negligence. Many people are also especially bothered by deaths resulting from the person's own actions, either immediate (suicide) or long term (lung cancer as a result of smoking). When the circumstances are especially tragic, most people will have special difficulty facing and accepting the person's death.

Environment. Most people have strong desires about who or what is nearby when they die. Many people want to die at home, with their family near them, both for comfort and to have an opportunity to say their last good-byes. Less frequently, some people prefer to die alone and in a strange environment.

Age. Most people wish to die (and to have their loved ones die) old, having lived a long life. Conversely, we think the death of a young person is especially tragic.

Perspective. If a person has had a long, productive, and satisfying life, she is less likely to fear death, and others are more likely to think the death is less tragic. However, if she has significant regrets, or important unfinished plans (she didn't put away enough money for her children's education), then she, along with her friends and family, are more likely to find the death especially sad. This is connected with the previous element. After all, most people are afraid of dying young in part because, at an early age, they think they have not lived a full and productive life, and so have more regrets about things they did not do, places they did not see.

Not everyone will have precisely the same understanding of, or give the same weight to, each element. Still, using these we can broadly specify what would constitute a "good death": It would be for someone to die relatively painlessly, not as the result of human action, with their friends around, at a ripe old age, having lived a full and satisfying life. We can likewise specify what would constitute a terrible death: one that is exceedingly painful or deteriorating, caused by human agency, in a wholly strange environment, at a young age, and with significant regrets about her life.

Of course these elements rarely occur in such neat clusters. Some elements of a good death are often mixed with elements of a bad one. They may even be in tension. In making heroic efforts to keep a young person alive, we may cause her considerable pain. If that pain is necessary to her continued and long-term survival, it is worth it. However, if she dies anyway, only now having suffered intensely, then that seems to make her death even worse.

As we shall see, understanding what people consider a good death will play an important role in arguments for and against PAS. Now we turn to examine the most common arguments against PAS.

Reasons for Thinking Euthanasia is Wrong

The value of life

We generally assume people will not intentionally destroy things that they think are valuable. Life is valuable and PAS destroys life. Therefore, PAS is incompatible with the value of life.

This argument looks plausible. To successfully rebut it defenders must explain why PAS does not diminish value. They have an answer. They claim PAS respects the value of people's lives, while forbidding PAS diminishes it. Forcing someone to live in a seriously diminished or continuously painful condition denies her value. It makes her a mere means to other people's beliefs. Conversely, letting her choose the time and place to die affirms the value of her life as a whole. Most opposed to PAS disagree. They think that allowing someone to end her own life, no matter why, denies her life's value. How do we adjudicate between these diametrically opposed claims? We must first understand what each side means by "the value of life." This will help not only evaluate this specific argument, it will give us a better sense of what is really at stake in the debate over PAS.

Proponents of PAS describe life's value in fairly ordinary ways. They say we should consult informed people and see which abilities, experiences, relationships, and endeavors they value (Mill 1998/1863: 81–2). What do they value? They value freedom, love, knowledge, happiness, friendship, family, care, responsibility, self-improvement, character, etc. Nothing fishy or mysterious here.

We can see the simplicity and appeal of this answer if we engage in a bit of science fiction. Suppose we meet Jocyx, an intelligent, happy, sentient Martian who has a family and treats other Martians (and us) well, etc. In short, she has all the features of a good human life. Most people would think that she has a valuable life. That value limits what we can legitimately do to and with her. We shouldn't skin her, lock her up, or confiscate her space ship.

Advocates of PAS claim that once we acknowledge that these characteristics capture life's value, we see that PAS recognizes – not diminishes – the value of human life. In two ways. One, if we think freedom is important, we will want to respect a person's choices whenever possible. If that includes the desire to end one's life, then, barring some special contravening reasons, we should respect her desire. Two, since these features capture life's value, then the absence of some number of them will diminish life's quality. Of special relevance to this debate are those conditions (losing their mental faculties or being in severe pain) that make some people wish to hasten their deaths. To respect the wishes of people who think that the quality of their lives has been seriously diminished does not ignore their value: it respects them.

Opponents of PAS will object. They claim that we ignore or downplay people's value by saying that some people have a diminished quality of life. I don't see why. These are the reasons people give for thinking *their* lives are diminished. And some of these are reasons people give for thinking their lives are no longer worth living. Still, the fear seems to be that saying someone's life is qualitatively inferior is to say that her life has no value, and therefore that we can do with her whatever we want. That is a groundless fear. We can insist that people's lives have equal value, *in the sense that the lives should be given equal moral consideration*, without having to deny the obvious claim that not everyone's life is qualitatively identical. After all, would you rather be happy, fulfilled, and loved, or miserable, hated, and a failure? The only plausible response is: "Is this a trick question?" All of us realize the first life is qualitatively superior to the second. However, nothing untoward comes from this admission unless you assume that we can do whatever we wish to people with lower-quality lives. Why should we assume that?

Consider the following analogy: all students are equal. If we interpret this as saying that all students are equally bright, insightful, hard-working, well-trained, or moti- vated, that each merits the same grade, or that each was an equally good student, the claim is demonstrably false. However, there is a more plausible interpretation of "all students are equal," namely, that the interests of each student – as student – should count the same (Singer 1990/1975: 5). We cannot refuse to teach a student because she is less bright nor abuse a student because she is less insightful. If she con- tinues to be a student she must be treated with the same respect, and given the same consideration, as every other student. We should not, for instance, place extra requirements on a weaker student or hold her to higher grading standards. However, that does not mean that all students should receive the same grades no matter what their performance. Nor must all students be allowed to take all the same courses. We can justifiably exclude a poorly trained freshman from a senior seminar for majors.

In the same way, we can grant the equal value of human life while denying that all lives are qualitatively equal. Having a qualitatively inferior life does not mean that a person should die. It certainly does not mean we should take her life against her will. What it does mean is that if an autonomous person is at the end of her life, is in pain or rapidly deteriorating, and wants to die, then we should respect her wishes.

Opponents to PAS will still disagree. They think human life is uniquely valuable (Cohen 1986; Smith 2003). They think that human life is sacred.

Life is sacred

What do people mean by this claim? Some use this phrase as if it were equivalent to the claim that "life is valuable." Since I discussed that option in an earlier section, I focus here on a uniquely religious interpretation of the phrase. On this view we should not take a life, even when the person is in considerable pain, because doing so is "playing god." "Human life is a gift of the creator," and only god should decide when someone's life ends (Jans 2002: 2). That is what is standardly meant by the claim that life is sacred. That is why these people think PAS is immoral.

There are two issues. One is whether this principle is true. In the previous chapter, I identified some difficulties with a purely religious ethic; I will not raise those issues again here. The second is whether this claim, even if true, shows that PAS is immoral. I don't think it does. This principle is either inconsistent with other principles most religious people embrace or it is consistent but untenable. Let me explain. *Very* few religious people are categorically opposed to the taking of a human life. Virtually all of them support killing in self-defense and in war; many support capital punishment. All think that sacrificing one's life to save others is permissible, e.g., by shielding someone from an oncoming bullet or by jumping on a grenade in wartime. In each case individuals "play god": they decide to end someone else's (or their own) life.

If it is sometimes justifiable to end someone's life, and if in ending a life one always "plays god," then it cannot be categorically wrong to "play god." This undercuts the simple version of the "life is sacred" argument against PAS. If critics of PAS want to continue to use this argument in its current form, they must oppose *all* taking of human life. That, they are unwilling to do. Therefore, they must recast the "life is sacred" argument if they wish to use it at all. They must claim that (a) we do not always "play god" when intentionally ending a life, or that (b) "playing god" is not always wrong. Then they must also show why PAS – but not war, capital punishment, etc. – is an impermissible instance of playing god. It is hard to know how they could do that.

There is one final problem with this argument. Many religious people are prone to say after someone's death that "that was god's plan." What do they mean? If they mean that all deaths occur according to god's plan, then it is *impossible* to play god: everyone's life ends exactly when it should. I assume that is not what these critics of PAS mean. They think that although people can play god, they shouldn't. This has a worrisome implication. They must assume that it is possible "to take a human life (our own or someone else's) before God wants it ended, but . . . ⟨that it is not possible to⟩ preserve it after God wants it ended" (Hardwig 2001/1997: 50). However, that possibility makes no sense. If we can end a life before god wants (e.g., through suicide, physician-assisted suicide, or murder), then we can also prolong it longer than god wants. Keeping someone alive by artificial means would sometimes be a instance of the latter. That is why, Hardwig claims, the religious person cannot categorically oppose physician-assisted suicide. She must always ask whether, by continuing to keep someone alive, she is prolonging the person's life longer than god wants. And, indeed, many religious people would agree. Perhaps it is just this sort of reasoning that lead the Rev. Charles Parker to form the Euthanasia Society of America in 1938.

In sum, the "life is sacred" objection is insufficient to show that PAS is always wrong. At most it shows that we should be careful before ending a life. And so we should. There are dangers in having, encouraging, or legally permitting PAS, dangers we will address later. First we will examine the most common reasons for PAS.

Arguments for Physician-assisted Suicide

The most prominent argument for PAS is an argument from autonomy. On this view people have the moral right, and should have the legal right, to end their own lives. In its unqualified form it would justify a blanket right to assisted suicide. However, most defenders of PAS won't support that. Instead they will combine the autonomy argument with a "quality of life" argument, so that people have a right to assistance to end their lives only if they are autonomous *and* they are suffering from a debilitating or painful disease for which there is no remedy. These people want both elements since they think PAS is immoral if only one is present. We could imagine someone whose life is qualitatively diminished but does not want to die. We could also imagine someone who wanted to die although they have what appears to be a qualitatively superior life (they have faced only minor setbacks to their life plans). In both cases physicians should not help these people end their lives.

To understand the autonomy argument, we must examine both elements. We look at the second element first.

Quality of life

The earlier discussion helps us state more clearly what it means to say that someone has a quality of life that would warrant her wanting to hasten her own death. An example will illustrate. Josephine had lived a full, happy, and satisfying life. Now she is 85 years old, has terminal cancer, is in considerable pain, has lost most of her family, and has no remaining significant goals. Her life has less quality now than when she was 45, healthy, active, and had a close family life. This affects how she and others think about her death. Those who still care for her will remember her life fondly and think that she has now been released from pain. Although the pain of her last days was regrettable, the other elements of her death were as positive as anyone might reasonably hope. Of course her death would have also been worse had she died 40 years earlier. It would also be worse if she had to live debilitated and in pain for another three years. The latter consideration partly motivates the use of PAS.

Decades ago I heard a news story about a truck driver who was trapped in his burning cab. He could not be rescued and was in excruciating pain. He begged people near the truck to shoot him, to put him out of his misery. No one did. The trucker lived too long, even if it was only a few minutes too long. Less dramatically, but no less real, are the thousands who, like the trucker, are miserable and want to die more quickly. Unlike the truck driver, these people will live weeks, months, or even years too long.

Our great-great-grandparents regularly faced the first problem – dying too early. But they didn't worry about dying too late; there was little people could do to postpone death. However, mid-century, the tandem of public health measures and medical advancement began to lengthen human life. Overall these changes were enormously beneficial. But they have a downside. The same factors can diminish, as well as enhance, the quality of the person's last months and years. Many people die in a hospital, hooked up to assorted machines, often without their loved ones nearby. Because of our technological gadgets they are also more likely to live too long. So these medical advances give us choices we didn't have before. We must decide when, how, and how long to sustain life, or whether to end it – or at least not to make extraordinary efforts to sustain it.

Here, as elsewhere, having choices is good, but not unqualifiedly so. If I am powerless, then I am not to blame for what happens. Conversely, if I have power, I am at least partly responsible for the outcome of my actions (Bergmann 1977). If the stakes are high, the cost of error is high. And the stakes here are very high. We should be careful not to terminate someone's (including our own) life prematurely. We should also be concerned that we also don't prolong it inappropriately.

Autonomy

Most people in Western societies highly value freedom. Freedom promotes important social goods – truth, progress, creativity, democracy – and it protects, promotes, and permits the ability to make wise choices (Mill 1985/1885): it promotes autonomy. "Autonomy," as we shall see later, has four distinct meanings. Here we focus on two: normative and descriptive autonomy. People are "normatively autonomous" if they have the legal right to control their lives. If they actually control their lives, they are said to be descriptively autonomous (Haworth 1986: 1).

These are importantly different. Some people may have the authority to control their own lives but rarely exercise it. Others may control their own lives despite significant social and legal barriers to doing so. Although distinct, these notions are deeply related. We want normative autonomy precisely because it makes descriptive autonomy more achievable. We especially want to be able to do as we want when the decision is important. Deciding when, where, and how to die is clearly important. That is why defenders of PAS think we should have the legal right to do so.

Objectors disagree. They claim the autonomy argument is vulnerable to three criticisms. One, if someone is autonomous, then her life is still worth living; the quality of her life is not diminished. Two, if a dying person is no longer autonomous, then we cannot respect her autonomy, including her desire to die. Moreover, since we know that pain clouds people's judgment, we have reason to doubt that she knows or can clearly articulate what she wants. Three, the way to avoid problems one and two is by accepting people's previous wishes, as expressed in their living wills and durable powers of attorney. However, people sometimes change their minds. We should not make people die because of earlier decisions.

All these worries are important. I cannot do full justice to any of them here. Still, I can quickly summarize plausible responses by defenders of PAS. One, just because someone is autonomous does not mean that she has a high quality life. Autonomy is an element of a human life worth living; it does not guarantee such a life. An autonomous person can realize that what once gave her life meaning is gone.

Two, a person may still be autonomous even though debilitated and in pain. Of course, we should be suspicious of someone who, when suffering, begged to be put out of her misery even though she had never expressed such a wish before. Nonetheless, even then we would not automatically dismiss her claims. After all, it is the pain – and her belief that it will be unrelenting – that undergirds her judgment that the quality of her life has been compromised. If she continues to express such a wish over time, particularly if she can give a cogent account of why she wants to die, then we should conclude that she is autonomous. The decision is obviously much easier if she expresses a view that, although prompted by present pain, is consonant with her previously expressed wishes over the past 20 years.

This suggests that we should not have excessively demanding criteria for "descriptive autonomy." If the criteria are too demanding (or perhaps even middling), then all of us are sometimes (and perhaps often) not descriptively autonomous. Yet most of us think we should have the right to make purely personal choices. We must therefore be careful not to adopt criteria of descriptive autonomy that we are unwilling to live with in other contexts. If we do, then many of us will not have the legal right to make basic decisions about our lives.

It we adopt weaker and more defensible criteria, then many dying people will be sufficiently autonomous to decide their own fate. We can, of course, ask them questions; we can talk to their friends and family to better discern their wishes. We should be sensitive to ways that pain and depression can skew people's better judgment. In making decisions about life and death, we should be cautious.

Three, the critic is correct that people sometimes change their minds: they state preferences they latter disavow. If we have reason to think that is true for a patient, we should not force her to die because of a previous declaration she now rejects. However, the purpose of the living will is not to commit someone to an action she later disavows. It is to make her wishes clear and binding on others; and it is to give guidance to medical personnel when she cannot express her current wishes.

So what do we do if a patient is unconscious or in some other way non-autonomous? If we have evidence that she no longer agrees with her previous declarations, and we think she will soon regain her autonomy, then we should wait. However, if medical opinion agrees that she will continue to be non-autonomous, then, unless something has transpired to indicate that she has changed her mind (while still autonomous), we should honor her expressed wishes. After all, the living will is (by hypothesis) the only statement of her desires that we have. And these are precisely the conditions she wanted covered when she wrote it.

Objectors will not find this argument convincing. Some will claim that although it is morally permissible for a patient to refuse treatment – in so doing they are just letting the disease take its normal course – it is not morally appropriate for them to be killed. And that is what PAS does. In short, they rely on the doing/allowing distinction, which we have seen before, and will discuss more fully in Chapter 17.

Defenders of PAS might make two quick responses. One, no one buys this distinction when deciding the fate of non-human animals. We think it is not just permissible to euthanize an animal in pain; we think it would be grossly inhumane to allow an animal to die slowly and painfully, to let nature take its course. Therefore, this distinction could undergird a successful argument against PAS only if it applies merely to humans. That would be very odd. Most people believe we should treat humans *better* than we treat non-human animals. Yet here, it seems, we are morally permitted to treat dying animals, but not dying humans, humanely.

Two, even if the doing/allowing distinction were serviceable in some cases, it is inappropriate here given doctors' special obligation to care for their patients. As Beauchamp puts it:

> In cases in which patients make reasonable requests for assistance in dying, it is a misconception to suppose that doctors can escape responsibility for their decisions if they refrain from helping their patients die. No physician can say "I am not responsible for outcomes when I choose not to act on a patient's request." There has long been a vague sense in the physician and legal community that if only the doctor lets nature take its course, then one is not responsible for the outcome of death. But a physician is always responsible for any decision taken and the consequent action or inaction. The physician who complies with a patient's request is therefore responsible in exactly the way physicians who refuse to comply with the request are responsible (2002/1997: 43).

Worries about Legalizing Physician-assisted Suicide

Some people opposed to PAS acknowledge that there are reasons why a terminally ill person in serious pain should be able, in consultation with her doctor, to end her own life. But that, they insist, is not the only issue. We must also ask whether legalizing PAS will have sufficiently long-term negative consequences that we should not make this a legally permissible option. Tom Beauchamp clearly expresses both concerns:

> The core of the argument in favor of the moral justifiability of acts of physician-assisted suicide and voluntary active euthanasia is that relief from suffering and a voluntary request justify our doing what we otherwise would not do: implement a plan to end a human life. This action has its strongest defense when: (1) a condition is extremely burdensome and the burden outweighs any benefits, (2) pain management cannot be

made adequate, (3) only a physician is capable of bringing relief, and (4) the patient makes an informed request (Beauchamp 2002/1997: 45).

But that is not the only issue, Beauchamp claims:

> Although particular acts of assistance in dying might be morally justified on some occasions, the social consequences of sanctioning practices of killing would involve serious risks of abuse and misuse and, on balance, would cause more harm than benefit to society . . . The argument is not that these negative consequences will occur immediately after legalization, but that they will grow incrementally over time. Society might start with innocent beginnings by developing policies that carefully restrict the number of patients who qualify for assistance in suicide or euthanasia. Whatever restrictions are initially built into our policies will be revised and expanded over time, with ever-increasing possibilities in the system for unjustified killing. Unscrupulous persons will learn how to abuse the system . . . (2002/1997: 46).

This fear is far from crazy. Even if it is insufficient to make us oppose PAS, it gives us compelling reason to be careful in designing and executing this policy. A full discussion of how to evaluate such dangers awaits a more detailed discussion of the slippery slope argument in the next chapter. Here I will explain the basis for this argument and briefly suggest how defenders of PAS might respond.

Suppose Papa is 85 years old, has terminal cancer, is unable to live on his own, and neither he nor his children can pay for nursing care. He expresses a clear wish to continue to live, whatever the cost. His daughter quits work and becomes his full-time nursemaid (Brody 1990). Papa eventually realizes how much he is hurting his daughter and the rest of his family. He now says that he wishes to die. Likely he says this – so the argument goes – because he feels pressured to end his life. It is not what he really wants to do.

Is this possible? Sure. Is this a reason to categorically forbid the terminally ill from ending their own lives? I do not see how. It is obvious that if we establish PAS, some people will be hurt by it. But that is true of all institutions. The question is, how likely will this be? For we also know that disallowing PAS will force some number of patients to live longer than they want. That is also bad. From my experience it is also likely.

Second, this scenario assumes that Papa has simply bowed to family pressure. It seems more likely that as part of a loving family he has just realized how burdensome he has become. He does not want to be a burden. Given his options, he prefers to die (Hardwig 1997, 2001/1997). On the other hand, if his is not a loving family, then I doubt that they could pressure Papa to do what he does not want to do.

Third, perhaps Papa is one of those people who would genuinely feel put upon. He wishes he could continue to live without being a burden to those he loves. However, he lives in the United States, is not wealthy, and relies on Medicare. For him, his only options are to die earlier than he might like or to psychologically and physically cripple his family. Given that choice, he thinks dying is preferable. He may not like the choices. We may not either. If so, we can try to change the health system so he does not have to choose between dying early and being a financial and personal burden to those he loves. But in the meantime, he must choose within the available options.

Perhaps the worry, though, is slightly different. Critics may claim that the practice of physician-assisted suicide will so change our thinking about death that we will come to expect people to die whenever their continued living becomes even a slight burden on the family. To assess this line of argument fully, we will need to look more carefully at slippery slope arguments, which we will do in the next chapter. Then, in the following chapter, we return to further examine the notion of autonomy, initially in the rearing of children and, later, in evaluating paternalistic laws, most especially, laws against the use of certain drugs.

REFERENCES

American Medical Association (2002) "Elements of Quality Care for Patients in the Last Phase of Life." (Online) Available at: http://www.ama-assn.org/ama/pub/printcat/7567.html. (Accessed June 20, 2002.)

Beauchamp, T. L. (2002/1997) "Justifying Physician-assisted Deaths." In H. LaFollette (ed.), *Ethics in Practice: An Anthology*, 2nd edn. Oxford: Blackwell Publishers, 40–7.

Bergmann, F. (1977) *On Being Free*. Notre Dame: University of Notre Dame Press.

Brody, E. M. (1990) *Women in the Middle: Their Parent-Care Years*. New York: Springer.

Cohen, C. (1986) "The Case for the Use of Animals in Biomedical Research," *New England Journal of Medicine* 315: 865–70.

Hardwig, J. (1997) "Is There a Duty to Die?" *Hastings Center Report* 27 (2): 34–42.

Hardwig, J. (2001/1997) "Dying at the Right Time." In H. LaFollette (ed.), *Ethics in Practice: An Anthology*, 2nd edn. Oxford: Blackwell Publishers, 48–58.

Harris Poll (2005) "By a Near Four-to-One Margin, US Adults Favor Not Taking Additional Steps to Prolong the Lives of Patients in a Persistent Vegetative State." (Online) Available at: http://www.harrisinteractive.com/news/allnewsbydate.asp?NewsID=909. (Accessed July 27, 2005.)

Haworth, L. (1986) *Autonomy: An Essay in Philosophical Psychology and Ethics*. New Haven, CT: Yale University Press.

Jans, J. (2002) "Christian Churches and Euthanasia in the Low Countries: Background, Argumentation and Commentary," *Ethical Perspectives* 9: 119–33.

Mill, J. S. (1998/1863) *Utilitarianism*. New York: Oxford University Press.

Mill, J. S. (1985/1885) *On Liberty*. Indianapolis, IN: Hackett.

Rollin, B. (1985) *Last Wish*. New York: Linden Press/Simon & Schuster.

Singer, P. (1990/1975) *Animal Liberation: A New Ethics for Our Treatment of Animals*, 2nd edn. New York: New York Review, distributed by Random House.

Smith, W. J. (2003) "Kass, in the Firing Line." *National Review Online*. (Online) Available at: http://www.nationalreview.com/comment/smith200312050930.asp. (Accessed July 29, 2005.)

NINE

Slippery Slope Arguments

Slippery slope arguments are frequently used to criticize physician-assisted suicide (PAS). People using these arguments often acknowledge the appeal of allowing individuals to end their lives quickly, if necessary with the assistance of their physicians. The problem is not what happens in individual cases. The problem is that legalizing PAS will have disastrous consequences. Therefore, we should not legally permit it.

Later in this chapter I will address these particular arguments. However, I begin by discussing *causal* slippery slope arguments more generally. Since these are commonly employed in debates on a variety of moral and political issues, it will be helpful to broadly understand their nature and use. That will then help us to better evaluate their use in the PAS debate.

Understanding Slippery Slope Arguments

The moral roads on which we travel are slippery. Our individual and collective actions inevitably affect others, ourselves, and our institutions. They shape the people we become and the kind of world we inhabit. They increase or decrease the likelihood, however slight, that certain futures will occur. Sometimes those consequences are positive, a giant leap for moral humankind. Other times they are detrimental or morally regressive. Since change is ubiquitous, we should not try to avoid slippery terrain. Rather we should find ways to successfully navigate it.

If change is inevitable, then what is the function of causal slippery slope arguments in moral debate? Do they just point out the obvious? No. If that were all they did, then they would be part of every moral assessment. They aren't. They have one primary role: to defend the status quo by making us fear change. Change, of course, is sometimes bad – but not inevitably. Change is also the engine of progress, moral and otherwise. What *is* inevitable is that we, our relationships, and our institutions are not static. So fearing change is irrational.

That helps explain why, although (a) life is slippery, and (b) we can sometimes develop cogent slippery slope arguments (Volokh 2003; Walton 1992; B. Williams

1995), given their principal usage, (c) we should banish them from moral and political debate. They are often fallacious and have often been used for ill. I recognize that this proposal seems hasty. After all, all argument forms are sometimes offered with false premises and are sometimes used for ill. Yet that doesn't lead us to jettison common logical principles (e.g., modus ponens). Why slippery slope arguments? There are three reasons. One, slippery slope arguments are especially prone to be vague and ill-formed. Two, people are easily swayed by them – more easily than by faulty instances of modus ponens. They sound suggestive even when argumentative details are vague or absent. Three, even when they are cogent, we can always find alternative, usually preferable, arguments that capture their insights without carrying their argumentative baggage. These three problems do not plague the use of modus ponens.

Before we can evaluate causal slippery slope arguments, we must first get clearer about exactly what they are.

The structure of causal slippery slope arguments

The philosophical and legal literature is replete with competing, and sometimes wholly incompatible, accounts of slippery slope arguments. Those who regularly use them may employ several versions. This makes their positions difficult to critique since if people object to one formulation, the defenders may shift to another. Since I cannot canvas them all, I will briefly outline one prominent alternative and then contrast it to my own. Throughout the first section I will explain why I think my account is preferable to alternatives. I will then evaluate their use.

Although Eugene Volokh's account explicitly concerns only social policies, his description captures the nub of all causal slippery slope arguments. "You think A might be a fairly good idea on its own, or at least not a very bad one. But you're afraid that A might eventually lead other legislators, voters, or judges to implement policy B, which you strongly oppose." So you oppose A (2003: 1028).

There is clearly something right about his account. Slippery slope arguments do claim that we should reject some proposed behaviors or policies because we judge that their likely consequences will be bad. However, his definition is too broad. Just because we reject an action or policy because of projected bad consequences does not mean we are using a slippery slope argument (SSA). If I say that a student shouldn't cheat because she will be caught and punished, I am saying the student shouldn't engage in the behavior because of likely negative consequences. But that is not a SSA. What distinguishes them? Most often it is the mechanism that leads from what he dubs "A" to "B". Specifically, I propose that causal slippery slope arguments have the following general structure:

1. Action x is *prima facie* morally permissible, that is, it is an action that, barring special reasons, it is not wrong to do.
2. If we do x, then, through a series of small analogous steps, circumstances y will probably occur.

3. Circumstances y are immoral.
4. Therefore, action x is (probably) immoral.

Let me say something about each element. First, although there are philosophical disputes about the precise meaning of "*prima facie*," these differences have no bearing on the current discussion. Volokh's language is sufficient, x must be "a fairly good idea on its own, or at least not a very bad one." If we could stop after taking the first (and perhaps a few additional) step(s), then we would have done nothing (very) wrong. However, given the kinds of creatures we are, the nature of institutions we inhabit, or the types of laws we employ, we are unlikely to stop after the first step. That is why the first step (action x) is immoral. It is not immoral in itself; it is immoral because it probably leads to consequences that are. Second, the mechanism of slippery slope arguments is a series of small analogous steps which presumably lead us from an action that is *prima facie* permissible to one that is not. Finally, all assume that the latter action or circumstances (y) are, in fact, immoral.

Differentiating slippery slopes from related argument forms

To understand and evaluate these arguments, we should differentiate them from other argument forms with which they are often confused or conflated. Some of these forms are quite plausible and thereby lead us to think slippery slope arguments are more forceful than they are.

One form clearly distinguishable from slippery slopes

Although the consistency argument is clearly not a slippery slope argument, it is sometimes confused with it. The consistency argument is schematized as follows:

C1: We should do x for reason R.
C2: Reason R justifies doing y.
C3: Y is immoral. Therefore,
C4: Doing x is not justified by reason R.

Some people treat these as slippery slope arguments (Volokh 2003: 1037). However, since their second premise is critically different, we should distinguish them (Schauer 1985: 363, 369). Consider the following consistency argument. I think the FBI should be allowed to tap Achmad's telephone simply because a field agent judges that that would promote American security. If it is acceptable to a field agent to tap a phone because she thinks it will promote American security, then she could tap my telephone. It would be immoral for her to tap my phone. Therefore we should not tap Achmad's phone just because an individual agent thinks it will promote American security. Like all consistency arguments, this claims that the reasons that justify doing x straightforwardly justify doing y. In contrast, slippery slope arguments claim that x leads to y by means of some series of small analogous steps (allowing the agent to tap Achmad's phone will ultimatey lead to allowing her to arrest and detain suspects indefinitely, without granting them any legal protections). We challenge consistency arguments by demonstrating that x and y are relevantly different and, therefore, that although R will justify doing x, it does not justify doing y. We challenge slippery slope arguments by denying that action x will probably lead to y.

Two forms more closely related to slippery slopes

The following two argument forms are more closely related to slippery slope arguments and, therefore, are sometimes difficult to distinguish from them. What I shall show, though, is that for each we face a dilemma. If someone has a *strong* instance of these arguments then she would not recast it as a slippery slope argument. That would be argumentatively anemic. People use slippery slope arguments rather than these forms precisely because the evidence for the conclusion is weak.

Straightforward inductive generalizations

Suppose someone proposes that we raise the speed limit on interstate highways to 90 mph. I would argue that the death rate from automobile accidents will skyrocket; therefore, we should resist the proposal. But this is not a slippery slope. It is a simple inductive generalization (Salman 1989: 90). We have ample empirical data about how changes in speed limit impact death rates from automobile accidents. We saw what happened when we increased speed limits from 55 mph to 65 mph. The same evidence suggests death rates would increase if we raised speed limits to 90 mph.

The reasoning employed in slippery slope arguments differs. Each step down the slope differs from, but is analogous to, the previous step. It is not a straightforward generalization. Of course one might use a slippery slope argument to oppose increases in speed limits. But someone would do so only if she lacked solid empirical evidence of the effects of this change in policy. If she had the evidence, she would use an inductive generalization instead.

Straightforward causal arguments

Although slippery slope arguments are distinct from "straightforward causal arguments," in some cases they bleed into them. But as with inductive generalizations, someone would use a slippery slope argument only if she lacked the empirical evidence to support a straightforward causal argument. To explain why, consider the following example. Frank intentionally drops a Ming vase from six feet above a bare concrete floor. The vase breaks. It would have been silly to have mounted a slippery slope argument against his dropping the vase since dropping the vase, barring something or someone to cushion the fall, just is to break the vase. Increasing the temporal gap between x and y does not alter the facts. My detonating strategically placed explosives atop a Swiss mountain is not the first step down a slippery slope to killing people at the bottom; rather, barring some freakish intervention, I kill villagers below *by means of* an avalanche. Adding a month-long timer does not relevantly change matters, although it does slightly increase the probability that something or someone might intervene, thereby making the consequences a bit less certain, albeit still clearly causal. In each case x starts the causal chain that standardly leads to y. Such chains are "more reminiscent of a cliff or a wall than a slope" (Lode 1999: 1477). In short, the mechanisms of change in paradigm slippery slope arguments differ from paradigm cases of straightforward causal arguments.

Some causes are direct (e.g., the water from the leaking gutter erodes the foundation of the house) while others are probabilistic (e.g., smoking causes cancer). But in each case there is a clear causal chain from x to y. If I get lung cancer from smoke, it is because I myself smoked or regularly inhaled second-hand smoke. In contrast, slippery slope arguments hold that x leads to y by means of small, usually barely indistinguishable, analogous steps. To use the example from the last chapter, some opposed to physician-assisted suicide claim that even (seemingly) justifiable instances of PAS would ultimately lead some other physicians to take *their* patients' lives inappropriately (Bok 1998). How? Presumably successive physicians will make analogous (slightly different albeit similar) exceptions to the "rules" against taking patients' lives; these changes in agents' perspectives will "accumulate" over time, diminishing doctors' psychological repugnance to killing. Eventually some doctors will kill some patients unjustifiably (Wright 2000: 82–4). The earlier changes causally pave the way for later ones. However, the causal connection is not causal in the ordinary sense. For instance, the doctors who will purportedly kill later patients are not the same ones who helped the first patients end their lives, nor did the former doctors *make* the latter doctors kill their patients. Because the mechanism is different, the probability that y will occur is also far less than one.

Yet people offering slippery slope arguments rarely conclude that doing x is *probably* immoral. They conclude or imply that doing x *is* immoral. Perhaps this omission is rhetorical since acknowledging it would diminish their arguments' ability to sway public opinion. It could also be that they think it is immoral to do x even if x only probably leads to the immoral y. If the probabilities were high enough, that might be plausible. Nonetheless, this claim should be clearly stated and defended. Additionally, I would think that if we object to x only because of these deleterious consequences, then our moral disdain for doing x would be less than if we had independent reasons for thinking it is immoral. If nothing else, we should regret that we cannot do x – after all, x is *prima facie* morally permissible, apparently desirable, and only probably leads to immoral consequences. Yet many who employ slippery slope arguments have the same disdain for x as they have for actions they deem intrinsically immoral. That is the first suggestion that the common *use* of slippery slope arguments is rhetorical.

Evaluating Slippery Slopes

To evaluate causal slippery slope arguments, I begin indirectly, by examining several cases in which slippery slope arguments have been or might be used, and contrast them with a clear case where such arguments would never be used. These will help us better identify the nature, function, and reliability of these arguments.

Looking at some cases

Cases where slippery slopes look plausible

If a parent wants to convince her child to be honest with her friend Susie, she might use a slippery slope-sounding argument. "I understand why you want to tell Susie a 'white lie' about why you cannot attend her party. That seems like a good idea right now. But be careful. By telling this small lie now, you will be more likely to later lie about more important matters," the parent might say. "With each lie you will become less inclined to tell the truth, and more prone to lie about more serious matters. If you do not want to become a liar, you should resist the urge to lie to Susie" (an argument suggested by Bok's insightful discussion of lying in chapter 5, 1978).

Or suppose Bob, an alcoholic who has not had a drink for two years, asks his counselor whether he could have a drink at an office party the coming weekend. The counselor will almost surely say "No." "Although you might think it would be acceptable to take a drink just this once, under these unusual circumstances," she might say, "even if this first use will not make you drunk, you will become more likely to drink again later. After all, you think, 'I took a drink *that* time and didn't get drunk.' Each time you drink again, you will increase both the frequency and amount that you drink. Before long, you will regularly be getting drunk. So don't drink – not even once" (for different examples see Lode 1999: 1504; Mayo 1990–91: 91). Even if oversimplified, the counselor and the parents offer sound advice. Both claim that a *relatively* harmless and plausibly permissible action may increase the propensity of acting badly later. This propensity makes doing the initial actions immoral. These kinds of cases lend credence to slippery slope arguments.

Cases where slippery slopes are implausible

Not all slippery slopes are so plausible. Some are ludicrous. You and your spouse are devoted parents. You are rarely away from your children. But you want an evening alone, without interruption from the kids. You go out for dinner together and leave your children with a sitter. Your children would prefer that you be home, but the sitter is adequate. You also spend money on yourselves, money you could have spent on the children.

Suppose someone offers a slippery slope argument against your going out. They argue that by going out this evening with your spouse rather than doing something with and for your kids you have started down a treacherous slide. Your action will probably lead you to do something more extravagant for yourself. Before long you may mortgage your children's college education and even their health so you and your spouse can take a five-star around-the-world cruise. These consequences are so horrendous that you should not start down this road. That is why it would be wrong of you to go out to dinner with your spouse, even this once.

This argument, unlike the first two, is absurd because the projected consequences are so clearly improbable, and because few people, if any, seriously believe it would be wrong of you to go out for dinner occasionally. Barring some special knowledge about you, we have no reason to think these disastrous consequences are more than the faintest of faint possibilities. In fact, given our background knowledge of what often happens to parents of young children, we have far more reason to think that failing to go out for dinner in these circumstances will create or reinforce a habit of neglecting your spouse to spend time with your children. That failure would likely have serious consequences for your marriage.

Cases where slippery slopes are morally disastrous

The history of moral debate is littered with slippery slope arguments used to defend morally horrific behavior. Such arguments were regularly used to resist abolition. For example, a prominent Protestant preacher claimed that we should not grant "colored men" freedom because of the "terrible consequences" to which that would lead:

> Then a colored man might be the next governor; and colored men might constitute their Legislature, and set on the bench as judges in their courts. Thus the entire administration of the government in those States would be placed in the hands of degraded men, wholly ignorant of the principles of law and government (Rice 1846: 33).

These arguments did not end with the Civil War or with the turn of the twentieth century. Growing up in Nashville, I regularly heard slippery slope arguments against granting equal rights to blacks. In my town blacks were required to ride on the back of the bus, to drink at separate water fountains, and to use different toilets. Proposals to change these practices were met by racists who claimed that even small changes to these rules would ultimately lead to more fundamental (and "clearly immoral") changes: before long blacks might want to marry our daughters or our sisters!

What these cases show

By reflecting on these cases, by understanding when slippery slope arguments are — and are not — used, we can isolate what is insightful and worrisome about them.

The importance of habit

The arguments against single instances of lying and drinking gain their plausibility by exploiting a significant psychological and moral truth that we have seen before: our previous choices, actions, and deliberations inevitably shape our current behavior, while current choices and actions shape future behavior. Yet in using slippery slope arguments to evaluate only some behaviors, we imply that this is an episodic feature of human life. It is not. It is the heart of human life. We call it "learning." We consciously learn words and syntax so we are able to speak and think. We consciously attend to what is around us so that we will be "spontaneously" attentive in the future. We consciously reflect on our action so that we become predictably self-critical. Although the precise ways that we use language, attend to our surroundings, and reflect on our behavior and beliefs are sometimes conscious, the character of these conscious deliberations is likewise shaped by earlier actions, choices, and behavior. When we understand human action, we see why it is misleading to say that a propensity to be dishonest is a *mere* consequence of lying to Suzie. That implies a false separation between the later event and the earlier behavior. It is like saying that coughing without covering your mouth has, as a consequence, the release of germs into the air. Not so. Coughing without covering one's mouth just is, in this world, to release germs into the air. Of course there is a temporal gap between your daughter's initial lie to Suzie and your daughter's becoming a liar (and between my coughing and germs being released into the air). That means another factor (another person, circumstances beyond one's control, or the person's other habits) might intervene so that the later behavior does not occur. However, when the connection between an action and what follows is sufficiently tight, we do not ordinarily distinguish the action and its consequence. One way of describing this is to say that human action is temporally thick: it is not something we do once, in some narrow slice of time. An action is what it is in important measure because of the ways it typically extends into the future. This may sound like a truism. But if it is, it is a truism we have oft forgotten when we think about ethics. Slippery slope arguments gain much of their credence by exploiting this phenomenon, but they do so in ways that mask habits' central role in human behavior.

The use of such arguments also implies that all habits are negative – that all slopes lead downward. They thereby create an "undifferentiated risk aversion" (Schauer 1985: 376), an irrational fear of change. They make us "slopeaphobic." But that is to be life phobic since *all* actions occur on a slope. That is the kind of creatures we are and the kind of world we inhabit. We are changing creatures living in a world of change in which each choice affects the direction and character of that change. Sure, some slopes do lead downward, but others lead upward (we call them "learning curves"). Whether we tend to move up or down the slope depends, in part, on how we view change, and whether we have experience of traveling on slippery terrain. We can learn to better traverse downward slopes – to slip and occasionally slide – without sliding all the way down to the bottom. We can also learn how to ascend after having slipped on a downward slope: we can learn from a bad experience.

Omissions, as well as actions, can create habits

Our habits – our propensities for future action – are created not only by what we do, but also by what we fail to do. Habits emerging from omissions differ from those shaped by actions. They diminish, rather than increase, the propensities for particular future actions. Every day I fail to do my scheduled exercise or practice the piano

(Mayo 1990–1: 91), I initiate or reinforce a habit of missing exercise or practice. That does not mean that I will become a couch potato, but it does make it less likely, albeit slightly, that I will make or sustain a successful regimen of exercise or practice. Every time I am indifferent to the needs of a friend, I initiate or reinforce a habit of being indifferent. That does not mean that I will become a selfish pig, it just makes that more likely, albeit slightly. This is a phenomenon of which most of us ordinary mortals are well aware.

Once we recognize that both actions and omissions shape my propensities for future behavior, it is apparent that slopes cannot be avoided. Rather we should learn how to navigate them successfully.

The importance of empirical data

The counselor's argument against Bob's (the alcoholic) taking a drink is plausible not because of some vague causal connection presumably tracked by slippery slope arguments, but because she has strong empirical evidence of Bob's inability to handle alcohol. A slippery slope argument not only does not add anything, it detracts from the counselor's argument. It is far more powerful for her to present Bob with the clear empirical evidence: his history of alcoholism, his past attempts to "drink just once," and how even a single drink repeatedly led to his resuming his alcoholic behavior. The counselor might use slippery slope-sounding language, but if she does, she does so to present the evidence, not as a substitute for it. Absent such evidence, there is no good reason to tell Bob not to drink.

Once we step back and understand these arguments' function, we see that they persuade (or fail to persuade) people based almost entirely on the listener's current beliefs about what is right and wrong. When people are predisposed to think that the initial behavior (x) is acceptable, then they are rarely swayed by slippery slope arguments. For instance, since most parents want to go out for dinner with their spouses, they are not afraid of what will happen if they do. That is why the second argument has no bite. Conversely, if the listener is already inclined to believe that x is wrong, then they will be receptive to slippery slope arguments and will not be inclined to notice the absence of empirical evidence in support of premise two. Those already opposed to euthanasia will likely think that slippery slope arguments against it are telling. This is the second reason for thinking that such arguments' primary use is rhetorical.

Their function is conservative

Small changes not only can, but sometimes do lead to more substantial changes. About this, those who use slippery slope arguments are right. We are creatures who learn and adapt to new environments; our previous actions change propensities for future action. Where they went wrong was in implying that all changes are morally objectionable. Many people would not have recognized that racism and sexism were fundamentally wrong until they first took those moral baby steps. That is why those

small changes were not immoral. They dislodged people from their immoral behavior. Change is not inevitably bad. Change can be beneficial, as when we learn from
experience. Yet the standard use of slippery slope arguments ignores this by presup-
posing the moral status quo. If premise three is false, then the conclusion is not supported. This is worrisome since, as the historical examples reveal, the moral status
quo is always debatable, is not infrequently inappropriate, and is sometimes seriously
unjust. Yet these are precisely the circumstances in which slippery slope arguments
are normally brandished: to defend assaults on the moral status quo. These are the
same conditions under which such arguments are unacceptable. Once someone has
mounted a critique against the status quo, we cannot defend the status quo by simply
reasserting it. Yet, as Glanville Williams put it:

> it is the trump card of the traditionalist, because no proposal for reform, however
> strong the argument in its favor, is immune from the wedge objection. In fact, the
> stronger the argument in favor of reform, the more likely it is that the traditionalist
> will take the wedge objection – it is then the only one he has (G. Williams
> 1986/1958: 426).

In such cases, their real use is rhetorical.

Their real use is rhetorical

Let's rehearse some of our findings. Causal slippery slope arguments are plausible
only if the second premise is true, yet we have no reason to believe the second
premise is true unless we have evidence of the causal link between x and y. The counselor's advice to the alcoholic makes good sense only if she has specific evidence of
the alcoholic's past; without that evidence, the advice is unduly cautious. Many
people drink without becoming alcoholics. However, if we do have this evidence, we
do not need slippery slope arguments. So why do people use them? They use them
as rhetorical tools. This rhetorical use may not always be objectionable. A presenter
might have the required evidence to support the second premise but does not put it
forward because she believes the recipient cannot understand it. As a heuristic device
(Volokh 2003: 1125), this may be sensible. Even so, this use is defensible only if the
speaker has the necessary evidence. If pressed in philosophical debate, she should be
able to produce it. If she can, then within that debate, the slippery slope argument
adds nothing. If she cannot produce the evidence, then the slippery slope argument
is just a rhetorical device that plays on the listeners' fears or prejudices.

Social-political versions of the slippery slope

The habitual nature of humans partly explains how social mores evolve and how past
political decisions shape future choices. Moreover, a central aim of social institutions
and political decisions is to enable some options and foreclose others. This combination of institutional aims and our psychological natures seems to support the moves

exploited by the second premise of slippery slope arguments in the political arena. Here are four examples of these arguments.

Four examples

First, political theorists, legal scholars, and judges sometimes employ slippery slope arguments to defend free speech. Although free speech is fundamentally important to the flourishing of individuals and the state, there are instances where each of us would like to curtail some speech. We might even think we would be justified in doing so in select cases. However, if we forbade speech in these presumably justified cases, we would lessen the political and legal barriers to more frequent and substantial limitations on speech, and thereby increase the likelihood that the state will squelch speech that we need. Even when that is not a likely consequence, limitations on speech will have a "chilling effect" on desirable speech. Citizens will increasingly be afraid to air their views in public, even if their speech would have passed constitutional muster. Rather than opening the possibility that the government will limit important speech (and even engage in wholehearted censorship), we should permit forms of speech we find grossly objectionable. We must stick by our general principles; otherwise we start down the slippery slope (Arthur 1997).

Second, as we saw in the previous chapter, slippery slope arguments are often used to criticize physician-assisted suicide. Those using this argument claim that permitting PAS will lead, over time, to detrimental changes. To avoid these immoral results, we should refuse to take the first step.

Third, people occasionally offer what van der Burg calls the "apocalyptic slippery slope" (van der Burg 1991: 43). In these cases the proponents claim not that y is especially likely, but rather that y is so terrible that the mere risk of its happening is sufficient to justify refraining from doing x. This form of the argument has been used to condemn the nuclear arms race, extensive reliance on nuclear power, recombinant DNA research, and cloning.

Fourth, people sometimes critique proposals simply because of who supports them – what Volokh calls the "ad hominem heuristic" (2003: 1075). Members of an identifiable – and by your lights, distasteful – group offer a proposal that you think acceptable, or perhaps just a bit misguided. Nonetheless, you fear that if the group is given a political inch, then they will, over time, gain more power, and begin to institute significant and severely negative changes.

The problems with these arguments

It is not difficult to see why each of these examples is rhetorically persuasive. However, I would contend that, like the personal versions canvassed before, they are either (a) not slippery slope arguments, (b) are flawed, or (c) that their insights, however valuable, can be accommodated as well, if not better, in other ways. To explain, let us briefly look at each example, and especially the discussion of PAS.

(1)   Although the free speech argument is plausible, in its strongest form it is not really a slippery slope argument. Proponents claim that if we prohibit Nazis from speaking then we thereby license the majority to prohibit any speech they deem immoral. That is true, however, only if the reason we prohibit the Nazis' speech is that *the majority objects to it*. If so, then this is a claim about what our reasons commit us to. It is an argument from consistency, not a slippery slope.

(2)   Slippery slope arguments against PAS take several forms. One common move is to argue that even advocates of PAS must recognize that "the logic of justi- fication for active euthanasia is identical to that of PAS" (Arras 1999: 276). As stated, however, this is not a slippery slope argument but a consistency argument. It claims that since PAS is relevantly similar to active euthanasia, then if we permit one, we must permit the other. It does not claim that permitting one will lead us, via small analogous steps, to permitting the other. Furthermore, this argument assumes that active euthanasia is morally objectionable. If it were not morally objectionable, the argument has no bite. Yet Arras does not say why it is morally objectionable.

Even if Arras were to mount such an argument, this general strategy, oft employed in the euthanasia debate, drives home the earlier point that slippery slope arguments are the preferred weapons against social change – including some changes that we now regard as significant moral progress. Not only were these arguments used to battle equal rights for blacks and women, they were also used to challenge public education, the forty-hour working week, government-supported retirement and medical care, etc. When someone challenges that moral status quo with a plausible argument, then (a) we need to defend the status quo, and (b) we cannot defend it merely by reasserting it. In arguments about social institutions as in arguments about persons, the third premise can be false. And all social institutions, like persons, are on a slope. Incremental change can be bad, but it can also be the engine of improve- ment. Given the creatures we are and the institutions we inhabit, we would not have decided overnight that blacks are equal to whites or that women should have the right to vote. We reached these desirable moral ends only by first taking small steps on the slippery slope of life.

Arras and other critics of PAS, however, rarely rely on a single slippery slope argu- ment. Arras argues that permitting even seemingly permissible cases of PAS will likely lead to abuse: (a) physicians may euthanize patients even when their "decisions" are not "sufficiently voluntary"; (b) the practice will have more detrimental effects on "the poor and members of minority groups"; (c) physicians' failures to "adequately respond to pain and suffering" will lead some ill people to prematurely choose death; and (d) we will not establish a reporting system that "would adequately monitor these practices" (1999: 277).

Arras has isolated some serious worries, ones we would be ill-advised to ignore. These should give us pause before permitting active euthanasia. If we proceed, we should seek ways to lessen the probability of those detrimental effects, and proceed only if the gains are worth the costs. Nonetheless, I fail to see that his points vindi- cate the use of the slippery slope. First, PAS did not create the problems Arras men- tions. Doctors and philosophers disagree now about what constitutes a "sufficiently voluntary" action. Doctors now fail to give adequate pain relief, the current US health system is often unfair to the poor and minorities, and medical reporting in that system is shoddy (ibid.).

Second, to whatever extent that these worries are legitimate, it is not because seemingly permissible actions will be transmuted via small analogous steps into morally objectionable ones. Rather, we can note the significant failings of our current health care system, and straightforwardly predict what will happen if we permit physician-assisted suicide unless we take due care. That is, we can inductively generalize, as we might in speculating about the likely consequences of electing an incompetent president or of raising the speed limit to 90 mph. But such speculations have nothing to do with slippery slope arguments. To use a slippery slope argument to make any of these points would be argumentatively weak.

Third, we must not forget that forbidding PAS will also have demonstrable costs, that forbidding physician-assisted suicide may be "the callous abandonment of patients to their pain and suffering" (1999: 279). I think the conclusion we should draw is that whether we legalize PAS, we should make significant changes in our medical system. Once we make these changes, we can conduct a careful risk analysis of the benefits of permitting and forbidding PAS.

(3)   The importance of empirical evidence is most vivid when considering apocalyptic versions of the slippery slope. Those who employ this version claim that since x might lead to some supremely terrible y, then we should refuse to do x, no matter how appealing. Such arguments have been used to criticize cloning, certain forms of genetic engineering, and our reliance on nuclear power. Consider, for example, the claim that widespread use of nuclear power could lead to two different, but related, supremely terrible results: (a) a nuclear "accident," more serious than that at Chernobyl, and (b) long-term contamination of the earth from disposal of radioactive wastes.

To see why this does not vindicate the use of slippery slope arguments, let us compare it with two structurally similar, but wildly implausible, slippery slope arguments. In the first, the same x (using nuclear power) presumably leads to a different but still terrible y (the moral collapse of the country). In the second, a different x (educating the poor) is claimed to lead to the same terrible y (a nuclear meltdown). Unlike the original case, these arguments are laughable. Why? Because we have no evidence that either x will lead to either y. Without such evidence, the mere terribleness of y gives us *no* reason to refrain from x. None. After all, any action *could* lead to terrible consequences. The original argument about nuclear power, on the other hand, is plausible precisely because we can see a possible causal connection between x and y.

Once again we see that we can – and must – assess this claim without employing slippery slope arguments. We should make an informed judgment of risk. We must determine the seriousness and likelihood of the risk and compare it with the importance and likelihood of the benefits. As the likelihood and seriousness of harm increase, we have increased reason to refrain from acting, while as the likelihood and importance of the benefits increase, we have increased reasons to act. We should ask

(a) just how risky is using nuclear power, and (b) how beneficial is it? To the extent that we have real evidence for thinking that it might have these disastrous consequences, then that should give us some pause in relying on nuclear power. Minimally it should compel us to make serious efforts at ensuring safety. Of course, that is precisely what we do. We make stringent safety demands of nuclear power plants, and we do so because we have empirical evidence that a meltdown could occur. We also know about the dangers of storing radioactive materials.

Of course, knowing these risks of using nuclear power, even if substantial, does not solve the issue, for omissions, as well as actions, have consequences. The failure to use nuclear power plants would arguably make power exorbitantly expensive, and that could lead to our country's financial demise. Minimally it could make us too dependent on fossil fuels. These consequences are also terrible, and someone might argue that these risks, although perhaps less terrible, are far more likely than the consequences of a meltdown. I cannot here defend either argument – nor the range of other possibilities. What I do know is that slippery slope arguments, as they are regularly used, are poor substitutes for a careful assessment of risk.

(4)   This leads to the last form of the social political version. Such arguments are used by both sides of the political spectrum: some people use these to critique any changes in abortion laws. They fear that if they permit so-called "right to life" groups to win on any point, no matter how small, the groups will be emboldened and empowered to seek more serious restrictions on abortion rights. Others may use this argument to resist any gun registration law, no matter how minor, on the grounds that if these laws are adopted, gun control groups will seek to confiscate guns.

I understand the appeal of these arguments. They are far from crazy. However, they are not slippery slope arguments. The issue in these cases is not, strictly speaking, whether slightly limiting abortions (or having minimal gun registration) will transform, via small analogous steps, into more significant restrictions on abortion or guns. The issue is whether giving a group you dislike a political victory, however small, empowers them to make more substantial and unwanted changes (Volokh 2003: 1075–80). These are plausible claims, but only inasmuch as they are sound inductive generalizations, grounded in knowledge of the group in question and our appreciation of the temporal thickness of action.

Living on a Slippery Slope

I have not argued that all slippery slope arguments are faulty, although many are. I have not claimed that slippery arguments never isolate morally relevant features of action, for many do. What I have argued is that given the way they function in moral debate, we should avoid them. They do not add anything and often do more harm than good. Moreover, by making us fear slopes, these arguments make us more likely to slide on the slopes we must traverse. Consider the following analogy: people who must walk on slippery surfaces might not know that the slopes are slippery. Others might fear them. Still others might know the surfaces are slippery but are prepared to navigate them. Who can best move on slippery surfaces? The first person, being unaware of the nature of the surface, is most likely to slip. The second person is so afraid of slipping that she doesn't venture out, while the third person will have the surest footing.

This resembles living on the slippery slope of life. Those who do not understand the propensities of current action to shape future behavior (for example, young children) are more likely to make mistakes. Those who are unduly afraid of slippery surfaces – who unduly fear change – will stay crouched in their moral corners, afraid to do anything new, different, or innovative, because any new action *might* lead to perdition. And those who understand that all life is on a slope – those sensitive to the ways in which current choices and actions have morally relevant consequences – will be better prepared to navigate those slopes. They will see the ways that personal actions and social changes can have detrimental effects, and will be on guard against them, and, when feasible, find ways of insuring the detrimental effects do not occur. These people will have the conceptual boots to give them a relatively firm grip and the experience of walking on slippery surfaces that gives them more secure footing.

In short, the knowledge that actions occur on a slope should neither incapacitate us nor make us unduly fearful. If we did not change, then we could not learn, grow, improve, and progress. What we thought was a descending slope might turn out to be ascending. In other cases we may discover what every hiker knows, that a partial descent down one slope is often required to climb to a higher neighboring peak (Depew and Weber 1996: 282–4). Finally, even when we are on a descending slope, we can often descend part of the way without sliding to the bottom.

Whether we can and do depends, in large measure, on our recognition of the moral terrain on which we travel, and our experience in traversing such terrain. Of course, change is not always for the good. It must be watched, scrutinized, and evaluated. However, that is just to say that we should reflect on what we do. We will then be more likely to intelligently guide our conduct: to act when we should, to refrain from acting when appropriate, and to have the wisdom to discern the difference.

In the next chapter we turn to further discuss the notion of autonomy, which also played a critical role in the debate over physician-assisted suicide.

REFERENCES

Arras, J. D. (1999) "Physician-assisted Suicide: A Tragic View." In J. D. Arras and B. Steinbock (eds.), *Ethical Issues in Modern Medicine*, 5th edn. Palo Alto, CA: Mayfield, 274–80.

Arthur, J. (1997) "Sticks and Stones." In H. LaFollette (ed.), *Ethics in Practice: An Anthology*, 2nd edn. Oxford: Blackwell Publishers, 364–75.

Bok, S. (1978) *Lying: Moral Choice in Public and Private Life*. New York: Pantheon Books.

Bok, S. (1998) "Part Two." In G. Dworkin, R. G. Frey, and S. Bok (eds.), *Euthanasia and Physician-assisted Suicide: For and Against*. Cambridge: Cambridge University Press, 83–139.

Depew, D. J. and Weber, B. (1996) *Darwinism Evolving.* Cambridge, MA: MIT Press.

Lode, E. (1999) "Slippery Slope Arguments and Legal Reasoning," *California Law Review* 87 (6): 1469–544.

Mayo, D. J. (1990–1) "The Role of Slippery Slope Arguments in Public Policy Debates," *Philosophic Exchange* 20–21: 81–97.

Rice, N. L. (1846) *A Debate on Slavery.* New York: Wm. H. Moore.

Salman, M. H. (1989) *Logic and Critical Thinking.* San Diego, CA: Harcourt Brace Jovanovich.

Schauer, F. (1985) "Slippery Slopes," *Harvard Law Review* 99: 361–83.

van der Burg, W. (1991) "The Slippery Slope Argument," *Ethics* 102 (1): 42–65.

Volokh, E. (2003) "The Mechanisms of the Slippery Slope," *Harvard Law Review* 116: 1026–134.

Walton, D. (1992) *Slippery Slope Arguments.* Oxford: Clarendon Press.

Williams, B. (1995) "Which Slopes are Slippery?" In B. Williams (ed.), *Making Sense of Humanity and Other Philosophical Papers, 1982–1993.* Cambridge: Cambridge University Press, 213–23.

Williams, G. (1986/1958) "Euthanasia Legislation: A Rejoinder to the Nonreligious Objections." In T. A. Mappes and J. S. Zembaty (eds.), *Biomedical Ethics.* New York: McGraw-Hill.

Wright, W. (2000) "Historical Analogies, Slippery Slopes, and the Question of Euthanasia," *Journal of Law, Medicine, and Ethics* 28 (2): 176–86.

PART FOUR

Autonomy, Responsibility, and Risk

TEN

Autonomy, Children, and Paternalism

The discussion of physician-assisted suicide (PAS) in Chapter 8 ended with two unresolved issues. The first concerned the cogency of slippery slope arguments, an argument form frequently used to criticize PAS. I discussed this in the previous chapter. The second was the notion of autonomy, which plays a central role in arguments defending PAS. I address that issue here.

What is Autonomy?

As we saw earlier, "autonomy" is ambiguous. It is used to describe four different but interrelated notions: (1) the *capacity* for autonomy, (2) the *ability* to be autonomous, (3) *realized autonomy*, and (4) *normative autonomy*. The first three are *descriptions* about what someone (1) can eventually be able to do, (2) is now able to do, or (3) now does, while the fourth is *normative*, a claim about what people should be allowed to do.

Realized autonomy is the primary descriptive term. To realize one's autonomy someone must be "one's own person, to be directed by considerations, desires, conditions, and characteristics that are not simply imposed externally upon one, but are part of what can somehow be considered one's authentic self" (Christman 2003). As elsewhere, abilities and capacities can only be understood by reference to a realized ability. Someone with the ability to run in the Boston Marathon would be someone who could compete if she so chose, while someone with the capacity to run in the Boston Marathon would be someone who, with time and practice, could compete. Someone with the *ability* to be autonomous could control her life now (could realize autonomy), even if she does not standardly do so. People with the *capacity* for autonomy will, barring some problem, eventually develop that ability.

Since realized autonomy is the core descriptive notion, should we infer that someone must have *realized* autonomy before they are granted normative autonomy? No. If that were true, then adults who do not control their own lives should be denied normative autonomy. Yet we normally think adults have the right to make their own choices, as long as they do not harm others. Besides, an individual can usually realize autonomy only if she has normative autonomy. So, realized autonomy cannot be required before the state grants someone normative autonomy. On the other hand, the bare capacity for autonomy is too weak. Even newborns have the capacity to be autonomous (i.e., barring some problem they will eventually develop that ability). Yet we don't think newborns should have authority to run their own lives. That is why for the last several hundred years, most moral and political philosophers thought that the *ability* to be autonomous was sufficient for normative autonomy: that governments and individuals should generally not interfere with the choices of those who have these abilities, even if they are only marginally realized (Mill 1985/1885: 54–73).

Put differently, we assume we should not generally treat normal adult human beings paternalistically. We should not force a normal adult to act (or forbear from acting) simply because we think it will be in her best interests. For instance, most people would be outraged if the government were to pass laws forcing adults to exercise, eat four servings of vegetables daily, give up smoking, etc. Everyone thinks paternalistic laws toward adults require justification; some object to all paternalistic laws (Husak 1994, 2002).

The nature and scope of autonomy is not only important in its own right, it is deeply connected to other issues with important implications for ethics: paternalism, responsibility, and moral education. Here I will focus on the notions of autonomy and the justification of paternalism. In the following chapter I discuss responsibility. My strategy here is to better understand autonomy and paternalism by exploring the standard ways we treat children relative to adults. We will identify the skills and knowledge that make autonomy possible. It will also help us better understand the scope of and justifications for paternalism.

To start, we should distinguish three questions: (1) Do children have the ability to be autonomous: do they have the rational and experiential wherewithal to make informed decisions about their futures? (2) Should parents (or guardians) permit children to make (some) decisions about their futures? (3) Should the state promote children's acquisition of autonomy, and, if so, how? The first question concerns children's intellectual and volitional abilities. The second and third questions are two aspects of *normative autonomy*. In this chapter I focus on the second, although I will end with a few observations about the proper role of the state.

We often get the wrong answer to these questions because we assume that (a) the ability for autonomy is all or nothing – that an individual either has or lacks it, and that (b) if someone has the ability, then she is normatively autonomous, while if she lacks it, she is not. Conjoin these beliefs with the descriptive belief that adults, but not children, have this ability, and we must conclude that adults, but not children, are normatively autonomous. However, this argument puts excessive weight on questionable empirical claims and blurry conceptual distinctions.

There are two interrelated problems with these assumptions. One concerns the ways we determine whether someone has the ability to be autonomous. The other is the belief that the ability to be autonomous is all or nothing. Both are bad for children and for adults. Current practice confines children to practical purgatory where they have no socially recognized control over their lives until, upon reaching the magical age of 17, 18, or 21 (depending on where they live), they suddenly are given "complete" say. This view also makes us inappropriately opposed to all paternalism toward adults. These confusions make it harder to understand the role of autonomy in end-of-life decisions. To explain these claims, I will first examine the arguments for the claim that children should not be normatively autonomous. At the end of this chapter, I will then speculate on its implications for thinking about PAS.

Why People Think Children Should Not Be Normatively Autonomous

Most people assume that parents can tell their children – especially their very young children – how to act "for their own good." We assume parents can require children to go to bed at a reasonable time, to do their schoolwork, to eat their spinach, and to refrain from viewing movies with "adult content." Not only can parents legitimately exert this control, most people think they should. They think parents who give their kids free rein have not fulfilled their parental responsibilities. Yet we also assume that once a child becomes an adult, others can no longer treat her as a child. Paternalism toward adults is (generally) wrong; it always needs to be justified.

Those who think a child should not have substantial liberty to make her own decisions typically offer one of two arguments. First, they may argue that children are incapable of making a real decision, let alone a *good one*. Thus, parents can protect the capacity for autonomy. However, that is not done by giving children freedom.

Second, some claim that even if some child were able to be autonomous to some degree, giving her significant authority over her life will create an environment that is antithetical to her – or other children's – best interests. Some thinkers combine these objections to explain why children should not generally be given authority to make their own choices.

> Children are not just miniature adults; they need time to mature and develop the traits that make it possible for adults to live good lives. These morally relevant differences undermine the attempt to show that it is unjust to deny children the same rights as adults; they also suggest that the consequences of equal rights would be harmful to children and society as a whole (Purdy 1992: 369).

There is a profound sense in which Purdy is correct. Very young children have limited abilities and giving them extensive say too early, and without appropriate training, will harm them. However, people often make questionable inferences about what this means for the proper treatment of children and for a full understanding of autonomy.

Children's inability to be autonomous

Much depends on what Purdy means by "a child." Is she referring to a two-year-old who is not yet potty trained, a 12-year-old who does not want to take calculus, or a 15-year-old who is deciding whether and where to go to church? If it is the two-year-old, then, of course, the child cannot understand the options, let alone make an informed choice. It would be not merely misguided to let the child have a choice, but it wouldn't make sense. If, however, she is referring to either of the latter children, then I would suggest that, barring special evidence to the contrary, of course they can make some informed choices, and, indeed, ought to have a defeasible say in them.

Those defending current practices would likely respond that this ignores the profound intellectual and volitional deficiencies of children relative to normal adults. These theorists claim we are not justified in making basic decisions for (most) adults since their cognitive and volitional abilities are sufficiently well developed so that their decisions are rational, even when unreasonable. Children, on the other hand, do not just make bad decisions, they are unable to make good ones.

Deficiencies which undermine the ability to be autonomous

To assess this claim we must first identify the deficiencies that limit people's ability to be autonomous, deficiencies people assume children are more likely than adults to have. There are five relevant factors: (1) an inability to mentally process information, (2) ignorance of relevant factors, (3) insufficient understanding of the implications of one's actions for the future, (4) emotional instability, and (5) temporary incapacity. I will not say much about the first factor. Still, we could all agree that someone who is severely retarded will have limited abilities to make wise decisions. Here, though, we will focus exclusively on intellectually normal children and adults.

Ignorance. Ignorance straightforwardly constrains people's ability to make a reasonable decision. If I do not know the relevant facts, then I cannot weigh those facts. If I do not weigh those facts, then my decision cannot be based on the evidence. I might stumble on the proper decision. However, that would be luck, not wisdom. Young children rarely know the relevant facts; therefore, they are less likely than adults to make wise decisions. A child who does not know that arsenic is dangerous will not be able to rationally decide whether to drink it. A child who does not understand addiction cannot rationally decide whether to smoke.

Lack of appreciation of consequences. It is not enough that someone knows the relevant factors; she must also know and appreciate the consequences of her choices. Most young children do not grasp the consequences of smoking, of unprotected sex, or of a failure to study in school. Even if they abstractly understand these consequences – they can recite what someone else told them – they fail to appreciate either their *likelihood* or *seriousness*. That is why parents are disinclined to let children decide whether to smoke or study.

Emotional instability. Even if someone knows the facts and appreciates their significance, she may make an irrational choice if she lacks emotional strength, perseverance, or personal confidence. Even if emotional deficiencies do not bar her from making a good choice, they may stop her from executing that choice. Someone who lacks self-confidence or is emotionally fragile may be swayed at the last minute by irrelevant factors, while someone who procrastinates or gives up quickly may fail to do what she thinks she ought to do.

Temporary incapacity. Finally, if someone is temporarily incapacitated – if she is extremely angry, ill, exhausted, inebriated, or depressed – then she will be less likely both to know and act on what she judges to be reasonable.

No doubt these are obstacles to wholly rational choices. No doubt the first three deficiencies are more prevalent in children than in adults. That is why we have reason to think that children are generally less able than adults to be autonomous. However, this does not support the common belief that we can standardly treat children paternalistically, while never (or rarely) doing so to adults. Why? Even if most children are more deficient than most adults, they are not wholly deficient. Moreover, most adults are often ignorant of relevant facts; some fail to appreciate the consequences of their actions; others lack the necessary emotional stability. In short, the abilities of children relative to adults are not as great as many people suppose. Finally, it is difficult to draw a clear distinction between the unreasonable and the irrational. Without it, we cannot sustain the dramatically different ways that we treat children relative to adults.

The unreasonable and the irrational

Although we can conceptually distinguish between the two terms, we cannot conclude that unreasonableness is wholly distinct from irrationality. Irrationality is nothing more than the disposition to act unreasonably. This is apparent once we try to distinguish an irrational person from one who is rational but always makes unreasonable choices. The latter person might display a knowledge of logic; she might cite presumed reasons for her behavior. However, if she standardly made unreasonable choices, we cannot conclude she is really rational. Rationality is exhibited by what a person does.

Consider Feinberg's claim that children's cognitive disabilities are "not only inabilities to make correct inferences, but also failures of attention and memory, failures to understand communications, and even failures to *care* about a belief's grounding and implications, leading in turn to a failure to grasp its full import, or adequately to appreciate its full significance" (Feinberg 1980: 317–18). On his view, a 15-year-old is incapable of having a "full visceral appreciation of the significance of an irrevocable transaction for his future interests over the course of a lifetime." That is why we should not let him make important decisions (ibid. 325).

This sounds convincing enough. Surely we do not want children to suffer long-term damage because of their inability to grasp the significance of their decisions. Yet any way we specify this second disability will either (a) fail to justify our decision to *systematically* deny children a say in important matters, or (b) justify us in intervening in adults' lives far more often than we would countenance. For although it is doubtless true that the run-of-the-mill 15-year-old will fail to have a "full visceral appreciation of the significance of an irrevocable transaction for his future interests over the course of a lifetime," those adults among us having such an appreciation should throw the first paternalistic stone. Adults – like children – often fail to appreciate the long-term effects of our choices. To the extent that we can appreciate them, it is because we learned it by trial and error, not through a clear application of principles of reason we see clearly and children see only darkly. Consequently, although a diluted version of the claim is surely true – e.g., that the 15-year-old fails to *largely* appreciate the significance of a *difficult-to-revoke* transaction for her future interests over many years – it is equally true of the 40-year-old chain smoker and the 29-year-old helmetless cyclist. Yet if we weaken the criteria of reasonableness so that most adults are properly deemed reasonable, then we can no longer plausibly claim that many children, and certainly most older children, have substantially impaired capacities. Research indicates that at least by the age of 15, "the capacity for adolescent competence in decision-making is apparent" (Mann et al. 1989: 272).

Forcing Children to be Adults: Worries about Normative Autonomy

When pressed, most people recognize that many children beyond infancy are not wholly incapable of making rational choices. Nonetheless, they maintain that neither parents nor the state should grant children normative autonomy. These objectors fear that granting children some normative autonomy will force them to make significant personal decisions they are ill prepared to make. This is a sensible concern, especially if we are talking about a five-year-old making a complex decision with important consequences for the remainder of her life. What, though, about older children facing such decisions? As the research cited above shows, even late preteens are, in relevant cognitive and volitional respects, already reasonable and mature enough to have important, albeit perhaps defeasible, say in making significant decisions. They are more like adults than infants. Although they are less able than many adults, they are more able than others; certainly they are not wholly unreasonable.

However, let us consider a child who is admittedly less rational than most adults. Suppose Sue is an emotionally limited 12-year-old whose parents are divorcing. Does that justify automatically ignoring her wishes? Should they pretend to heed her wishes – by asking her what she wants – and then ignore what she says if they disagree? Or should her parents give her preferences about where and with whom she will live significant (even if not final) weight? I think so. For as ill-formed and ill-informed as her views may be, to refuse to heed her wishes, especially if they are strong, simply makes her a pawn of the parents. There is reason to think that even with her limited abilities, she has some sense of where her life would go best. Moreover, letting her have a say in the decision makes her more involved with, and perhaps more understanding of, the final resolution.

Doubtless there are dangers here: Sue may not want to choose; she could feel incredibly burdened by that choice. However, there is no good way to avoid these burdens. If parents ask her what she wants to do, even if they have no intention of heeding her wishes, then she could be as burdened as she would be if her decision really counted. The only way to completely avoid this burden is for the parents to steadfastly refuse to solicit or entertain her views – to tell her up front that her wishes in the matter are irrelevant. However, the stakes for her are just too high to not even hear or heed her views on the matter.

Still, there may be grounds for worry. By giving Sue some say, we may establish legal and social institutions that give children too much responsibility to determine their futures. That may well damage many other children's chances of being well prepared for life as adults. If the dangers to other children are substantial, perhaps we must sacrifice children like Sue to protect these other, already luckier, children.

However, I think we should be morally queasy about denying children in such situations a voice in determining where they live. Moreover, before buying this argument, we should be clearer about the nature of the dangers children will face if we grant them (limited) normative autonomy. Some people imply that hordes of children will scramble to sue their parents because their parents did not give them an adequate allowance or forced them to eat their spinach. However, I see no reason to think this is a serious likelihood, and even less reason to think courts would permit these children to act on their preferences.

This objection is more plausible if interpreted as a worry about the indirect costs of giving children normative autonomy. To give children autonomy is to grant them certain rights. However, if children and their parents get mired in squabbles about which rights children have, it will create an atmosphere detrimental to children. As Frances Schrag puts, this would create relationships

> . . . defined increasingly by mutual rights and obligations and that the natural affection and sympathy most parents feel for their children would be undermined. Parents would focus more and more on meeting their obligations or if not on meeting them, at least appearing to meet them in the eyes of the law. Parents would begin to practice "defensive parenting", i.e., the art of meeting the letter of the law to forestall the threat of a future suit. . . . Parents . . . would tend to see themselves more and more as sub-contractors to the state performing a definite service in exchange for pay . . . The present relationship of a competent nurse to a psychiatric patient would be the paradigm for the new relationship (1980: 246–7).

These are legitimate worries. Injecting rights talk into any intimate relationship can damage it. That is true not only of relationships between parents and children, but also between adults who are good friends, partners, or spouses (Hardwig 1984). However, adults would never consider that the appropriate way to avoid this problem is to deny that their friends, partners, or spouses are autonomous. Rather, they would find a way to understand close relationships between autonomous beings who nonetheless care about each other. Such relationships will not be guided by concern for rights, nor will partners regularly appeal to their rights. In a similar way, parents can respect their children, even as they love and care for them. They can sometimes let them choose for themselves, even when we may think their decisions are misguided (LaFollette 1996).

Additionally, Schrag's worries, though perhaps legitimate for very young children, seem wholly irrelevant when discussing some cases, for example, the fate of an older child whose parents are divorcing. Here the child finds herself in circumstances that *demand* that she make a choice. Perhaps she is not as well equipped to make as wise a decision as she will be able to later in life (let us hope she isn't). Perhaps it is unfortunate that she must make such a choice. In a different world, political, legal, and social institutions might make it easier for children to maintain regular contact with *both* parents. Nonetheless, in our world, circumstances often demand that a decision be made, and it is difficult to know why the child – whose welfare is directly and substantially affected by this decision – should not have a say. More generally, I think we can acknowledge the power of Schrag's concerns without completely denying children normative autonomy, especially if there is a better option. And there is. We can reject the common view that one either has or lacks the ability to be autonomous and that one either does or does not realize autonomy.

Rethinking Autonomy for Children

Circumscribed autonomy

Parents could control their children's decisions only if they supervised them around the clock. Even the most overprotective parents cannot do that. Whether we "permit" it or not, children do make important decisions when they are away from their parents. They decide whether to take drugs, to have sex, to tell lies, to steal, to join gangs, etc. The question is not whether parents should let them make these decisions. Children make them. The question is whether their parents have equipped them to make good decisions (the argument in this section was first developed in LaFollette 1999).

To well equip their children, parents must acknowledge their children's intellectual and volitional deficiencies. But the reason for doing so is not to have an excuse for denying their autonomy, but to help them shed these deficiencies. We must understand how children acquire knowledge, how they become more aware of the significance and relevant consequences of their actions, how to make them better able to discern and resist extraneous impulses, and to become more emotionally stable. Then we should help them develop these abilities. For, like all human abilities, they do not descend on children from heaven. They come only with practice.

Lack of practice is thus a sixth factor that undermines autonomy, a factor ignored in the standard accounts. Yet at some level everyone recognizes that the ability to make informed choices is acquired only by effort and practice. Like all skills, it is not acquired overnight. It is developed over years, by practice in the laboratory of life. As Mill puts it:

> The human faculties of perception, judgment, discriminative feeling, mental activity, and even moral preference, are exercised only in making a choice . . . The mental and moral, like the muscular powers, are improved only by being used. The faculties are called into no exercise by doing a thing merely because others do it, no more than by believing a thing only because others believe it (Mill 1978).

The lack of volitional exercise not only directly diminishes autonomy, it also intensifies the second and third deficiencies. If someone has never had to live with the consequences of her decisions, then she is unlikely to know which factors are relevant. Likewise, someone who has not made important decisions cannot really appreciate their significance. Simply hearing someone say that our decisions matter is not the same as discovering that they matter. If someone always intervenes to save us from our bad choices, then we will neither see nor appreciate the need to make wise ones.

In summary, the standard view of children's autonomy errs in two ways: One, it assumes children are less capable of making informed decisions than they are. Two, it ignores the crucial fact that the only way children can develop the ability to be autonomous, and have any hope of realizing autonomy, is by first being permitted to act on their developing ability. As Dewey aptly put it:

> A child as he grows older finds responsibilities thrust upon him. This is surely not because freedom of the will has suddenly been inserted into him, but because his assumption of them is a necessary factor in his *future* growth and movement (Dewey 1976: 195).

However, this does not require that we give infants (or even older children) complete normative autonomy. The solution: giving children circumscribed normative autonomy, in the following order.

1. *Administered autonomy.* When children are very young, they have little ability to decide, let alone make good decisions. But that is true of all skills. They are acquired by practice, ideally starting at an early age. Yet, parents and the state must be careful to protect children from their own unwise decisions. So, although parents should give very young children some prerogatives, these should be carefully administered in small doses, the way one might administer a medication. The parent tries to let her child acquire a sense of making choices and of taking responsibilities in small matters. Still, the choices are more apparent than real since the parent is always ready to step in.

   A related strategy is to give the young child certain responsibilities, and then expect the child to fulfill them: for instance, expecting the child to carry out the garbage. This can help the child to see that success or failure matters. Although this may help the child learn to assume responsibility, unless the child also has some autonomy, even if limited, she is unlikely to learn how to make wise choices, rather than simply fulfilling the demands of others.

2. *Monitored autonomy.* When children are still quite young, but after they have coped with the minimal doses of administered autonomy, the parent should give them greater choice and greater responsibility. At this stage of development parents should not parcel out autonomy in small doses. Rather they should give the children wide scope to make their own choices and assume responsibility for them: to let the child cope with the consequences of her actions. Still, the parents will loosely monitor their child's choices. They will let the child act in ways that hurt her a bit; but they are prepared to intervene if it appears the decision is dangerous or highly detrimental. They will not intervene as quickly or as often as they would in the previous stage.

3. *Minimally constrained autonomy.* As a child becomes a teen and has developed the intellectual means and emotional stability to generally make wise choices, parents must give her increasing autonomy. The parent will knowingly let the child make more serious errors than they would have at earlier stages, although they might still intervene in ways they would not intervene in the life of an adult. If the parents have brought the children through the first two stages, typically they can often simply talk with the child.

Autonomy, multiculturalism, and the culture wars

"But wait," an objector might say, "this entire argument is based on highly contentious claims about the importance of autonomy, the nature of the good society, and the nature of the family." The belief that autonomy is highly valuable already commits one to an account of the good which some people reject. The parents should educate the child for her life as an adult. They do that not by making her autonomous, but by inculcating their values in her. As Callan puts it, "Raising a child engages our deepest values and yearnings." We should not, therefore, construe "the parent's role in ways that make individual parents no more than instruments of their children's good" (Callan 1997).

Callan is surely right that parents are not mere "instruments of their children's good." Within families people's interests sometimes clash, and parents' interests should not be ignored or systematically sacrificed for their children. At the same time, children are not there just for their parents. At least sometimes – and perhaps often – the children's good is paramount. A pivotal part of that good is to prepare them for life as adults. I contend that requires enabling them to make their own decisions.

This seems to be at odds with some conceptions of the good life, notably those in which each generation gives their children "the tradition" – the conception of the good life they (the parents) have adopted. However, this isn't at odds with my proposal, or, if it is, so much the worse for this conception. Here's why. Those parents claim that (a) the state has no right to tell them how to live yet (b) they have a right to tell their children how to live. Why is this? The only faintly plausible answer is that the parents are capable of making their own choices while the children are not. This answer assumes that when a person is autonomous, others should not tell them how they live, while, if a person is not, others can so tell them. That is to acknowledge that autonomy is a significant value.

If autonomy is a value, and the best way for an adult to become autonomous is for her to have been given increasing normative autonomy while she was a child, then parents cannot instruct their child in just any way they want. They must train her to be autonomous, in part by giving her increasing normative autonomy in the ways described in the previous section.

This in no way denies that parents can instill their values in their children. They should do this. Those beliefs and values give older children a starting point from which they can entertain and judge competing ideas. Moreover, it shows the child that ideas matter. That is a crucial part of helping a child become autonomous (LaFollette 1989: 85).

David Archard does not find this argument compelling. He thinks it misstates the traditionalists' arguments.

> What the parents assert is a right to the unobstructed practice of their values. They do not claim a right to the free or autonomous choice of these values. They do not claim this because, as imagined, they do not think of their values as ones that are freely chosen. The group esteems liberty not autonomy. It is not thus inconsistent of them to demand that their children have no choice over which values they acquire. For the parents do not think of these values as autonomously chosen. However they would want their children, once adults, to be as free as they, as parents, now are to live by these values (Archard 2002: 154).

However, this approach makes sense only if (a) no lifestyle is *really* preferable to any other, or (b) the truth that one lifestyle is preferable cannot be rationally ascertained, but acquired only through proper instruction. Perhaps some people who want such wide latitude in the rearing of their children believe their own views are neither autonomously chosen nor true. However, that is not what most of them believe. Typically these people are part of a religious or ethnic community that thinks their way of life is superior to others; it is not just one option on the smorgasbord of life. That is precisely why they think they should be permitted to so instruct their children.

Yet if they think that, then consistency demands that they permit their children the latitude to choose their own lifestyle, and that requires giving them the mental wherewithal to make their own decisions when they become adults. That likely also requires giving the child exposure to some options.

The parent and the state

The earlier discussion explains why the parents rather than the state play the pivotal role in giving children normative autonomy. The child's metamorphosis from the irrational through the partly rational to the mostly rational must be overseen by a caring and proximate parent, not a distant judge. Judges may occasionally be required to intervene if the relationship between child and parents fails. In the ideal world, though, astute parents will give imperceptibly increasing normative autonomy to their increasingly able children. We have no rules telling parents precisely how much autonomy to grant, or where precisely they should give them increasing prerogatives. Parents must be attentive to the ways in which their children have behaved in the past, and be alert to what they can do to enable their children to make better decisions. Often the best way is by letting them make decisions for themselves and then to expect them to cope with the consequences. Still, the state plays an important role. It can encourage and even teach parents how to empower their children to become autonomous adults. It can do so directly by placing expectations on parents. It can do so indirectly by respecting the adult's autonomy. That shows the adult just how important autonomy really is.

Of course, there is no denying the potential dangers of granting children too much normative autonomy too quickly. However, there are still greater dangers to children, and to society, if we do not let children be autonomous in degrees. Although there is no formula for walking this child-rearing line, that is not a sign of sloppy parental thinking, but a faithful rendering of the confusing psychological facts and fuzzy moral boundary between the unreasonable and the irrational. There is no easy way to decide precisely what a child's abilities are or of deciding precisely just how able a child must be before we consider them *able enough*.

Implications for Physician-assisted Suicide

Both the ability to be autonomous and realized autonomy are matters of degree. That undercuts several common objections to physician-assisted suicide. As we saw in the previous chapter, some objectors claim that people who are dying cannot make autonomous choices when they are in pain, anxious, and depressed. Pain and suffering do skew a person's judgment, sometimes sufficiently so that we might discount her stated preferences. Some dying people may feel pressured to end their own lives: we should protect them from that pressure.

However, this argument proceeds too quickly. No one ever fully realizes their autonomy. Besides, someone does not need to realize her autonomy before we grant her normative autonomy. So the fact that someone is in pain and depressed does not automatically show that we can legitimately ignore her dying wishes. We must ask: "Is she autonomous *enough*?" We cannot say precisely just how autonomous that would be. What we do know is that our criteria cannot be so demanding that adults are regularly judged to be irrational and therefore subject to paternalism. Any plausible criteria will surely hold that many dying people are rational enough to make informed decisions about the ends of their lives, decisions we should respect – especially if, prior to becoming ill, they clearly stated their preferences about how they should be treated when they are dying.

The critic of PAS might claim, though, that this approach ignores the seriousness of the decision. When the decision is a matter of life and death, we should demand compelling evidence that the person is acting rationally and without undue pressure. I suppose ideally that might be nice. However, the importance of this decision also gives us reason to not place the bar too high. We should be leery of forcing people to stay alive against their express wishes merely because they do not reach some impossibly high standard of realized autonomy. The costs are monumental if we use these considerations to bar all physician-assisted suicides.

REFERENCES

Archard, D. (2002) "Children, Multiculturalism, and Education." In D. Archard and C. MacLeod (eds.), *The Moral and Political Status of Children*. Oxford: Oxford University Press, 142–59.

Callan, E. (1997) *Creating Citizens: Political Education and Liberal Democracy*. Oxford: Clarendon Press.

Christman, J. (2003) "Autonomy in Moral and Political Philosophy." *Stanford Encyclopedia of Philosophy*. (Online) Available at: http://plato.stanford.edu/entries/autonomy-moral/. (Accessed August 6, 2003.)

Dewey, J. (1976) *The Middle Works, 1899–1924*. Carbondale, IL: Southern Illinois University Press.

Dewey, J. (1994) *The Moral Writings of John Dewey*, rev. edn. Amherst, NY: Prometheus Books.

Feinberg, J. (1980) "The Child's Right to an Open Future." In W. Aiken and H. LaFollette (eds.), *Whose Child? Children's Rights, State Power, and Parental Authority*. Totowa, NJ: Rowman & Littlefield, 124–53.

Hardwig, J. (1984) "Should Women Think in Terms of Rights?" *Ethics* 91: 441–5.

Husak, D. N. (1994) "Is Drunk Driving a Serious Offense?" *Philosophy and Public Affairs* 23: 52–73.

Husak, D. N. (2002) *Legalize This! The Case for Decriminalizing Drugs*. New York: Verso.

LaFollette, H. (1989) "Freedom of Religion and Children," *Public Affairs Quarterly* 3: 75–87.

LaFollette, H. (1996) *Personal Relationships: Love, Identity, and Morality*. Oxford: Blackwell Publishers.

LaFollette, H. (1999) "Circumscribed Autonomy: Children, Care, and Custody." In J. Bartkowiak and U. Narayan (eds.), *Having and Raising Children*. State College, PA: Penn State University Press, 212–37.

Mann, L., Harmoni, R., and Power, C. (1989) "Adolescent Decision-Making: The Development of Competence," *Journal of Adolescence* 12: 265–78.

Mill, J. S. (1978) *On Liberty*. Indianapolis, IN: Hackett.

Mill, J. S. (1985/1885) *On Liberty*. Indianapolis, IN: Hackett.

Purdy, L. (1992) *In Their Best Interests? The Case against Equal Rights for Children*. Ithaca, NY: Cornell University Press.

Schrag, F. (1980) "Children: Their Rights and Needs." In W. Aiken and H. LaFollette (eds.), *Whose Child? Children's Rights, Parental Authority, and State Power*. Totowa, NJ: Rowman & Littlefield, 237–53.

ELEVEN

Punishment

In the early chapters of the book we discussed capital punishment. We tend to think that issue is exhausted by debates about the value of life and whether it deters potential murders. Those are surely important aspects of the issue. They do not exhaust it. Capital punishment is just one form of punishment. Therefore, we cannot know if it is justified until we know whether the institution of punishment is justified. After all, the criminal justice system treats people in ways that, if unjustified, would be criminal. When we imprison people, we capture them against their will and restrain them; were punishment not justified, we would be guilty of kidnapping. When we fine people, we take their money against their will; were punishment not justified, we would be guilty of theft. When we execute criminals, we kill them against their will; were the death penalty not justified, we would be guilty of murder. Moreover, when we investigate crimes we interrogate people, we search their houses and cars, tap their phones, check their confidential bank records, follow them, and may imprison them while they await trial. Were these practices not justified, we would be trespassing, invading people's privacy, harassing them, and kidnapping them.

We conveniently forget these facts. We should not. We need to justify not only (a) the institution of punishment but also (b) our decisions to make certain actions criminal, (c) the forms of punishment we employ, and (d) our procedures for investigating crimes and determining guilt. Unless we do, we commit the very crimes that we claim merit punishment.

Three Theories

Most justifications of punishment are either forward looking or backward looking. Forward-looking theories hold that we can justify punishment only by its results, especially whether it decreases crime and increases public safety. Backward-looking theories hold that we can justify punishment only after looking at the past, by seeing what the perpetrators have done. Communicative theories attempt to blend forward- and backward-looking elements into a single theory – although some of its advocates think the theory is primarily forward looking (Braithwaite and Pettit 1990), while others argue that such a theory is primarily backward looking (Duff 2001).

The contrast between the first two broad types of theory tracks the distinction between consequentialist and deontological moral theories. Forward-looking theories of punishment are consequentialist, while backward-looking theories are deontological. Many objections critics raise to forward-looking theories of punishment are species of more general criticisms of consequentialist theories, while many objections critics raise to backward-looking theories of punishment are instances of more general criticisms of deontological theories.

Forward-looking theories

There are several variations of forward-looking theories, with deterrence theories being the most common.

Deterrence

Deterrence theorists claim that we punish criminals to lessen crime and promote public safety. We threaten punishment to dissuade people from engaging in criminal behavior. We punish criminals so that people considering crime will see that our threats are serious (general deterrence), and that individuals we punish will not revert to criminal behavior upon their release (special deterrence).

It is easy to see why deterrence is a popular theory of punishment. The theory is based on five widely held beliefs – three moral and two empirical. The moral claims are that (a) we are justified in establishing and enforcing laws that promote public safety, that (b) we are justified in promoting public safety by lessening crime, and that (c) we are justified in harming people to lessen crime. The empirical claims are that punishment is (d) a necessary and (e) on its own an effective means of lessening crime. All these claims seem plausible. Most people just take it for granted that the institution of punishment is justified. Deterrence seems like an excellent justification for the practice.

There are two further forward-looking aims of punishment. These are not full-blown theories; rather, they are used to justify particular forms of punishment.

Incapacitation

Over the last two decades, American officials have taken heightened interest in the use of incapacitation to lessen crime. While deterrence aims to lower crime and enhance public safety by stopping people (the convict and others) from committing crimes in the future, incapacitation seeks to lessen crime and elevate safety *now* by getting and keeping felons off the street. Given the plausible belief that a few people are responsible for a preponderance of crime, the rationale of this approach is clear. We will lessen crime if we keep repeat offenders off the street.

Rehabilitation

Like incapacitation, rehabilitation is more about how to punish than whether to punish. Its central claim is that if someone is going to be punished, then it is better to rehabilitate them, since that will (1) lessen crime and (2) make former criminals more productive members of society. This claim seems plausible if, as incapacitation theory asserts, a few people commit most crimes. Although its principal aims are forward looking, some versions contain retributive elements. To better understand these elements we will first discuss the most common backward-looking theories.

Backward-looking theories

Most backward-looking theories are retributivist, although some rehabilitative theories also contain backward-looking assumptions.

Retribution

These theories always include the negative claim that we should punish only the guilty. However, since most theories hold this, what commonly defines them are two positive claims: that we *should* punish the guilty, and that the punishment should fit the crime.

Like deterrence, retributivism is an appealing theory. It reflects our common belief that we should reward or punish people according to their behavior, according to what they deserve (Rachels 2002/1997). We generally think that the best runner should win the race, that the most qualified person should get the raise or the promotion, and a benevolent person should be praised. We also think that the slouch should not get the job, that the fool should not be elected, and that the scoundrel should be condemned. If we import these beliefs into our criminal punishment system, the implications are clear: that the criminal (and not the innocent person) should be punished, and that her punishment should fit, or be proportional to, her crime.

It is not enough that the person commits the crime. She must do so voluntarily. If the person could not have avoided committing the crime, then she did not act voluntarily; if she did not act voluntarily, then she cannot be responsible for what she did. If a bridge on which I am walking collapses, and my body falls on a passerby and kills him, *I* did not kill him and cannot properly be charged with murder. Likewise, if I lack the appropriate mental capacity to appreciate what I am doing, then *I* (as an agent) did not do it, and I cannot deserve punishment (or praise). We do not blame or punish either a four-year-old or a *severely* retarded person. Since they lack the mental ability to fully understand what they have done, then although we might choose to incapacitate them on grounds of public safety, we cannot justifiably punish or blame them.

Rehabilitation

Rehabilitation is primarily a forward-looking theory since its aim is to lessen crime and make former criminals productive members of society. Nonetheless, it standardly also includes retributivist elements. Many of these theorists think criminals should get what they deserve; that is determined by what they voluntarily do. However, these theorists also believe that many criminals pursue crime because of environmental factors largely beyond their control. Therefore, the responsibility for their actions is somewhat mitigated. Although it is appropriate to punish them since they are partly to blame, we should punish them in ways that recognize and seek to correct their deficiencies. In rehabilitating them we seek to make criminals more responsible, and thus less likely to commit future crimes.

Blended theories

As we will see, there are serious objections to both pure consequentialist and pure deontological theories of punishment. That has led some theorists to blend the theories: to find a way to incorporate their best, and avoid their most objectionable, elements. Most of these are communicative or expressive theories (Duff 2001; Feinberg 1994/1970).

Communicative (or expressive or paternalistic) theories of punishment are less familiar than the first two. Communicative theories provide a comprehensive justification for punishment by blending significant features of retribution, deterrence, and rehabilitation – but with important twists. The core idea is that through punishment the community communicates to the offender its condemnation of her behavior. This theory includes a retributive element since it insists that punishment must be based on the criminal's own wrongdoing: the criminal is censured because she flouts the community's values. It also includes consequential elements since a crucial aim of communication is to make the offender, and others, less likely to commit crime. Finally, it includes rehabilitative elements inasmuch as punishment seeks to have "the person censured accept the censure as justified" (Duff 2003: 345). If they accept the censure, they will be less likely to commit future crimes.

Of course, since communicative theories embrace elements of each major theory, they reject others. Since two of its aims are to promote safety and change the criminal's propensity for future crime, it is at odds with pure backward-looking theories; since one of its aims is to give criminals what they deserve, then it is at odds with pure forward-looking theories.

Although these are best seen as blended theories, some advocates from each side have tried to show that, despite appearances, communicative theories really are best thought to be pure forward-looking theories (Braithwaite and Pettit 1990) or pure backward-looking theories (Duff 2003: 342–4). Whether either position can make good on this claim is another matter. However, neither claim is preposterous. That fits with an earlier observation: we can often make the same theoretical point in different ways.

Assessing the Theories

All the theories are somewhat plausible. The question is whether any can justify punishment on its own; if not, is there any way to blend them? If so, how? In this section I will discuss some difficulties with each theory.

Forward-looking theories

Although the moral and empirical elements undergirding forward-looking theories are plausible, when stated unqualifiedly each is vulnerable to criticism.

Value judgments

A central aim of government is to protect its citizens. But that is not its only aim. If the state acts as if it were – as it sometimes does – it will sacrifice other valuable aims. We could lessen crime by installing closed-circuit televisions in everyone's home and randomly strip-searching pedestrians. However, these actions would seriously diminish people's privacy; we would likely come to fear the state more than we now fear the common criminal. We could lessen petty theft by publicly beheading thieves. However, we think that penalty is grossly disproportionate to the severity of the crime.

In short, although deterrence is important, it is not enough. We must consider other effects of punishment. Unfortunately, although we recognize this·in the abstract, we often forget it in the concrete. After terrorists flew commercial airliners into the World Trade Center and the Pentagon in the fall of 2001, Congress passed the so-called Patriot Act, almost without objection. Although protecting ourselves from terrorism is surely important, it does not exhaust the state's legitimate concerns. The Patriot Act widely expanded police powers in ways that seriously invade people's privacy. Within a year of its passage, the majority of Americans began to object to some features of that act.

As I noted in Chapter 2, this is a common problem of all forward-looking reasoning – whether prudential or moral. We often draw our ends too narrowly. In employing consequentialist reasoning, we consider only select ends; in achieving them, we set back others. We often do this in prudential reasoning when we focus on an immediate end, say, having a tasty meal, to the detriment of other long-term ends, say, maintaining a healthy weight. Or we may focus on one long-term end (getting a promotion) and ignore others (our families or our health). We have a similar tendency in political and moral reasoning: we focus on one legitimate end (obtaining cheap power) at the cost of long-term ends (having renewable resources, a healthy environment, and a sound ecology). We do something similar in our criminal justice system. In our quest to protect ourselves from criminals we often don't worry about punishing the innocent or punishing the guilty excessively.

The second value claim – that we are justified in promoting public safety by limiting crime – seems uncontentious until we see that behind this innocent-looking claim is the debatable assumption that limiting (street) crime invariably promotes public safety. Although it surely promotes safety in some respects, it may diminish it in others, for instance, by vastly increasing police powers.

The third value claim – that we are justified in harming people as a way of lessening crime – is debatable on its face. It holds that we can cause harm to prevent harm. That claim may be true, but it needs defense.

Empirical claims

Deterrence theory seems to assume that people choose to commit crimes only after calculating the costs and benefits of alternative actions. The state threatens punishment to change those costs and benefits, and, therefore, to change individuals' judgment about the most desirable alternative. This makes citizens less likely to commit crime.

On this model people are fully informed and wholly rational: they always (a) know the costs and benefits of available actions, (b) correctly weigh those costs and benefits, and then (c) choose the action with the best likely outcome. All three assumptions are false; even weaker versions of them are dubious. No one is fully informed of the available outcomes; many people are nearly oblivious. Second, even when we know the available outcomes, we are often bad at judging their relative likelihoods. Third, even when we "know" the outcomes and their likelihoods, we sometimes fail to act on what we know. We know that it is bad for us to smoke, to drink excessively, to eat poorly, and to be a couch potato. Yet that does not stop many of us from smoking, getting sloshed, eating junk food, and failing to exercise.

In short, no one always decides what to do based on a careful calculation of costs and benefits. Most do not do it regularly. In deciding whether to watch a movie, to make love, to eat dinner, or to talk with a friend, we rarely consciously calculate the costs and benefits of action. We do not; we could not; and we should not. If we tried to make conscious choices about everything we did, we would be immobilized. If nothing else, we just do not have the time (for a vivid example in medicine, see Gawande 2002: 228–52). Human behavior is not consciously directed in the way this model of punishment presupposes. As we have seen before, behavior is more habitual than most philosophical accounts grant.

If ordinary people do not regularly make decisions in these ways, criminals are even less likely to do so. Criminals tend to be poorer, less well educated, and have less self-control than non-criminals. So they are more likely to make unreasonable judgments and less likely to act on their judgments even when they do know what is best – especially since most criminals assume they will not be caught, or, if caught, not convicted, and, if convicted, not punished. We have even less reason to think the threat of punishment regularly deters spontaneous crimes or crimes of passion. That is why those whom the state most needs to deter are least likely to be deterred by the threat of punishment.

This is the case at least on standard renditions of deterrence theory. However, deterrence theory need not hold that the threat of punishment deters crime only consciously. It can also deter subconsciously, indirectly. When society becomes aware of the seriousness of an offense, it often increases criminal penalties against it. In so doing the society signals to its citizens that the crime is especially serious. Potential criminals may be deterred, then, not so much by the threat of increased punishment as by their awareness of society's disapproval. Here's one example. Alcohol-related fatal traffic accidents declined by 8 percent from 1993 to 1998 despite an increase in the number of miles driven (Greenfield and Henneberg 2001: 29). Why? Primarily because people's patterns of drinking changed. Not so many years ago, many people did not balk at driving home from a bar tipsy – if not completely sloshed. In contrast, more people now go to bars or parties only if they have a designated driver, and they are more careful not to leave the bar or party drunk. More people offer rides to inebriated friends. Bars may call cabs for drunk customers. Why did this behavior change? I think the best explanation is an increased awareness of, concern about, and social disapproval of, drunk driving. Increased social disapproval of drunk driving works unconsciously: it shapes people's habits and dispositions. It leads more people to be careful not to drive while under the influence. It shapes people's behavior by influencing what they will even consider doing. True, the laws have gotten tougher, and it would be silly to claim that has not made any difference. However, it seems more likely that social disapproval explains both the changes in behavior and the increased punishments than to think that the punishments, by themselves, changed people's drinking behavior. If this explanation is plausible, then deterrence might still work even if it does not work directly.

Armchair considerations, then, do not give us decisive reasons to think that punishments do deter. We must consult the empirical literature. And the literature is clear. According to criminologists, "not a single meta-analytic review of the research literature has found that deterrence-based interventions reduce recidivism" (Wright and Cullen 2006). (For references to those 12 meta-analyses, see the Wright and Cullen article.)

An argument that any purely forward-looking theory cannot work

The previous discussion isolates several worries about any purely forward-looking theory of punishment. As these theories are ordinarily articulated, they seem to depend on "facts" about human rationality, deliberation, and motivation that are dubious. However, the most serious criticisms of them are moral criticisms. As we saw in Chapter 2, any pure forward-looking (consequentialist) theory seems to countenance injustice. If the only aim of punishment is to produce the most desirable results, then it appears we could sometimes appropriately punish innocent people and that we could punish guilty ones more (or less) severely than they deserve.

Consequentialists respond that such actions would rarely – and perhaps never – be justified if one considers all relevant consequences. The retributivist would retort that even if a consequentialist would never, in fact, countenance such behavior, she cannot accurately explain why these behaviors are wrong. Consequentialism would bar injustice because it so happens that it does not promote the best ends. However, the proper explanation, the retributivist claims, is simply that it is unjust. It is akin to giving a stellar student an A *because she agreed with me*, rather than *because she deserved it*. It would be the right result for the wrong reason.

Finally, even if consequentialism would not countenance punishing the innocent, it punishes the guilty to make people safer. And, that, some have argued, is still to treat people as a mere means to public safety (J. G. Murphy 1994/1973: 48–9). As Hegel put it: it is akin "to the act of a man who lifts his stick to a dog. It is to treat a man like a dog instead of with the freedom and respect due to him as a man" (1967/1821: 246). These criticisms show, so the objection goes, that deterrence cannot by itself justify the practice of punishment.

However, Kant does not forbid treating people as a means, but only treating them as a mere means. It is not clear why punishing guilty people to deter crime must treat them as *mere* means. Many public practices treat people as means, yet we not only tolerate them, we think they are justified. The government requires all citizens to pay taxes to raise money for government services. The government does not thereby treat taxpayers as a mere means to this public good. If the process treats people respectfully (that is, if it does not demean them), and the process serves legitimate social aims (by providing police protection, education, roads, etc.), then it does not treat them as mere means.

Something similar happens when training surgeons. Surgeons must have not only information but certain physical skills. A surgeon cannot learn to take blood, put in a central line, or acquire a new technique for bypass surgery except by taking blood, putting in central lines, and doing bypass surgery. In doing so, she will make some mistakes. Patients are means whereby physicians acquire these skills. Is this morally objectionable? I think not. There is no other way for physicians to gain these skills. Besides, most people know – or could know – that when they go to a teaching hospital, they may be treated by a novice. They choose such hospitals because those doctors teaching the aspiring physicians are tops in their respective fields (Gawande 2002).

Even accomplished surgeons must regularly acquire new surgical techniques; at least they must do so if they want to give their patients the best care. The first patients on whom they use the new techniques may suffer or even die; later patients will benefit. Gawande illustrates this point by describing a new procedure on babies with "a severe heart defect, known as transposition of the great arteries" (2002: 27). There was a standard and reliable procedure that could prolong children's lives into their early twenties. It was eventually replaced by a procedure that promised to lengthen the life of such children substantially, with fewer fatalities. However, refining the procedure required first using it on 70 babies, of whom one-fourth immediately died – compared to 6 percent who would have died had the doctors used the old procedure. Then the benefits of the new technique began to appear: the number of deaths declined far below the rate of the old procedure.

To put it crudely, 19 percent of these first 70 babies died as a means to the doctors' refining the procedure. Should we then mount a Hegelian objection against this practice of medicine? No. Although its consequences justified the change in the procedure, the babies were not being used as *mere* means to that end. The doctors tried to save the babies, and the children they saved would live longer. Moreover, the doctors informed (or should have informed) the parents about both procedures.

It seems we can apply similar reasoning to criminal punishment. We can use punishment to achieve an important social good, while still treating criminals with the appropriate respect. Whether we do treat them with respect is determined not by whether we are consequentialists or retributivists, but by the ways that the law, the officers of the court, and the prisons treat them.

Perhaps this is a suitable response. We cannot decide here. What we will do is now examine backward-looking theories.

Backward-looking theories

Retribution, the most common backward-looking theory, is based on the idea that people deserve to be punished. Not just any punishment will do. The punishment should be neither too lax (a literal slap on the wrist for multiple murders) nor too stern (beheading someone for jaywalking). The punishment should be proportional to (fit) the crime. A common interpretation of the retributivist ideal is expressed in the biblical adage, "an eye for an eye."

If we take this literally, then our most common punishments (imprisonment and fines) would "fit" only the crimes of kidnapping and robbery. Therefore, that cannot be what *lex talionis* means. "Proportionality" must mean something different. Von Hirsch offers one promising account of what it means (1994: 128–9). He does not speak of a punishment as strictly fitting the crime. Rather he specifies three ways that punishments can be proportional to the crime, and to other punishments:

- *parity*: similar offenses deserve similar punishments;
- *rank-ordering*: more serious crimes should be treated more seriously;
- *spacing*: more serious crimes should be punished much more seriously.

Exactly what this means in concrete cases will be highly debatable. Nonetheless, I find this account sufficiently precise to broadly explain what it means to make the punishment appropriate to the crime. Inasmuch as most people's views about punishment would include these elements, then they are features any adequate theory must accommodate, or else it must show why, contrary to first appearances, they should not be jettisoned.

Nonetheless, there is an important ambiguity here. As stated, the principle does not specify which element of "the crime" should fit the punishment. The law requires two elements for criminal guilt: the person must not only do the proscribed behavior (the *actus reus*), she must have a certain mental state (the *mens rea*) (Gross 1979: 4–5, 48–9, 74–6). Sometimes a person may meet one of these requirements but not the other. If someone does a criminal action (killing someone, taking their property, etc.) but lacks a guilty mind (they may not be doing it intentionally and they may not be culpably negligent), then she has not committed a crime. Or if someone has a guilty mind (wants to kill someone, take their property, etc.), but does not do the criminal action, then she also does not commit a crime. In less dramatic cases, a person may have both elements, but in significantly different proportions: the person may do an especially heinous act with a partly guilty mind or a mildly bad deed with malicious intent.

Does the principle specify that the punishment should be proportional to the *actus reus* or to the *mens rea*? When someone commits a seriously wrong behavior with a fully guilty mind, this distinction effectively disappears. In other cases it is crucial. A punishment that fits the act might not be proportional to the character of the criminal's mind, while a punishment that fits (is proportional to) the criminal's mind, might be disproportionate (either too stringent or too lax) to the criminal act. So how should we punish these people? To know, we must get clearer about what it means to have a guilty mind, and, to use the language from the previous chapter, what it means to be responsible for one's behavior.

Intention, character, and choice

We have seen these issues before. In the first chapter we discussed conditions that might excuse or mitigate a person's responsibility for a capital crime. The same factors can excuse or mitigate a person's responsibility for any crime. To better understand what those factors might be, we can import some lessons from our discussion of autonomy. For whatever else it means to have a guilty mind, the guilty person must at least be able to be autonomous.

In the previous chapter we identified five factors than can diminish a person's autonomy, and thus, diminish her responsibility for action: (1) an inability to mentally process information, (2) ignorance of relevant factors, (3) insufficient understanding of the implications of one's actions for the future, (4) emotional instability, and (5) temporary incapacity. Each disability, if severe enough, would be grounds for completely excusing someone of criminal responsibility; if less severe it would just attenuate her responsibility. For example, someone who is *severely* retarded could not have a guilty mind, and thus, cannot be responsible for her actions, while if she were only mildly retarded, we might think she was responsible, even if not wholly so. In the former case, the courts would likely consign her to a mental institution, in the same way that we might forcibly quarantine the carrier of a highly infectious disease. In the latter case we would punish her, albeit less severely than we would have had she been normal. The problem, of course, is knowing where to draw the line between a disability that mitigates responsibility and one that eliminates it (Austin 1979; Feinberg 1970/1968; J. G. Murphy 1994/1973). I will not pursue this issue further here. However, I have no reason to think that retributivists cannot provide an account of excusing and mitigating conditions. Nor do I see why they will have more trouble doing so than other theorists; all theories will need such an account. A deterrence theorist, for example, must know whether a criminal's action is voluntary, for if a person is incapable of judging rationally, then she cannot be deterred.

In short, although this is an important issue, it is not a serious problem for pure retributivism. However, I do think that theory faces some insurmountable problems.

An argument against pure retributivism

In its negative form, retributivism is a central element of any defensible account of punishment. In explaining why we should punish James rather than Joan, the answer must be because James, rather than Joan, committed some crime. However, determining whom to punish is not the only moral question. Although retributivism seems especially suited to deciding whether we should punish some particular person, there are five elements of our justice system that it cannot explain: (1) the institution of punishment as a whole; (2) the investigation and prosecution of crimes; (3) hospitalizing seriously retarded or seriously mentally ill criminals; (4) assessing punitive damages in civil trials; and (5) passing laws defining what is criminal. Let me explain each.

We did not establish the institution of punishment because we wanted a mechanism for giving people what they deserve (Dolinko 1991: 542–3). We established it to protect society, to prevent harm. If Dolinko is right, is there a way to salvage the central insights of retributivism? Hart (1968: 9–11) and Rawls (2002/1997) think so. We need only distinguish between the purpose of the institution (to protect people from harm) and the justification for punishing particular individuals (that they committed the crime). As Waldron puts it:

> The ideas of guilt, innocence and punishment cannot feature in the first principles ⟨justifying the practice of punishment⟩, though, of course, once the first principles are in place and the idea of punishment has been justified, then they may be used in any statement of moral principle that sums up the gist of the whole (Waldron 1992: 28).

As developed, this argument does not show that retributivism plays no role in the account of punishment. The theory still plays a role once we have established the institution of punishment, but less of a role, I think, than Hart and Rawls realized. It is not enough to justify the institution and decisions about whom, specifically, we should punish. We must also justify the practices of police and prosecutors: investigating people, watching them, checking their bank records, tapping their phones, and interrogating them. And we must justify charging and detaining people while we determine their guilt or innocence.

Pure retributivism cannot justify any of these critical elements of the criminal justice system. Retributivism claims we are justified in punishing people if and only if they deserve to be punished. There is nothing within the theory that even addresses the treatment of people before the determination of guilt (Kant 2002/1785: 36). Until we have determined a person's guilt, she does not deserve to be punished; hence, we have no reason to think she deserves being scrutinized, having her privacy invaded, or imprisoning her before trial. If retributivism were the sole justification for punishment, then we would not be justified in treating suspected criminals in this way. I suppose a retributivist might claim that once we have determined an individual's guilt, then we could retrospectively justify our intrusion into her life. However, this cannot justify those intrusions when they occurred. When she was investigated, interrogated, detained, and tried, the powers that be did not know she was guilty, at least not by any appropriate legal standard. Even if this argument worked for those who are eventually convicted, it won't work for those who are investigated, charged, or tried, but not convicted. This is not to say that these intrusions cannot be justified. I think they can be. Just not in retributive terms. However, if we must use non-retributive considerations to justify these practices, as well as the whole institution of punishment, then why assume that pure retributivism is sufficient to determine whom we should punish, and how severely? It seems consequentialist arguments play a far greater role than even Rawls and Hart thought. Retributivism's inability to explain still other legal practices further strengthens this conclusion.

Retributivism is also unable to explain the practice of incapacitating people who commit crimes when they are insane or mentally deficient. The theory tells us only that we should not punish them. It does not tell us that we can legitimately restrain them against their will. Consequentialism seems better equipped to explain this: we restrain them to promote public safety. I assume the retributivist will not disagree. However, if treating incapacitated people in these ways is permissible and for these reasons it is unclear why punishing normal adults in these ways and for these reasons is categorically wrong.

Neither can retributivism explain the use of *punitive* fines in civil trials. Although civil trials differ from criminal trials (since the defendant cannot receive prison time), some of these include a punitive element. Suppose a company has discharged an untreated and toxic chemical into the local groundwater. Five years later ten local children are diagnosed with leukemia. If the company's actions caused the cancers, then courts will award the children (and their families) significant monetary damages. Typically these are compensatory damages to remunerate the child and the family for their physical and emotional damage. If the courts also determine that the company knowingly endangered citizens – or was even grossly negligent – then the jury can also award punitive damages to the plaintiff. Since these are punitive awards, it seems they should be justified in the same way that we justify criminal punishments.

However, punitive damages – as they are given now – could not be justified on purely retributive grounds. If punitive awards were based solely on the nature of the wrong, then two companies who engaged in the same behavior would have to pay the same punitive damages. They are not. A small company might have to pay a $1 million fine, while an international conglomerate might have to pay $50 million. This is grotesquely unfair on purely retributive grounds. However, giving the same awards would undercut the central rationale for punitive awards, namely, to deter other companies tempted to engage in similar behavior. Assessing a $1 million penalty against the small company would arguably be a strong deterrent to them and to other similarly sized companies. However, it would not faze a global conglomerate. If the fine is going to deter them or other similarly sized companies, their fine must be much larger. While most people think this is appropriate, the pure retributivist must demur. Certainly it is unclear how they might try to account for this phenomenon in wholly retributive terms.

There is one last important problem facing retributivists. Any system of criminal justice will inevitably punish some innocent people. We can avoid this possibility only by not having a system. This is a serious moral difficulty for all theorists. It is a special problem for the retributivist. For if the *only* justification for punishing someone for a crime is that she is guilty (really guilty – and not just "found" guilty), then retributivism cannot countenance any system that punishes some innocent people. Since all systems will occasionally punish the innocent, retributivism cannot justify punishment. Even if they could find some way to permit such a system, it would hurt their case since it would undermine perhaps their strongest objection to consequentialism: that it justifies punishing the innocent. The only way they might avoid this last objection is to claim that while the consequentialist would justify intentionally punishing the innocent, the retributivist would not. Punishing the innocent would be *only* a foreseen but unintended consequence of the system. Whether this response is adequate will depend upon the adequacy of the purported moral distinction between what we intend to do and what we merely foresee. We will have more to say about that distinction in Chapter 17.

Given these problems, a modified Rawls/Hart position appears to be more defensible than pure retributivism – or even Rawls's and Hart's original proposal. On this modified view we justify the criminal justice system as a necessary means of promoting public safety. Then we make the obvious point that the system cannot achieve those valuable aims without a mechanism for identifying and convicting criminals, including a system to investigate, interrogate, detain, and try those we think committed a crime. Neither can we protect the public unless the state has the authority to incarcerate dangerous people, even if they are not legally responsible for their actions. Finally, even the best system will occasionally punish the innocent. But since public safety is vitally important, then everyone – even those innocently convicted – can at least understand the reasoning for the practice. Retributivism, however, can neither explain nor countenance these elements of our criminal justice system.

Summation: Fate of pure deontological and consequentialist theories

In discussions throughout the book, we have seen that both unqualified deontological and consequentialist theories are subject to telling criticisms. Each seems tenable only if supplemented. We see this again in discussing punishment. Neither retributive (deontological) nor deterrence (consequentialist) theories are wholly adequate. Perhaps the best solution is not to choose one, but to find an alternative that accommodates the insights of – and avoids the problems of – both.

Communicative theories

A communicative or expressive theory is an attempt to blend forward- and backward-looking elements, although different communicative theorists emphasize one element over the other (Braithwaite and Pettit 1990; Duff 2001, 2003). We communicate our displeasure to criminals but not to trees in our backyards. Why? The deontologically oriented communicative theory claims we do that "because the tree is not an autonomous object, and, hence, does not deserve our censure." In contrast, a consequentialistically inclined communicative theorist will claim that we do not communicate our displeasure to a tree because it is a waste of time. The tree cannot alter its behavior. Which answer is preferable? Perhaps we need not choose. After all, the notion of autonomy applies only to creatures who are able to change their behavior in reaction to the censure of, or threats of punishment by, others. This suggests that the gap between the two standard theories may not be all that great; that in some respects, at least, they are two different ways of making the same point. This is not an issue I can resolve here. Before we leave this topic, I want to address one issue that has been lurking in the background of many of these discussions: How does being in an unjust society alter our justifications for punishment?

Can We Have Just Punishment in an Unjust Society?

In our discussion of racism, we saw that our society is unjust in significant ways. This is not to condemn our society; others are much worse. Although that may be some consolation, it does not excuse our unwillingness to change our system. We should try to be better than we are.

This is a problem that worries both deontologists and consequentialists (Morris 1994/1981; Tonry 1994/1993). They worry whether it is just (or efficacious) to punish people who, because of poverty, bad homes, and inadequate education, have severely limited opportunities. Those of us who have been relatively privileged may not understand the predicament of the disadvantaged. Yet were we in their shoes, we might conclude that crime is a wise strategy, or at least not a silly one. Minimally we should accept some responsibility for creating and sustaining conditions that make crime more likely (J. Murphy 2002/1997: 480).

That has led some to suggest that the best way to lower crime is to remove inclinations to crime, rather than punishing crime after it occurs. John Q. Wilson disagrees.

> The hope, widespread in the 1960s, that job creation and job training programmes would solve many social problems, including crime, led to countless efforts both to prevent crime by supplying jobs to crime-prone young and to reduce crime among convicted offenders by supplying them with better job opportunities upon their release from prison.

What those who propose such efforts fail to realize is that removing incentives to crime is not fundamentally different than punishing people to discourage crime.

> Deterrence and job-creation are not different crime fighting strategies, they are two sides of the same strategy. The former emphasizes (and tries to increase) the costs of

crime; the latter emphasizes (and tries to increase) the benefits of non-crime. Both depend on the assumption that we are dealing with reasonably rational persons who respond to incentives (Wilson 1994/1983: 184).

Although these strategies are flip sides of the same motivational coin, they do not work equally well. Attempts to remove incentives to crime have generally failed (Wilson 1994/1983:198, 200), while we now know that "it is possible to lower the crime rate by increasing the certainty of sanctions . . ." (ibid. 204).

There is something right about Wilson's claim. However, he goes far beyond the evidence when he claims that this shows that we should exert more effort to insure swift punishments than to remove incentives to crime. There are four problems with his inference. One, the evidence he cites is not about the severity of punishments, but about their certainty. However, there is no attractive way to increase the certainty of punishment since criminals are rarely caught, charged, prosecuted, and convicted. The only way to solve this problem is to allow the police to substantially intrude into our lives. That, I think, is unacceptable.

Two, as we saw earlier, there is no empirical evidence that punishing people with the sole aim of deterring others works (Wright and Cullen 2006).

Three, the extent to which his claim is true depends largely on the individual's starting point. Someone who has a decent education, a good job, and a satisfying family life generally has little to gain from crime and a great deal to lose. Conversely, someone who is unemployed, poorly educated, and generally has a less than satisfying life could have much to gain from crime.

Four, Wilson is likely wrong that punishment and reward are two sides of the same coin. Punishment aims to stop particular behavior. Even when it succeeds, it often redirects the undesirable behavior to another behavior that is often as bad, or even worse. In contrast, since positive reinforcement (reward) aims to encourage socially desirable behavior, e.g., being gainfully employed, there is no bad behavior to be displaced (Skinner 1953). If Skinner is right, then criminal punishment occasionally encourages antisocial behavior, while opening opportunities for disadvantaged citizens makes them less inclined to resort to crime by changing what they think it is reasonable to do.

Finally, whether a person pursues crime is largely a matter of habit. It is not merely that the person with a good education and a good job has incentives to continue living a (generally) law-abiding life – which is true enough; she has no real inclination to commit a felony. Most of us would never even consider knocking off a liquor store. Other people not only do not have incentives to be law-abiding, they are habitually disposed to consider crime.

The proper conclusion, then, is not that efforts to change crime by changing social conditions are futile. Nor is the conclusion that punishment serves no legitimate social purpose. Rather, we should understand that these are problems that we cannot solve overnight. We must use every tool in our possession. We should both increase options and employ punishments.

As Dewey so eloquently summed it up:

Courses of action which put the blame exclusively on a person as if his evil were the sole cause of wrong-doing and those which condone offense on account of the share of social conditions in producing bad dispositions, are equally ways of making unreal separations of man and his surroundings, mind from the world . . . By killing an evil-doer or shutting him up behind stone walls, we are able to forget both him and our part in creating him. Society excuses itself by laying blame on the criminal; he retorts by putting the blame on early bad surroundings, the temptation of others, the lack of opportunities, and the persecutions of officers of the law. Both are right, except in the wholesale nature of their recriminations . . . No amount of guilt on the part of the evil-doer absolves us from the responsibility for the consequences on him and others of our way of treating him, or from our continuing responsibility for the conditions under which persons develop perverse habits (Dewey 1988/1922: 20–1).

In the following chapter we explore the issue of gun control. That issue obviously has deep connections to the issue of punishment since (a) many crimes are committed with guns, and (b) the main way we control the use of guns is through the criminal law. We will also get a better understanding of the importance of risk, which we briefly discussed in the chapter on slippery slope arguments. Finally, we will get our first look at the language of rights.

REFERENCES

Austin, J. L. (1979) "A Plea for Excuses." In *Philosophical Papers*, 3rd edn. Oxford: Oxford University Press, 175–204.

Braithwaite, J. and Pettit, P. (1990) *Not Just Deserts: A Republican Theory of Criminal Justice*. Oxford: Oxford University Press.

Dewey, J. (1988/1922) *Human Nature and Conduct*. Carbondale, IL: Southern Illinois University Press.

Dolinko, D. (1991) "Some Thoughts About Retributivism," *Ethics* 101: 537–59.

Duff, R. A. (2001) *Punishment, Communication, and Community*. Oxford: Oxford University Press.

Duff, R. A. (2003) "Punishment." In H. LaFollette (ed.), *Oxford Handbook of Practical Ethics*. Oxford: Oxford University Press, 331–57.

Feinberg, J. (1970/1968) "What's So Special About Mental Illness." In J. Feinberg (ed.), *Doing and Deserving: Essays on Responsibility*. Princeton, NJ: Princeton University Press, 272–92.

Feinberg, J. (1994/1970) "The Expressive Function of Punishment." In R. A. Duff and D. Garland (eds.), *A Reader on Punishment*. Oxford: Oxford University Press, 92–111.

Gawande, A. (2002) *Complications: A Surgeon's Notes on an Imperfect Science*. New York: Henry Holt.

Greenfield, L. A. and Henneberg, M. A. (2001) "Victim and Offender Self-Reports of Alcohol Involvement in Crime," *Alcohol Research and Health* 25 (1): 20–31. (Online) Available at: http://www.niaaa.nih.gov/publications/arh25–1/20–31.pdf. (Accessed August 10, 2005.)

Gross, H. (1979) *A Theory of Criminal Justice*. New York: Oxford University Press.

Hart, H. L. A. (1968) *Punishment and Responsibility: Essays in the Philosophy of Law*. Oxford: Clarendon Press.

Hegel, G. W. F. (1967/1821) *Philosophy of Right.* New York: Oxford University Press.

Hudson, B. (1987) *Justice through Punishment.* Basingstoke: Macmillan.

Kant, I. (2002/1785) *Groundwork for the Metaphysics of Morals.* Oxford: Oxford University Press.

Morris, H. (1994/1981) "A Paternalistic Theory of Punishment." In R. A. Duff and D. Garland (eds.), *A Reader on Punishment.* Oxford: Oxford University Press, 92–111.

Murphy, J. (2002/1997) "Repentance and Punishment." In H. LaFollette (ed.), *Ethics in Practice: An Anthology*, 2nd edn. Oxford: Blackwell Publishers, 475–80.

Murphy, J. G. (1994/1973) "Marxism and Retributivism." In R. A. Duff and D. Garland (eds.), *A Reader on Punishment.* Oxford: Oxford University Press, 44–70.

Rachels, J. (2002/1997) "Punishment and Desert." In H. LaFollette (ed.), *Ethics in Practice: An Anthology*, 2nd edn. Oxford: Blackwell Publishers, 466–74.

Rawls, J. (2002/1997) "Two Concepts of Rules." In H. LaFollette (ed.), *Ethics in Practice: An Anthology*. Oxford: Oxford University Press, 480–86.

Skinner, B. F. (1953) *Science and Human Behavior.* New York: Macmillan.

Tonry, M. (1994/1993) "Proportionality, Parsimony, and Interchangeability of Punishments." In R. A. Duff and D. Garland (eds.), *A Reader on Punishment.* Oxford: Oxford University Press, 112–60.

von Hirsch, A. (1994) "Censure and Proportionality." In R. A. Duff and D. Garland (eds.), *A Reader on Punishment.* Oxford: Oxford University Press, 112–60.

Waldron, J. (1992) "Lex Talionis," *Arizona Law Review* 34: 25–51.

Wilson, J. Q. (1994/1983) "Penalties and Opportunities." In R. A. Duff and D. Garland (eds.), *A Reader on Punishment.* Oxford: Oxford University Press, 174–209.

Wright, J. P., Cullen, F. T., and Beaver, D. M. (2007) "Does Punishment Work?" In H. LaFollette (ed.), *Ethics in Practice*, 3rd edn. Oxford: Blackwell Publishers, 531–542.

TWELVE

Gun Control

Many of us assume we must either oppose or support gun control. Not so. We have a range of alternatives. Even this way of speaking oversimplifies our choices since there are two distinct scales on which to place alternatives. One scale concerns the degree (if at all) to which guns should be abolished. This scale moves from those who want no abolition (NA) of any guns, through those who want moderate abolition (MA) – to forbid access to some subclasses of guns – to those who want absolute abolition (AA). The second scale concerns the restrictions (if any) on those guns that are available to private citizens. This scale moves from those who want absolute restrictions (AR) through those who want moderate restrictions (MR) to those who want no restrictions (NR) at all. Restrictions vary not only in strength but also in content. We could restrict who owns guns, how they obtain them, where and how they store them, and where and how they can carry them.

Our options are further complicated by the union of these scales. On one extreme no private citizen can own any guns (AA, which is functionally equivalent to AR), while at the other extreme, every private citizen can own any gun, with no restrictions (NA + NR). But once we leave those extremes, which few people hold, the options are defined by a pair of coordinates along these distinct scales. While most people embrace positions on the "same" end of both scales, others embrace more exotic mixtures: some will want few weapons available to private citizens, but virtually no restrictions on those guns that are available (MA + NR), while others may prefer making most guns available, but want to seriously restrict them (NA + MR).

So our choice is not merely to support or oppose gun control, but to decide *who* can own *which* guns, under *what conditions*. Although I cannot pretend to provide a definitive account here, I can isolate the central issues and offer the broad outline of an appropriate solution. To simplify discussion, I adopt the following locutions: those opposed to most abolition and most restrictions advocate a "serious right to bear arms," while those supporting more widespread abolition and more substantial restrictions are "gun control advocates." This simplification masks significant disagreements among advocates of each position. However, it does let us better see the issues at stake.

Justifying Private Ownership of Guns

A moral question

Do citizens have a "serious right to bear arms"? This is a moral question, not a constitutional one. For even if the Constitution did grant this right, we should determine if there are sufficiently compelling arguments against private gun ownership to warrant changing the Constitution. On the other hand, if this were not a constitutional right, we should determine if there are strong reasons why the state should not ban or control guns, and if these reasons are sufficiently compelling to make this a constitutional right. Most defenders of private gun ownership claim we have a moral right – as well as a constitutional one – and that this right is not an ordinary right, but a fundamental one.

A fundamental right

If they are correct, they would have the justificatory upper hand. Were this a fundamental right, it would not be enough to show that society would benefit from controlling access to guns (Hughes and Hunt 2000). The arguments for gun control would have to be overwhelming. Yet there is also a hefty cost in claiming that this is a fundamental right: the evidence for the right must meet especially rigorous standards.

What makes a right fundamental? A fundamental right is a non-derivative right protecting a *fundamental* interest. Not every interest we individually cherish is fundamental. Since most interests are prized by someone, such a notion of "fundamental interest" would be anemic, serving no special justificatory role. Fundamental interests are special: they are integrally related to a person's chance of living a good life, *whatever her particular interests, desires, and beliefs happen to be*. For example, living in a society that protects speech creates an environment within which each of us can pursue our particular interests, goals, needs, and development, whatever our interests happen to be. Is the purported right to bear arms like this paradigmatic fundamental right?

Even if it were, that would not straightforwardly establish that it is impermissible to abolish or restrict private ownership of guns. After all, fundamental rights standardly have conditions, boundaries, or restrictions on them. Some rights, like the right to vote, are *conditional* upon reaching a specified age, and they can be *forfeited* by emigrants and imprisoned felons. Additionally, most right tokens can be *restricted* or *overridden* when the exercise of that right harms others. For example, my right to free religious expression gives me wide discretion in how I exercise my religion. I can remove my kids from high school and exclude them from selected school activities (*Wisconsin v. Yoder*, 406 U.S. 205 [1972]; *Moody v. Cronin*, 484 F. Supp. 270 [1979]). I can sacrifice animals (*Church of the Lukumi Babalu Aye v. City of Hialeah*, 508 U.S. 520 [1993]). Nonetheless, it does not permit me to sacrifice humans. Nor does my right to free speech permit me to slander someone or to preach outside her window at 2:00 a.m.

Of course rights would not be worth much if they were straightforwardly subject to the wishes of the majority. We fiercely defend fundamental right types although their tokens sometimes undercut society's interests. We cannot restrict or put conditions on fundamental rights except for compelling reasons, and individuals cannot forfeit their fundamental rights (if they can forfeit them at all) except for overwhelming reasons. Still, although tokens of a right sometimes run counter to the majority's wishes (Dworkin 1977), we should not infer that rights – especially fundamental rights – standardly undermine the public interest. Freedom of speech and freedom of association benefit society as well as individuals. These are the best – and arguably the only – way for society to discover the truth (Mill 1985/1885). Of course, not every right has such a significant social payoff – although most fundamental rights do. Still, we generally assume fundamental rights (right types) do not harm society.

This provides a framework for evaluating people's claims that a right is fundamental. Advocates must show that and how granting the right protects individuals' fundamental interests, and they must be prepared to respond to objections that granting that right type will harm society. These are serious obstacles for gun advocates. It is difficult to see that a serious right to bear arms satisfies either of these requirements, let alone both.

First, I see no compelling reason to think that owning a gun is a fundamental interest. Other fundamental interests are necessary to one's flourishing no matter what one's particular desires, interests, and beliefs. It is difficult to see how this is true of guns. Moreover, the interests protected by paradigmatic fundamental rights – our interests in unfettered speech, freedom of religion, and freedom of association – are not merely means to my flourishing, they are elements constituting it. By contrast, having a gun in my bed stand, in my closet, or on my person might be a means for me to achieve my ends, but they are not constitutive elements of my flourishing. Hence, owning guns is not a fundamental interest.

Wheeler disagrees. He argues that the right to bear arms is fundamental since guns are the best way to protect our fundamental interest in self-defense (1997). Even on his view, guns are not inherently valuable; they are valuable only as a means of self-defense (ibid. 433–8). I fail to see how this could make the right to bear arms fundamental. Not every means to a fundamental interest is a fundamental right. That would arguably make most actions protected by fundamental rights. Nonetheless, the connection between owning guns and self-defense is sufficiently important that I will address it later.

Others might claim that gun ownership is an essential element for the flourishing of a proper citizen. A proper citizen, on this view, is one capable of providing for and defending his family. Although each citizen can (generally) fend for himself, citizens come together to form a limited government to provide those few needs they cannot easily satisfy on their own. However, this vision of the citizen is very controversial, more controversial than the interest in gun ownership it seeks to justify. It assumes each of us has far more control over our lives than we arguably do have. Furthermore, even if this conception were defensible, it would not establish a

fundamental right to bear arms since guns are mere means to independent citizenship; they are not constitutive of that citizenship. Hence, it is doubtful that the purported right to bear arms satisfies the first requirement of a fundamental right.

Second, we have evidence that granting this right type does harm society. If this
evidence is at all credible, then granting this purported right would not satisfy the
second requirement either.

But this does not resolve the issue. Although people do not have a fundamental
right to own guns, gun control might be wrong because it violates some derivative
right or simply because it is bad public policy.

A derivative right

Suppose we determined that "the right to bear arms" is not a fundamental right, but
a derivative right. This would still be a significant finding since derivative rights, like
fundamental ones, cannot be restricted without good reason. *Prima facie*, I think we
have such a derivative right. Each of us has a fundamental right of non-interference:
we should be allowed to live our lives as we wish, so long as we do not thereby harm
others. This is a right each of us needs, no matter what our particular interests. That
general right derivatively protects personally important activities.

For instance, I would be furious if the state forbade me from sharing a pint with
a friend. Nonetheless, although consuming alcohol is a particular interest and enjoyment I have, it is not a constitutive element of the good life in the way that the free-
doms of speech, press, and association are. That is why I do not have a fundamental
right to consume alcohol. Consequently, the conditions under which my consumption of alcohol can be legitimately restricted are more lax than they would be if the
activity were a fundamental interest.

Nonetheless, since I have a *prima facie* derivative right to consume alcohol, the
state can legitimately abolish or restrict alcohol consumption only if they can show
that so doing is an effective means of protecting the public from harm. They can do
that in some cases: people who consume substantial amounts of alcohol are dangerous drivers. Since this behavior is unacceptably risky to others, the state can legitimately restrict drinking while driving. Whether privately owning guns is similarly
risky is something we must discover.

Bad public policy

If private gun ownership were not a derivative right, it might still be bad policy to
substantially restrict or abolish guns. There are always costs of enforcing a law. Sometimes these costs are prohibitive, especially when the public does not support that
law. If the public will not voluntarily comply with the law, then the state must try to
force compliance. In its efforts to do so, it invariably employs excessively intrusive
methods. Such methods never entirely succeed, and, to the extent that they do, they
undermine public confidence in and support for all law. Consider America's experience with Prohibition. Although one of Prohibition's aims — to protect innocents

from harm caused by those under the influence — was laudable, the law was unen-
forceable and excessively costly. Consequently, less than two decades after Prohibition was passed via Constitutional amendment, it was repealed.

The cost of enforcing any law — and especially an unpopular law — weighs against
making any behavior illegal unless we have solid evidence that the behavior is seriously harmful. If we adopt a weaker standard — if we criminalize every action type
whose tokens occasionally lead to some harm — then we would criminalize most
behavior. Consequently, even if there were no right to bear arms, we should still not
seek to substantially limit private ownership of guns unless we have good reason to
think that will prevent serious harm.

Summing up: justifying the private ownership of guns

The preceding analysis isolates three questions we must answer in deciding whether
people should be permitted to own guns: (1) How important is owning a gun to
some people? (2) What are the consequences of private gun ownership? (3) Is abol-
ishing or restricting private ownership of guns bad policy? Although gun ownership
is not a fundamental interest, many people want to own guns and think they have
good reason to do so. That is sufficient to show that serious gun control would undermine gun owners' interests. Moreover, there is some reason to think that serious gun
control in countries with a strong tradition of gun ownership would be bad policy.
Therefore, we should certainly not abolish, and arguably should not restrict, private
ownership of guns without good reason. Are there good reasons? To answer this question, we must determine the effects of private gun ownership: (a) how likely is it
that private gun ownership seriously harms others?; (b) are there substantial benefits of gun ownership that might counterbalance any harm?

Harm, Danger, and Risk

We must be careful when we say that guns cause harm. Guns kill people because
agents use them to kill people (or misuse them in ways that cause people to be killed).
As the National Rifle Association (NRA) puts it: "Guns don't kill people, people do."
In one sense their claim is uncontroversial: murder is the act of an agent, and guns
are not agents. In another way, the claim is irrelevant. No gun control advocate
claims, hints, or suggests that guns are moral agents. Guns are objects and objects
do no evil. But not all objects are created equal. Imagine the NNWA (National
Nuclear Weapons Association) claiming, "Tactical nuclear weapons don't kill people,
people do." In one sense their claim would be true. In a more profound way, it would
be ludicrous.

Of course guns are not nuclear weapons. Guns are not as dangerous as nuclear
weapons and some guns have seemingly legitimate uses. The question is whether the
character of guns makes them especially harmful. We know that tactical nuclear

weapons, biochemical weapons, live grenades, etc., are much more dangerous than feathers, ice cream, and butter knives. Where do guns fall along this continuum?

There are two distinct but related questions: (1) are guns "inherently dangerous"?; and (2) what is the empirical probability that they cause serious harm? "Inherently dangerous" objects are those whose nature or design is sufficient to justify our prediction that they will cause harm, independently of any empirical evidence. We do not need double-blind empirical studies to know that nuclear weapons are inherently dangerous: they were designed to cause harm, and their nature is such that we can confidently predict they will cause harm. The two questions are intricately related since inherently dangerous objects are more likely to cause serious harm. Yet they are separable because some dangerous objects are not inherently so. Automobiles, alcohol, and cigarettes were not designed to cause harm, but all are causally implicated in many people's deaths. Other things being equal, we are more prone to control inherently dangerous objects than objects that harm others as an unwanted side effect.

Guns, unlike autos, are inherently dangerous. Guns were invented for the military; they were designed to cause (and threaten) harm (Singer et al. 1956). The same aims determine the ways that guns are redesigned: they are changed to make them more efficient at causing harm. In contrast, a significant aim of redesigning automobiles is to make them less dangerous. To some extent these efforts have succeeded. Although the absolute number of annual traffic fatalities has not noticeably declined, the number of fatalities per mile traveled has declined 75 percent since the 1950s (Hemenway 1995). We have enhanced the auto's original aim of efficient transportation while lessening harmful side effects. That is why we can sensibly say that the automobile is not inherently dangerous despite the fact that it causes harm. We cannot say the same for guns.

The literature of gun advocates supports my contention that guns are inherently dangerous. They advocate the private ownership of guns to prevent crime and to arm the militia. Guns can serve these purposes only because they are effective means of inflicting and threatening harm. Even guns normally not used to harm humans have purposes that ride piggy-back on this fundamental purpose. Shotguns are used to kill animals, and target guns are designed to be especially accurate. Taken together, this evidence supports the common view that guns are inherently dangerous. That is why we have special reasons to regulate them.

Although inherently dangerous, guns are far less dangerous than weapons of mass destruction, and they do have seemingly legitimate uses. That is why we must see how risky they are before we can legitimately abolish or seriously restrict them. We must also determine if they have sufficient benefits so that we should permit them, even if they are risky.

An intermediate conclusion

We have shown that owning guns is not a fundamental interest and that guns are inherently dangerous. That is why we cannot categorically dismiss all forms of gun control. However, this is a weak conclusion, for although guns are inherently dangerous, they may not be so dangerous as to justify more than a system of minimal registration. What seems clear is that their inherent dangerousness precludes the idea that guns cannot be subject to governmental control. Before determining the actual danger that guns present, we should first determine how risky an action must be before we can justifiably restrict it.

Risk

Humans are notoriously bad at judging risk. Often we are unaware of, or are inattentive to, the seriousness of risks: we may drive inebriated. At other times we overestimate the risks: we may refuse to fly because we think it is too dangerous. A proper determination of risk would be based on a careful accounting of the action's costs and benefits. We should determine (1) the probability of harm, (2) the seriousness of harm (the product of the gravity and extent of the harm), (3) the probability of achieving the benefits, (4) the significance of the benefits (the product of the importance and extent of the benefit), and then act accordingly. Of course, even if we reached the same determination to the above questions, we might still disagree about whether to act: we might disagree about what risks are worth which benefits. Nonetheless, we can all agree that (a) as the likelihood and seriousness of harm increase, we have increased reason to refrain from acting, while (b) as the likelihood and importance of the benefits increase, we have increased reasons to act. We can import these lessons into the law.

Legal rules

But not straightforwardly. The issue is not whether we should own guns if they are legal, although that is a fascinating question. The question is whether the state should curtail private gun ownership. The foregoing considerations are relevant but not decisive. The decision to permit private ownership of guns is shaped by two factors pulling in opposite directions. First, even if we think Roger (an adult) stupidly engages in a dangerous activity (sky diving or boxing or racing), we might think Roger's autonomy requires that we permit it. Our commitment to individual liberty weighs against the government's abolishing or restricting the private ownership of guns as a way of limiting harm (Hughes and Hunt 2000). Second, some actions (smoking in public places) that are acceptably risky to Roger might be unacceptably risky to others. Are guns unacceptably risky to others?

Put differently, gun control does not concern what private individuals should do, but what governments should allow private individuals to do. We must determine the risk of permitting the private ownership of guns, constrained by these complicating considerations. To illustrate how this might work, consider the following example. We have evidence that a number of wrecks are caused by drivers using cell phones. Roger wants to use his cell phone while commuting to work. He decides the inconvenience of not using the cell phone is worse than the small probability of personal harm. He might overestimate the inconvenience of not being able to use his cell phone or insufficiently appreciate the seriousness of the risk. However, since he is an adult, we might think we should not interfere with his decision to use a cell phone while driving. That is what autonomy requires. Yet Roger is not the only person at risk. Passengers in his or others' cars may also be harmed. The seriousness of harm to them must also be considered in deciding to permit or restrict drivers' use of cell phones.

These judgments of risk must be further tempered by the costs of enforcement mentioned earlier. Although we know that using cell phones while driving may lead to accidents, we also know other activities may do the same – drinking coffee while driving, eating a donut, looking at a map, talking to a passenger, driving more than two hours without stopping, driving on less than six hours of sleep, driving home after a bad day at the office. Presumably we should not make all these illegal. The probabilities of serious harm are small and enforcing such laws would require far-reaching intrusions into everyone's life. However, as the probability of serious and widespread harm increases, then, other things being equal, we should criminalize the action.

For instance, when people are released from prison (and not just on parole) they have "paid their debt to society." Yet we do not permit them to own a gun. We judge that they are more likely to harm others. Of course not all of them – and likely not a majority of them – would harm others if they were permitted to own a gun. They are prevented from owning guns because they are members of a group statistically more likely to cause harm: we judge that allowing former felons to own guns is unacceptably risky. The National Rifle Association and most other gun advocates agree.

Someone might counter, though, that we deny felons the right to own guns not because we judge that permitting them to own guns is risky, but that they, by their actions, have *forfeited* the right to own guns. However, that is not the best justification for our action. Why should felons forfeit their right after they have served their time and are free of all obligations to the state? For instance, while imprisoned in the United States, felons do forfeit their right against unlawful searches and seizures. But once they are released from prison (and are no longer on parole or probation), a former felon has an unconditional right against unlawful searches and seizures – the same as every other United States resident.

At first glance, there is some reason to think felons who use guns in commission of a crime could forfeit their right to own a gun, in the same way that drunk drivers lose their licenses. However, drunk drivers do not lose their licenses forever, while in most jurisdictions felons are *never* permitted to own guns. Moreover the prohibition against former felons' owning guns is not limited to those who used guns in the commission of a crime. Hence, it is more plausible to think that we can prevent released felons from owning guns because we judge that they are more likely to commit crimes with guns.

This is our rationale for all laws proscribing risky actions. Every drunk driver does not cause an accident. Most do not. Yet we do not flinch at laws forbidding drunk driving. For it is not merely that drunk drivers are statistically more likely to cause harm, they are more likely to cause harm because they are inebriated. We can arguably use the same rationale to justify restricting access to guns. We restrict access not only because guns are inherently dangerous, but because – if gun control advocates are right – permitting private ownership of guns is very risky.

What we need to know

We can now specify what we must know to intelligently decide whether to prohibit or restrict gun ownership (or any other risky action). (1) Is there a statistically significant correlation between the action (private ownership of guns) and harm (homicides, accidental deaths, suicides, armed robbery)? (2) Do we have good reason to think this correlation indicates that the purportedly risky action causes the harm? (3) How serious are these resultant harms? (4) How important is the activity that the state wishes to control (a) to the individual agent and (b) to the society?

In deciding whether to restrict the behavior, we must balance these considerations using the following general guidelines:

1.   If we have evidence that the behavior causes harm, then we have some reason to limit the behavior. As the evidence increases, the reasons for prohibiting the behavior increase. As the probability that the behavior will lead to harm (the product of the gravity and extent of the harm) approaches certainly, then the reasons for forbidding the behavior become very strong.
2.   The more grave and widespread the potential harm, the more reason we have to constrain the behavior. If the gravity and extent of the harm are substantial, we might constrain the behavior even if our evidence that the behavior causes harm is moderate.
3.   The higher the probability that allowing the action will have important benefits, the stronger the reason to permit it. The greater the benefits, the greater the reason to permit it.

Libertarians might claim that individuals' rights are so strong that the state cannot justifiably intervene, even to constrain those who put others at extreme risk. The state should not proscribe risky actions, although they can intervene after harm has occurred. This use of "risk" is misleading. If on one occasion I drive while inebriated, I engage in a risky action: there is some probability that I – and others – will be harmed. However, permitting people to drive inebriated will definitely cause harm, although we cannot specify in advance who will be harmed. A personal decision to own a gun is risky in the former sense. A decision to permit citizens to privately own guns is – depending on the evidence – risky in the latter sense. If gun control advocates are right about the evidence, then we have good grounds to constrain private gun use. The question is: are they right?

Assessing the Evidence

Armchair arguments

Debates over gun control typically begin, and sometimes end, with armchair arguments. Both sides offer armchair explanations of why (and how) the presence (or

absence) of guns will increase (or decrease) violent crime. It is tempting to categorically dismiss armchair arguments since they seem to be poor substitutes for
empirical evidence. However, we cannot devise sound empirical studies nor understand their results without armchair arguments. In a study to discover if widespread
availability of guns increases homicides or decreases crimes, we need armchair arguments to tell us which variables we should control (e.g., Lott 1998: 21–4). Without
them we would not know that we should control for the extent of poverty, the incidence of drug use, increases in the number of police officers, or the introduction of
tougher (or more lax) penalties. Without them we would not know that we do not
need to control for the price of mayonnaise, the criminal's eye color, or who won
the last World Series.

Armchair arguments also take center stage in evaluating empirical studies, in criticizing experimental design, and in reinterpreting the reported findings (Black and
Nagin 1998; Cook et al. 1995; Cook et al. 1997; Hemenway 1997b, 1998; Lott
1998; Wheeler 1997). So before I discuss the empirical evidence, I summarize some
significant armchair arguments employed by gun advocates and gun control advocates.

More weapons, more violence

Gun control supporters offer empirical evidence of a positive correlation between
murder rates and the availability of guns (especially handguns). Availability of guns
is also positively correlated with suicide and accident rates. This empirical evidence
is best understood against the background of the following armchair argument: (1)
Guns (and especially handguns) are the easiest way to kill others or oneself. People
can stand at a relatively safe distance and pull the trigger. (2) When people are angry,
they act in ways they do not normally act. They may strike out at others. If they have
a gun close to hand, they are more likely to use that gun. Although they could resort
to a knife or a baseball bat, they are less likely to do so, and, even if they do, those
weapons are less likely to cause a serious or fatal injury. (3) When people are
depressed, they act in ways they would not act normally. If they have a gun close to
hand, they are more likely to kill themselves. Although they might slit their wrists
or take pills, they are less likely to do so, and, even if they do, they are less likely to
kill themselves. (4) When people handle guns, even for a legitimate purpose, the
probability of serious or fatal injury to themselves or others increases. When children have access to guns, the likelihood of an accident increases still more.

The conclusion of the armchair argument is clear: the more widely available
guns are, the more people will be murdered, will commit suicide, and will die
of accidents. This is a plausible armchair prediction. Perhaps it is wrong. Maybe it
is reasonable but overinflated. Or it might be that the prediction is well founded,
but that the widespread availability of guns is nonetheless justified. What is apparent
is that the claim that widespread availability of guns increases the number of homicides, suicides, and accidental deaths is highly plausible. It is difficult to imagine it
is false.

Availability of guns prevents or stops crimes

Pro-gun supporters offer empirical evidence supporting the claim that guns prevent crime; their armchair arguments undergird and explain those studies. The motivating idea is simple: most criminals want to minimize their risks when committing a crime. If they know that someone in a house is armed, they will be less likely to enter that house, at least when the person is home and awake. Potential criminals are also less likely to assault or rob someone whom they believe is carrying a weapon. Finally, when criminals try to rob or assault an armed person, the person is more likely to foil the crime. This, too, is a plausible armchair prediction. Perhaps it is wrong. Maybe the claim is overinflated. Perhaps guns have these benefits, but there are other effects of owning guns – e.g., those mentioned above – which outweigh them. What is apparent is that the claim that the widespread availability of guns would prevent or thwart some crimes is highly plausible. It is difficult to imagine that it is false.

Of course, we cannot stop with these armchair arguments. We must assess the empirical evidence.

The data

The empirical evidence is difficult to assess, and, to the extent that we can, it does not univocally support either side. You might not know that from listening to the public policy debate. Some gun control advocates imply that strict gun laws would all but eliminate murder, while some gun advocates imply that having a gun in every home would virtually end crime. Both claims are unfounded. Gun control will not virtually eliminate murder; arming all citizens will not virtually eliminate crime – about that we can be confident. The problem is determining the precise effects of permitting or restricting guns. The available evidence is strong, but not overwhelming.

The connection between availability of guns and murder

There is a positive correlation between murder rates and the availability of guns (especially handguns). The more widely available guns (especially handguns) are, the more people are murdered. The figures are duplicated time and again in country after country. Here is the bottom line: "the correlation between any-gun prevalence and the overall murder rate is .67, while it is .84 between handgun prevalence and overall murder rate . . ."(Carter 1997: 3). These figures are significant to the .01 level; that is, the chance that these correlations could occur merely by chance is less than one out of 100. This correlation meets the statisticians' gold standard.

But this does not resolve the issue, for it does not establish what gun control advocates claim it shows, namely, that gun control is an effective way of substantially lessening the murder rate. First, a statistical correlation shows that two things are linked, but it does not tell us if the first caused the second, the second caused the first, or if there is some third factor which caused both. Second, even if the items are causally related, we do not know that changing the cause will automatically and straightforwardly change the effect since another factor might intervene to sustain the effect.

Gun advocates proffer their own armchair explanation for the correlations: these correlations reflect the character of the respective social and political systems. European countries are more racially homogeneous and socially cohesive than the United States. Although I doubt these points explain all the correlation, I am confident they explain some of it. Were the United States to regulate guns as tightly as most European countries, our murder rates would arguably fall, but they would not immediately plummet to European levels.

We might be able to finally settle the issue if we conducted controlled experiments, randomly dividing our population in half, giving half of them guns, removing all the guns from the other half, and then monitoring the murder rate. Of course, that would be morally unacceptable, politically unrealistic, and probably even scientifically unachievable. Before we had enough time to exclude all possible intervening causes, sufficient time might have elapsed so that new intervening causes could have emerged. But we are not in the dark. We have empirical evidence that helps adjudicate between competing explanations of the correlation.

First, we have empirical evidence, bolstered by armchair arguments, that guns are more lethal than other weapons. Some claim the ratio is 5 : 1; no estimates are lower than 2 : 1 (Reiss and Roth 1993: 260). This partly explains the strong correlation between guns and homicides. When people harm others out of anger, those using the most lethal weapons are more likely to kill their victims.

Second, the nature of secondary gun markets helps explain how the widespread availability of guns increases crime in general, and homicides in specific. Various opponents of gun control claim that, "If we outlaw guns, only outlaws will have guns." Armchair arguments suggest why this is a silly claim. Where, one might ask, do criminals get their guns? They often steal them or buy them from those who purchased them legally. Even guns obtained from other criminals are usually traceable to people who purchased them legally. Empirical evidence supports this armchair supposition. Most criminals report having stolen their guns, received them from a friend or family member, or purchased them from someone who had stolen it. At least half a million guns are stolen each year (Cook et al. 1995: 81), and these swell the numbers of guns available illegally.

Not only does the primary (legal) market affect the availability of guns on secondary (illegal) markets, it also affects the price of guns on those markets, much "like the analogous markets for motor vehicles or prescription drugs" (ibid. 71). As we restrict availability of guns in the primary market, the supply of guns in the secondary markets decreases and their cost increases (ibid. 73). Since teenagers are least able to afford hefty prices, this will diminish their ability to obtain guns. Since teenagers commit most deadly crimes, decreasing the availability of legal guns will indirectly decrease the number of homicides. Conversely, having huge numbers of legally available guns increases the number of guns on secondary markets and typically lowers their price. This makes it easier for prospective criminals, including teenagers, to obtain guns.

The evidence of the connection between gun availability and homicide rates is not limited to the United States. A study that compared the 26 most developed nations of the world "shows a highly significant correlation between total homicide rates and both proxies for gun availability" (Hemenway and Miller 2000: 3). There are, of course, always worries about comparisons across countries since countries may collect and categorize the data in different ways. Nonetheless, this comparison is plausible since, by comparing developed countries with each other, we lessen the chance that differential economic and social conditions caused the different death rates. Moreover, this data squares with the Carter data given earlier, and with other studies (Baker 1985; Brill 1977; Krug et al. 1998; Reiss and Roth 1993).

Other costs of owning guns

Many costs of gun ownership fall especially heavily on young children. A comparison of the rates of homicides, suicides, and accidental deaths among 5- to 14-year-olds in 25 of the most prosperous countries in the world showed that US children are 17 times more likely to be killed by a gun (and six times more likely to be killed by any means), twice as likely to commit suicide (and ten times more likely to do so with a gun), nine times more likely to die of an accidental gunshot wound (Centers for Disease Control 1997; Hemenway and Miller 2000). This finding squares with a meta-analysis of all available studies (Hemenway and Miller 1999: 73).

Finally, we should not forget the enormous personal and financial costs of *non-fatal* gunshot injuries. According to the most recent study, the costs of "treating all gunshot injuries in 1994 was $2.3 billion. Of these costs, we estimate that $1.1 billion was paid by government" (Cook et al. 1999: 553).

These are all significant costs. But they are not the only relevant considerations.

The use of guns to prevent crime

Gun advocates claim that having (and perhaps carrying) a gun prevents crime. As I noted earlier, this is a sensible armchair claim. Someone contemplating a robbery is more likely to proceed if she thinks she can succeed with little risk to herself. If a prospective robber believes the tenants are at home and have a gun they know how to use, then she is more likely to seek another target. Two surveys support this belief. According to one survey, 4 percent of all Americans have used a handgun in the past five years to avert a crime. Given those figures, researchers estimate that there are at least 600,000 defensive uses of guns per year. Kleck uses these results, in conjunction with another survey, to claim that the number might be as high as 2.5 million (Kleck 1991: 105–6). Given the number of violent crimes using guns, "the best evidence indicates that guns are used about as often for defensive purposes as for criminal purposes" (ibid. 107). If true, that is a powerful reason to resist attempts to limit availability of guns (Kleck 1997). Such statistics, particularly when bolstered by

moving anecdotes of those who have saved their lives by having a gun, cannot be cavalierly dismissed by gun control advocates.

However, these figures are inflated, likely dramatically so. First, Kleck's methodology is questionable. Surveys have an inherent tendency to overestimate rare events.
Kleck made his estimates based on phone interviews with people in 5,000 dwelling
units. One percent of those units claimed to have used a gun defensively in the past
year. Kleck inferred from these responses that there are 2.5 million defensive
handgun uses per year. However, since this inference is based on an affirmative answer
by one person out of a hundred, that means for every chance for a false negative
(someone who falsely denies using a gun defensively) there are ninety-nine chances
for a false positive (someone who falsely claims to have used a gun defensively)
(Hemenway 1997b). The probability that this or some other bias skews the findings
is substantial.

Second, Kleck's findings are inconsistent with findings by the National Crime Victimization Survey (NCVS) (US Department of Justice 1996), which interviewed far
more people, and interviewed them more regularly. Kleck's estimates even clash with
the NCVS findings on the incidence and circumstances of robberies (which seems
less subject to reporting bias). If Kleck's figures were correct, then "Kleck asks us to
believe that burglary victims in gun owning households use their guns in self-defense
more than 100% of the time, even though most were initially asleep" (Hemenway
1997a: 1442). For other criticisms of his study see Alba and Messner (1995).

Finally, if there were 2.5 million defensive gun uses each year, how many of those
were necessary? Given the negative results of private gun ownership, gun advocates
should show not only that guns deter crime, but that they are the *best* way of doing
so. Some people plausibly claim that owning a dog is an effective deterrent. Presumably having an alarm and a "neighborhood watch" are also deterrents. If true,
then some number of people who used a gun defensively could have achieved the
same results without the accompanying danger. In summary, there is no doubt that
guns deter some crime and stop the completion of other crimes. Just not in the
numbers that Kleck claims.

John Lott supplements Kleck's argument by claiming that the widespread use of
concealed weapons would decrease the annual number of homicides by 1,400, rapes
by 4,200, aggravated assaults by 60,000, and robberies by 12,000 (Lott 1998: 54).
If true, and if there were no countervailing costs, this would be a powerful reason
not only to permit guns but to encourage people to have and carry them. However,
Lott's conclusions have also come under severe criticism.

> The central problem is that crime moves in waves, yet Lott's analysis does not include
> variables that can explain these cycles. For example, he used no variables on gangs, on
> drug consumption, or community policing. As a result, many of Lott's findings make
> no sense. He finds for instance, that both increasing the rate of unemployment and
> reducing income reduces the rate of violent crimes . . . (Hemenway 1998: 2029).

Perhaps the most compelling critique comes from Jens Ludwig, who compares the
rate of violent crime toward youths and adults in states that passed shall-issue car-

rying permits. Most of these states issue gun permits only to people over 21. Arm-chair considerations predict that younger people, who cannot legally carry, will not receive the full benefits from the purported deterrent effect of shall-issue laws. Indeed, you would think they would be more vulnerable to crime. Thus, those under 21 years of age are a natural control group to track general swings in crime. Once statisticians included this factor, they found that shall-issue laws lead to higher – not lower – homicide and robbery rates (Ludwig 1998).

I also have an overarching worry about Lott's conclusions. The one correlation in the gun control debate that is seemingly beyond dispute is the high correlation between the presence of guns – especially handguns – and homicide rates. Gun advo-cates offer explanations for the correlation, but no one I have seen seriously chal-lenges it. I find it difficult to square this correlation with Kleck's and Lott's claims that having more guns – and toting them with us – will lower crime.

An overall assessment of the empirical evidence

The strong correlation between the presence of guns and higher murder rate is com-pelling. Since the correlation is statistically significant to a .01 level, it is difficult to believe that limiting private gun ownership will not have a noticeable effect on the number of murders. Gun advocates disagree: they claim that cultural factors explain the correlation. Although I think they are partly correct, they draw the wrong infer-ence. For one crucial difference between European and American cultures is the widespread presence of guns. Each culture is the way it is, at least in part, because of the role guns (or their absence) played in its creation and maintenance. Therefore, curtailing the private possession of guns might well change the American culture so that it would become less violent. Consequently, it is not only that fewer guns would directly cause some decline in violent crimes – which it should. It is also likely to reshape the cultural values, which, along with ready availability of deadly weapons, lead to such an extraordinarily high murder rate in America.

On the other hand, the statistical evidence that guns prevent or thwart crimes is suggestive and cannot be ignored, despite its identified weaknesses. In summary, the overall statistical evidence tilts in favor of gun control advocates, although the evi-dence is disputable. However, we should not expect nor do we need indisputable evidence. We can act on the best evidence we have, while being open to new evi-dence. If widespread availability of guns were responsible for even one-fourth of the increase in the number of murders, that would be a significant harm the state should prevent if it could do so in a relatively unintrusive and morally acceptable way.

There is little doubt that we can do that, at least to some degree. If nothing else we could control some types of guns and ammunition. To take one obvious example, Teflon-coated bullets are designed to pierce protective vests. People do not use these bullets to pierce the vests on a deer or a squirrel, on a target or a skeet. They use them to pierce the vests on people, usually law enforcement officers. This ammuni-tion has no purpose except to cause harm. Hence, I think we are justified in abol-ishing these bullets and in establishing severe criminal penalties for anyone possessing them. This would not save large numbers of lives. But, assuming this ban's enforcement is not impractical, then, if it saved even a few lives, that would be a compelling reason to outlaw them.

On the other hand, some guns have a much wider use, even if they are occasionally used for ill. People have seemingly legitimate uses for shotguns and single-shot rifles. Consequently, barring strong evidence to the contrary, we should not abolish them. We should, however, study their contributory role in causing harm, and explore ways we might lessen this harm in a relatively unintrusive way.

The central debate concerns handguns. The evidence we have shows that handguns are disproportionately used in homicides and in robberies. Although "there are approximately three times as many long guns as handguns in the US, more than 80% of gun homicides and 90% of gun robberies involve handguns" (Hemenway 1995: 60). The experience in Canada also suggests that criminals will not switch to long guns if handguns are unavailable. Given the special role handguns play in causing harm, we have compelling reasons to extensively control, or perhaps even abolish, them. However, policy considerations, mentioned earlier, should give us pause.

A Third Way

In the past we not only assumed that we must either support or oppose gun control, we assumed that the only way to control guns was to legally proscribe access to them. We should consider other options. Although I find the idea of a world without handguns immensely appealing, there are reasons to seek alternatives, especially in countries like the United States with a deeply entrenched gun culture. In the present political climate, the abolition or serious control of guns in the United States is unlikely to work and even less unlikely to happen. There are far too many people who desperately want guns. There are far too many people who own guns. Any attempt to disarm the society would be beset with the problems like those that plagued Prohibition. We have other possibilities.

We could employ elements of a policy we use to control another inherently dangerous object: dynamite. Dynamite has many beneficial uses. That is why we permit people to own it under specifiable conditions, e.g., to build a road. But it is also inherently dangerous. That is why we heavily restrict its purchase, storage, and use. I cannot own dynamite for recreation (I like the flash), for hunting (I am a lousy shot) or for self-protection. Owning dynamite is rarely a significant interest, and never a fundamental one. More important to the present point, even when we do permit people to own dynamite, we subject them to strict legal liability. The owner is financially liable for any harm caused by his dynamite, even if he was not negligent.

I propose we make handgun owners (and perhaps all gun owners) strictly liable for harm caused by the use of their guns. If Jones's child takes his gun and kills someone while committing a crime, then Jones will be financially responsible to those harmed. If Jones's child accidentally kills a neighbor's child, Jones will be financially responsible to the child's family. If someone steals Jones's gun and kills someone while robbing them, then Jones will owe the victim compensatory damages. And if Jones were negligent in the storing of the gun, he could be subject to punitive damages as well. Perhaps if he were grossly negligent in storing the gun (he left if lying in his front yard, next to a playground), we might even charge him with negligent homicide.

This procedure is justified since guns are inherently dangerous, and it is only reasonable to expect people to take responsibility for their risky actions. The benefits are notable: many people would be disinclined to own guns, while those owning guns would likely take greater care in storing, handling, and using them. This could arguably achieve the central aims of gun control without direct government intervention. Doubtless that means that some people will be forced to pay for the misdeeds or mistakes of others in ways we might dislike. However, that is a more attractive policy than continuing the current scheme in which guns are easily obtained in the United States or than in completely denying individuals' interest in owning guns.

To make this option more palatable, we could let gun owners purchase liability insurance to cover potential losses. We might even require them to do so. After all, most states require drivers to have automobile insurance. This insurance-backed system of strict liability would make people take more care with any guns they own, while providing financial remuneration to those harmed by the use of those guns. Perhaps this will not work. Other proposals might work better. What seems clear to me is that we need to do something: we cannot continue with the status quo.

REFERENCES

Alba, R. D. and Messner, S. F. (1995) " 'Point Blank' against Itself: Evidence and Inference About Guns, Crime, and Gun Control," *Journal of Quantitative Criminology* 11: 391–410.

Baker, S. P. (1985) "Without Guns, Do People Kill People?" *American Journal of Public Health* 75: 587–8.

Black, D. and Nagin, D. (1998) "Do Right-to-Carry Laws Deter Violent Crime?" *The Journal of Legal Studies* 27 (1): 209–20.

Brill, S. (1977) *Firearm Abuse: A Research and Policy Report*. Washington, DC: Police Foundation.

Carter, G. L. (1997) *The Gun Control Movement*. New York: Twayne Publishers.

Centers for Disease Control (1997) "Rates of Homicide, Suicide, and Firearm-Related Death among Children – 26 Industrialized Countries," *MMWR Weekly* 46 (5): 101–5.

Cook, P. J., Lawrence, B. A., Ludwig, J., and Miller, T. R. (1999) "The Medical Costs of Gunshot Injuries in the United States," *JAMA* 282 (5): 447–54.

Cook, P. J., Ludwig, J., and Hemenway, D. (1997) "The Gun Debate's New Mythical Number: How Many Defensive Uses Per Year?" *Journal of Policy Analysis and Management* 16 (3): 463–9.

Cook, P. J., Mollinoni, S., and Cole, T. B. (1995) "Regulating Gun Markets," *The Journal of Criminal Law and Criminology* 86 (1): 59–92.

Dworkin, R. M. (1977) *Taking Rights Seriously*. London: Duckworth.

Hemenway, D. (1995) "Guns, Public Health, and Public Safety." In D. A. Henigan, E. B. Nicholson, and D. Hemenway (eds.), *Guns and the Constitution*. Northhampton, MA: Aletheia Press, 49–82.

Hemenway, D. (1997a) "The Myth of Millions of Annual Self-Defense Gun Uses: A Case Study of Survey Overestimates of Rare Events," *Chance* 10 (3): 6–10.

Hemenway, D. (1997b) "Survey Research and Self-Defense Gun Use: An Explanation of Extreme Overestimates," *The Journal of Criminal Law and Criminology* 87 (4): 1430–45.

Hemenway, D. (1998) "Review of More Guns, Less Crime," *New England Journal of Medicine* 339: 2029–30.

Hemenway, D. and Miller, M. (1999) "The Relationship between Firearms and Suicide: A Review of the Literature," *Aggression and Violent Behavior* 4 (1): 59–75.

Hemenway, D. and Miller, M. (2000) "Firearm Availability and Homicide Rates across 26 High-Income Countries," *The Journal of Trauma* 49 (6): 1–4.

Hughes, T. C. and Hunt, L. H. (2000) "The Liberal Basis of the Right to Bear Arms," *Public Affairs Quarterly* 14 (1): 1–25.

Kleck, G. (1991) *Point Blank: Guns and Violence in America*. New York: Aldine de Gruyter.

Kleck, G. (1997) *Targeting Guns: Firearms and Their Control*. New York: Aldine De Gruyter.

Krug, E. G., Mercy, J. A., Dahlberg, L. L., and Powell, K. E. (1998) "Firearm and Non-Firearm-Related Homicide among Children," *Homicide Studies* 2: 83–95.

Lott, J. R. (1998) *More Guns, Less Crime: Understanding Crime and Gun-Control Laws*. Chicago, IL: University of Chicago Press.

Ludwig, J. (1998) "Concealed Gun-Carrying Laws and Violent Crime: Evidence from State Panel Data," *International Review of Law and Economics* 18: 239–54.

Mill, J. S. (1985/1885) *On Liberty*. Indianapolis, IN: Hackett.

Reiss, A. J., Jr. and Roth, J. A. (eds.) (1993) *Understanding and Preventing Violence*. Washington, DC: National Academy Press.

Singer, C., Holmyard, E. J., Hall, A. R., and Williams, T. (1956) *A History of Technology*, vol. 2. Oxford: Oxford University Press.

US Department of Justice (1996) *Criminal Victimization in the United States, 1993: A National Crime Victimization Survey*. Washington, DC: US Government Printing Office.

Wheeler, S. C., Jr. (1997) "Self-Defense: Rights and Coerced Risk Acceptance," *Public Affairs Quarterly* 11 (4): 431–43.

PART FIVE

Living Morally

THIRTEEN

Everyday Morality

Most issues we discussed have significant political, social, or legal dimensions. I chose to emphasize these issues for two reasons. First, many people have a narrow view of morality: they think morality is primarily private, concerning what each individual chooses to do. A few even continue to think (or imply by their focus) that morality primarily concerns sex: that we can distinguish the moral from the immoral person simply by knowing when, how, where, and with whom she sleeps. The discussions so far should demonstrate why such views are untenable. Second, the actions on which I have focused impact many people, and impact them in vital ways. Millions of people starve; hundreds of thousands of people face decisions about prolonging or not prolonging their lives; millions of people are victims of racism. Given the number of people affected, and the extent to which they are affected, it seems only sensible that we be very concerned about these issues.

But we must be careful. There are four interrelated ways in which everyday behavior seems morally more significant than the "larger" social issues we discussed.

1. We are often in a position not only to especially benefit, but also especially harm, our family and friends.
2. We interact repeatedly with the same people. Even if no one action toward a person is especially significant, the effect of all our actions on her may be.
3. Even if the effects of our actions on any one person are minor, the cumulative effects of all our interactions with people close to us may be more significant than our influence over social, political, and legal issues.
4. Especially since most of us seem to lack substantial influence over these issues.

Together these explain why an adequate account of morality must attend to everyday ethics: the ways in which we talk, listen, treat, behave with and around our friends, family, colleagues, neighbors, and brief acquaintances. All defensible theories consider everyday interactions morally significant. Unfortunately, a casual reader might not know that by looking at the literature. Few books explicitly discuss everyday ethics (Benatar 2001; Martin 1995; Sommers et al. 1996), and a few others deal with aspects of everyday life such as friendship and family (Badhwar 1993; Friedman 1993; LaFollette 1996).

I cannot identify all elements of everyday morality, let alone discuss them thoroughly. Instead, I simply give the flavor of how we might think about everyday morality. I will do so in ways that highlight the connections between everyday ethics and the more profound political and social issues on which we have focused. I first isolate elements of morality that played a central role in our thinking about these larger ethical issues; then I explore ways these inform everyday moral decisions.

Factors Strengthening Moral Behavior

Looking back on the discussions throughout this book, we can isolate five factors that enhance our moral thought and whose absence constrain it. These are:

- knowledge of the morally relevant facts;
- knowledge of the effects of our actions;
- having a vivid moral imagination;
- caring about others;
- interpreting others' behavior.

Each is singularly important; most are interrelated. None will guarantee that we will act morally; however, we cannot regularly act morally without them.

We can profitably subdivide them into three groups: knowledge of context, psychological dispositions, and interpreting others' behavior.

Knowledge of the context

I will not regularly make good moral choices if I do not attend to the context within which I act. Context is critical, but not just for morality. We must know the context to make sense of every human action. Saying, "I love you," to my wife is rather different than saying "I love you" to a piece of paper lying on my floor. Moving my right hand in a jabbing motion "means" one thing if I am in a boxing ring, another if I am three feet from my boss, and still another if I am shadow boxing in my den. Saying, "The square of the hypotenuse of a right triangle is the sum of the squares of the other two sides," in response to the question, "What is the Pythagorean Theorem," is very different from saying it when asked, in a criminal trial, whether I saw the defendant fleeing the scene of a murder. Everyone recognizes the importance of context. Unfortunately, what we recognize in the abstract, we forget in the concrete. We rarely make sufficient effort to discern the context of our moral choices: to identify the morally relevant facts and to trace the likely effects of our actions.

If I am ignorant of the relevant facts, I cannot make the appropriate moral decision, or if I do, it is a matter of luck. Unless I know the needs and interests of those affected by my action, then I cannot effectively assist them. And, if I am deciding whether a term is racist, whether my comment about my secretary's blouse is sexist, or whether I should support affirmative action, I must understand the context as shaped by current practice and relevant history. As I explained in Chapters 5 and 6, if I am ignorant about the extensive historical discrimination against blacks and women, and if I do not understand the ways previous discrimination has ongoing effects, then I will not understand why using some epithet or commenting on my secretary's blouse might be objectionable or why affirmative action might be justified.

It is not enough to be able to recite current and historical facts. I must use that information to predict the likely effects of my and others' actions, otherwise I cannot make a good moral decision, or, if I do, it is luck. All theories acknowledge, to different degrees and for different reasons, the moral relevance of the effects of our action. These effects obviously matter to the consequentialist: they directly determine what is moral. They also matter indirectly to deontologists and virtue theorists (which I discuss in the next chapter). I cannot correctly describe most actions or virtues unless I know their likely consequences. For instance, we cannot know if an act is attempted murder unless we know that the behavior in question (pulling the trigger on my handgun) standardly leads to someone's death. And we cannot understand what benevolence is unless we know the behavior standardly helps others. That is why my decisions will be morally questionable if I do not know the relevant consequences of my actions. Unless I see the ways that discrimination has ripple effects into the future, I cannot understand what is wrong with the status quo. Unless I know the likely consequences of implementing proposals making drugs or guns (il)legal, I will not know whether to support them.

However, it is not enough to know the context of our actions. We must also have the appropriate psychological dispositions; specifically, we need a vivid imagination and we must care about other people.

Psychological factors

It is not enough that I abstractly know the facts and the likely consequences of my action. I also need the moral imagination to "see" how those facts shape the context for my action. Imagination helps me see what I might have missed from a mere canvas of the facts. Although I can recite statistics about the rates of incarceration and the nature of prisons, I may not appreciate prisoners' plight if I lack a vivid moral imagination. I need to imagine the ways in which incarceration can increase the propensity for recidivism and appreciate the legal and social obstacles to a released felon's reintegration into society. Likewise, if I cannot imaginatively empathize with someone who is dying and in excruciating pain, I may be baffled by her request for physician-assisted suicide.

I can also know all the facts, understand the effects of my actions, and can vividly imagine the ways my actions affect others. However, unless I care about others, I will not standardly act morally. If I am indifferent to prisoners, I will not be morally moved to do anything about the criminal justice system, even if I understand all the facts and can fully envision the treatment of felons.

Interpreting others' behavior

Each of the previous factors contributes to what might broadly be described as our ability to understand others. But they do not exhaust this ability. To be able to respond appropriately to another person we often must also know something about what makes her tick, what motivates her. In short, we must know something about her character. For if we misunderstand her character, we will likely misinterpret much that she says and does, and will subsequently respond inappropriately. For instance, we may be inappropriately trusting or excessively guarded. After all, we relate to those we believe are trustworthy one way, and those we believe are shysters, another; to those we think are honest, one way, and those we think are liars, another; to those we deem compassionate, one way, and those we deem selfish, another. If we mis-judge their character, then we will relate to them inappropriately. That is why this so important: it affects whether we act morally in relation to others.

We act as if this were easy. We assume (or act as if we assume) that we can just watch how a person acts and listen to what she says, and then straightforwardly gen-eralize about her character. We can't. We cannot see what a person does and hear what she says in some pristine way, without interpretation or evaluation. What we see and hear is already shaped by our beliefs about what motivates that agent (or most people). Put differently, we rarely see or describe others' actions in morally neutral terms ("Joan raised her arm and slowly unclenched her fist"). We standardly see them as "benevolent" or "mean," "careful" or "sloppy," "intelligent" or "dull," "tol-erant" or "close-minded," "refined" or "crass," "spontaneous" or "rigid," "hard-working" or "lazy," "sincere" or "deceptive," "thoughtful" or "flippant."

This might not be a problem if everyone evaluated the same behaviors in the same ways, but we don't. Two people often "see" the same behavior in different – even wholly incompatible – ways. So we must decide which interpretation is best. If Jane says something that sounds intelligent, she might be bright, lucky, or have cribbed the idea. If Bob says something inane, he might be ignorant, tired, or mistaken. If Lisa gives Ron a gift she may be generous or angling for some benefit. If Richard hits Ralph, he may be assaulting Ralph, having a seizure, or defending himself from Ralph's assault. Which interpretation is correct?

We again see the importance of context. We cannot understand an action unless we know the contexts within which Jane, Bob, Lisa, and Richard act. Did Barbara tell Jane what to say? Is Bob being serious or is he joking? Does Lisa want to become a member of the local Chamber of Commerce of which Ron is a board member? Has Ralph been threatening Richard for months?

Key elements of that context – ones we have not yet emphasized – are the respec-tive characters of Jane, Bob, Lisa, and Richard. Our interpretations of their current behavior are shaped by our views of their character (LaFollette 1996: chapter 6). We are more likely to describe a current behavior in ways that are "in character," as behav-ior we see as springing from the person's basic dispositions. We are less likely to ascribe motives that we think are "out of character" – ways that are at odds with what we take to be her deeper traits. If someone we think wise says something stupid, we tend to ignore it as an aberration or else we assume there is some deep truth we missed. If someone we think kind acts in a way that seems mean-spirited, we tend to think that we have misunderstood her action – or that she has acted out of character. And so we should. It is reasonable for our overall judgments of someone's character to shape our attributions of motive for her current behavior. We would be imprudent if we trusted someone we know to be a liar; we would be gullible if we took a known shyster's seemingly benevolent action at face value. In each case we see these people's actions as exhibiting a stable (and unwholesome) character.

The problem with this line of thinking should be clear: this explanation looks circular. We look at individual actions to determine a person's character, and we use our judgments about someone's character to inform our interpretations of their actions. As I will explain, that is often a serious problem – not one that can be wholly avoided. We have no other plausible way to judge people's actions or characters. We cannot determine someone's character except by watching how she acts and listening to what she says. Ouija boards are no substitute. Moreover, our judgments of individual actions are – and should be – framed by our judgments about a person's character.

However, although circular in one sense, it is not viciously circular. Think about a non-moral trait like intelligence. What make us decide that someone is intelligent? It should not be based on any single thing that they say. At most we can describe such single actions by saying that they *sound* intelligent. However, we know there are always multiple explanations for intelligent-sounding behavior – one of which is that the person really is intelligent. Maybe, though, she got lucky or remembered what someone else told her; perhaps she is intelligent about this one subject but not generally so. Our judgments of someone's character must always be based on *patterns* of behavior, not isolated behaviors. If she continues to act in similar ways, then we start to move from the claim that someone's behavior seemed intelligent to the claim that that person is intelligent. Once we make that judgment, it begins to shape how we view the next thing she says or does. This is both inevitable and prudent. However, that does not – or should not – mean that the judgment is unchangeable. If we begin to witness consistently stupid behavior, we should revise our judgments. To that extent, it does seem that the judgments of individual acts are chronologically prior. However, they are not wholly independent upon our background judgments about this person, all people, or some subclass of people (e.g., physicians).

However, as I hinted earlier, this approach is dangerous. For if no single act does a trait make, and we use our beliefs about a person's traits to interpret her acts, how can we be confident when ascribing traits to another? The answer is that many of us can't really be – even though that doesn't stop most of us from feeling confident. We often make biased or hasty judgments about others. Then, these quick judgments shape how we respond and relate to them. What we then see usually reinforces our initial views, no matter how ill informed.

The problem becomes acute once we notice that we tend to apply these insights in two diametrically opposed ways. If our or our friends' action can be construed positively, that is what we usually do: we see it as indicating some favorable trait, or we excuse, rationalize, or dismiss the action as "out of character." We conveniently forget the myriad ways we (and our friends) are inconsiderate, rude, unkind, cantankerous, or stingy. In contrast, when interpreting the behavior of those we dislike, we tend to treat their single actions as indicating a deep character flaw, or we interpret seemingly laudable behavior as sneaky or manipulative.

These subconscious biases are exacerbated by the absence of any of the first five factors that influence moral understanding. We misjudge people's character if we base our interpretations of their behavior on false, ill-informed, biased, or hasty views, and without any serious attempt to imaginatively understand their actions. Unfortunately these biases are neither rare nor restricted to the ignorant few. All of us have these propensities sometimes and to some degree, and many of us have them in spades. Knowing we all have these propensities, you would think we would be more cautious and self-reflective – that we would take concrete steps to counter them. Unfortunately we do not. And that increases the chance that we relate to others inappropriately.

Some Common Interactions

Let us now use those elements to talk about some common interactions where we morally founder. Here are four examples of ordinary behavior of which most of us are at least sometimes guilty. I know I am.

Driving

Getting behind the wheel of a car changes some people from calm, seemingly sensitive human beings, into raving lunatics. People may speed through neighborhoods where young children live; they may cut in front of cars in a rush to get to their destinations; they may refuse to let a waiting driver out of a parking lot, even when they can do could so with little (if any) inconvenience; they may beep at someone who does not move the instant a light changes; they may drive down the road well below the speed limit, carrying on a conversation with their passengers – or looking for an address – oblivious to the ever-growing line of cars snaking behind.

I think these behaviors are morally inappropriate. They might indicate raw egoism. But most don't. These occur primarily because we are inattentive to the interests of others and the effects of our behavior on them. Since we do not see or appreciate their interests, we act inappropriately. When we are on the receiving end of similar behavior, we see all too well why such behavior is inappropriate. However, we fail to equate our speeding or beeping or chatting with our passenger with the same behavior committed by others. Even if we occasionally recognize these behaviors in ourselves, we quickly forget it the next time we are in a hurry, want to chat with our passengers, etc.

Relating to functionaries

It can be frustrating to deal with bureaucrats, whether in business or government. A company fouls up our order, sells us a defective computer, fails to record a bill we paid, or promises to send a repairperson, who fails to show up for a scheduled service call. We call or visit the company to straighten out the problem. If we call, we must first navigate the rabbit warren of electronic answering machines, only to discover that it does not provide us the option we really want (nothing like, "to strangle the manager, press seven"). We finally get a voice on the phone or a body in front of us. We explain the problem. They claim they cannot handle it. They shunt us to someone else. Our frustration mounts. After being shuttled back and forth, we get angry. Often, however, the person at whom we get angry did not make the policy, is not empowered to change it or make an exception to it. Yet we vent our frustration with the product, the company, and the policy, on them. They become our scapegoat.

Perhaps there are circumstances in which anger is justifiable – for instance, if they blindly defend the company's policies, and especially if they become snippy. Although they did not set the policies and may be unable to change them, by their behavior they show that they endorse them. If so, then it seems as appropriate to get angry with them as it would be to get angry with someone who did have the power to change that policy. But likely it is inappropriate to get angry with either.

Nonetheless, it is appropriate to express dismay at the company's policy and ask the person to convey that dismay to the powers that be. If enough people express their disapproval, then the people with power will change the policy. Doubtless, too, some workers will not convey customer disapproval unless the customer gets at least mildly miffed. After all, I know that sometimes I do not appreciate the concerns of friends, family, or colleagues unless they get at least a bit angry with me. Although I may initially react badly to their anger, later, in an hour of cool reflection, I may see that they were justifiably disgruntled. However, I expect most workers are more likely to convey the customer's dissatisfaction if the customer treats them decently. Therefore, except under perhaps a few unusual circumstances, getting angry with a functionary is unproductive, unnecessary, and does not treat them with the appropriate respect.

Being snippy or rude

We have had a bad day. A friend asks a favor; a family member asks a question; someone calls on the phone; the dog barks; the computer goes on the fritz. We get snippy with our friends or family, rude with the caller, or scream at our computer or the dog. Such behavior is at least unbecoming and likely morally objectionable. Although it may not seriously damage others, it may hurt – if not harm – them.

Since we are prone to interpret our own behavior favorably, most of us are inclined to excuse it, while, if someone else acts the same way, we take offense. Bias makes us more likely to act immorally.

Gossiping

We all gossip: we tell stories about others, stories that put them in a bad light. Although some people do not think gossip is always (or perhaps not even often) bad, I think it usually is. First, in gossiping (or listening to gossip) we usually spread (or believe) exaggerations if not outright fabrications. These are indefensible on any plausible account of morality. Of course when most of us spread or listen to gossip, we do not *know* it to be false. Neither do we know it to be true. Often we have considerable evidence that it is false – if nothing else, because we heard it from notoriously unreliable sources. Because we do not know it to be a lie, we do not feel like liars. However, such gossip can harm others as much as can a lie. We gossip as if what we say were true, knowing that others will likely believe us. In so doing we shape how other people see and relate to the subject of the gossip. Others come to believe that she is untrustworthy or selfish or manipulative, and thereby adjust their behavior toward her accordingly. Since we are most likely to gossip about those we do not like, that is not a consequence we mind.

Some people disagree. They claim that gossip plays an important role in people's moral education. As we hear people gossip we come to understand what behaviors (they think) are good or bad, becoming or vile, and we subsequently know better how they expect us to act (Sabini and Silver 1982). There is no doubt that gossip can play that role, and it can do so even if the gossip is demonstrably false. That is, gossip teaches us what people *believe* to be immoral, unbecoming, inappropriate, etc. However, it is hard to imagine these benefits could justify telling falsehoods about others. Perhaps, though, these benefits may justify gossip if we have good reason to believe that the gossip is true. Is it wrong to tell unflattering truths about others? Sometimes not. If I know you may become business partners with Joe – whom I know to be unscrupulous – then I should warn you. However, in so doing I am not gossiping. I am not spreading unsubstantiated claims about Joe; nor am I just idly chatting about him. I am protecting you from harm. Certainly my action would not be wrong. Indeed, not telling you about Joe would be wrong. Since you have reason to think I would pass along relevant information that I had about Joe, then my failure to do so is a contributing factor to any subsequent harm he causes you. Even then, I should be honest and qualify my claims to the degree that I think they might be false.

Suppose, though, I am *just* gossiping, that I am telling unflattering truths about Joe without any specific, relevant, and appropriate purpose. That is still morally questionable even if what I say is true (Holland 1996). There are a variety of reasons why. Perhaps the most significant problem is that by relaying only unflattering truths about Joe – without mentioning his more positive traits – I give you a skewed, and therefore false, impression of him. Given the aforementioned role that background information plays in shaping our interpretation of other people's behavior, I harm him.

Everyday or Social Ethics?

The recognition that there are myriad ways in which our everyday behavior has significant moral implications might even lead some people to suggest that this book's emphasis on political and social issues is a common form of moral farsightedness, well captured by the following lyrics of a song from the 1966 Broadway musical *Hair*:

> How can people be so heartless; how can people be so cruel.
> Easy to be hard . . .
> Especially people who care about people,
> Who say they care about social injustice.
> Do you only care about the bleeding crowd,
> How about a needing friend?

The song exposes those who are so preoccupied with large social issues that they ignore the needs of those immediately around them – those whom they can help most, and help most easily. As a child of the 1960s, I can attest that there were people whom this did seem to describe. However, I think there were fewer than the song suggests.

More common, I think, were the "hangers-on" who joined student strikes and antiwar protests more to be "part of a movement" than to "make a difference." They enjoyed the camaraderie, the sense of belonging, and the excitement that accompanied anti-establishment resistance. However, they would have been no more willing to help the bleeding crowd than a needing friend. Conversely, those I knew who were genuinely devoted to "the cause" – who were concerned about suffering, pain, and injustice – were also more likely to be sensitive to those around them. Not always and not entirely, but generally and for the most part.

The interplay of everyday and social morality

There are two reasons for the last comment: (1) close personal relationships give us the knowledge and the motivation to develop an impartial morality; and (2) real intimacy flourishes in an environment that impartially recognizes the needs and interests of all. Let me explain. Suppose you are standing next to someone who has an epileptic seizure, but you have never heard of epilepsy, let alone witnessed a seizure. Or suppose you are stranded on an elevator with someone having a heart attack, but you don't know people have hearts, let alone that they can malfunction. In short, try to imagine that these happened when you were five years old. You would do nothing. If you tried, you would likely do more harm than good; success would be serendipitous.

We cannot promote interests we cannot identify, and the way we learn to identify people's specific interests is by having interacted with them. Most of us learned from our families how to recognize and respond to the needs of others. Our parents comforted us when we were hurt; they laughed with us when we were happy. We learned from their example. Without that experience, not only would we lack the requisite knowledge, we would also lack the appropriate motivation. Though I expect we may have some biologically inherited sympathetic tendencies, these will wither unless others care for us and we for them. If we then develop empathy toward our friends, then, since empathy is usually non-specific, we will be inclined to generalize that to others. Moreover, a society that recognizes the needs of strangers is typically one in which intimacy can flourish. A society that prizes empathy, caring, and honesty will be one that equips its citizens for close personal relationships.

Judging Others and Improving Oneself

The reader might conclude from the discussions throughout this book that the primary role of morality is to give us the knowledge whereby we can informatively judge others. If that is the primary conclusion the reader reaches, then I have, to some significant degree, failed. The primary aim of moral thinking is to help us be less cruel, more caring, fairer, and more just – in short, to make this a morally better world. The best way to do that is not by spending the bulk of our time judging or condemning others, but by morally improving ourselves.

This is not just to repeat the popular slogan, "Don't judge," for the fact is we do – and should – judge others, at least to some degree and in some ways. The problem is that the term "judge" is ambiguous between evaluating and condemning (and perhaps "sentencing"). We do evaluate circumstances, actions, and people. We judge that Randi's behavior harmed her friends or that Butch's behavior was inconsiderate. It is difficult to know why this is a problem. Yet in so doing we need not condemn the agent or make some grand judgment about her or her character. Consider the following analogy. As a teacher, my job is to evaluate my students. As a reviewer, my job is to evaluate an essay or a book. But neither activity requires that I think ill of the student or the author, let alone condemn either for their work or character. In fact, were I to regularly infer that a student who submitted a weak paper was a dunce or morally tainted, or infer that a professional who wrote (what I judged to be) a mediocre paper was either a dullard or unworthy of being a philosopher, then I would have failed in my job as a teacher or a reviewer. That is not to say that we might not make those judgments in certain circumstances; but they should not be the norm.

There are at least two reasons why such harsh judgments and round condemnations are usually morally inappropriate. Recall the discussion earlier in this chapter. Harsh judgments based on single actions are usually unwarranted generalizations (although some behaviors might be so outrageous as to warrant a harsh judgment about the person). Very good people occasionally do very bad things; very smart people occasionally say very stupid things. Furthermore, most hasty generalizations occur because we are ignorant of the relevant context. What seems ill advised or ignorant or self-centered or small-minded may not be; once we understand the full circumstances we may see that. That is a lesson that I know in the abstract, but often forget in the concrete.

With those warnings firmly in mind, it seems that the best route for moral development is to devote the bulk of our energies to determining how we, individually, can be most responsive and responsible – how we can be most moral. This approach recognizes that the limitations on judging others are not fully applicable to ourselves. Although we might deceive ourselves about what we do and why we do it, our ignorance is largely remediable, while correcting our ignorance of the relevant circumstances of others' action is more difficult. Moreover, in evaluating others, we do not directly change them or make them more moral. In fact, if done inappropriately, it might make them more stubborn or callous. I have limited power over others. However, I have considerable (although not unlimited) power to reshape myself in light of retrospection. That is why by focusing mostly on ourselves and what we can do, we are more likely to make a serious moral difference. Finally, although hypocrisy does not necessarily undermine the truth of what we say, it usually undermines its effectiveness. If we do not first have our own moral house in order, others will tend to discount our moral claims. That is why the most significant way of shaping other people's moral behavior is by what we do rather than what we say.

All this seems to suggest that maybe the best way of being moral, at least in everyday action, is to cultivate the appropriate habits, the appropriate dispositions to behave – the correct virtues. It is to that idea that we now turn.

REFERENCES

Badhwar, N. (ed.) (1993) *Friendship: A Philosophical Reader*. Ithaca, NY: Cornell University Press.
Benatar, D. (ed.) (2001) *Ethics for Everyday*. New York: McGraw-Hill.
Friedman, M. (1993) *What Are Friends For?* Ithaca, NY: Cornell University Press.
Holland, M. G. (1996) "What's Wrong with Telling the Truth? An Analysis of Gossip," *American Philosophical Quarterly* 33 (2): 197–209.
LaFollette, H. (1996) *Personal Relationships: Love, Identity, and Morality*. Oxford: Blackwell Publishers.
Martin, M. W. (1995) *Everyday Morality: An Introduction to Applied Ethics*, 2nd edn. Belmont, CA: Wadsworth Publishing Company.
Sabini, J. and Silver, M. (1982) *Moralities of Everyday Life*. New York: Oxford University Press.
Sommers, C. H., Sommers, F. T., and Fogelin, R. J. (1996) *Vice & Virtue in Everyday Life: Introductory Readings in Ethics*, 4th edn. San Diego, CA: Harcourt Brace Jovanovich.

FOURTEEN

Character, Virtue Ethics, and Pragmatism

If the best way to act morally is by cultivating the virtues, then it seems we must either amend the standard accounts of consequentialism and deontology or search for a theory that gives the virtues a more prominent role. Such a theory is available. Although this theory has a long theoretical life, stretching back several thousand years, it vanished from formal ethical discussion for more than a hundred years. Then, in the last 50 years, it has made a comeback. This revival has been largely spurred by the perceived failings of the standard alternatives.

Rationale for the Theory

Flaws with the standard alternatives

Deontologists and consequentialists have had a theoretical slugfest for several centuries, with each isolating seeming flaws in the other theory – at least, flaws in the ways the theories are often articulated. I have mentioned most of these before, so I will only summarize them here.

Problems with deontology

It is clear why many people find deontology appealing. Most of us first learned morality as a set of rules and most of us continue to think rules play an important role. Even so, most people acknowledge that (a) there are some exceptions to even seemingly ironclad moral rules; that (b) knowing the rules will not always help us decide what to do; and thus that (c) judgment is an essential element of any adequate conception of morality. Finally, it seems deontologists sometimes engage in rule worship: they care more about the rules than the people whose lives we affect.

As we saw in Chapter 2, most deontologists think they can accommodate these concerns; a few think these are not genuine problems. However, inasmuch as these are genuine concerns, we must either reject or supplement deontology. Virtue theorists claim their theory can better deal with "exceptions" to moral rules, and whereas judgment is an addendum to deontology, it plays a central role in virtue theory.

Problems with consequentialism

Consequentialism also captures some common moral impulses. However, as standardly formulated, it demands that we decide how to act based solely on the likely consequences of our actions. That view faces two potent criticisms. First, even when we know the precise effects of our actions, we sometimes think other factors are morally relevant, that we should sometimes stand our moral ground even when we can promote some valuable end by violating a moral rule. Second, although we know that we affect others, and we know generally which actions produce which results, we cannot predict the precise nature, extent, and contour of these effects.

As we saw in Chapter 2, most consequentialists think they can accommodate these concerns; a few think they can show why these are not genuine problems. However, inasmuch as these are genuine concerns, we must reject or supplement standard accounts of consequentialism. Virtue theorists claim that since we cannot accurately predict the future, we shouldn't even try. Rather we should put our efforts into those things we can control, most especially, our character. If we develop virtuous dispositions, then we will be able to judge what to do when we must act.

The centrality of judgment

Neither standard theory gives judgment a central role. The strictest versions of both do not appear to give it any role. On these models ethics resembles math. Moral calculations may require special patience and care. Just as one can rush through a math problem and make sloppy mistakes, one can also make mistakes in moral calculation. However, neither mathematical nor moral "calculations" require judgment in any robust sense. Skill, yes; judgment, no.

Although few modern-day deontologists or consequentialists hold such mechanical views of moral reasoning, neither theory gives judgment an independent status. For these theories judgment is simply a tool for determining how we should act. Deontologists use judgment to determine if an act is a type that is permitted, required, or forbidden by the relevant moral rule. Consequentialists use judgment to determine which features are morally relevant (and thus should be included in moral calculations), and to decide how to "balance" competing consequences. In contrast, virtue theory gives judgment center stage. It holds that what is right or wrong, good or bad, noble or ignoble, is *determined* by what a virtuous person judges that she should (or should not) do (Hursthouse 1999: 25–32). (It would be interesting to explore the ways that virtue theory resembles divine command theory ⟨discussed in Chapter 7⟩ since that theory claims that good is determined by what God judges.)

Arguments in the previous chapter suggest that judgment in some rich sense is required for "everyday morality." These interactions are too minor to warrant detailed scrutiny and too specific to be covered by rules. We need cultivated moral judgment to know how to act in these circumstances. Virtue theory seems especially able to capture this important element of the moral life. To further explain how virtue theory differs from deontology and consequentialism, let's look at an early proponent of it.

Aristotle's Ethics

Aristotle's theory differs radically from deontology and consequentialism as they are standardly formulated. Aristotle does not give a different answer to the question: "What should I morally do?" He (and the Greeks in general) asked and answered a different question. They wanted to know "How should I live?" The answer to the first question indicates (or is normally thought to indicate) that morality has a narrow focus, concerning only a subset of human behavior (whether you kill, steal, lie, etc.). The Greeks were concerned about all behavior that is plausibly part of the good life.

Happiness

A good life, Aristotle says, is one that seeks *eudaimonia*, a word that is often translated as "happiness." That is misleading since the Greek view of happiness differs from a more modern conception. Happiness is not mere pleasure. Nor is it something "out there" that a person could completely attain. Rather, happiness is a way of characterizing one's whole life. It is to have a good life, to live well and do well.

The good life

To understand what Aristotle means by "a good human life," we must first understand his notion of "the function of an object." Everything, the Greeks believed, is identified by its function. The function of a flute is to hit a range of musical notes with a particular sound. An excellent flute is one that fulfills this function well. That is the flute's "virtue." A flute that sounded like a Stradivarius might sound exquisite, but it would not be an excellent flute. A saw is a cutting tool. A dull saw is not an excellent saw, although it might serve admirably as a shim under the leg of a wobbly table. Animals also have functions. Only by understanding their function can we discern what it is to be an excellent instance of that animal. A toothless lion is not an excellent lion; a lame cheetah is not an excellent cheetah, etc. So what is the proper function of (and, therefore the virtue of) a human being? It is to live the best a human can live.

This profoundly alters our understanding of morality. Most people think morality constrains human behavior, that morality is a set of rules barring us from doing what we want to do, and occasionally demanding that we do things we had rather not. Not virtue theorists. They think morality is a prescription for the best life we can live; it is not an *imposition* on that life. Therefore, while the deontologist and the consequentialist must answer the question, "Why should I be moral?" the virtue theorist thinks the question is nonsense: it is equivalent to asking "Why should I live the best life I could live?"

Virtue

Aristotle holds that the virtuous person must: (1) do the appropriate action; (2) do so habitually (regularly, and in a variety of circumstances); (3) enjoy acting virtuously; (4) know *that* it is virtuous; and (5) know *why* it is virtuous. Why do we need each of these elements? Let me explain briefly.

Do the appropriate action

The virtue theorist's explanation of what it means to "do the appropriate action" sounds remarkably unsatisfying. What is the appropriate action? It is the action the virtuous person would do. That sounds circular. It is not the kind of answer we expect. We want a rule.

However, before we reject that answer out of hand, consider the following parallels:

- What is the best way to build a house? The way best builders build.
- What is the best way to teach? The way the best teachers teach.
- What is the best sentence to use? The one the best writers would write.

These are all plausible answers. Although in each case we can articulate rules describing what the best builders, teachers, and writers would do, we do not have an independent mechanism for doing so. Excellent practitioners help define excellent practice, whether the practice is building, teaching, writing, or acting morally.

Do so habitually (regularly, and in a variety of circumstances)

A person is virtuous only if she does the right thing habitually, that is, regularly and in a variety of circumstances. It is not enough to be right some of the time. As the old saw goes, even a broken watch is right twice a day. Stupid people may occasionally say intelligent-sounding things, and immoral people may occasionally do seemingly benevolent acts. However, if these acts are not habitual – if they are "out of character" – then we can infer that the intelligent-sounding language is a matter of luck, and the seemingly benevolent action is done from some ulterior motive, for instance, out of the person's belief that acting benevolently would pay off, perhaps by endearing them to a potential client or raising their reputation in the community.

The act must also be performed in a variety of circumstances. Otherwise we cannot know if the person has a localized rather than a global virtue. Al may be incredibly generous with and supportive of his fellow partners in crime. That doesn't imply that he is a generous or sympathetic person. Likewise, someone who is smart about only one thing is not smart. Rather, she has savant syndrome.

Enjoy acting virtuously

It is not enough that a person do what a virtuous person would do and that they do it regularly. They must also enjoy doing it. This element is in stark contrast with Kant's theory. Kant thought people demonstrated the highest moral worth when they act against their inclinations. Aristotle would have thought this claim incomprehensible. Perhaps for this reason, Aristotle does not really explain why he thinks virtuous people should enjoy being virtuous. However, I think he could offer four possible explanations.

The *first* is connected to the previous conditions. We assume a person who wants to be honest, benevolent, courageous, and so on is more likely to do so regularly, and in a wide variety of circumstances. We can fight inclination now and again, but not always. On Aristotle's view, we are habitual creatures. We respond quickly, according to our character.

Second, a person who acts benevolently, spontaneously, and because she enjoys it, is not only likely to be more reliable, but more effective. When we act against our inclinations, two factors typically conspire to make the action more rigid – less "us." One, patterns of action that are not habitual tend to be stiffer than habitual action. There's nothing mysterious here. Someone learning to type cannot type as fast or as accurately as an accomplished typist. A young child cannot walk as smoothly or as briskly as an older child. Someone learning to speak the language speaks more haltingly than someone who is fluent. The same is true of morally laden traits like benevolence. If a person really doesn't want to be benevolent, then since her action is not habitual, it is more rigid, less likely to be responsive to the recipient's needs, and less attuned to the relevant features of the context. Again, nothing mysterious. Someone learning to type *who doesn't want to type* will be, all things considered, less adept than the avid learner.

There are gradations between these extremes. Someone with developed habits of benevolence may not be inclined in some situations to do what she would normally want to do; she may be exhausted or depressed. Still, she may do it habitually, and the habit may modulate the action so that it is still effective. And someone who is working to inculcate the requisite habit, but has not yet succeeded, will also be more effective – even if less fluid – than if she lacked both the habit and the inclination. There are exceptional people who can learn even complicated behaviors quickly; others can quickly mimic the behavior of the virtuous with seemingly little effort. Even so, people who are virtuous will be more effective than those who are merely trying to be virtuous.

Third, we think people without the "appropriate feelings" are flawed even if we cannot see any way that the absence of those feelings shapes her behavior. We generally think it is bad for someone to take delight in others' misery.

Fourth, since the aim of the good life is to achieve *eudaimonia*, then being miserable while acting virtuously works against that ultimate aim.

Know that it is virtuous

The point here is somewhat akin to Kant's claim: it is not enough to act as a virtuous person would; the agent should know that her action is virtuous. However, unlike Kant, Aristotle does not require that this knowledge be wholly conscious, and certainly not wholly conscious at the time that she acts. It is enough that the person be aware, at least in retrospect, that she acted as a virtuous person would have. Why should this matter to Aristotle? If nothing else, the person who does not know that the act is moral is likely less reliable – less likely to do what is morally required in the future.

Know why it is virtuous

A person might know *that* the action was virtuous, but not know why it exemplified human excellence. Aristotle, as well as Kant, would find such a person flawed. Part of the explanation is doubtless that if she knows why it is virtuous, she is more likely to be reliably virtuous.

How can we develop the virtues?

According to Aristotle, there is only one way: by habituation. How do we inculcate a habit? We begin by mimicking those who have the virtue. We merely follow suit. This is true of any excellence. If one wants to become a builder, she works with a master builder and does what the builder does. If all goes well, she eventually starts to think like a master builder. Mimicking the great builder does not automatically make her a great builder. However, it is the only route to becoming a great builder. In listening to and reading a masterful writer one starts to learn how to become a better writer herself. Finally, mimicking a virtuous person does not yet make one virtuous; but it is only by doing what a virtuous person does that she can develop virtuous dispositions. Only then can she learn to enjoy being virtuous; only then can she come to "see" what is virtuous and why.

The problem, of course, is knowing how to move from just mimicking the behavior to exemplifying it. How does one stop aping a good writer and become a good writer? How does one stop aping a great builder and become a greater builder? Unfortunately, there is no formula. However, we do know that this does not happen all at once. Just as one doesn't go from being an infant to an adult all at once, one does not go from being a novice to an expert all at once. These changes are gradual. When someone acquires the skills of the master she simply finds after a while that she knows how to "go on" (Wittgenstein 2002/1953).

Pragmatism: A Better Alternative

Virtue ethics has obvious strengths: it emphasizes the need for cultivated judgment and gives habit a pivotal role in the moral life. However, as I will explain shortly, it is also vulnerable to several criticisms. Pragmatism can capture the theory's insights while jettisoning its disturbing features. To explain how, I will first say a bit about pragmatism before returning to detail the drawbacks of virtue ethics.

What pragmatism is

Pragmatism is a philosophical movement developed near the turn of the twentieth century in the work of several prominent American philosophers, most notably, Charles Sanders Peirce, William James, and John Dewey. What unified pragmatism was its rejection of standard epistemological assumptions about the nature of truth, objectivity, and rationality. The rejection of these assumptions springs from the pragmatist's belief that practice is primary in philosophy. Meaningful inquiry originates in practice. Theorizing is valuable, for sure, but its value arises from practice, is informed by practice, and its proper aim is to clarify, coordinate, and inform practice. Theorizing divorced from practice is useless. That commitment runs throughout this book. I hope that the benefits of this perspective are by now obvious.

Pragmatism is at once both familiar and radical – familiar in that it often begins with rather ordinary views; radical in that it often sees in those views insights that philosophers and lay people may miss or misunderstand. As I explained in "Moral Relativism," a pragmatic ethic (although I did not so label it there) is objective without being absolutist. It acknowledges that ethical judgments are relative, without being relativistic. And it tolerates – indeed, welcomes – some moral differences, without being irresolute.

Moreover, a pragmatic ethic can incorporate insights of other ethical theories without being just some ad hoc amalgam of them. For instance, a pragmatist uses moral criteria (rules, considerations of consequences, etc.) in moral reasoning, albeit not in the ways the standard ethical theories do. Many forms of these theories hold in some attenuated form that the relevant moral criteria are (a) fixed, (b) complete, and (c) directly applicable. Although many philosophers will deny that their views are criterial in these three senses, the character of many discussions suggests that this view is still influential if not dominant. For instance, the principle of utility is thought (a) to provide the means for determining what is moral for all people, at all times, in ways that (b) do not need to be supplemented, and (c) can be directly applied to specific cases. Likewise for many deontological theories. Using the model of law, they see morality as a collection of rules or principles that tell us how we ought to act. To this extent, most deontologists share one key presupposition of divine command theorists (Chapter 7), namely, that morality can be binding on us only if its source is independent of those whom it "binds."

Pragmatists disagree. They see criteria as tools isolating morally relevant features of action – features people should consider in making moral decisions. Criteria are not fixed since they can be, and often are, tweaked or even supplanted in light of experience. They are not complete, since elements of moral judgment cannot be subsumed under them. And they are not always directly applicable since principles cannot give us univocal direction on how we should behave in every circumstance.

The pragmatist's rejection of a criterial view of morality springs from its rejection of the notion of rationality undergirding that view. The belief that morality is primarily conscious adherence to prior and fixed criteria overrationalizes human beings; it fails to understand the pervasive role of habit in human action. We first glimpsed this role in the first chapter and discussed it more fully in "Racism." The notion of habits is pivotal for showing how pragmatism captures many of the insights of virtue theory while avoiding many of that theory's problems. To see how, we need to return to identify some of those problems.

Problems with virtue theory

Virtue theory is flawed in part because it puts undue emphasis on the agent, it fails to give an adequate account of social ethics, and it draws too sharp a distinction between motives, actions, and consequences.

Puts undue emphasis on the agent

As it is often developed, virtue theory puts excessive emphasis on the individual agent in two ways. It overemphasizes the agent's personal purity and the actions of individual agents, and it does so in ways that are psychologically implausible.

Overemphasizes the agent's personal purity

The virtue theorist claims that good just is what the virtuous person does. When virtuous people act, good consequences often follow; however, these consequences are not the agent's ultimate aim. Her aim is simply to be virtuous. However, I would contend that if someone must choose between doing an action that *really does* make the world better (in some robust and complete sense) and one that maintains her personal purity (by "being virtuous"), there are good reasons to think that she should sacrifice her purity for the greater good (see Walzer 1973). Minimally she should reevaluate what she takes to be virtuous. To explain why, consider the following phenomenon: moral actions do not invariably benefit others. After all, no single agent's behavior determines the way the world goes. Other people's actions and factors wholly beyond any particular person's control may intervene so that behavior that normally leads to a desirable result will not do so in some cases. That is why we cannot judge the virtues wholly by their effects.

Although both the virtue theorist and the pragmatist acknowledge this phenomenon, they understand it very differently. The virtue theorist might regret when her actions do not lead to good ends. However, in itself that failure would give her *no* reason to modify or abandon her understanding of the virtues. In some cases a pragmatist would agree. If a virtue (say, benevolence) that normally leads to desirable consequences "misfires" in unusual circumstances, then the pragmatist would not give the matter a second thought. After all, the evidence of this virtue's tendency to promote the interests of others is very strong.

Still, in many cases the pragmatist would see a virtue's failure to achieve good results as *a* reason to re-evaluate the nature or value of the virtue. If some virtue (say loyalty) regularly "misfired," or if its consequences were, even in a single case, especially objectionable, then a pragmatist would see that as a reason to consider that she has inculcated the wrong virtue, or that she had not entirely understood its nature or value. Judy may have thought that loyalty required her to defend her friends and family members against all charges, no matter the evidence. Then her son is charged with murder and the evidence against him is overwhelming. She might conclude that loyalty is not valuable; more likely she would rethink what loyalty requires. She might conclude that she can acknowledge his guilt while still loving him.

If we should re-evaluate virtues in such cases — as I think we should — then the virtues are valuable primarily because they are efficient or even necessary means of promoting the best consequences. (Deontologists might similarly argue that virtues are valuable primarily because they empower people to follow the requisite moral rules.) On these views having the virtues is very important morally. However, their value and their precise nature cannot be determined without understanding the ends they serve. This poses a dilemma. Virtue theory is a genuine alternative to the standard theories only if the virtues' value is independent of their likely effects in the world. However, if that is true, then virtue theory is largely — and perhaps exclusively — concerned with each agent's moral purity. I find that more than a bit worrisome.

Overemphasizes individual action over social, political, and economic institutions

Virtue theory focuses on the character of individual agents. Unless we make considerable adjustments to the theory, then that implies that the focus of moral change and moral action is always the individual. However, that is both morally and empirically dubious. Character, in the robust sense required for virtue theory, is arguably not the norm. Empirical evidence shows that most people's actions are far more likely to change because of slight changes in the external environment than any robust virtue theory can acknowledge, admit, or permit (Doris 2002). If an essential way to make people act morally is by focusing on social, political, and economic institutions rather than individual character, then that is where we should put our emphasis. As I have argued throughout the book, these institutions are morally important, often critically so. They establish the arena within which each of us acts. They can help or hinder our opportunities. They also encourage virtuous or vicious behavior. Unbridled capitalism rewards (and therefore encourages) greed and punishes (and therefore discourages) altruism. And the presence or absence of certain social institutions (public education, heath care, freedom of opportunity, etc.) will either harm or enhance the life chances of all but the very rich who can obtain these goods on

their own. Most people understand that much good and evil in this world are pro-
duced, shaped, and sustained by social, political, and economic institutions. That is
why, according to Doris, "we should invest more of our energy in attending to the
features of our environment that influence behavioral outcomes" (2002: 146).

Even if we reject Doris's strong claim that global character is rare, we ignore the
role of social institutions at our own peril. We must be attuned to ways that even
slight alterations in social, political, and economic systems can make moral action –
and the inculcation of the virtues – more or less likely. That suggests that virtue
theory will be unable to give an adequate account of social ethics.

Fails to give an adequate account of social ethics

Standard ethical theories not only give us guidance on how we should behave personally, they give us tools for developing, critiquing, and revising laws, social policies, and governmental regulations. We can offer moral arguments for public
education, provision of health care to the indigent, personal privacy, and a fair criminal justice system. It is not clear, though, how virtue theory will help us think about
these issues. In deciding whether to be honest, it seems plausible for us to ask: "What
would a virtuous person do?" However, when deciding whether to advocate universal health care, to permit physician-assisted suicide, to ban handguns, or institute a
tax to raise money to combat world hunger, I do not see how the same question
would give us any moral guidance.

I do not see that this problem can be solved. There is virtually nothing written by
virtue ethicists on social ethical issues – although Slote thinks virtue theory could
have a social morality (Slote 2000: 344–6). I am dubious that it can be done, at least
without so changing the theory that it no longer looks like virtue theory. I think this
problem, when coupled with the next, exposes serious flaws in the theory. It seems
better if we can find an alternative that permits us to address both personal and social
issues, and a theory that captures some central insights motivating virtue ethics. I
think pragmatism is just such a theory.

But first let us explore one last weakness with virtue ethics – and, indeed, with
deontology and consequentialism.

Excessively distinguishes between motives, acts, and consequences

All three major theories distinguish, albeit in different ways, between (a) acts and
consequences, (b) acts and motives, and (c) motives and consequences. These distinctions identify different factors we may consider when deciding what to do. To
that extent, these distinctions are helpful. Unfortunately, having made these distinctions, each major theory makes too much of them: they treat them as if these are
wholly separate features of human action, differences that allow us to distinguish the
theories. The first marks the theoretical divide between consequentialists and deontologists; the second, between deontologists and virtue theorists; the third, between

consequentialists and virtue theorists. However, none of these distinctions is sufficiently clear or hardy to sustain the presumed wall separating the theories.

Deontologists claim that right and wrong are determined by the character of
action, while consequences are "merely" the results of action, and hence, not central
(and perhaps irrelevant) for determining what is moral. Consequentialists draw the
distinction similarly but reach the opposite conclusion. They think an act is "merely"
the causal precursor of consequences, and hence, not central (and perhaps irrelevant) for determining what is moral. Both views imply acts and consequences are
events in narrow slices of time that are connected only causally. They just disagree
whether the acts or the consequences are morally relevant. Both views err by con-
struing this distinction as marking some deep moral or ontological divide.

Even the strictest deontologists and consequentialists must reject a rigid distinction between acts and their consequences. Act descriptions embed implicit or explicit
references to consequences, while morally significant descriptions of consequences
incorporate unstated act descriptions. Suppose I point a loaded gun at Joe's head and
pull the trigger. What, according to the deontologist, have I done? Have I twitched
my finger? Have I shot a gun? Have I murdered Joe? Have I orphaned his children?
Deontologists will presumably claim that the third is the preferred moral description, that the first two are incomplete descriptions, while the fourth identifies a mere
consequence. But why are the first two insufficient? Presumably because they fail to
include all the morally relevant features of "what I did." That is a plausible response,
however, only because pointing a loaded gun at someone's head and pulling the
trigger standardly leads to the other person's death. If they didn't, then "killing Joe"
would not be the preferred description. This "consequence" is so likely that it determines the act description.

Or consider a deontologist who thinks we can legitimately use animals for food
and experimentation, yet also thinks we should not be cruel to animals (Cohen
1986). How can he determine which actions toward animals are cruel (and are therefore impermissible) and which are not cruel (and therefore are permissible)? Why is
carving up an animal to strengthen my forearms cruel, while carving up an animal
to hone my skills as a surgeon is not? It won't do to just say the answer is provided
by the descriptions of the respective actions since we describe the two actions as we
do *only because* of their purported consequences. Cohen and other defenders of
experimentation claim we have evidence that surgeons need to carve on animals to
refine their skills – which we deem highly beneficial – but we do not think that
carving up dogs is a necessary prerequisite for strengthening people's forearms; nor
do we deem such strengthening as highly beneficial. However, if we did, we would
use different descriptions. If there were better ways for surgeons to master their
skills, we would also consider their carving on animals cruel, while if strengthening
my forearms were vitally important, and accomplished only by cutting dogs, we
would be less likely to think that was cruel.

The consequentialist will likewise have trouble wholly distinguishing acts from
their consequences, albeit for opposite reasons. She will obviously want to distinguish murder from self-defense. That, though, requires more than a simple descrip-

tion of the consequences (someone's dying). She must also refer to the context: whether the "victim" was threatening (or was reasonably thought to be threatening) to kill you or a member of your family. The consequentialist cannot circumvent this problem by claiming that the consequences were appropriate, excusable, or an instance of self-defense, since *these* descriptions also incorporate unstated act descriptions. In short, although there are sometimes practical reasons for distinguishing acts from consequences, we should not infer that these mark any fundamental moral divide.

A similar problem arises for the virtue theorist. Any attempt to sharply distinguish motives from either acts or consequences will be unsuccessful. For although we sometimes find reasons for speaking specifically about someone's motives rather than her acts or consequences, these distinctions do not carve the universe at its moral joints. Not every passing thought is a motive. We can correctly identify someone's motives and character (and she can correctly identify her own) only if we (she) know(s) how she is disposed to act in a variety of circumstances, and that requires understanding the likely consequences of her actions. Someone who is benevolently motivated will standardly do benevolent acts (which standardly lead to good consequences). Of course, our best motives occasionally misfire, and the most careful, thoughtful actions occasionally lead to disastrous results. But that is just the point: they misfire – we can explain why the motive did not lead to its normal action or the action did not have its normal consequences. Conversely, what makes something a benevolent action rather than a mean-spirited one – what makes it an action that typically leads to good consequences rather than rotten ones – is usually the agent's motives.

This isn't in the least mysterious when we think of other traits. People who regularly say intelligent things in a variety of circumstances are intelligent, and we expect intelligent people to normally say intelligent things. Making intelligent comments and acting on that reasoned information typically leads to better results. However, things occasionally misfire. Bright people sometimes say stupid things and stupid people sometimes say intelligent things. And sometimes acting on what we have good reason to believe (about the safety of airplanes or inoculations) occasionally has disastrous consequences. Why should this phenomenon be mysterious when it comes to morality?

There is a better way to conceptualize the relationship between acts, motives, and consequences. Acts, motives, and consequences, properly understood, are interrelated concepts having temporal depth and spatial breadth. As the previous discussion suggests, (1) we describe actions as we do because of their expected consequences and the actors' motivations; (2) we identify motives as we do because they are standardly followed by certain actions and consequences; and (3) we understand that consequences are what they are because they normally spring from certain motives and actions. None of these elements occurs in a thin slice of time in one locale. If I lie to you now, I am not just mouthing words, (a) my action springs from my habits (and thus, my motives), (b) I deceive you (or at least try), (c) in order to change your behavior, while (d) shaping the character of our relationship, and (e) strengthening my disposition to lie. If I am myopic, I may think of my action unidimensionally. However, that does not change my action's depth or breadth. A "lie" that did not spring from who I am would be a mistake (I did not realize the information I was telling you was false), not a lie. A "lie" that did not deceive in some morally objectionable way (e.g., bluffing in poker) would not be a lie. A "lie" that did not change (or seek to change) your behavior would likewise not be a lie. After all, the aim of a lie is to always to get someone to act – or not act – differently than they would have had they been told the truth. Therefore a lie that did not alter our relationship in any degree (by making you distrustful of me if you discovered it) would arguably not be a lie (discovering that you are a superb bluffer). And a lie that does not make me more prone (however slightly) to lie in the future, would arguably have been an accident and not an act. Understanding that each element of this triumvirate is temporally and spatially thick helps focus deliberation. We will primarily think about what we do now since that is most within our control. However, in thinking about what we do now, we should realize that our present action springs from who we are, and that our action standardly has certain consequences, including – and perhaps especially – consequences for making us certain kinds of people.

Here is an example from another domain that illustrates this point. What is it to be a good teacher? Is the good teacher the one who follows the proper rules for good teaching (be fair, explain the material clearly, use up-to-date information, etc.), the one who has inculcated the appropriate academic virtues (honesty, open-mindedness, rigor, clarity, etc.), or is she the one who has the best consequences (say, the students like her best or they score higher on standardized tests)?

It is clear in this context that there is something fishy about the question. Although, for certain purposes, we may focus on one of these elements to the relative exclusion of the others, none in isolation is a sufficient condition of being a good teacher. Indeed, these are all deeply interrelated and temporally thick criteria. Normally the good teacher is the one who generally follows the rules because she has the appropriate academic virtues, which usually means that students learn more from her. However, these are not identical: someone might have the appropriate virtues, yet for a variety of reasons, be unable to be effective in the classroom. Such a person would not be a good teacher.

Where the discussion has brought us

Our discussion has led to two observations about the nature of morality. The first is that we are neither epistemological nor moral islands. As we began to see in Chapter 5, we are who we are, believe what we believe, and have the opportunities we have in large measure because of our social, political, and economic environments. That is why any adequate account of morality must be concerned with these institutional structures. Second, we have the most direct control over what we, as individuals, do here and now.

These observations might appear to be in tension. They are not. Rather they are mutually supportive. We get in moral trouble if we focus exclusively on either. The virtue theorist is right that we should pay special attention to our own actions since these are most within our control. However, we want to make ourselves certain kinds of people in important part because we know we will then be better equipped to improve social, political, legal, and economic institutions. These institutions not only have profound effects on others, but changing them also becomes an indirect way of changing ourselves. The right institutions make us more likely to act morally, and less likely to experience morality's requirements as excessively demanding.

REFERENCES

Cohen, C. (1986) "The Case for the Use of Animals in Biomedical Research," *New England Journal of Medicine* 315: 865–70.

Crisp, R. and Slote, M. A. (eds.) (1997) *Virtue Ethics*. Oxford: Oxford University Press.

Doris, J. M. (2002) *Lack of Character: Personality and Moral Behavior*. Cambridge: Cambridge University Press.

Driver, J. (2001) *Uneasy Virtue*. Cambridge: Cambridge University Press.

Foot, P. (2001) *Natural Goodness*. Oxford: Oxford University Press.

Frey, R. G. (2000) "Act-Utilitarianism." In H. LaFollette (ed.), *The Blackwell Guide to Ethical Theory*. Oxford: Blackwell Publishers, 165–82.

Herman, B. (1993) *The Practice of Moral Judgment*. Cambridge, MA: Harvard University Press.

Hill, T. E., Jr. (1992) "Imperfect Duty and Supererogation." In *Dignity and Practical Reason in Kant's Moral Theory*. Ithaca, NY: Cornell University Press, 147–75.

Hurka, T. (2001) *Virtue, Vice, and Value*. Oxford: Oxford University Press.

Hursthouse, R. (1999) *On Virtue Ethics*. Oxford: Oxford University Press.

Korsgaard, C. M. (1996) *Creating the Kingdom of Ends*. Cambridge: Cambridge University Press.

Slote, M. A. (2000) "Virtue Ethics." In H. LaFollette (ed.), *The Blackwell Guide to Ethical Theory*. Oxford: Blackwell Publishers, 325–47.

Slote, M. A. (2001) *Morals from Motives*. Oxford: Oxford University Press.

Walzer, M. (1973) "Political Action: The Problem of Dirty Hands," *Philosophy and Public Affairs* 2: 160–80.

Wittgenstein, L. (2002/1953) *Philosophical Investigations*. Oxford: Blackwell Publishers.

FIFTEEN

Animals

Morality does not concern what rocks do. Nor, barring special circumstances, does morality concern what we do to rocks. The reason is simple: rocks don't do anything, nor can rocks be harmed. Only certain kinds of creatures can morally wrong others; only certain kinds of creatures can be wronged. Such creatures have "moral status." This idea is so obvious that we don't tend to think about it. Not do we tend to think critically about which objects have moral status. We typically just accept the views of our society, even when, in retrospect, we realize just how wrong its views were.

In the early 1800s blacks in many states had no moral status. They were treated as property. Other people at that time doubtless thought that slaves had *some* moral status. Nonetheless, they assumed blacks' status was dramatically less than that of whites. At that time, many people also thought that women lacked full moral status. Among other things, they thought that women should not be allowed to vote.

Although less obvious, assumptions about moral status also lay just beneath the surface of every ethical issue we have discussed. In deciding whether to lie, we assumed that the creatures who lie and those to whom they lie have moral status. Rocks, crickets, and radios cannot tell a lie nor can they be lied to. "I lied to my radio about why I was late coming home" is not something a sane person would say. Creatures must have advanced cognitive abilities to lie and to be deceived by lies. These are creatures with moral status.

The issue also lurked beneath our discussion of capital punishment. Only certain kinds of creatures can commit crimes or be harmed by crimes. Objects devoid of moral status can be neither victims nor criminals. I might steal Stephanie's VCR and use it for target practice. In so doing, I do not wrong the VCR; I wrong Stephanie. VCRs cannot be victims. Likewise, if a VCR malfunctions and electrocutes Stephanie, the VCR did not murder Stephanie; it would be ludicrous to send it to prison, fine it, or verbally chastise it (although we might curse at it!). Perhaps we might think that the manufacturer was negligent: that it should not have built electronic devices that would shock their owners. If so, then we might think the manufacturer wronged Stephanie; we might even hold it guilty of negligent homicide.

However, we haven't asked, until now, why we made these moral assumptions. We never asked how we determine if something has moral status, nor did we decide if all creatures with moral status have the same degree of moral status. If we think two creatures have different moral status, we never asked what justifies this difference. This is not some mysterious and abstract theoretical inquiry. It is a practical inquiry that shapes our answers to an array of practical questions, perhaps most especially racism and sexism. The same question also takes center stage in inquiries about the moral status of non-human animals, especially since we have morally schizophrenic views about non-human animals.

Non-human animals

Our schizophrenic views of non-human animals

In some respects we view and treat some non-human animals as if they had not just some, but considerable, moral worth. Yet in other ways we view and treat similar animals as if they were devoid of worth, as if they had no moral status. Let me explain.

Most of us believe it is wrong to wantonly kill or torture a higher-order mammal. Suppose we discover that Jones, our next-door neighbor, has a habit of picking up stray cats and decapitating them with his homemade guillotine; or that he smashes their heads with his sledgehammer to strengthen his arm muscles or to use their brains to create a collage on his basement wall. In the process he studies their reactions to stress and submits a paper outlining his results to a regional science journal. Almost everyone would conclude that Jones is immoral. We wouldn't want him to be our president, our friend, our next-door neighbor, or our son-in-law.

This view reflects most people's beliefs that there are moral limits on how we can treat non-human animals, and that these limits arise from the nature of the animals, not from the desires of other humans to see animals treated well. Jones's behavior is wrong because of what it does *to the animal*. That suggests that we believe that animals have moral status. Although most people think animals have less status than humans, they have sufficient status to morally constrain how we treat them.

That's half of our morally schizophrenic selves. The other half cavalierly uses animals for clothes, research, in the development of new drugs, and to determine the safety of household products. All these uses inflict some pain on animals; many inflict considerable pain. A chronicle of such uses is readily available in academic journals and books (Mason 1993; Ryder 1975; Singer 1990). I will not discuss these uses of animals here. However, I will focus briefly on the use of animals for food – by far humans' single biggest use of animals.

Factory farms and humane diets

The literature chronicling the treatment of animals on the contemporary farm is immense. Doubtless some claims about the treatment of animals are exaggerated or

out of context. Nonetheless, the evidence that many farm animals suffer considerable pain, distress, and stress is compelling (Mason and Singer 1990; Singer 1990:
chapter 3). This is not to say or imply that farmers are especially cruel. They aren't.
Rather, economic factors compel farmers to cram more and more animals in smaller
and smaller spaces (American Public Health Association 2003: 12). For instance,
farmers are required by law to give each chicken only two-thirds of a square foot of
space (United States Department of Agriculture 2003). Most people would be
appalled at a neighbor who kept his dog chained to a tree in the back yard or confined in a small kennel in the basement. Yet these domestic animals, no matter how
mistreated, are given much more room than factory-farmed animals.

The effects of overcrowding on these animals is predictable: they become aggres-
sive and ill. Having created these behavioral and medical problems, farmers must
then "solve" the resulting problems. To stop chickens from fighting, farmers will
debeak them. To stop sows from crushing their young in cramped quarters, farmers
will immobilize nursing sows. Cramped animals are (again, not surprisingly) more
likely to get ill, which then requires both medical intervention and prevention. One
"solution" is to give them massive amounts of antibiotics. Farm animals are now given
13 million pounds of antibiotics annually – more than four times the amount given
to all humans.

These factors conspire to make life for animals on a factory farm deeply distress-
ing. As James Rachels crisply puts it: "For these animals the slaughterhouse is not an
unpleasant end to an otherwise contented life. As terrifying as the process of slaugh-
ter is, for them it may actually be regarded as a merciful release" (1977: 189). (As
an aside, these conditions are also indirectly detrimental to humans [American Public
Health Association 2003: 12].)

What would justify doing this to animals just so we can eat them? Most people
probably think they must eat animals to be healthy. However, although there may
have been times and places when that was true, it is no longer true, except for some
few people with unusual medical conditions. Instead, there are compelling health
reasons to substantially limit or abandon meat (American Dietetic Association 2003).
So why do most people continue to eat meat? Perhaps because they like its taste.
However, is it morally acceptable to inflict substantial pain and suffering on animals
to satisfy our taste buds? How could it be? Everyone assumed that our fictional Jones
acts immorally. We think he inflicts considerable pain on animals to satisfy some
trivial end (having a colorful, textured collage on his wall), or a significant interest
(having strong arms) that he could satisfy in some other less objectionable way (e.g.,
lifting weights). That certainly seems like a compelling reason to think that he acts
immorally. However, it seems we can say precisely the same things about our practice of eating meat. By eating meat we satisfy one trivial end (compared to the
suffering of the animals), namely, exciting certain taste buds. We also satisfy a
significant end (getting nutrition), although this is an end we can satisfy in equally
good – if not better – ways. So why isn't eating meat just as bad as Jones's behavior? Why isn't it worse? After all, the cats Jones kills suffer little (he kills them

quickly), while most animals on a factory farm suffer a great deal over a long period of time.

Perhaps the better explanation for why most people continue to eat meat is simply that doing so is a deeply ingrained habit, one that is very difficult to break. Is it morally acceptable to inflict substantial pain on animals because we have trouble breaking the habit of eating them? Perhaps if the habit were equivalent to an addiction, that would mitigate our responsibility. However, we should be careful. For had Jones been reared to treat cats in the ways described, few people would think that would give us reason to excuse his behavior. He ought to stop treating cats in those ways, period.

Yet we continue to eat animals. That suggests that this half of our schizophrenic selves thinks that non-human animals have no moral status. Minimally it implies that we think they have far less status than do humans. When pushed, most people don't want to abandon either of these beliefs. They would be appalled at the suggestion that there was nothing wrong with decapitating wholly conscious cats for the fun of it. They would be equally – if not more – appalled at the suggestion that morality requires us to change our eating habits.

Do non-human animals have moral status?

So perhaps most people's reaction to the Jones example is just misguided. To decide, we must get clearer about the grounds for ascribing moral status. Let's begin again with the uncontroversial claim that ordinary rocks have no moral status, while humans do.

To say that rocks have no moral status is not to say that we should never include inanimate objects in our moral deliberations. Sometimes we should. But only when what someone does to them affects other humans' interests. For example, we shouldn't:

- demolish someone's private property, e.g., taking a sledgehammer to someone's rock garden;
- destroy objects humans need, e.g., an important mineral in manufacturing;
- blow up an historically significant artifact, e.g., the Pyramids; or
- spray-paint a landscape humans find especially pleasing, e.g., the Grand Canyon.

These actions harm people by damaging objects they own, need, want, or desire. However, we cannot *harm* the objects in any morally robust sense. That is why they have no moral status. (Although I do not discuss this issue here, many environmental ethicists reject this view. They think nature has certain intrinsic interests [Callicott 1989; Elliot and Gare 1983; Hargrove 1989; Johnson 1991; Rolston 1986, 1988; Taylor 1986].)

In contrast, we can harm humans. We think we shouldn't. That is what it means to say that humans, but not rocks, have moral status. Humans, as Kant would say, are not mere means to others' ends. It is wrong for Susan to hit Paula, not because other people like Paula or because other people would be offended by the violence, but simply because Paula is a person.

What about non-human animals? Where do they fall along this continuum? Should we treat them more like inanimate objects or more like humans – or perhaps somewhere in between these extremes? To treat them like inanimate objects is to think that they have no independent moral status; to treat them just like humans is to think they have full moral status; to treat them somewhat like humans is to think that they have some moral status, albeit less than humans. The reaction to the Jones example suggests that most people are inclined to this last option.

The ground of moral status

In asking whether a creature has moral status we are not asking if it has some identifiable physical characteristic like skin, arms, weight, or hair. Instead we are asking a normative question about how the creature should be treated. It is akin to asking, as we did in the discussion of punishment, if a person deserves to be punished. To be sure, in answering this normative question, we usually refer to the person's physical characteristics, her mental state, her behavior, and any relevant mitigating factors. But merely listing characteristics is never enough. We must explain why these characteristics and factors support our assessment of whether and why she is responsible for her actions. Of course, people may disagree about precisely which traits and behaviors justify an ascription of guilt; they are even more likely to disagree about the traits' precise relevance. Despite these disagreements, most people reject the practice of holding seriously retarded humans criminally liable. In the same way, we find some disagreement about which characteristics are necessary or sufficient for ascribing moral status. There are deeper disagreements about their precise relevance. Nonetheless, most people think that certain psychological traits and mental abilities – sensation, consciousness, thought, and emotion – are especially relevant to determining moral status. We are more concerned about creatures that can feel pain, anxiety, depression, etc. We think they have moral status because they have interests that can be advanced or set back.

Interests

Something can be harmed only if it has interests that can be set back by the actions of others. Something can be benefited only if it has interests that can be advanced by the actions of others. Since rocks have no interests, they cannot be harmed or benefited. The problem is knowing how to define interests and how to decide which interests generate how much moral worth. I cannot resolve that issue here. Still, we can agree that an adequate account of interests cannot be either too weak – so that most objects have interests and therefore moral status – or too strong – so that things we normally think have moral status do not. Let me explain. Suppose we say that an object has interests (and thus moral worth) if any of its functions can be enhanced or diminished by another's action. If this were true then a computer would have interests (and thus moral worth) since we could smash it. A rock lining my drive-way would also have interests (and thus moral worth) since we could crush it to make a new road. And grass would have interests (and thus moral worth) since we could uproot it. This notion of interest would be far too weak. On this view every-thing has interests (and thus moral worth). Therefore, virtually every action we take arguably sets back something's interests. That would make acting morally impossible.

Neither should we define the notion of interests too strongly. We do not want an account that denies moral status to creatures that we are confident have such status. Suppose someone proposes that something has interests only if it consciously asserts those interests. As stated, this account is far too restrictive. It would mean that no infants, severely retarded people, or comatose patients would have interests; there-fore they would have no moral status. This account would also imply that many fully functioning normal adults would lack some interests we think we have. After all, we all have some interests we do not – and perhaps cannot – articulate at the present time. We also likely have some interests we explicitly disavow.

Although being able to articulate one's interests is too strong to be a necessary condition of moral status, it is surely a sufficient condition. Only cognitively sophis-ticated creatures can articulate their interests. These creatures will standardly be capable of pain, suffering, desire, frustration, happiness, aversion, etc. They are crea-tures who not only have interests, they are capable of identifying and respecting others' interest. Some philosophers use this idea to explain why non-human animals do not have any serious moral status (Carruthers 1992; Cohen 1986; Fox 2002/1997).

The moral community

These philosophers argue that contractualism is the most defensible moral theory. Contractualism holds that morality is "the result of an imaginary contract between rational agents, who are agreeing upon rules to govern their subsequent behavior" (Carruthers 1992: 35). Such a theory is not only "at least as plausible as utilitarian-ism, but . . . [its] normative output is considerably more attractive" (ibid. 48). Can we explain all human morality as arising from an imaginary contract between rational agents? Perhaps. Certainly a number of prominent ethicists thought so (Gauthier 1986; Rawls 1999/1971; Scanlon 1998). However, even if it is an ade-quate moral theory, I do not think it implies that all non-human animals are devoid of moral status. To explain why, I return to address a question I raised at the begin-ning of this chapter.

Moral agents or moral patients

We saw earlier that only creatures with relatively sophisticated cognitive abilities can lie to others. Jo cannot lie to William unless she recognizes: (1) the difference between what is true and what is false, (2) that by acting in certain ways (verbal or otherwise) she encourages William to believe what is false, and (3) that, in so doing, she changes the way he behaves. If Jo is a normal functioning adult, she is capable of lying. For instance, she might tell William that she will buy his used car for more than the asking price if he holds it for two days. In fact, Jo intends to buy another car. She considers William's car a desirable backup if her preferred deal falls through.

However, a three-year-old child could not lie to William; she lacks the requisite cognitive sophistication. Moreover, no one can lie to creatures devoid of cognitive abilities. For instance, we cannot lie to rocks or rockets. However, although creatures who can lie and creatures who can be told lies must both have some cognitive abilities, they needn't have the same abilities. An infant can be deceived by a lie although she cannot tell one. As anyone who has been around very young children knows, they will believe whatever they are told. That explains why, among other things, they are easy prey for sexual predators.

Likewise, while a seriously retarded person (or an infant) lacks the cognitive ability to be guilty of murder, they can be murdered (or assaulted or raped). Those assaults, rapes, and murders would be wrongs against them. These people can be morally wronged even if they are not full agents. They are, in Regan's words, moral patients (1983: 152–4).

> Moral agents are individuals who have a variety of sophisticated abilities, including the particular ability to bring impartial moral principles to bear on the determination of what, all things considered, morally ought to be done, and having made this determination, to freely choose or fail to choose to act as morality . . . requires. Normal adult human beings are the paradigm individuals believed to be moral agents. . . .
>
> In contrast *moral patients* lack the prerequisites that would enable them to control their own behavior in ways that would make them morally accountable for what they do . . . Moral patients, in a word, cannot do what is right or proper to perform . . . [Nonetheless, some of these] have a sense of the future . . . , have an emotional life . . . , and have an experiential welfare : . . Moral patients can be on the receiving end of the right and wrong acts [and thus can be wronged]. (Regan 1983: 152–4).

This explains why non-human animals have moral status. They have interests and they are capable of suffering, even if they are insufficiently sophisticated to recognize similar interests in others.

Cohen, Fox, and Carruthers disagree. They insist that morality is reciprocal: that the only creatures who can have rights are creatures who respect others' rights. Since non-human animals lack the cognitive sophistication to recognize other people's moral status, then they have no serious moral status. The problem, as you might infer, is that this position seems to imply that infants and severely retarded humans also lack moral status. This helps frame a common argument for the moral status of non-human animals.

Marginal cases

One of the most powerful arguments that animals have moral status is the argument from marginal cases. A classic statement of the argument can be found in Peter Singer's *Animal Liberation* (Singer 1990/1975). Suppose, Singer asks, we compare higher animals with a severely brain-damaged infant. What do we find?

> Adult chimpanzees, dogs, pigs, and members of many other species far surpass the ability of the brain damaged infant to relate to others, act independently, be self-aware, and any other capacity that could reasonably be said to give value to life . . . The only thing that distinguishes the infant from the animal, in the eyes of those who claim it has a "right to life," is that it is, biologically speaking, a member of the species *homo sapiens*, whereas chimpanzees, dogs, and pigs are not. But to use *this* difference as a basis for granting a right to life to the infant and not to the other animals is, of course, pure speciesism. It is exactly the same kind of arbitrary difference that the most crude and overt kind of racist uses in attempting to justify racial discrimination (Singer 1990: 18).

Arguments from moral cases can take one of two forms. Sometimes they are offered in both guises by the same author. The first form is some version of the slippery slope argument; the second, a consistency argument. As I argued in Chapter 9, we should abandon slippery slope arguments in moral debate. So let us focus on the second, more persuasive, form. Those using this form claim that many non-human animals are cognitively similar to (or even more sophisticated than) infants and severely retarded humans. We grant these humans moral status. Consistency thus demands that we grant relevantly similar non-human animals the same status. The only response, I think, is for the contractualists to defend bare speciesism.

Bare speciesism

Cohen claims that we can justifiably treat severely retarded infants differently than we treat adult chimpanzees simply because they are human. He doesn't think this is inconsistent at all. As he puts it, "Speciesism is not merely plausible, it is essential for right conduct . . ." (Cohen 1986: 867). How, though, could he defend this position? I see no reason for thinking that a bare biological divide could be morally relevant. Recall our earlier discussion about racism and sexism. These practices are morally indefensible since they treat a mere biological divide as a significant moral divide. Of course, there are differences between the races and the sexes, but so what? The differences are merely biological. Of course, there are differences between humans and chimps, but so what?

However, Cohen thinks species differences are more fundamental than racial and sexual differences. But exactly what this means – and why he thinks species differences are morally relevant – is not obvious. Why should our "primary" classification (whatever that means) be our species rather than biological class (mammals), biological order (primates), subspecies distinctions (race), or cross-species distinctions (gender)? For some purposes (identifying units of evolutionary selection) species may be considered biologically primary; for other purposes (identifying creatures susceptible to sickle-cell anemia), subspecies distinctions may be primary; and for still other purposes (identifying creatures capable of giving birth) cross-species distinctions would be best. Finally, even if we could determine that one and only one of these classifications was biologically primary, how would that make this particular biological divide morally relevant?

Stephen Post offers one answer. He claims speciesism is grounded in "species loyalty" (Post 1993: 294). Species loyalty is "the outgrowth of millennia of human evolution shaped by natural selection . . . [This] 'kin selection' or 'kin altruism' is deeply ingrained in the human 'biogram'" (ibid. 295). In short, speciesism is morally justified because it is biologically natural to favor one's kin.

To say that such loyalty is natural, however, suggests it is unavoidable – something we do instinctively, something we cannot avoid. But, since some people are non-speciesists, speciesism cannot be natural in this strong sense. Hence, when Post claims favoritism toward kin is "natural," he must mean something weaker, namely, that biological creatures have a tendency to favor their own species. That may be true. However, why should we assume that such a tendency (if it exists) is morally permitted, let alone required? There are other biological tendencies we think morality should constrain. For instance, we probably have a tendency to prefer those who look like us – those who have the same tint of skin and slant of eye. (Perhaps we think of them as kin?) We may also have some biological tendencies toward aggression. Our hormones sometimes move us to have sex at inappropriate times. However, we do not encourage, praise, or morally sanctify these tendencies. We think morality should tame them, not lionize them.

The deficiencies of speciesism can be demonstrated by a bit of science fiction. Suppose aliens arrive on earth. They are phylogenetically discontinuous with humans – they are not even carbon-based life forms. We find them aesthetically repulsive. They look like giant slugs – and we call them Slugantots. We have no natural sympathies for them. However, their behavior reveals that they are intelligent, purposive, sentient creatures – although the exact contours of their abilities elude us because of their peculiar embodiment.

Post, Cohen, and other speciesists claim that species loyalty gives us the right to favor humans over them – all other things being equal. (It likewise gives the aliens the right to favor themselves over us.) However, neither our natural proclivities nor our aesthetic dislike for them would justify favoring a human over a similarly situated Slugantot, just as an affinity for people of like tint does not give Caucasians the moral right to mistreat people of color. Bare speciesism, like racism and sexism, is simply indefensible. It may be that humans have a greater moral status than non-human animals. But that doesn't mean we can do to them as we please.

Conclusion

If these arguments are correct then at least cognitively sophisticated non-human animals have moral status. We should consider their interests. Moreover, it seems their interests in avoiding pain and suffering are sufficiently strong that they will outweigh the desires of humans to satisfy their trivial interests. Put differently, we cannot just use them any way we wish. If the arguments in the early part of the chapter are correct, that means we should rethink our widespread use of animals for food.

Some people will contend that that conclusion just has to be wrong: any morality that requires that we change our diets demands too much of us. We return to confront that argument in Chapter 17.

REFERENCES

American Dietetic Association (2003) "Position of the American Dietetic Association: Vegetarian Diets," *Journal of the American Dietetic Association* 103: 748–65. (Online) Available at: http://www.eatright.org/Public/GovernmentAffairs/92_17084.cfm.

American Public Health Association (2003) "Precautionary Moratorium on New Concentrated Animal Feed Operations," *APHA Association News*, 12–14. (Online) Available at: http://www.apha.org/legislative/policy/2003/2003-007.pdf.

Callicott, J. B. (1989) *In Defense of the Land Ethic: Essays in Environmental Philosophy*. Albany, NY: State University of New York Press.

Carruthers, P. (1992) *The Animals Issue: Moral Theory in Practice*. Cambridge: Cambridge University Press.

Cohen, C. (1986) "The Case for the Use of Animals in Biomedical Research," *New England Journal of Medicine* 315: 865–70.

Elliot, R. and Gare, A. (1983) *Environmental Philosophy: A Collection of Readings*. St. Lucia, Queensland: University of Queensland Press.

Fox, M. A. (2002/1997) "The Moral Community." In H. LaFollette (ed.), *Ethics in Practice: An Anthology*, 2nd edn. Oxford: Blackwell Publishers, 117–27.

Gauthier, D. P. (1986) *Morals by Agreement*. Oxford: Oxford University Press.

Hargrove, E. C. (1989) *Foundations of Environmental Ethics*. Englewood Cliffs, NJ: Prentice-Hall.

Johnson, L. E. (1991) *A Morally Deep World: An Essay on Moral Significance and Environmental Ethics*. Cambridge: Cambridge University Press.

Mason, J. (1993) *An Unnatural Order: Uncovering the Roots of Our Domination of Nature and Each Other*. New York: Simon & Schuster.

Mason, J. and Singer, P. (1990) *Animal Factories*, 2nd edn. New York: Crown Publishing.

Post, S. (1993) "The Emergence of Species Impartiality: A Medical Critique of Biocentrism," *Perspectives in Biology and Medicine* 36: 289–300.

Rachels, J. (1977) "Vegetarianism and 'the Other Weight Problem'." In W. Aiken and H. LaFollette (eds.), *World Hunger and Moral Obligation*. Englewood Cliffs, NJ: Prentice-Hall, 180–93.

Rawls, J. (1999/1971) *A Theory of Justice*, 2nd edn. Cambridge, MA: Harvard University Press.

Regan, T. (1983) *The Case for Animal Rights*. Berkeley: University of California Press.

Rolston, H. (1986) *Philosophy Gone Wild: Essays in Environmental Ethics*. Buffalo, NY: Prometheus Books.

Rolston, H. (1988) *Environmental Ethics: Duties to and Values in the Natural World*. Philadelphia, PA: Temple University Press.

Ryder, R. D. (1975) *Victims of Science: The Use of Animals in Research*. London: Davis-Poynter.

Scanlon, T. M. (1998) *What We Owe to Each Other*. Cambridge, MA: The Belknap Press of Harvard University Press.

Singer, P. (1990/1975) *Animal Liberation: A New Ethics for Our Treatment of Animals*, 2nd edn. New York: New York Review, distributed by Random House.

Taylor, P. W. (1986) *Respect for Nature: A Theory of Environmental Ethics*. Princeton, NJ: Princeton University Press.

United States Department of Agriculture (2003) "World Egg Production," *International Egg and Poultry Review* 66: 1–3. (Online) Available at: http://www.ams.usda.gov/poultry/mncs/International/2003Reports/x111203.pdf.

PART SIX

The Demands of Morality

SIXTEEN

World Hunger

We are watching television, and an advertisement for UNICEF, OXFAM, or the Christian Children's Fund interrupts our favorite show. We grab our remotes and quickly flip to another channel. Perhaps we mosey to the kitchen for a snack. Maybe we just sit, trying not to watch. These machinations may banish these haunting images of destitute, starving children from our TVs and our thoughts, but they do not alter the brutal facts: millions of people in the world are undernourished; thousands die each day; most of those who suffer and die are children, and, with collective effort, we could end the suffering of millions without too much strain.

At the same time, many of us talk as if we were nearly indigent. Relative to the rich in our society we may be financially strapped. But relative to most citizens of the world, we are awash with money. Given that, what, if anything, should we do, individually or collectively, to alleviate their suffering and save their lives? Most of us interpret this as asking: "Should we be charitable, and, if so, how charitable?" That seems to be the guiding premise of organizations who implore us to send money: they tell us to open our hearts, to be generous, to give of ourselves, to help those in need. The character of their appeal reveals just how pervasive the "charity view" is. We think that although it would be nice of us to assist the starving, none of us is morally required to assist them – that we have done nothing (very) wrong if we ignore those strangers in need. Indeed, most people assume that if we help, then we are moral heroes.

There are those rare voices admonishing us to give, proclaiming that our failure to assist is not just tight-fisted, but wrong. Some of these will claim our obligation is based on a right of the starving to our assistance (Li 1996; Shue 1996), while others who claim we have strong obligations to assist will eschew talk of rights since their preferred ethical theories do not countenance them (Singer 1996/1972). But all these thinkers emphatically reject the charity view. They aver that assisting the destitute is not a moral option but a moral requirement.

There are fewer still who declare that we have a positive obligation *not* to help, since assistance, according to their predictions, would not only prolong the misery of the hungry, but increase the number of people dying (Hardin 1996/1974).

Despite these differences, advocates of these standard views frame the moral question similarly. They ask – as I did in the beginning – what, if anything, should the
relatively affluent do to aid the starving? The work of Sen and others has led an
increasing number of scholars to reject this formulation of the question (Drèze and
Sen 1989, 1991a, 1991b, 1991c; Sen 1981). These scholars state or imply that even
asking this question is a mistake – and likely a moral failing (Crocker 1997: 211).

The work of developmental theorists has illuminated aspects of world hunger not
operative in the standard ways of framing the debate. It has illuminated the circumstances surrounding, and the causes of, endemic and episodic hunger; and it offers
wise counsel about effective efforts to alleviate hunger. However, as we shall see, it
does not eliminate the need to address the standard moral questions. It merely
requires that we reframe them. We must still ascertain whether and how those of us
in relative affluence should morally respond to the brute facts of starvation – and to
the conditions that create and sustain it. However, we cannot correctly characterize
the issues until we first understand the standard options.

The Basic Options

Charity

Most people in the United States, and many in the developed world, embrace the
charity view in one of two incarnations. On one view *being* charitable is wholly voluntary, while on the other, *to whom* we are charitable is wholly voluntary. According
to the first variation, we have no duty to the needy (Hoenig 1999). According to the
second, traceable to Kant, we have an *imperfect duty* to help people in need. However,
although we ought to be charitable to some degree, there is no particular person
whom we are obligated to assist. Certainly no particular person can expect, let alone
demand, our assistance.

Despite their differences, both views hold (a) that no particular person can
demand or expect the assistance of others and (b) that governments cannot legitimately coerce us (e.g., via taxation) to be charitable (Narveson 2000: 317). Moreover, although the second view holds that we morally ought to be charitable, we can
fulfill that imperfect duty without helping anyone who is starving. We could, instead,
help the unemployed in our neighborhood, support a literacy program, or give to
Planned Parenthood. Some who hold this view might claim we are duty bound to
meet greater needs before meeting less substantial ones. However, since there are
pressing needs close to home, likely we could satisfy an imperfect duty of charity
without helping any of the world's starving. Thus, on both charity views, people who
fail to contribute to famine relief might be stingy or morally shortsighted, but they
would not necessarily be immoral.

In this chapter I will not directly discuss the charity view. I will simply assume it
is the best position if no defensible alternative can be found. Now I focus on those
alternatives; however, in discussing them I will indirectly address the charity view.

We should not aid the starving

Most of us think feeding the starving would be good even if it is something that we do not do. We think it is good because (a) we think it relieves human suffering and most accounts of morality hold that (b) relieving human suffering is at least permissible and perhaps morally required. Hardin disagrees. He thinks that (a) is false, and therefore concludes that we should not feed the starving.

Both the duty and the charity views, Hardin claims, assume that our ability to feed people is boundless. It is not. "A nation's land has a limited capacity to support a population and as the current energy crisis has shown us, in some ways we have already exceeded the carrying capacity of our land" (Hardin 1996/1974: 12). Given these limitations, some countries are like overcrowded lifeboats. Their land cannot support the country's current population – and certainly not future generations given current population growth rates. Although feeding starving people may temporarily keep some alive, in the long run it will increase the population to the point where we can no longer feed them, even if we wanted. That will dramatically increase suffering and endanger future generations. That is why assistance is morally wrong.

Here's an example to illustrate Hardin's point. At the time of Hardin's writing in the early 1970s, India had a population of 650 million people. Despite the large number of people dying from starvation, its population was growing at a rate of 2.6 percent per year. At that rate, India's population would double every 27 years. The problem was even more acute in Colombia, Ecuador, and Pakistan, which had annual population growth rates of greater than 3 percent. At that pace, their populations would double every 21 years. If those countries were unable to feed their current populations, how could they possibly feed a population twice or four times its current size – even with massive assistance from more affluent nations? Although our initial sympathetic impulse is to feed the starving, we should not. We should recognize just "how wrong generosity can be" (Fletcher 1977: 105).

A strong obligation to feed the starving

The claim that we have a strong obligation to assist the starving takes two broad forms, reflecting different theoretical commitments. The first claims that we have a positive obligation to ease suffering and promote happiness; hence, we should assist the starving (Singer 1977/1972: 28). The second claims people have a right to food, and that right grounds our obligation to assist them. Of course rights, absent compelling obligations or duties, are effectively empty (Pogge 2000). That is why even those who claim that people have a right to food will claim that the relatively affluent have a strong correlative positive obligation to assist those in need. Therefore, although the distinction between these two positions is theoretically intriguing, and could well have *some* practical significance, for present purposes I will ignore the difference and simply talk about the strong obligation to assist the starving.

Those who claim the relatively affluent have this strong obligation must, among other things, show why Hardin's projections are either (a) morally irrelevant or (b) mistaken. A hearty few take the former tack: they claim we have a strong obligation to aid the starving even if in our efforts to keep many of them from starving, we eventually become malnourished ourselves. These folks think that surviving on "lifeboat earth," only by letting others drown in the sea of starvation, would signify an indignity and callousness worse than extinction (Watson 1977). They think it would be morally preferable to die struggling to create a decent life for all than to continue to live at the expense of the starving.

However, most who think we ought to feed the starving take the second approach. They claim, or imply, that *if* feeding the starving had the terrible consequences Hardin predicts, then we should not feed them (Singer 1977/1972: 34). Consequently, most who reject Hardin's neo-Malthusian conclusion argue that his projected consequences are implausible, if not demonstrably wrong. To set the stage for showing that Hardin's views are wrong, I must first describe the developmental alternative.

The developmental alternative

The basic idea

Most discussions of world hunger state or imply that (a) starvation is caused by a shortage of food in a region, (b) which is usually caused by a natural disaster (drought, floods, etc.). Given these assumptions, we then ask: (c) what, if anything, should we morally do to help people escape the effects of this famine? If we assume someone should assist them, then (d) we must decide "*who* is responsible for providing this help" (McKinley 1981).

Jean Drèze and Amartya Sen argue that this way of framing the issue mistakenly treats hunger as a naturally induced phenomenon unconnected to the social, political, and economic institutions within which it arises (1989; 1991a, 1991b; 1991c). This is not true, they claim, even for a farmer who owns her own land. The farmer's ability to obtain enough food depends not only on the size and quality of her land, a normal rainfall, and her hard work, but also on the actions of others. Will people living upstream dam up or pollute the water flowing through her land? Will they permit their animals to overgraze the land so there is no grass for hers? Will others sell her the supplies she needs: seed, animal feed, farm equipment, etc.? Will others buy her products so she has money to buy the supplies she needs? Will they pay her a fair price? Will they assist her if some disaster interferes with her crop or prevents her from harvesting it? Unless these and other factors are satisfied, then all the land and hard work in the world will not suffice to feed her family. That is why families' inability to feed themselves often has little to do with the general availability of food in the area.

History supports this armchair reasoning. During the 1974 famine in Bangladesh, the amount of food per capita in the country was the third highest during a ten-year period (Drèze and Sen 1989: 27). The same was true in the country's regions worst hit by famine. "One of the famine districts (Dinajpur) had the *highest* availability of food in the entire country, and indeed, all four of the famine districts were among the top five in terms of food availability per head" (ibid. 28). The problem, Drèze and Sen explain, is that the families had insufficient "entitlements" to food. That is, they lacked the money and the ability to buy food and the government did not make food or employment available to them (Sen 1981: 4).

This shows why we cannot determine the causes of either episodic or endemic hunger by simply asking whether the country's overall level of food has declined. We must determine whether the people have sufficient entitlements to food. Of course, the overall availability of food is one factor determining people's entitlements (Drèze and Sen 1989: 25–9). Although some detractors claim it is the single most important factor determining whether people are fed (Bowbrick 1987), most researchers agree with Drèze and Sen that its significance is overemphasized (Parikh 1991; Sobham 1991). I cannot wholly resolve this debate here, although my later discussion about Hardin bears on these empirical issues. However, even if food availability were the most important factor, it is not the only one. Whether a decline in overall food availability leads to starvation depends on a variety of social, political, economic, and governmental factors.

The moral implications

This developmental perspective requires that we explore broader questions about the political, social, and economic relationships within and between countries. But this does not obviate the need to answer the moral question: what, if anything, should those of us in affluent nations do to help impoverished countries and individuals, especially those facing episodic or endemic hunger? It just slightly changes it. We should now ask: "Are we obliged to insure that they have adequate food entitlements?" That requires us to ask several derivative questions: do we have obligations to encourage (or coerce) their governments to enhance their entitlements? Are we obligated to establish ongoing trade relations with these countries to enhance their citizens' entitlements? Do we have obligations to send food or to help distribute food when the country cannot do so on its own? Although the developmental perspective does not resolve these moral questions, it has prescriptive implications. Minimally it obliterates any simple version of Hardin's argument. Conversely, seeing why Hardin's argument fails elucidates significant features of the developmental perspective.

Hardin claims that a country's ability to feed its people depends solely on the land's ability to produce sufficient food. Developmental theorists counter that the land's fertility is far less important than are the country's (a) internal economic and political strength and its (b) transnational economic and political agreements. These factors show how dependent we all are on others – both within and between countries. No person and no country is wholly self-reliant. If any US citizens doubted this, I suspect the damage wrought by Hurricane Katrina eliminated that doubt forever. The fate of thousands of people was determined not just by the Category 4 winds that ravaged the eastern Gulf of Mexico or the storm surge that slammed into the coast. Their fate was also determined by the snail's pace at which assistance

arrived, and the failure to fund various preventative measures, including the necessary upgrade of New Orleans's levees. Citizens of New Orleans did not have complete control over their lives. They still don't.

Although less dramatic, we see that most European countries import goods valued
at greater than one-third of their respective GNPs (United Nations Development
Program 2000: 213). These countries are able to feed their citizens only because they
have material goods and human skills to trade for food and other essential goods,
and they usually have the militaries to insure that they are treated fairly in world
markets.

Morever, Hardin's projections, like those of Malthus before him, have turned out
to be wildly mistaken. In the early 1970s he projected that the world's population
at the turn of the century would be 6.6 billion. It was, in fact, slightly more than
5.8 billion (United Nations Development Program 2000: 226). And India, which,
according to Hardin, had a population growth rate of 2.6 percent in 1973, had a rate
of 2 percent by the turn of the century; that is projected to decline to 1.2 percent
by the year 2015 (United Nations Development Program 2000: 225). There are
surely limits to how many people the land can support, but we are not approaching
those limits at the breakneck speed Hardin claimed.

It is not enough to know that his projections failed. It is crucial to understand why
they failed. The explanation for their failure reveals significant facts about the nature
of hunger and suggests potent strategies for its control. Population trends are best
explained by the "demographic transition theory" (DTT), a sociological theory which
has been around since long before Hardin first advanced his views on hunger. According to one prominent formulation of DTT, population trends move through four distinct stages. In the first, the combination of a high birth rate and a high death rate
produces a steady population. In the second stage, death rates decline while birth
rates remain high, leading to high population growth rates. In the third, birth rates
decline more rapidly than death rates; consequently, population rates increase but at
a much slower pace. In the final stage, population becomes stable as low birth rates
parallel low death rates. We have long since passed the first stage, and the declining
population rates worldwide suggest that most of the world has passed the peak of
the second stage. Even those undeveloped countries still in the second stage are
ambling toward the third, while countries in the highly developed West are already
comfortably settled into the fourth. In these later stages population growth rates sta-
bilize even while death rates decline. That shows that we need not "let 'em starve"
to control population growth. General economic development can propel countries
into these latter stages in which people have no reason to have large families and
heightened reason to have smaller ones (Heer 1975: 13–14).

Although it does not explain all perturbations in population (Caldwell 1997),
demographic transition theory is both theoretically plausible and it squares with the
empirical data. Its theoretical plausibility is clear: impoverished people have strong
incentives to have large families, especially in countries with poor medical care. In
an environment with high infant mortality rates, people can reasonably expect to
have surviving children only by having many of them. Having more children means

having more hands to feed the family, either by working in the fields, or working in neighboring cities to supplement the family income. They are also the aged person's only source of income in countries without a social security program.

Conversely, relatively affluent countries do not have high infant mortality, nor do its citizens need children to supplement the family income or to care for them in old age. Such countries also have high educational attainment. Although education may enlighten students about the scope of the population problem, its most powerful influences on population growth are indirect. First, post-secondary education delays marriage and consequently decreases the number of children any woman can bear. Second, it opens new vocational opportunities for women of childbearing age. Third, people with higher educations tend to have higher incomes, and are thus less likely to need children to provide old-age security. Fourth, in states with compulsory education, the child cannot substantially contribute to the family finances; instead, they drain economic resources. Fifth, states with compulsory education are more likely to have social security for the elderly (Caldwell 1976: 339–44).

These factors collectively explain population growth rates. They predict that as long as people remain uneducated, lack economic security, and live in a country with high infant mortality and no social security, then they will have large families. Conversely, as health care increases, infant mortality decreases, and governments fund social security programs and establish compulsory education, then birth rates will decline even as death rates decline. These theoretical predictions have been borne out time and again by epidemiological facts (World Health Organization 1999: 3–23). The difference in population growth rates between countries is dramatic. In 1998 rates in the lowest developed countries averaged 1.9 percent; in medium developed countries, 1.6 percent; and in the highest developed countries, 0.6 percent (United Nations Development Program 2000: 226). Finally, the Human Development Index (a compilation of factors reflecting health and economic well-being) has increased worldwide over the last quarter century (United Nations Development Program 2000: 178–85). This trend almost perfectly parallels the decline in the number of people starving (Bread for the World 2000: 4). The DTT is a theory well established in fact.

Hence, we have compelling theoretical and empirical evidence that Hardin's proposal would likely have a result opposite of that predicted. That's not quite right. Aid that simply kept the starving alive and did nothing to change their overall well-being might well have his predicted result. It would arguably prolong the second stage of transition, and increase suffering. However, immediate food aid and medical assistance, coupled with developmental assistance to enhance economic security, lower infant mortality rates, and improve the educational attainment of a country's citizens would remove incentives for large families and replace them with incentives for smaller ones.

Since Hardin's position is both theoretically and empirically flawed, we are left with two options. However, as I stated earlier, I take the charity position to be the default. If the claim that we have a strong obligation to assist cannot be defended, then we should conclude that assisting is morally permissible but not morally obligatory. Whether that strong obligation can be defended is what we will now determine.

Strong obligation to assist

A responsibility to help the vulnerable

The most familiar ground for claiming that we have a strong duty to assist is simply that, if we can alleviate people's suffering or prevent their dying at little personal cost, then we morally ought to do it (Singer 1996/1972: 28). This seems especially plausible when those in need are in no way responsible for their own plight. Since the overwhelming majority of those who are seriously undernourished are children who are paradigmatically innocent and vulnerable (Bread for the World 2000: 100–2), then their need would arguably demand our assistance (LaFollette and May 1995).

Our dependence on others

Although some people, and especially children, are more vulnerable than others, all of us were and are dependent on others. None of us is – or could be – wholly self-sufficient. Most of us recognize that our parents had to care for us lest we die. But that is only the beginning of the debt to others. Our abilities to speak a language, to read literature, to appreciate art, to live in cities, to travel the world, and to purchase the goods we need arose only because of the efforts of those who came before. "It is of grace and not of ourselves that we live civilized lives" (Dewey 1988/1922: 19). We are likewise dependent on our contemporaries, both near and far.

Nations, like individuals, are also vulnerable. In the distant past, countries may have been relatively self-sufficient. No longer. Now every country is vulnerable to others' actions. As the earlier data on global imports indicated, we heavily depend on other countries' trading with us. Indeed, the more developed a country's economy, the more dependent it is on others, although its immense power may mask that vulnerability. For example, the powerful economies of the United States, Japan, and Western Europe cannot survive without imported oil and raw minerals that drive their respective industries – and this has been so for more than 30 years (Brown 1974: 75–98). Our global economy makes our mutual dependence clear. In such a system, responding to the pressing needs of distant others is morality's way of acknowledging our reciprocal vulnerability, our common humanity. It reflects the fact that we now globally live in the circumstances of justice (Hume 1978/1740: Book III, Section II, Part II). To put it differently, we could think of reciprocal caring as a form of moral insurance (Shue 1996: 119–22). After all, any country can be severely damaged by a natural disaster.

Protecting the vulnerable

Robert Goodin offers an intriguing and powerful variant of this argument. He argues that our obligation to assist the vulnerable is not a unique positive responsibility, but is rather a general moral duty that undergirds all special role responsibilities (1985).

In so doing he challenges the view that special obligations are especially demanding and arise entirely from our voluntary choices (Hart 1955: 183–4). Goodin disagrees. The entire panoply of special rights is far better explained as arising from others' vulnerability in relation to us. "It is vulnerability, however engendered, that plays the crucial role in generating special responsibilities" (Goodin 1985: 107).

The voluntarist model cannot even adequately explain the presence – let alone strength – of our duties to keep promises. For promises when nothing is at stake are only minimally binding – and then only for purely consequentialist reasons. If, on a lark, I promise you that I will breathe at exactly 2:45 this afternoon, then, barring some unusual explanation for the importance of my doing so, no one is going to worry whether this is a promise I keep, or even remember.

At other times, we are obligated to fulfill others' expectations if they are especially vulnerable to our action, even if we did not make an explicit promise to help them. This obligation is even codified in the current law (the doctrine of estoppel) (Goodin 1985: 42–8). If Goodin is right that we have this general duty, then we should help those who are especially vulnerable to us, particularly when we can assist them at relatively little cost to ourselves. When others are especially vulnerable to the actions of entire groups, then those groups – and derivatively their members – bear a special responsibility to help (Goodin 1985: 135–41).

This account, if plausible, would bolster the common view that we have an obligation to save the vulnerable, especially since we can collectively and individually assist them at relatively little cost to ourselves. And the fact is, we can save the lives of many. According to Bread for the World, the United States could halve the number of its own and the world's hungry with an investment of $6 billion a year, just slightly more than $20 a person (Bread for the World 2000: 3). Even if this underestimated the cost by half, we can, through concerted action, largely end world hunger by investing $100 per US citizen per year, with the amounts diminishing over time. If the rest of the developed world also contributed their fair share, we could, for that same amount of money, likely end hunger and go some distance toward generally improving the lot for the more than one billion people who currently live in poverty (less than $1 per day [World Bank 2000: 46]). It is difficult to imagine what argument could be mustered to suggest that (a) this investment is not worth that cost or that (b) any tolerably decent human being would not be willing to pay that cost. It would be, in Goodin's words, just the fulfillment of our collective and individual responsibilities.

However, the argument need not stop here – although often it does. Our mutual interdependence and the extreme vulnerability of the poor paves the way for a second, potentially more potent, argument – an argument that, if sound, shows why even a libertarian would claim that we have an obligation to assist the starving.

A duty to rectify injustice

Most discussions of world hunger ask simply whether the relatively affluent should aid the starving (Cullity 1996, for example, makes this explicit). They imply or assume that the starving are relatively distant, and, in some important sense, wholly independent of us. Even Drèze and Sen often speak this way: they speak of the "problems" of famines and chronic hunger and the "need" (not requirement) for "public action" (Drèze and Sen 1989: 17). However, this understates our relation to the malnourished, not only within our country but throughout the world. It assumes that we are in no way responsible for their plight. Yet if that assumption is false, then we arguably have a potent "negative" obligation to assist them – to rectify the wrongs we helped create, the suffering we sustain, and the inequalities from which we benefit.

Here's why. According to most moral theories we have especially strong negative obligations not to cause harm. If we subsequently harm someone, then we have a powerful obligation to undo that harm, to make recompense for our misdeeds. We have reason to think that those of us in affluent nations partly caused the plight of the undernourished, that we actively sustain their impoverishment, and that we benefit from their diminished condition. If *any* of these claims are true, then we have not only the "ordinary" positive obligation to assist the vulnerable, but also a negative obligation, arising from the harm that we caused and/or sustain. If all are true, then the negative obligation would be compelling. Let us look at each in turn.

We caused their plight

The same economic, social, and political interdependencies that explain our mutual vulnerabilities suggest that we likely partially caused the starving people's plight. Decisions in one part of the world have economic ripples elsewhere. Some ripples become tidal waves. We have no doubt about this when those waves crash onto our own economic shores. When OPEC hikes gasoline prices, it increases our costs of living and we are infuriated. When Japan boosts tariffs, it hits our wallets. When we are on the short end of the economic stick, we quickly recognize that others' decisions to sell or withhold goods, or to increase tariffs, negatively impacts our economies. Yet, as we have noted throughout this book, most of us tend to conveniently forget the impact of our actions, in this case, the impacts of our economies on others. That is a factual and moral mistake. For as potent as the actions of others are on us, our actions are even more significant for them. The West is economically so powerful that even seemingly insignificant actions can have dramatic effects, especially on Third World countries.

These effects reveal two different ways we arguably cause the suffering of the world's impoverished peoples. Consider two variations on a single analogy. In the first, I place unwilling gladiators into an arena with lions. When some are killed, I cannot wash my hands of their deaths. Although the lions – and not I – were the immediate cause of their deaths, I am responsible since I placed them in this vulnerable position. Two, I do not place gladiators into this arena. Rather, I "offer" men in the region the "option" of becoming gladiators. I do so knowing full well that my arena is the only source of income. I assuage my guilt by claiming that since these men have volunteered to fight the lions, then I am not responsible for their deaths.

Nonetheless, by using their extreme vulnerability to get them to do what no sane person would do if they had an option, I am still responsible for any harm that results. Again, we have no problem acknowledging this if we are the vulnerable parties; why should we deny it when we are the exploiters?

Arguably we (partially) caused the plight of the starving in one of these senses. We are highly advantaged people whose economic, social, and political institutions are "causally deeply entangled in the misery of the poor" (Pogge 1997: 505; 2000). Moreover, our relative social starting positions "have emerged from a single historical process that was pervaded by grievous wrongs" (1997: 509). That is why: "We should not tolerate such radical inequalities in social starting positions if the allocation of those positions depends upon historical processes in which all important moral (and legal) rules and principles were massively violated" (ibid.).

Admittedly, the causal networks of which Pogge speaks are astoundingly complex. That is why my gladiator example is somewhat disanalogous. In that case, I placed (or enticed) them into the arena with the lions. However, no one person or country single-handedly created the conditions that led to starvation. That is why no one is wholly responsible for the plight of the impoverished and starving. Our world and our global economy result from a confluence of factors, including the choices of billions of people over an extended time. Certainly some much smaller number of players, actors, and events are especially significant in this causal chain. However, we rarely know precisely who caused what. Many of us assume this ignorance lets us off the moral hook.

I do not see why. We need not be the sole cause of an event to be (partially) responsible for it. After all, we are never strictly the sole cause of any event: actions have consequences only within certain contexts and background conditions (Hart and Honoré 1973) (which is why the OPEC nations are not solely responsible for skyrocketing oil prices either!). If we were morally responsible only for those things for which we were the sole cause, then arguably we would not be responsible for anything. And, if we were morally responsible only for those things for which we were the predominant cause, we would be responsible for very little. No doubt in select cases, where background conditions are predictably stable, we might feel justified in ascribing sole responsibility for some actions. But that is rare. For most of what is important in our lives, the question is not whether I am *solely* or even *predominantly* responsible for harm, but whether I am *responsible enough*. We must ask: did I play a *sufficiently important* role that it is proper to attribute responsibility to me – to blame me for mistakes (and to expect me to atone for them) or to praise me for my successes (Staub 1989: 51–67, 81–90, 262–4)?

Let me give two examples. My parents were surely pivotal forces making me who I am. Nonetheless, it would be a mistake to think they are wholly responsible. There are myriad other factors, some of which I know, others of which I am ignorant. Despite the presence of these other factors, we would be foolish to deny my parents' causal role in making me who I am.

Two, professors are not wholly responsible for the successes and failures of their students. To think they are assumes professors have far more power than they do.

This is a mistake that both administrators and students often make. Yet we should not err on the other extreme by inferring that professors are not responsible at all for student learning. The fact is: student learning is a function of a variety of factors, one of which is surely the professor.

There is a childlike part of us that wants to place all the moral responsibility (and especially the moral blame) on a few shoulders; we like neatly dividing the world into the good guys and the bad guys. But that does not reflect the way the world works. As the previous examples indicate, the forces that make us who we are, and the forces that create significant political, social, and economic changes, are not singular, but arise from a convergence of factors. That is true not only of work habits or student learning, but also – of special relevance to the current issue – of endemic and episodic hunger.

In short, we need not precisely determine everyone's contributory role before accepting or assigning responsibility. Once we know that we played a contributory role in creating the harm, then we should acknowledge partial responsibility and a heightened obligation to assist – to help undo the effects of what we have done. Since the economies of the Western world substantially influence people in the Third World – and our well-being has come, to some degree, at their expense – then we should accept some responsibility for their plight.

We actively sustain their impoverishment

Some might think it is too strong to say that we caused the conditions that make widespread hunger likely. Even if that were true, we often act in ways that sustain the conditions of the malnourished. To use the earlier analogy, if I had nothing to do with placing people in the arena with the lions, but subsequently opened a chain of hotels catering to fans who came to watch, then my actions actively support the exploitative practice. I am partly responsible for the death of the gladiators.

The relevance to world hunger is clear. We are voracious consumers. Because we want fresh fruits, coffee, and spices – and we want them at a minimal cost – we bring it about (cause) or support (sustain) efforts to convert an area's most arable lands from growing staples for the locals to growing niceties for us. Sometimes this is devastating to the local poor (even if desired by the local rich), especially if the demand for these luxuries abates, as it often does. Further, in our quest for cheap goods, we financially reward those businesses engaging in exploitative hiring practices in the Third World, thereby partially causing the suffering of the vulnerable (Wolff 2002). We also politically support the international borrowing and resource privileges that burden democratic regimes with debts generated by former dictators, and that allow those dictators to legally abscond with the country's natural resources (Pogge 2001b: 20–1). Although we may occasionally complain about these (and other related) practices, the fact that we support them through our consumption and political decisions shows that we sustain the impoverishment of the worst off, and are thereby partial causes in their continuation (United Nations Development Program 2005).

We benefit from their suffering

Even if we do not actively support the systems that harm the impoverished, most people in the Western world benefit from the predicament of the poor and do nothing to stop it. In that way we are causal contributors to their deprivation. Some might claim that our causal role – and our moral responsibility – is diminished since we simply failed to stop the harm. In other contexts, however, we recognize that inaction can cause harm. If a state fails to properly educate or provide affordable health care to its children, then the government has caused their illiteracy or ill-health; if a government fails to have an emergency system for coping with natural disasters, then it is responsible for deaths they could have prevented. (As I write this, this is clearly the view of the majority of Americans in the wake of Hurricane Katrina.) And if I fail to stop an assault on a third party, especially if the cost or risk of intervening is minimal, then most of us will say that my inaction contributes to any harm befalling the victim. This is especially true if I benefit from that harm (the victim has me in her will). For then my refusal signals that my action is, in some sense, intentional.

Responsibility in the real world

These three arguments give us reason to think that we have a negative responsibility to ensure that the poor of the world are fed. However, these arguments, though powerful, are not invincible. Does this give us a reason to do nothing? Of course not. We should act on the best evidence we have. The degree of epistemological certainty we require before acting depends on the relative costs of action versus inaction. Before assessing criminal penalties – where the costs to accused criminals are enormous – we reasonably demand very strong evidence of their guilt. However, under most circumstances we do not use nor would we countenance such an exacting standard.

We should employ the same standards of evidence when (a) accepting praise, (b) holding others responsible for harms they partially cause, sustain, or could remedy, and (c) accepting responsibility for similar harms we partially cause, sustain, or could remedy. Unfortunately, we usually don't. We tend to use relaxed standards of evidence when accepting (and expecting) praise for our successes and when attributing blame to people who harm us; and we often use very demanding standards when determining our own responsibility. If nothing else should be obvious from the arguments throughout the book, such bias is morally untenable. If we hold ourselves to the same standards that we hold others, then we will recognize some causal responsibility for the plight of the impoverished in our world. And, if Goodin is correct – that we needn't be causally responsible for harm to have a responsibility to reduce harm (Goodin 1985: 126–7) – then we should help, especially since we can remedy their condition at relatively little cost to ourselves.

Conclusion

We have a multilayered argument that suggests we have a strong obligation to bolster the well-being of the seriously impoverished. First, we have a positive obligation to assist those who are vulnerable to our actions. Second, we also have reason to think we are partially responsible for the suffering of the world's poor, and hence, have a strong negative obligation to stop further harm. Third, we could feed them and ease their suffering and pain with relatively little effort. If we do nothing in the face of these arguments, we have reason to think that we are complicit in the deaths of many people. We might be wrong, but when, with only a relatively small sacrifice, we can avoid the decided possibility that we are accomplices in many people's deaths, then morally we ought to act.

Knowing precisely how to act is more unclear. Doubtless isolated individuals have limited power to remedy these problems. To empower and feed the impoverished we need collective action and a change in global institutions (Shue 1996: 128–9). Specifically, if the arguments in the last section are correct, then our first efforts should be to cease acting in ways that cause or sustain others' impoverishment. Then we should (a) work to bring international efforts to bear on especially corrupt governments, (b) use global resources (Pogge 1997) to promote broad development that will make endemic hunger a painful note from our collective past, and (c) establish systems which effectively respond to episodic hunger.

Likely, though, bare political efforts will not entirely discharge our duties to the impoverished – since we know that governments are unlikely to soon change their ways or give the support they should. Hence, we should also contribute to non-government organizations with proven track records in eliminating hunger, promoting development, and empowering the poor. These contributions will not only assist the needy, they will show others that we are serious about the need for governmental and institutional change. The extent to which we should contribute is, of course, controversial – it raises the ever-pressing issue about the degree to which morality can be demanding (Kagan 1989; Scheffler 1992; Williams 1985). That is the issue to which I now turn.

REFERENCES

Bowbrick, P. (1987) "Rejoinder: An Untenable Hypothesis on the Causes of Famine," *Food Policy* 12 (1): 5–9.

Bread for the World (2000) *A Program to End Hunger*. Silver Spring, MD: Bread for the World.

Brown, L. R. (1974) *In the Human Interest*. New York: Norton.

Caldwell, J. C. (1976) "Toward a Restatement of Demographic Transition Theory," *Population and Development Review* 2 (3/4): 321–66.

Caldwell, J. C. (1997) "The Global Fertility Transition: The Need for a Unifying Theory," *Population and Development Review* 23 (4): 803–12.

Crocker, D. (1997) "Hunger, Capacity, and Development." In W. Aiken and H. LaFollette (eds.), *World Hunger and Morality*, 2nd edn. Upper Saddle River, NJ: Prentice-Hall, 211–30.

Cullity, G. (1996) "The Life Saving Analogy." In W. Aiken and H. LaFollette (eds.), *World Hunger and Morality*, 2nd edn. Upper Saddle River, NJ: Prentice-Hall, 51–69.

Dewey, J. (1988/1922) *Human Nature and Conduct*. Carbondale, IL: Southern Illinois University Press.

Drèze, J. and Sen, A. (1989) *Hunger and Political Action*. Oxford: Oxford University Press.

Drèze, J. and Sen, A. (eds.) (1991a) *The Political Economy of Hunger: Endemic Hunger* (vol. III). Oxford: Oxford University Press.

Drèze, J. and Sen, A. (eds.) (1991b) *The Political Economy of Hunger: Entitlement and Well-Being* (vol. I). Oxford: Oxford University Press.

Drèze, J. and Sen, A. (eds.) (1991c) *The Political Economy of Hunger: Famine Prevention* (vol. II). Oxford: Oxford University Press.

Fletcher, J. (1977) "Give If It Helps, but Not If It Hurts." In W. Aiken and H. LaFollette (eds.), *World Hunger and Moral Obligation*. Englewood Cliffs, NJ: Prentice-Hall, 103–14.

Goodin, R. E. (1985) *Protecting the Vulnerable: A Reanalysis of Our Social Responsibilities*. Chicago, IL: University of Chicago Press.

Hardin, G. (1996/1974) "Lifeboat Ethics: The Case against Helping the Poor." In W. Aiken and H. LaFollette (eds.), *World Hunger and Morality*, 2nd edn. Upper Saddle River, NJ: Prentice-Hall, 5–15.

Hart, H. L. A. (1955) "Are There Any Natural Rights?" *Philosophical Review* 64, 175–91.

Hart, H. L. A. and Honoré, T. (1973) *Causation in the Law*. Oxford: Clarendon Press.

Heer, D. M. (1975) *Society and Population*, 2nd edn. Englewood Cliffs, NJ: Prentice-Hall.

Hoenig, J. (1999) *Greed is Good: The Capitalist Pig Guide to Investing*. New York: HarperCollins Publishers.

Hume, D. (1978/1740) *A Treatise of Human Nature*, 2nd edn. Oxford: Oxford University Press.

Ignatieff, M. (1985) *The Needs of Strangers*. New York: Viking.

Kagan, S. (1989) *The Limits of Morality*. Oxford: Oxford University Press.

LaFollette, H. and May, L. (1995) "Suffer the Little Children: Responsibility and Hunger." In W. Aiken and H. LaFollette (eds.), *World Hunger and Morality*. Upper Saddle River, NJ: Prentice-Hall, 70–84.

Li, X. (1996) "Making Sense of the Right to Food." In W. Aiken and H. LaFollette (eds.), *World Hunger and Morality*, 2nd edn. Upper Saddle River, NJ: Prentice-Hall, 153–70.

McKinley, M. (1981) "Obligations to the Starving," *Noûs* 15: 309–24.

Narveson, J. (2000) "Libertarianism." In H. LaFollette (ed.), *The Blackwell Guide to Ethical Theory*. Oxford: Blackwell Publishers, 306–24.

Parikh, K. S. (1991) "Chronic Hunger in the World: Impact of International Policies." In J. Drèze and A. Sen (eds.), *The Political Economy of Hunger: Entitlement and Well-Being* (vol. I). Oxford: Oxford University Press.

Pogge, T. W. (1992) "An Institutional Approach to Human Intervention," *Public Affairs Quarterly* 6 (1): 89–103.

Pogge, T. W. (1997) "A Global Resources Dividend." In D. Crocker and T. Linden (eds.), *Ethics of Consumption*. Totowa, NJ: Rowman and Littlefield, 501–38.

Pogge, T. W. (2000) "International Significance of Human Rights," *Journal of Ethics* 4 (1/2): 45–69.

Pogge, T. W. (2001a) "Preemptive Humanitarian Intervention." In I. Carter and M. Riccardi (eds.), *Freedom, Power and Political Morality: Essays for Felix Oppenheim*. Basingstoke: Palgrave.

Pogge, T. W. (2001b) "Priorities of Global Justice," *Metaphilosophy* 32 (1/2): 6–24.

Scheffler, S. (1992) *Human Morality*. Oxford: Oxford University Press.

Sen, A. (1981) *Poverty and Famines: An Essay on Entitlement and Deprivation*. Oxford: Oxford University Press.

Shue, H. (1980) *Basic Rights: Subsistence, Affluence, and U.S. Foreign Policy*. Princeton, NJ: Princeton University Press.

Shue, H. (1996) "Solidarity among Strangers and the Right to Food." In W. Aiken and H. LaFollette (eds.), *World Hunger and Morality*, 2nd edn. Upper Saddle River, NJ: Prentice-Hall, 113–22.

Singer, P. (1977/1972) "Famine, Affluence, and Morality." In W. Aiken and H. LaFollette (eds.), *World Hunger and Moral Obligation*. Englewood Cliffs, NJ: Prentice-Hall, 22–37.

Singer, P. (1996/1972) "Famine, Affluence, and Morality." In W. Aiken and H. LaFollette (eds.), *World Hunger and Morality*, 2nd edn. Upper Saddle River, NJ: Prentice-Hall, 26–38.

Sobham, R. (1991) "The Politics of Hunger and Entitlement." In J. Drèze and A. Sen (eds.), *The Political Economy of Hunger: Entitlement and Well-Being* (vol. I). Oxford: Oxford University Press.

Staub, E. (1989) *The Roots of Evil: The Origins of Genocide and Other Group Violence*. Cambridge: Cambridge University Press.

United Nations Development Program (2000) *Human Development Report 2000*. Oxford: Oxford University Press.

United Nations Development Program (2005) *Human Development Report 2005: International Cooperation at a Crossroads: Aid, Trade and Security in an Unequal World*. Oxford: Oxford University Press.

Watson, R.A. (1977) "Reason and Morality in a World of Limited Food." In W. Aiken and H. LaFollette (eds.), *World Hunger and Moral Obligation*. Englewood Cliffs, NJ: Prentice-Hall, 115–23.

Williams, B. (1985) *Ethics and the Limits of Philosophy*. Cambridge, MA: Harvard University Press.

Wolff, J. (2002) "Economic Competition: Should We Care about the Losers?" In H. LaFollette (ed.), *Ethics in Practice: An Anthology*, 2nd edn. Oxford: Blackwell Publishers.

World Bank (2000) *World Development Report 2000/2001*. Oxford: Oxford University Press.

World Health Organization (1999) *World Health Report*. Geneva: World Health Organization.

World Health Organization (2000) *World Health Report*. Geneva: World Health Organization.

SEVENTEEN

Is Morality Demanding?

Arguments in the previous chapter give us some reason to think we have a strong moral obligation to assist the starving and seriously impoverished. If Singer is correct then that duty may be sufficiently strong that we must sacrifice much that we personally value in life. Many people find this view absurd. They think morality could never demand that much of us. On this view, we somehow know just how much morality can reasonably demand of us. We know that any morality which demands that we dramatically change our lives to help strangers is mistaken.

We have seen this concern before, in our discussions of both utilitarianism and religion. It is now time to explicitly discuss whether and how morality is demanding. Some people think morality is – at least in this world – quite demanding. At the other end of this continuum is the minimalist who claims that morality is quite lax, that it demands very little of us. In the middle is the moderate who claims morality is somewhat demanding. And there are many variations amid these three basic options (Kagan 1989).

Understanding the Debate

A brief summary of the three alternatives

Morality is demanding

A few hardy souls think morality is quite demanding – at least in a world like ours with so much pain, suffering, and need. As we saw in the previous chapter, Singer claims that given (a) our relative wealth, (b) the extent of hunger and suffering, and (c) the relative indifference of most people, morality requires that we should help relieve this suffering even if that means we must abandon anything devoid of moral significance (and, on his strong view, anything of less moral significance). Even on Singer's weak view, we should give up many leisure activities and send money we save to famine relief. We should also abandon many leisure activities and spend that time working to relieve the suffering of the starving and impoverished.

Moderate (ordinary) morality

Ordinary morality makes some demands on us: sometimes we should act in ways that subvert our personal interests. It forbids us from harming others, and occasionally requires us to aid others in need. However, it does not require significant sacrifices simply to aid others. Such sacrifices, although laudable, are not required. Ordinary morality is a moderate morality. Many people find it attractive precisely because it is moderate. Bernard Williams explains the appeal of a moderate morality with his now classic argument against any moral theory that implies that morality is very demanding. His aim is to show we must reject any morality requiring us to guide our life by impartial moral principles. Suppose, he says, two people are drowning and a rescuer can save only one; one is the rescuer's wife. An impartial moral theory, Williams claims, will require the rescuer to decide whom to save by some neutral means, for example, by flipping a coin. Or, even if it permits the rescuer to save his wife, it at least requires an impartial reason for why he can do so.

Williams disagrees. He claims the rescuer should straightforwardly save his wife; his choice requires no justification. It is not merely that the impartialist moral perspective does not make the proper prescription in this case – although Williams thinks it often does. His concern is that even when the impartialist gives the right answer, she has the wrong explanation for it.

> The consideration that it was his wife is certainly, for instance, an explanation which should silence comment. But something more ambitious than this is usually intended [in someone's saying that he was justified in his action], essentially involving the idea that moral principle can legitimate his preference, yielding the conclusion that in situations of this kind it is at least all right (morally permissible) to save one's wife. . . . But this construction provides the agent with one question too many: it might have been hoped by some (for instance, his wife) that his motivating thought, fully spelled out, would be the thought that it was his wife, not that it was his wife and that in situations of this kind it is permissible to save one's wife (Williams 1981/1976: 18).

Williams claims this shows that it is sometimes inappropriate to guide – or even consider guiding – our actions by impartial moral standards, especially when close personal relationships or significant personal projects are at stake. Morality cannot demand that we abandon our relationships or personal projects since, without them "there will not be enough substance or conviction in a man's life to compel allegiance to life itself" (ibid.).

Minimalist morality

While the moderate objects to any demanding morality, the minimalist contends that even ordinary morality is too demanding. For instance, libertarians claim that our only (enforceable) obligations are to not directly harm others. We have no obligations to assist others within our own country, let alone elsewhere in the world. We are not morally required to support those who are disabled or out of work; nor are we required to support public education (although it might be wise to do so). Arguably it would be nice of us to assist others; we should even encourage people to be charitable. However, we are not *obliged* to help (Narveson 2000). Any morality that requires us to do so is too demanding.

Three Elements

These characterizations suggest demandingness is a single feature of morality. It is not. It is better to think of demandingness as constituted by three interrelated elements. To use Scheffler's language (1992), these are:

1. *Pervasiveness.* What is morality's scope? Should all our actions be evaluated morally? Or are only some of them within morality's domain?
2. *Stringency.* Within its scope, does morality make heavy demands on us? Or are its demands relatively lax so that most can fulfill them relatively easily?
3. *Overridingness.* When the demands of morality clash with non-moral demands or interests, should we always do what morality requires? Or can non-moral demands or personal interests sometimes trump moral requirements?

Using these distinctions, we can specify that morality is demanding to the extent that it is stringent within its scope, is (reasonably) pervasive, and (usually) overriding. Conversely, morality is not demanding to the extent that it is not stringent within its scope, has a narrow scope, or can be (easily) overridden by non-moral interests. The minimalist will claim morality is lax, and may also claim that it is narrow in scope and not overriding. The moderate will claim that morality is not too stringent; they may also claim that morality is neither overriding nor non-pervasive.

Although these elements are logically separable, they are practically intertwined. If morality were non-stringent, there would be few circumstances in which morality's demands substantially clash with personal interests, and hence, few circumstances in which we might ask whether morality's demands are overriding. If morality were non-stringent, then it would not matter practically if it were pervasive since a lax morality would not substantially constrain personal interests. And if morality were not overriding, then it might matter little if it were pervasive and stringent since any significant demands might be trumped by personal concerns. Although these elements are practically interrelated, it is better to begin by keeping them separate, both in explaining and then evaluating the claim(s) that morality is (or is not) demanding.

A Closer Look at the Three Elements

Since I think stringency is the most important of these elements, that is where I will focus. However, I will briefly discuss the other elements first.

Pervasiveness

What it is

Most people talk as if morality were not pervasive. Books like this feed that supposition by discussing a few issues, barely mentioning others, and never mentioning
many. This suggests that morality concerns a relatively short list of specific actions,
and any actions not on the list are outside the domain of morality, actions about
which we need never morally fret. Thus, many people claim that lying, adultery,
capital punishment, physician-assisted suicide, and pornography are moral issues,
while premarital kissing, water skiing, and the length of a person's fingernails are
not. Of course, not everyone offers the same list, and even those with highly similar
lists may disagree whether buying a lottery ticket, having oral sex with one's spouse,
or telling a "white lie" are moral issues. Despite these disagreements, many people
think (or imply) that many actions are forever beyond morality's reach – that anyone
who worries (much) about the morality of getting a drink of water, reading a novel,
eating berries, telephoning our children, or taking a nap is an old-fashioned prude.

That is why the claim that morality is pervasive cannot mean that we need to
morally evaluate every action. Consider the following analogy. Most people think we
should be prudent – that we should (within moral limits) advance our interests. If
we can choose between an action that neither harms nor advances our interests and
one that substantially advances them, then, barring moral constraints or unusual circumstances, we should do the latter. However, not even the most thoroughgoing
egoist thinks we should scrutinize every action to ensure that we maximally advance
our interests. In deciding whether to eat a cookie, go for a walk, or read a book, we
should not consciously assess the long-term personal consequences of the alternatives. Does that mean that some experience is beyond the reach of prudential judgment? No. Experience teaches us that many actions have few, if any, implications for
our long-term interests. That is why we need not consciously evaluate them.

Experience also teaches us that other actions – choosing a career or a spouse,
making a hefty investment, and deciding whether to have children – have dramatic
effects for our well-being. These we should carefully scrutinize. In short, we use
experience to divide actions into those about which we should carefully deliberate
and those about which we need not. We can revise our "lists" in light of later experience and new knowledge. We may learn that we were mistaken: I once thought
that eating quickly had no significant impact on my long-term best interests and,
therefore, was something about which I need not reason or worry. Then I realized
that wolfing down food inclined me to eat more and, therefore, to gain weight; it
was also more likely to give me indigestion. I saw that a seemingly insignificant act
was relevant to my long-term well-being and, therefore, should be evaluated pru-
dentially. Although I may sometimes revise or suspend some rules, that does not
require me to consciously deliberate about each action to insure that I maximize my
self-interests. Why should someone who thinks morality is pervasive be saddled with
such a ludicrous corollary?

The real disagreement, then, is not between those that think we should morally evaluate every action and those who do not – for no one embraces the former view. The disagreement is between those who (seem to) think that some actions are always beyond the reach of morality and those who do not. Those who think morality is not pervasive think we needn't morally evaluate some actions *because* they are forever outside morality's domain. Those who think morality is pervasive believe that although we learn from experience that we normally needn't morally fret about some actions, we can never know that an action (described in morally neutral terms) is forever beyond morality's reach. We cannot automatically assume that watching a film, mouthing certain words, giving someone an injection, or asking someone on a date should or should not be evaluated morally. In most circumstances these actions are morally innocent, while in others these could be respectively: viewing pornography, engaging in hate speech, assisting a suicide, or harassing an employee.

Is morality pervasive?

That does not mean there is no disagreement here. Considerable practical distance remains between those who think more acts, in more circumstances, fall outside the purview of morality and those who think there are few such actions. Those who hold the latter position are more inclined to think morality *legitimately* expects a great deal of us. The former people do not. That is the first hint that the fundamental disagreement over demandingness is a disagreement about stringency. This will become more apparent after we discuss the element of overridingness.

Overridingness

What it is

Some people claim or imply that morality is not overriding. Several philosophers have taken up Williams's mantle (Nagel 1986, 1991; Stocker 1976, 1989; Wolf 1982). They claim that our personal relationships, our important projects, and our personal integrity sometimes (or often) override moral demands.

A tangential issue

I do not find this approach plausible. This makes it seem as if we must have some overarching (non-moral) perspective from which to assess a person's life. From that perspective, people's personal projects trump morality. This approach requires a new category of evaluation bridging prudence and morality. However, we have enough trouble employing notions of prudence and morality; adding another evaluative layer would only complicate matters.

What really is going on here, I think, is the belief that morality, properly understood, is not impartial: it gives precedence to people's personal relationships and projects. Think about Williams's drowning wife case. I think it is designed to reveal a conflict between personal integrity and *an impartial* morality. What makes people sympathetic to the case is not the belief that morality cannot override the man's personal commitment to his wife, but something stronger, a belief that the husband *should* save his wife and save her *for the right reasons* (because she is his wife).

If Williams thought only that morality did not require us to abandon our personal projects, then he would have to think that a man who embraced an impartial morality as his deepest personal project should *not* automatically save his wife. Williams clearly thinks that would be wrong. Properly understood, morality gives such preference to personal projects and relationships that we can pursue them straightway, without morally deliberating.

Impartialists will obviously disagree. Why the disagreement? The answer, I think, is that while Williams thinks morality is not stringent, impartialists think it is. If I am correct, then denying either the pervasiveness or the overridingness of morality is usually a circuitous way of denying that morality is stringent. It would be very odd to hold that morality *really does* make heavy demands of us, but that it is nonetheless wholly appropriate to ignore these demands.

Stringency

What it is

Those who argue that morality should not be too stringent imply that we have a moral yardstick – akin to the standard meter stored in Paris – whereby we know just how stringent morality can be. However, we have no fixed moral yardstick to measure stringency. We must always judge it relative to a baseline (Murphy 2000: 34–62).

What is the baseline?

Consider the following analogy. Students complain that Professor Jones is "too difficult." To evaluate their claims, we must ask: "too difficult relative to what?" Perhaps the students are intellectually limited, and arguably should not be in college. If so, they will find any demands excessive. Perhaps they are sufficiently bright but had poor schooling from kindergarten onwards; relative to their preparation, Jones expects too much. Or perhaps these students' previous teachers were lax; therefore they think Jones's requirements are excessive. They may think his expectations are *confining* inasmuch as they constrain their time, and *costly* inasmuch as they are stressed by Jones's requirements. However, just because someone thinks the demands are excessive does not show that they are.

We should employ a similar strategy in the current discussion. When deciding if morality is stringent, we must always ask: relative to what? To (a) people's abilities, (b) external circumstances, (c) their expectations, or (d) some defensible moral norm? Each dimension is important in understanding and assessing how stringent morality is, as well as how stringent people perceive it to be.

Relative to abilities

What may be simple for someone who is talented may be difficult for ordinary folks – and impossible for someone who is intellectually challenged. How should this shape our understanding of morality's demands? Should morality make precisely the same demands on everyone – the genius, the intellectually challenged, and "the person on the street"? Or should it make equally costly and confining demands? If it makes precisely the same demands on everyone, then morality will *effectively* require more of the less talented than of the most talented – it will be less costly or less confining or both. That seems unfair. We do not make the same demands of children as of adults, and we do not make the same demands of the severely retarded as we do of the normally intelligent. So, barring some forceful argument explaining why the talented should get off *relatively* easily, it seems appropriate to expect more from the genius than from ordinary folk. We should, to use the biblical dictum, hold that "to whom much has been given, much shall be expected." This is an issue I explore in more detail in the last chapter.

Relative to circumstances

Stringency is relative to circumstances along three dimensions: (1) people's moral instruction, (2) others' needs, and (3) the actions of others to meet those needs.

First, just as someone with only a passing acquaintance with math would find simple algebra inscrutable, people who had little moral instruction would find even minimal requirements difficult to satisfy. To that extent morality *effectively* demands more of such people than it does of those reared in loving homes, by parents who inculcated them with a sense of moral responsibility. Second, what we morally ought to do is also relative to others' needs. This is true even of "special" responsibilities to one's children and parents. No matter how lucky a parent is, her children will sometimes be ill, have trouble in school or with their friends. At those times, there are heavy demands on being a responsible parent. As we grow older, our parents (if they are still alive) need our care and attention more than they did when we were young. That can be a heavy moral demand. The extent of others' needs affects how demanding morality is.

Of course, if we live in a land of abundance, with little illness and few natural catastrophes, then others' needs will be slight and morality will not demand much of us. It would rarely confine (limit our options) or cost us (require us to abandon our significant interests) (Murphy 2000: 16–20; Scheffler 1992: 98). However, this is not our world. Although we can see why someone would think that it is unfair to have to help others, especially if there are many in need, it is also true that needing help and not getting it also seems unfair.

Third, what each of us should do morally depends in part on what others do. Even if many people had significant needs, if everyone capable of helping did their reasonable share, then morality would likely not seriously confine us or cost us much. For instance, if we had robust governments that provided substantial opportunities for all citizens, and safety nets for all in need, then individuals would not face significant demands beyond those of paying taxes. However, that is not our world. Of those who can help, some are ignorant, others are indifferent, and some are greedy. And governments have done little to meet the needs of their own citizens, let alone those of other countries. There is much unmet need. Does this change our moral responsibilities? Most people think so, although they disagree about just how much. Consider Singer's example. Suppose I am walking by a pond where a child is drowning. I can rescue the drowning child with relatively little effort and no danger to myself. Singer thinks most of us will recognize that I ought to save the child. Given what students have said to me over the years, I think he is right.

Now imagine that ten people are standing around a pond where two children are drowning. I jump in and save one. The indolent nine do nothing. Singer claims that under these circumstances I am obligated to rescue the second as well. Had others fulfilled their responsibilities, I would not have had to do so; perhaps I would not have had to save even the first. However, they did not act; there is still a child in need and I can rescue her with relatively little effort and at no risk to myself.

Some people will reject Singer's claim that I am obligated to save even the first child. These people would obviously think I have no obligation to save the second. However, most who agree that I should save the first child will also think that I should save the second if others do nothing. I can encourage others to act and chide them if they do not. By saving the one child, I may prompt them to act. However, if they do nothing, I should save the second child as well. Doubtless there is some point at which I can legitimately say: "No more!" The problem is knowing where that point is. However, since many people agree that others' inaction alters my responsibility, we see that morality can be stringent in some circumstances.

If our obligations increase relative to unmet need, morality seems to require much of us in this world given the extent of that need. After all, widespread malnutrition is not our only serious problem. Many of these problems are sufficiently common that they cannot be met by isolated individuals, but only by people acting in concert with others. If so, then arguably the only way to fulfill our (relatively) stringent duties is not only to personally aid others but to reshape society, our economic system, and our governments. Many of us would also find these duties highly confining and extremely costly. The degree to which they seem so depends, in part, on our expectations.

Relative to expectations

Recall the earlier analogy. A student for whom little has been expected will find even minor demands onerous. Likewise, someone reared thinking that morality is not demanding will find small moral demands excessive, and selfish people, especially if they live in a self-centered society, will perceive moral molehills as moral mountains. These people will experience even minimal moral requirements as exceedingly demanding. Conversely, people living in societies in which people are concerned about others will find morality less stringent because (1) the demands will *be* less confining and costly since others will be doing more, leaving less for each individually, and (2) they will *seem* less demanding since all citizens are expected to do more.

Relative to some defensible norm

The central question is whether it is reasonable for people to expect themselves (and others) to meet stringent moral demands. Put differently, we must determine which moral norms are defensible. I address the issue indirectly by exploring arguments for the stringency of morality. Since stringency is the most significant element of demandingness, we will ask: just how demanding can morality legitimately be?

How Can We Determine the Limits of Morality?

Some natural limits on morality's demands

Morality cannot require that we do what we cannot in any way do. That is what is meant by the "ought implies can" principle, which is deeply entrenched in morality and law. Some individuals, because of their age, ability, or condition, cannot understand or do what we expect ordinary people to do. Therefore, they are not responsible for their actions, even when their actions are inappropriate, undesirable, or bad.

However, we should be cautious in employing the "ought implies can" principle. Suppose I knowingly pollute the ground water in a region, causing hundreds of people to suffer and many to die. I am later incapable of compensating all the victims. On a non-critical reading of the "ought implies can" principle, that would imply that I am free of my responsibility to them. That cannot be right. At least I can be legitimately criticized for creating their predicament, even if I cannot now rectify it. Moreover, I should make partial recompense. Finally, I should feel guilty for what I have done, and be willing to accept the criticism – even condemnation – of others.

The real issue

Although the "ought implies can" principle does identify some limits on morality, the central issue is not whether a demanding morality is beyond our reach. We *could* spend more time and money helping others; we could take more care to insure that we do not harm or take advantage of others. We could adhere to moral standards that are costly and confining. The question is whether we are obligated to do so. Put differently, the issue is not what we can do, but what we should have to do. To help us determine the limits of morality, we should first discuss morality's role.

The role of morality

The overarching aim of morality is not to describe or understand what is right and wrong. If it were, those aims could be satisfied by people who fully understood but

never fulfilled their obligations. Thinking about morality is important; but it is important because it empowers us to act morally. Once we grasp its practical aim we better
understand the rationale for the "ought implies can" principle. Morality's aim is to
guide people's behavior. If someone cannot guide her behavior by moral considerations, then it is senseless to require her to do so. By itself this does not identify the
limits of morality. However, we can profitably extend that reasoning. For if we cannot
require people to do what they cannot do, we also cannot require them to do more
than we can *reasonably expect* them to do. Consider the following analogy. What can
an employer reasonably expect of her employees? Someone obsessed with her work
might spend every waking moment fulfilling her assigned tasks and, if she is highly
efficient, she may make monumental achievements. An employer would love it, of
course, if all her employees were similarly dedicated or efficient. But she cannot
demand it. Likewise, we should not set legal and moral expectations so high that
they can be understood only by the brilliant and performed only by the extraordinarily talented. If we do then most people would run seriously afoul of the law and
morality. Put differently, moral demands must be "motivationally accessible"
(Scheffler 1992: 124). Of course, how can we decide which demands are "accessible"? We must know the baseline. How might we decide? We might employ a golden
rule for moral expectations: "It is reasonable to expect of others what we reasonably
expect of ourselves." This will not tell us precisely what we should do. Nonetheless,
it does tell us that we cannot rationally expect more of others than we expect of
ourselves. Given our propensities to make exceptions in our own case, this is an
important acknowledgment. It suggests that our moral code should require some
effort, but should not be effectively beyond the reach of most of us. What would that
code be? The defender of ordinary morality has an answer.

Is Morality Demanding?

Ordinary morality and minimalism

Ordinary morality holds that morality cannot be too demanding – neither too confining nor too costly. However, ordinary morality is somewhat demanding inasmuch
as it *constrains* us against acting in ways that harm others, even when those actions
would advance either our personal interests or the greatest good. I may not kill or
restrict or steal from others to benefit myself or to promote the general good. Yet
ordinary morality is limited since we have *options* to pursue our own interests, even
if we thereby fail to promote the general good. (I adapt many of the following arguments from Kagan 1989.) I can spend money on myself even if others have more
pressing needs. Or, to use Williams's example, I can save my wife even if it means
others who are more deserving die.

   This nifty-looking way of categorizing the demands and limits of morality faces
three immediate problems. First, options and constraints are logically independent.
It is unclear why morality needs both, or why either options or constraints must have

the contours they do in ordinary morality. A system of options could include not only the option to allow harm, but also the option to do harm; constraints might not simply prohibit harm, but also prohibit pursuing one's own interests by neglecting the interests of others. Second, if morality has both options and constraints they will sometimes conflict. When they do, which is weightier?

Third, in ordinary (moderate) morality, neither options nor constraints are absolute. We do not have options to pursue minor personal interests rather than to substantially advance the overall good. To use a variation on an earlier example, I cannot scratch my back or eat a box of popcorn rather than easily save a drowning child. Nor are the constraints so strong that we can never violate them if we must do so to promote a substantial good. If I am lost in the woods and could starve or die from exposure to the cold, then I may break into your cabin to save my life. Or I may "borrow" your boat without asking if that is the only way I can save a drowning child.

The minimalist tries to avoid these problems by advocating a morality that makes even fewer demands. The minimalist claims options are limited only by constraints, while constraints are absolute. That is why we will never have an enforceable general obligation to assist others or to advance the good. To use the earlier example, although it would be nice of me to dirty my new shoes to save a drowning child, barring some special agreement I am not obligated to do so.

Although most people do not think that morality is very demanding, they think minimalism is too lax. They think we are obligated to help others in need, at least when the need is great and the personal cost is small. The problem is that moderates must defend their view against both the minimalist and against those who hold that morality is quite demanding. Whatever arguments the moderate uses against demanding moral views, the minimalist deploys against the moderate. She claims the moderate either unduly restricts options or cavalierly permits overriding constraints. The minimalist will want to know: if the purpose of options is to establish a sphere within which I can act, why should that ever be limited by the need to promote the good? At the same time, those who think morality is demanding will ask the moderate: if constraints are justified to insure that we are not subject to the acts of others, why should we not also be free of their indifference, especially if we are in great need? To answer these objections the moderate must identify some threshold, some place where the costs of respecting options and constraints is so high that we can justifiably ignore them (Kagan 1989: 50–1).

The minimalist faces her own set of problems: if people should never be expected to give up their personal projects to maximize the good, why should they be expected to give up their personal projects to recognize constraints on others? While if they should sometimes abandon their personal projects to respect constraints, why should they not sometimes abandon their personal projects to promote the good (LaFollette 1979)?

To adjudicate between these alternatives, we must decide if: (1) are we ever morally required to abandon our own interests to advance the interests of others, and, if so, (2) why should morality be confining and costly only when recognizing constraints and not also to assist others in pressing need? (Kagan 1989: 50–1) I focus on the second question for two reasons. First, although many people live as if they believe minimalism, few openly endorse it. Second, in addressing the second issue I indirectly address the first. I return to explicitly discuss the first question in the following chapter.

Why the difference?

All three approaches agree that some moral requirements can be demanding. We could easily imagine situations in which:

- the only way I can avoid bankruptcy is to embezzle from my company;
- the only way to get the job I want is to falsify my school records, to cheat on an exam, or to tell lies about my competition;
- the only way to avoid losing my driver's license is to flee from the scene of an accident.

All three approaches hold that these are actions I should not do, even if they are both confining and costly. Why are these demands thought to be a legitimate part of morality while feeding the distant hungry is thought to be too confining or too costly or both? Put differently, why should morality not be stringent? The most common answer is that a stringent morality ignores the moral distinction between doing and allowing. We have seen this distinction before. It is high time to discuss it in detail.

Doing/Allowing

Those who think morality is demanding do not think that doings are much (if at all) more important than allowings; the minimalist thinks there is an unbridgeable moral chasm separating them such that we are responsible only for our doings. The moderate thinks the moral distance between doings and allowings is a rift rather than a chasm. Still, they typically think acts are some considerable moral distance from omissions (Kamm 1998, 2000; McMahan 1993). If the distinction in either form is morally defensible, then we could explain the ordinary belief that morality cannot generally be stringent, except for a few behaviors. Is this distinction defensible?

To see why most people think so, consider the following examples. In the first, Elmer wants his wealthy grandfather's inheritance, and he is afraid his grandfather is about to change his will. So he poisons his grandfather. In the second case, Elaine works overtime so she can buy her six-year-old daughter a new toy. Elaine could have sent that extra money to OXFAM, thereby saving two starving Nigerian children. Perhaps Elaine did not know that she could have saved a starving child, but even if she did, she would have bought the toy anyway.

Elmer committed murder and should be punished. Elaine simply bought her child a toy; at most she allowed the Nigerian child to die. Not only did the law not seek to punish her, she would likely be praised for working extra hours to give her child this gift. Even those few who think she should have sent the money to OXFAM would say she did nothing remotely similar to what Elmer did. Virtually everyone would agree with this assessment in broad brush, myself included. However, that does not yet show that doings are standardly – let alone inevitably – more morally weighty than allowings.

Clarifying the distinction

Philosophers once referred to this as the act/omission distinction or as the active/passive distinction. Since many of these debates concerned euthanasia, it was also often linked to, or seen as coextensive with, the distinction between killing and letting die (McMahan 1993: 250). The preferred philosophical terminology has changed, and not just to reflect linguistic taste. After all, the language of doings and allowings is less elegant than that of actions and omissions. However, those defending the moral relevance of this distinction realized that not all actions leading to harm are doings, and not all omissions are allowings (Foot 1978: 26; McMahan 1993: 251). What is an example of an action that is not a doing? Joe is drowning and Bill swims to save him. Joe panics and starts clawing at Bill. Bill cannot save Joe, and can save himself only by pushing Joe away. This involves action, but it is not a doing: Bill does not kill Joe.

What is an example of an inaction that might be a killing? Failing to feed one's infant child – that action is wrong and usually considered a killing. To account for these cases, philosophers subsequently suggested a more arcane distinction between doing and allowing. They now describe this as the difference between "(i) initiating or sustaining a harmful causal sequence, and (ii) allowing or enabling a causal sequence to run its course" (Rickless 1997: 555).

Two dimensions

This discussion suggests that the distinction between doing and allowing is, or is not, morally relevant. These are not the only options. Indeed, few people hold either extreme. Most people think the distinction is morally relevant *in some sense*. However, there are significant disagreements about the *nature* and the *strength* of the difference. Both dimensions are matters of degree.

Nature

Some think that the *bare* distinction between doing and allowing is morally relevant. They claim that *even when all other morally relevant factors are the same*, the *mere* fact that something is a doing rather than an allowing should alter our moral evaluation of it. Others claim that although the bare distinction is not morally relevant, the distinction is important since other morally relevant factors are more often associated with doings than with allowings. Thus the distinction is a helpful epistemological tool that identifies a moral difference between two otherwise seemingly similar cases. Most

who think the bare difference is morally relevant also think the distinction is indirectly relevant. In addition to whatever moral difference the bare distinction makes,
the distinction is also typically associated with a host of other morally relevant
factors.

The range of options moves from those who think the distinction is morally significantly only indirectly, through those who think that the bare difference also makes
some moral difference, to those who think the bare difference is profoundly
significant.

Strength

Those who think the distinction is fundamental and those who think it is indirectly
relevant may disagree about the *strength* of the difference. Those on one end of this
spectrum hold (or seem to hold) that the bare distinction marks an unbridgeable
moral gulf so that doing an evil, no matter how minor, is always worse than allowing an evil, no matter how great. On the other end of the spectrum are those who
think the distinction, although indirectly morally relevant, marks the tiniest of moral
differences. Most people hold positions somewhere between these extremes. They
hold that the moral difference between the cases is significant, but bridgeable. For
these people, allowing an evil will sometimes be worse than causing one. Just how
often, is what they must decide.

Possible rationales for thinking the distinction is fundamental

There are three common arguments for thinking that there is a fundamental moral
difference between doings and allowings.

Intuition

Some people think we know by intuition that doings are morally more significant
than allowings. A few of these might think that we can straightforwardly intuit that
the distinction is morally relevant. More commonly these people offer a range of
real and fictional cases and then argue that the best explanation for people's intuitions about the cases is that there the distinction marks a morally relevant difference. Since most people have similar intuitions about a wide range of cases, they
infer that the distinction is not just important, but fundamental (McMahan 2000).

This is a highly suggestive argument. If the majority of people really are convinced
in case after case that doings are morally more significant that allowings, then we
have a *prima facie* reason for thinking this difference matters morally. However, the
argument is not quite as convincing as it first appears. First, the distinction is so difficult to draw that even philosophers sympathetic to it propose varying and even
incompatible accounts (Foot 1978; Kamm 1998, 2000; Malm 1989; McMahan 1993,
2000; Quinn 1989). Second – and relatedly – most people's intuitions support the
act/omission distinction, not the distinction between doings and allowings. Third,

even if we had a clear and univocal account of the distinction, this argument could not show that the *bare* difference between acts and omissions is morally relevant. It might simply be that acts are more likely than omissions to be associated with other characteristics that are morally relevant, and it is this association that leads people to think that bare acts are morally more significant than omissions.

Here I set these worries aside. I will instead challenge the claim that most people's intuitions support the doing/allowing distinction, at least the claim that the distinction is fundamentally relevant. Let's look at a couple of cases. Admittedly the first includes arguably extraneous factors. However, most real cases, about which our intuitions are best informed, are complicated in just these ways. Moreover, I think we can learn more about the distinction by seeing the way it operates in real-life cases.

As I mentioned in Chapter 3, it appears that most people who support the death penalty do so because of its purported results, namely, preventing other murders from occurring. In short, they justify doing one wrong (what would be wrong were it not justified) to prevent another one.

Second, we establish systems of punishment knowing that at least some innocent people will be harmed. Many innocent people will be investigated for and charged with crimes they did not commit. Even if they are eventually exonerated, the harm to them will be immense. We establish and maintain this system of punishment to protect ourselves. We clearly think it is better to have a system that deters crime, incapacitates dangerous people, and punishes guilty ones, than to have one in which *no* innocent people are punished. We do precisely what the doing/allowing distinction presumably forbids: we undertake a policy we know will harm some innocent people to prevent harm to others. Since virtually everyone thinks this is a satisfactory tradeoff, it seems people do not think there is a *fundamental* moral difference between doing and allowing.

Causal responsibility

The most common explanation for the fundamental significance of the doing/allowing distinction is a two-pronged claim that (a) we are morally responsible only for conditions we cause, and (b) we can cause conditions only by positive action (see, e.g., Kamm 2000: 209; McMahan 1993: 277).

Understanding responsibility

This argument has a certain plausibility. However, if a parent fails to feed her child and the child dies, most people will not only hold the parent responsible for the death, they would claim that the parent caused the death. Most people would say the parent killed the child (although, somewhat to my surprise, McMahan disagrees 1993: 270). Yet the parent did not do anything. That was the problem. She did not do anything, and it is her absence of action that we cite as the cause of the death, and as the grounds for holding the parent responsible.

Of course, as the earlier discussion showed, someone who embraces the doing/allowing distinction would likely claim that this case is different because the parent has a special moral responsibility to care for the child. However, even if this explains why we think the parent is responsible, this response gives shape to a dilemma for those advancing the causal responsibility argument. Either someone (in this case, the parent) can be held morally responsible for something she did not cause, or people can cause harm by allowings as well as doings. Each claim undercuts one premise of the causal responsibility argument.

There are other cases where claims of special moral responsibility are even less plausible. To vary a case offered by Jonathan Bennett, we would say: "I hurt my friend's feelings by not calling her on her birthday." We would not say: "I allowed my friend's feelings to be hurt" (1995: 72). My inaction harmed my friend. The doing/allowing distinction precludes inactions from being causes.

Negative causation

The second premise of the causal responsibility argument claims that allowings can never be causes. As the previous examples show, that does not seem to be true, at least in special relationships (parents and children, doctors and patients, lifeguards and bathers). In such cases we speak of parents' or professionals' *allowings* (failures to act) as the causes of subsequent harm. These are not the only examples. In some circumstances we cite failures as the causes of later conditions. Why did we lose so many crops last year? Because of the lack of rain or nitrogen in the soil. Why did the Bengali child die? Because of the lack of nutrition.

To identify the circumstances under which we properly cite allowings as causes, we must understand that we always make causal claims against a background of expectations (Hart and Honoré 1973). When normal background conditions are present, we ignore them and focus on any different factors. For instance, I cannot open a door without working hinges, and the door does not work properly in the absence of gravitational forces. These are necessary causal conditions that permit me to open the door. However, we ordinarily expect hinges to work, and we always expect to be subject to gravitational forces. So in most circumstances we ignore those conditions, and focus on what is different: usually whether someone turns the knob and pulls on (or pushes) the door.

This illuminates our explanations for why the crops failed and the child died. We cite an absence as a cause only if (1) certain background conditions must be satisfied before the event can occur (the crops grow and the child lives), (2) we ordinarily expect these conditions to be present (that water is available and that the child is fed), *and* (3) in these cases, the necessary conditions are absent. All three elements are required to cite an absence as a cause. For instance, we do not normally expect water in the desert. Thus, when crops do not grow there, we do not blame the lack of rain. However, if the land is irrigated and the crops fail, we will blame the irrigation system. And if we think that someone (say, the government) should have provided an irrigation system, we may also blame them.

We need to keep this in mind when morally evaluating individuals and institutions. We cannot take certain background conditions – or their absence – for granted. When we have it within our power to create or sustain background conditions that significantly affect people's interest, then we must decide that is something we should do. For instance, most countries have decided that the government should collect and treat human sewage, provide clean drinking water, reduce pollution, and educate its citizens. We make judgments against the background of these assumptions. When I flush my toilet, I expect the government to treat and purify the water before dumping it into the river. If that were not so, by flushing I set a dangerous causal sequence in motion. However, since my expectations are reasonable, I do not do anything untoward. If untreated waste is dumped into the river, it is not my fault but the fault of the local utility board. I also expect the government to maintain clean air and water. If it does not, then we blame the government for subsequent harm. Are these appropriate expectations? I sure think so. Most people agree. If so, then allowings can be properly cited as causes if we think people or institutions have a responsibility to perform an action that would have prevented a harm. The doing/allowing distinction can neither explain nor countenance this.

The chance for intervening factors

This third argument is related to the previous one, but since it raises some additional considerations, I will briefly discuss it. In most circumstances, when a person acts, she sets a causal chain in motion that, barring intervention, will have certain results. When these results are detrimental to others, we cite her as the cause of these harms. Normally we do not cite others' failures to intervene as the cause. At most, we think they merely allowed the causal chain to continue. Why might we think the doing/allowing distinction is morally relevant here? Here's one explanation: one person's failure to intervene does not preclude other agents or fortuitous events from intervening in ways that prevent the harm from occurring. Not saving the drowning child does not stop the person standing next to me from doing so. If I fail to feed Joani, someone else might feed her, she might find food on her own, etc. Although these facts might support the claim that in these cases doings are morally more significant than allowings, it does not show that the bare difference is morally relevant. I do not see how it could.

Two additional reasons for denying this strong thesis

We can now identify two additional reasons why we should reject a strong moral distinction between doings and allowings.

It cannot accommodate the practice of prohibiting risky actions

As I explained in Chapter 12, we forbid not only actions that harm others, but also risky actions – those likely to harm others, e.g., driving drunk, toting machine guns, and storing dynamite in one's bedroom. We calculate the likelihood and seriousness of the risk and "balance" it against the importance of the risky action. We subsequently limit people's behaviors if the cost of allowing the actions is greater than the cost of preventing it. This is consequentialist reasoning of the sort that the doing/allowing distinction is supposed to block. Although one person does think these laws are inappropriate (Husak 2004), most thinkers take them for granted. If protecting people from risky action is appropriate, then it appears that the doing/allowing distinction does not mark a fundamental or especially strong moral difference.

It has a defective view of human agency

Lurking around is the assumption that when an agent acts she is in "complete control with the capacity to ensure that the event will happen" (Harris 1980: 110), while if she refrains from acting, she is powerless. Both claims are false. I may point a gun at someone and pull a trigger, but that does not insure that they die. The gun must be loaded, I must be a good (or "lucky") shot, medical personnel must not intervene quickly to save him, etc. Conversely, in certain circumstances my inaction is the best explanation of a detrimental effect. If I fail to feed my infant, then I am not only responsible for the death, I killed her.

Conclusion

We have concluded that morality may well be more demanding than most people suppose. However, there are still two further objections to this claim, which we consider in the next chapter.

REFERENCES

Bennett, J. F. (1995) *The Act Itself.* Oxford: Clarendon Press.
Foot, P. (1978) "The Problem of Abortion and the Doctrine of Double Effect." In *Virtues and Vices and Other Essays in Moral Philosophy*. Berkeley: University of California Press, 19–32.
Harris, J. (1980) *Violence and Responsibility.* London: Routledge & Kegan Paul.
Hart, H. L. A. and Honoré, T. (1973) *Causation in the Law.* Oxford: Clarendon Press.
Husak, D. N. (2004) "Guns and Drugs: Case Studies on the Principled Limits of the Criminal Sanction," *Law and Philosophy* 23 (5): 437–93.
Kagan, S. (1989) *The Limits of Morality.* Oxford: Oxford University Press.
Kamm, F. M. (1998) "Moral Intuitions, Cognitive Psychology, and the Harming-Versus-Not-Aiding Distinction," *Ethics* 108 (3): 463–88.
Kamm, F. M. (2000) "Nonconsequentialism." In H. LaFollette (ed.), *The Blackwell Guide to Ethical Theory*. Oxford: Blackwell Publishers, 205–26.
LaFollette, H. (1979) "Why Libertarianism is Mistaken." In J. Arthur and W. H. Shaw (eds.), *Justice and Economic Distribution*. Englewood Cliffs, NJ: Prentice-Hall, 194–206.
Malm, H. M. (1989) "Killing, Letting Die, and Simple Conflicts," *Philosophy and Public Affairs* 18: 238–58.
McMahan, J. (1993) "Killing, Letting Die, and Withdrawing Aid," *Ethics* 103 (2): 250–79.

McMahan, J. (2000) "Moral Intuition." In H. LaFollette (ed.), *The Blackwell Guide to Ethical Theory*. Oxford: Blackwell Publishers, 92–110.

Murphy, L. (2000) *Moral Demands in Non-Ideal Theory*. Oxford: Oxford University Press.

Nagel, T. (1986) *The View from Nowhere*. New York: Oxford University Press.

Nagel, T. (1991) *Equality and Partiality*. New York: Oxford University Press.

Narveson, J. (2000) "Libertarianism." In H. LaFollette (ed.), *The Blackwell Guide to Ethical Theory*. Oxford: Blackwell Publishers, 306–24.

Quinn, W. (1989) "Actions, Intentions, and Consequences: The Doctrine of Doing and Allowing," *The Philosophical Review* 98 (3): 287–312.

Rickless, S. C. (1997) "The Doctrine of Doing and Allowing," *The Philosophical Review* 106 (4): 555–75.

Scheffler, S. (1992) *Human Morality*. Oxford: Oxford University Press.

Stocker, M. (1976) "The Schizophrenia of Modern Ethical Theories," *The Journal of Philosophy* 73: 453–66.

Stocker, M. (1989) *Plural and Conflicting Values*. Oxford: Clarendon Press.

Williams, B. (1981/1976) "Persons, Character, and Morality." In *Moral Luck: Philosophical Papers, 1973–1980*. Cambridge: Cambridge University Press, 1–19.

Wolf, S. (1982) "Moral Saints," *Journal of Philosophy* 79: 410–39.

EIGHTEEN

Egoism: Psychological and Moral

As we saw in the last chapter, some people claim that morality either cannot be or should not be demanding. Those who hold the former view think most people are simply unable to meet hefty moral requirements. Often this view rests on *psychological egoism*, the theory that everyone's actions are always and completely self-interested. Those who hold the latter view claim that although people might be able to satisfy significant moral demands, they should not be required to do so. This second view comes in myriad forms, several of which we discussed in the previous chapter. One form of this view is *ethical egoism*: the claim that people ought to always and only act to promote their own self-interests. Let us explore both forms of egoism.

Psychological Egoism

It is not hard to see why psychological egoism (hereafter PE) has widespread appeal. It seems to fit ordinary observations about what motivates people. Mother Teresa spent her life caring for the poor and the infirm while Bill Gates spends his life directing Microsoft. Although we might be unhappy doing what they do, we assume they are satisfied. Mother Teresa enjoyed her work and would have been miserable if she had to mastermind corporate takeovers or design software. Gates would be wretched if he had to care for lepers and live in a slum.

If we reflect on our own lives and the lives of our friends, we are no different. Doing what we want often makes us happy, while we are usually dissatisfied if we cannot do what we want. That is true whether we want to be missionaries or CEOs. What does this show us about the relationship between self-interest and morality? The psychological egoist claims it shows that everyone always seeks to promote her own interests. We will engage in moral behavior only if we think that it is the best way to advance our interests.

This thesis is widely held by non-philosophers. Yet many philosophers repudiate it. Why the divergence of opinion? As I shall show, some versions are indefensible. Nonetheless, ethicists are often so anxious to defeat PE that they fail to notice a germ of truth in it – a psychological observation with important implications for moral psychology. Here I will identify this insight and argue for its significance. Before I can do that, I must first identify the intuitive appeal of PE, and then explain why the theory, in its standard forms, is false.

The intuitive appeal of psychological egoism

There are three primary factors that lend credence to the thesis. First, everyone recognizes that we are frequently motivated to promote our self-interest. Second, in reflective moments we all realize we were occasionally mistaken when we thought that we were not motivated by self-interest. We initially thought that we acted out of concern for others or from commitment to moral principle, yet retrospectively discern that the principal, if not sole, motivation was self-satisfaction, e.g., we expect others to return the favor, we want a better image in the community, etc. Psychological egoists exploit this acknowledgment. They argue that since most of us understand that we are often motivated by self-interest even when we initially thought otherwise, then it is likely that we are always fooled when we think we are motivated by concern for others or adherence to principle. Third, PE is further bolstered by the realization, mentioned at the beginning of this chapter, that an individual is normally satisfied when she does what she wants to do, regardless of her purported motive. People who act morally are usually satisfied by the realization that they are (and are perceived to be) moral. Loving spouses and parents often achieve great satisfaction from caring for their children and significant others. Moral saints reap immense satisfaction from their work. It is difficult to cite a case where an individual acts in ways which she knows will never in any way satisfy her.

These observations elucidate the appeal of PE. These facts must be accounted for by any adequate theory of motivation, either by incorporating and explaining them, or by showing them to be illusory. My contention is that these observations can be best accounted for by the following egoistic-looking thesis: *a person will continually engage in an activity only if it has the effect of satisfying what she perceives to be in her own self-interest.* Though this thesis is obviously similar to PE, it differs from it in pivotal respects. To understand just how much it differs, I must first isolate the errors in standard PE.

What's wrong with psychological egoism

PE's appeal arises primarily from its ambiguous formulation. The thesis can be interpreted in several distinct ways. When an opponent objects to one characterization, the advocate shifts to a defense of another. When that version is successfully criticized, still another is forwarded. When the ambiguities are swept away, the thesis is demonstrably false. My initial task, then, will be to specify these ambiguities. The recognition of a single ambiguity is insufficient to undermine PE; nonetheless, when taken together they will. Since it is easy to slide back and forth between diverse formulations, keep each in mind as you read the following sections.

Motives or consequences

The first ambiguity arises because of the egoist's tendency to blur or ignore the distinction between the motive for and the consequences of an action. Simply because an act has a consequence does not imply that the agent was motivated by it. All acts have consequences of which the actor is ignorant; hence she could not have been motivated to achieve them all. Someone may also act in ways that she reasonably predicts will have certain effects, yet not be motivated to achieve those effects. Barbara might cook an anniversary meal for her spouse in order to make him happy, although she would doubtless be thrilled if he adores the meal. After all, she loves him. What sense could we make of someone for whom it was regularly otherwise: "I am doing something I know my spouse – the love of my life – will appreciate, and it makes me absolutely miserable"? Although feeling satisfied is one effect of Barbara's action, to claim she acted in order to gain satisfaction misdescribes what she did. Of course, some women might have ulterior motives for cooking meals for their husbands. We all know people who purportedly act for others when they are concerned only about themselves. However, just because some people are so motivated, we should not conclude that all or even most are. There are clear differences between these cases, and any adequate theory of motivation should acknowledge it. Even if we have difficulty determining an agent's motives in some cases, there is a fundamental difference between those who are motivated to help others, yet are consequently satisfied by doing so, and those who help others merely as a means of helping themselves. We can see this difference by looking at each person's behavior. The first person would have cooked the meal even if, she knew her spouse's being happy would not satisfy her; the second person wouldn't have. After all, she was only cooking the meal as an indirect way of satisfying herself.

One self's interest or one's self-interest

These observations illuminate an important related distinction PE obscures, the distinction between an action's being in one's interest and its being in one's self-interest (Hocutt unpublished). This distinction further elucidates the difference between the wife who cooks the meal to make her spouse feel better, and one who cooks the meal to make herself feel better.

The first wife has an interest in her spouse. She wants to make him feel cherished: she wants him to be happy. Likely she will be pleased if she succeeds. However, that does not imply that she was motivated to please herself. The second wishes only to promote her own self-interest; she cooks the meal for her husband only as a means to that end.

Psychological egoists gloss over this important distinction. They begin with the evident fact that individuals pursue their interests. Whenever an individual articulates *a* reason for action, she articulates *her* reasons. However, that simply identifies the locus of the interests (they are hers, not mine). It says nothing about their nature or object. Some of her interests may be self-interests – interests merely in her own welfare. She may also be interested in other people, in promoting the public good, or in becoming virtuous. Even if she is satisfied when she achieves these latter interests, we should not infer that her motivating interest was self-interest. As before, we can describe these differences behaviorally. An individual seeking her self-interests would gladly forgo efforts to help others if she could satisfy her self-interests in some alternative way; the one motivated to help others would not.

If PE is understood in the first way – as saying people always act to promote their interests – it is true, but uninteresting. That is just to say that each person's interests are hers and not someone else's (whose would they be?). It does not tell us which interests she has. In particular, it does not tell us if some of her interests are interests in other people. If PE is understood in the second way – as saying people always seek to promote their self-interests – evidence strongly suggests it is false.

That is why PE fails as a theory of human motivation. It treats pleasure or happiness as the sole end that everyone seeks. On this view people wander through the world in search of happiness and will do anything that will promote that end. However, happiness is not a thing we can grab or a state we automatically achieve by following a "happiness recipe." Knowing that Mother Teresa was happy caring for lepers does not mean we need only care for lepers to be happy. Knowing that Bill Gates is happy running Microsoft does not mean that would make us happy. Happiness is not an end best pursued directly; it is a byproduct of activity. Attempts to pursue it directly almost always fail.

If we cannot automatically be happy by doing what makes others happy, what can we do to be happy? The psychological egoist claims there is a simple formula: we pursue our self-interest. However, that is unhelpful advice since it does not tell us what that means. People are very different. What makes me happy might make you miserable, and vice versa. People have varied self-interests and, under the right conditions, they can be happy doing any number of activities. "We all have an immense capacity . . . for modifying our behavior in response to what we learn. The result is a remarkable behavioral flexibility. . . . We are able to devise alternative patterns of 'behavior' for virtually every circumstance or life . . ." (Lenski and Lenski 1968: 31). What often determines which of these actions people find satisfying is whether it is an action that they want to do. As Derek Parfit puts it, "what is in our interests partly depends on what our motives and desires are" (Parfit 1984: 87). Put differently, often we come to desire something not because we are satisfied by it; rather we are satisfied by it because we desire it.

Of course, there are limits to what will make someone happy. If nothing else, genetics limits the range of things that we could desire, the kinds of actions that could satisfy us. However, within those limits most people can develop any of a wide range of non-self interests. Fulfilling these interests will usually satisfy us, but only because they are our interests; they are not our interests (let alone our self-interests) because they are satisfying. As Nowell-Smith put it:

> If I want to relieve the stress of the beggar, I want to relieve the stress of the beggar;
> I do not want my own happiness, pleasure or satisfaction. Likewise, if I like giving

pleasure to my sick aunt, what I like is giving pleasure to my sick aunt, not my own liking, or even the glow I might receive from being benevolent. Indeed, if the latter were what I really liked, I should be doomed to eternal disappointment, because I could never get just that glow unless I acted for the sake of giving pleasure and not for the sake of the glow (Nowell-Smith 1957: 142).

In sum, psychological egoists claim to explain why we act as we do. It is a miserable failure. They can point out that we act in accordance with our interests, but they cannot explain why we have the interests we have. And the theory has no resources for telling us which interests we should develop.

Real interests or perceived interests

Thirdly, PE is ambiguous between the claim that individuals always act in ways (whether they realize it or not) that *do* promote their genuine interests and the claim that they act in ways that *they think* promote their interests. The egoist moves back and forth between these alternatives, making the thesis appear explanatorily potent. However, neither alternative is singularly plausible. The first alternative is faulty on empirical grounds. People sometimes fail miserably to promote their own interests, even when they try to do so. In some of these cases a person is temporarily satisfied since she does what she wants to do. However, she may ultimately find the action unsatisfying if those desires were simply adopted from others: Someone who becomes a doctor simply because her parents pressured her to do so may discover she does not like being a doctor. In short, people do not always act to promote what is, in fact, in their interests.

The second alternative is likewise implausible, particularly once we remember the aforementioned distinction between something's being in one's interest and its being in her self-interest. Even if it were true that an individual always acts to promote what she *believes* to be in her interests (itself a dubious claim), it is not true that she always acts to promote what she believes to be *in her self-interest*. Not infrequently individuals believe themselves to act from non-self-interested motives. Even if they are sometimes mistaken, that does not bolster the egoist's case. Successful disclosure of hidden motives shows only that an individual was mistaken about what her motive really was. It would not show that she was mistaken about what she believed her motive to be. Since she believed she was motivated to promote her non-self-interests, the second alternative is likewise defective.

Always self-interest or only self-interest

Finally, the thesis is ambiguous between the claim that people always seek to promote their self-interest to some degree or another, and the claim that they always choose that action that they think will promote their self-interest better than any known available option.

Although on the first interpretation the thesis might turn out to be true, it would be relatively uninteresting. We rarely have a single motive for what we do. One of those motives is often self-interest. Even when a person is motivated to help others she may, at the same time, also be motivated to promote her self-interest. If nothing else, she is likely aware of the ways that morality can be satisfying. However, this does not support an interesting or controversial interpretation of PE. Once we admit that any motives besides self-interest are operative then PE, in the strict sense, is undermined. Here's an easy way to see that. Consider a case where agent A has two options: option X promotes her self-interest, but option Y does so even better and she realizes this. If self-interest were her only motive she would automatically choose Y. However, if she has any non-self-interests, then at least in some cases, the slight increase in self-interest promoted by Y would be outweighed by a combination of self- and non-self-interests promoted by X. Seen in this way, PE is compatible with all forms of altruism. That undermines PE's aim.

Therefore PE must be understood as making the stronger claim: that people always choose that action they think will promote their self-interest better than any known available option. However, this stronger claim is counter-intuitive, particularly when coupled with previous distinctions. Even when people report themselves as pursuing their self-interest, many would claim to be likewise pursuing non-self-interests. And, although they might be mistaken about their real motive, they are not mistaken about what they believe their motive to be. Hence, they are not acting in ways they believe will promote their self-interest better than any known available option.

Summary

We now see that several of these formulations of PE are true, but trivially so. For example, the claim that people always act to promote their interests may be true, but in a sense no one would deny. These formulations are not really egoistic. If we were to devise a precise and non-trivial formulation of PE it would have to be this: *all human beings always act to promote only what they believe to be in their highest self-interest*. The earlier arguments, taken together, show why this thesis is false. So why do people continue to embrace PE? I think it is because (a) most people fail to see these ambiguities and (b) they are moved by the insights isolated at the beginning of this chapter. It is time to elaborate on those insights and state a revised thesis that incorporates and explains them without embracing the negative consequences of PE as traditionally understood. I will not pretend to provide an indubitable argument nor a final statement of the revised thesis; that would require a complete psychology. Nonetheless, I will offer arguments indicating its plausibility.

The insight of the thesis

The embedded insight is this: *a person will continually engage in an activity only if it has the effect of satisfying what she perceives to be in her self-interest*.

This thesis differs from the traditional version of PE in three significant and interrelated respects, all isolated in the previous discussions. First, it does not assert that a person is always motivated by promotion of her self-interest; it claims only that she will not continually act in ways that fail to promote her self-interest. Second, it recognizes that some of a person's interests are non-self-interests. An individual may have interests in other people, in political causes, in private charities, or in cultivating character. Nonetheless, when she realizes those interests she is normally satisfied. Third, it does not require that self-interest be the decisive, most weighty interest. Non-self-interests will at least sometimes predominate.

Why it is plausible

This thesis is plausible when seen against the backdrop of my previous arguments against PE. It recognizes that humans are often motivated by self-interest but does not require that self-interest be the only motive. Standard PE also cannot explain why we select some options or lifestyles over others. Since many options could be satisfying *if we adopted them*, then unless we choose the options *only* because we think they would be the most satisfying it cannot be that we choose them *in order to be* satisfied. Other motives – some non-self-interests – must be operative. That is why PE (in its controversial form) is false.

However, we are psychologically so constituted that acting on our interests – even our non-self-interests – is typically satisfying. As Dewey explains, "Almost any activity continued until it becomes a habit becomes pleasurable and when discontinued becomes a source of pain and dissatisfaction" (Dewey 1976: 23). This phenomenon, as Daniel Dennett puts it, "is not just part of a possible explanation of human behavior, but of any possible adequate explanation of behavior" (Dennett 1978: 72–3; Slote 1964). It is hard to imagine how we could have survived as a species without this psychological predisposition. That is why the revised thesis, once clearly stated, seems evident. Perhaps many philosophers recognize the truth of this claim, but claim that it is trivially true. I suppose in a sense it is. Unfortunately we sometimes ignore trivial truths to our detriment. This is one such case. It is regrettable that we do. The thesis has obvious and direct implications for moral psychology and moral theory.

Implications

According to this thesis, an individual will not continue to act morally unless doing so eventually has the effect of promoting her self-interests, even if it does not promote them better than available alternatives. Why does this matter? It requires us to rethink how to inculcate moral behavior in children and how we can improve our own moral behavior. Although we must sometimes battle our "natural" inclinations, that should not be our principal preoccupation. We should, instead, work to mold our interests so that they coincide with the demands of morality (an idea of Mill's I mentioned earlier). We do that by developing non-self-interests in others and by developing a second-order interest in being moral. If most people within a society do so, then (a) when people act they will standardly promote others' interests, and

(b) when people satisfy their non-self-interests in morality, they will normally also satisfy (as a side-effect) their own self-interests.

Of course, some people may not find the moral life satisfying. That is why we need laws to enforce a minimal level of decency: legal sanctions make compliance more attractive. Generally, though, most people in a well-ordered and just society are not motivated primarily by fear of punishment. They comply voluntarily with moral standards. It is not hard to see why. For many humans in normal circumstances (see the discussion of the "circumstances of justice" in Hume 1978/1740; Rawls 1999/1971), being moral is part of the most satisfying life they could lead. However, this strong conjecture need not be true for people to act morally; it need only be true that living morally is *generally* satisfying. And it is: considering and looking after the interests of others often does bring (to borrow Nowell-Smith's phrase) a certain glow unattainable in other ways. Opening oneself to love and caring allows one to enjoy human satisfactions attainable only in concert with others. Knowing this does not give a person a reason to act morally if she has no interest in doing so. What it does do is give her a reason not to abandon morality out of the fear that morality requires squelching her interests. This further explains why we should develop a second-order interest in being moral. If we do, we are more likely to act morally even when we are temperamentally or momentarily disinclined to do so. We will be willing to sometimes do what is moral just because it is moral, and we will likely be satisfied by doing so. However, this "piggyback" satisfaction will generally be insufficient to motivate us to continually act morally.

This is why merely imploring people to be moral will likely produce nothing more than frustrated individuals who make vain attempts to be moral. We must think about how to make morality "motivationally accessible" (Scheffler 1992: 124). To assume otherwise "is the greatest bar to intelligent social progress. It bars the way because it makes us neglect intelligent inquiry to discover the means which will produce a desired result, and intelligent intervention to procure the means. In short, it leaves out the importance of intelligently controlled habit" (Dewey 1988/1922: 28).

Unfortunately I fear that is what many of us (philosophers and teachers) do. We encourage individuals to be moral without offering guidance on how to do that. To make matters worse, we so denigrate self-interest that when an individual is satisfied by acting morally, she assumes her behavior is morally suspect. It is not. When moral training succeeds, the line between one's interests and self-interest blurs. The wife's obtaining what she wants may be as important to the husband's happiness as is his achieving what he wants for himself. The couple's interests become so pervasively intertwined that it is difficult for him to distinguish her welfare from his and vice versa. Likewise, when one's interests in being moral become important, then being moral becomes immensely satisfying, even when it may, in other ways, hinder other self-interests. That explains how someone like Mother Teresa could find working with lepers so intensely satisfying. And it explains why a doctor or lawyer or teacher is satisfied when she is conscientious and effective, even though she likely sacrifices some immediate self-interests in her quest for professional excellence.

Illustrating the thesis

Let me briefly describe a case that illustrates the revised egoistic-looking thesis. Suppose someone who has been reared a carnivore confronts the familiar arguments for vegetarianism (LaFollette 1989; Regan 1983; Singer 1990/1975). After some mental wrestling she decides – rightly or wrongly – that she ought to give up eating meat even though she rather enjoys its taste and texture. If my modified thesis is correct, she is unlikely to become a completely committed vegetarian overnight. The carnivorous habit is too strong; breaking it is too difficult. Even if she manages to live up to her convictions temporarily, she will eventually fail unless she comes to be directly satisfied by her new diet. As it turns out, many people will find the vegetarian diet satisfying, at least if they can successfully inculcate new eating habits. They are more likely to create this habit if they wish to be moral and believe morality requires them to give up meat. If, for whatever reason, they do not eventually find the habit intrinsically satisfying, they will eventually return to eating meat. They will either continue to think that they ought to be vegetarians – and feel guilty for being weak – or they will manage to "convince" themselves that their original assessment of the arguments was all wrong – that morality does not really demand that they be vegetarians.

This example illustrates one way that pragmatism blends the insights of competing standard theories. Consider the claims of Aristotle (as an exponent of virtue theory) and Kant (as an exponent of deontology). In trying to isolate important features of the moral life, each overemphasizes one part of it. Aristotle has a somewhat reflexive conception of habits (*Nichomachean Ethics*, Book 11), but has little to say about their original motivation. Kant denigrates the person who acts habitually even if the acts are normally thought to be good. We find goodness only in acts done out of a sense of duty.

The pragmatist thinks both theories capture important elements of the moral life. Consider again the example of the carnivore-turned-vegetarian. At some point in this person's life, she has a conflict between duty and inclination. Thinking that duty demands a change in eating habits, she gives up meat. She is acting out of duty, not inclination. She resists her current carnivorous habit. Here Kant has isolated an important feature of the moral life. Morality occasionally conflicts with inclination and self-interest. If she were to simply do what she has always done habitually, she would not do what she thinks she ought. Once she has begun to make the change, the situation differs. Within a few months our vegetarian becomes increasingly acclimated to her new diet. She now finds the diet normal; the thought of eating meat becomes increasingly less appealing. Soon the desire to be a vegetarian becomes embodied in her eating habits. She now does habitually what she once forced herself to do. She is satisfied by doing so. If my revised egoistic thesis is correct, she would not have continued to do so unless the diet had become satisfying – in this case by her becoming habituated to the new eating style. Hence the insight from Aristotle.

Since we are largely creatures of habit, it could not have been any other way. To the extent that Kant misses this important fact, he has gone awry. But if he has gone awry, it is not because he thinks morality demands that we sometimes act against inclination – for surely we must. Rather he fails to recognize that we are psychologically so constituted that if we become habituated to an action, particularly if it is one we desire to perform – for instance, out of a second-order desire to be moral – then we will find that action satisfactory and do it out of inclination.

Put differently, the pragmatist understands the moral life as a cooperative venture between conscious adherence to duty and cultivated habit. We are, from youth, taught certain moral principles. If our training is successful, then we will habitually act in ways we were trained to act. If we were taught the proper moral rules and attitudes, so much the better for us and everyone else. Nonetheless, it is just where habit fails, e.g., because we were improperly trained, that conscious adherence to duty needs to step in. Since we all received some improper or uninformed moral instruction, then all of us must scrutinize our habits, our inculcated moral beliefs. We will sometimes find we must change them. When we must, we must fight inclination out of a sense of duty. Duty is a powerful impetus to inculcate a new habit, one which, we hope, will enable us to be more moral.

Both sides of this tandem are essential. Without either we would be morally frail. And without understanding the germ of truth in PE we would fail to perceive and appreciate the proper interaction of duty and habit in the making of the moral life.

Ethical Egoism

An ethical egoist is not an immoralist. The immoralist says there is no such thing as morality. Such a view is untenable, for, according to the theory, others would not act wrongly if they killed or assaulted her. No one could rationally embrace such a claim. Yet in rejecting this claim, people acknowledge that there is at least one moral standard: they think it is wrong to kill or assault others. To acknowledge that is to deny the truth of immoralism.

The ethical egoist is not vulnerable to such a quick dismissal. She claims there is one moral standard: namely, that each of us should act in ways that maximize our own self-interest. Morality cannot require that we sacrifice our self-interest for others – or that they must sacrifice their interests for us. That does not mean that we should abuse, mistreat, or take advantage of others. That would be imprudent. It would work against our own best interests and that, according to the ethical egoist, would be immoral. An enlightened ethical egoist would recognize that it is in her interest to embrace some legal and moral protections against violence and theft since these are essential means for promoting her interests. Finally, each of us benefits from having other people around to provide enjoyment, satisfaction, company, and comfort. Others can give our life meaning that it would lack if we were alone.

In these senses the gap between egoism and standard moral theories is perhaps not as great as it first seems. Still, the gap is substantial enough. The egoist embraces the aforementioned "moral" restrictions only inasmuch as they promote her interests. Other people's value, according to the ethical egoist, is for us; and our value is for them.

Why might the egoist hold this view? It is that she thinks that the world is properly seen, understood, defined, and experienced from each individual's perspective. Each person is the moral, ontological, and epistemological center of her own universe. Just as we may consider the interests of others if doing so is the best way to promote our own interests, we may also listen to others if we think that doing so helps us (say, by enhancing our knowledge). Put differently, the egoist thinks all knowledge and morality begin within each individual. Other people may be brought into our epistemological and moral spheres, but only because of what they can do for us. And we can be brought into their sphere inasmuch as it benefits them.

Such a view is deeply mistaken. It reverses the true epistemological and moral priority. It is not that we are epistemological and moral hermits who eventually choose to learn from and interact with others. As we have seen throughout the book, our lives are inescapably intertwined with others from the beginning. We owe our lives as we know them to others. Civilization emerged over millennia, with each successive generation building on the knowledge, insights, values, and accomplishments of its ancestors. Without them we could not have art, history, science, or even language. Without language we could not speak. Nor could we think, or, if we could, our thoughts would only vaguely resemble thought as we know it. All our initial beliefs, interests, wishes, and values come from, and continue to be shaped by, others. We can deny these plain facts only at great peril.

None of this means that I should blindly adopt my society's views. I have argued throughout the book that blind adherence to the beliefs and values of others is arguably the principal source of moral evil. We must think for ourselves. However, in so doing we should not forget that we are able to do so only because of the intellectual gifts of those who came before. Others gave us language, exposed us to diverse ideas, taught us critical skills, and provided suitable background knowledge informing our deliberation.

Put more generally, our epistemological and moral dependence on others is primary, not derivative. We can come to think, live, and act on our own – but only to some degree, for we will always need others for physical and mental sustenance. We cannot provide for all our physical needs; we cannot make wise choices without information and critical feedback others provide. The extent to which we can become "independent" is itself heavily influenced by others. Independence more commonly arises in environments supporting independence. Some societies encourage free thinking, individual differences, and social experiments. Others encourage compliance and narrow-mindedness. It is not difficult to figure out which societies will have more free thinkers or more experiments in living, and which societies are more likely populated by herds of conformists. Ethical egoism is incompatible with these plain facts of human psychology. That is why ethical egoism is untenable.

Perhaps, though, a weaker form of egoism might be tenable. For instance, someone might recognize our dependence on and indebtedness to others yet contend that the best society would be one that teaches and encourages ethical egoism. I will confess, I cannot imagine that this is true; I think we are all far too vulnerable to factors over which we have no control (e.g., a hurricane that decimates our city). Still, we could allow small "experiments in living" to see. We can also evaluate their claims about how much interest one does, could, and should have in the interests of others – that was a central issue of the previous chapter. I think that arguments about stringency there can be extended to show why any strong form of ethical egoism is untenable.

REFERENCES

Dennett, D. (1978) *Brainstorms: Philosophical Essays on Mind and Psychology*. Cambridge, MA: MIT Press.

Dewey, J. (1976) *Lectures on Psychological and Political Ethics, 1898*. New York: Hafner Press.

Dewey, J. (1988/1922) *Human Nature and Conduct*. Carbondale, IL: Southern Illinois University Press.

Hocutt, M. (unpublished) "Interests, Self-Interests, and Egoism."

Hume, D. (1978/1740) *A Treatise of Human Nature*, 2nd edn. Oxford: Oxford University Press.

LaFollette, H. (1989) "Animal Rights and Human Wrongs." In N. Dower (ed.), *Ethics and the Environment*. Edinburgh: Gower Press, 79–90.

Lenski, G. and Lenski, F. (1968) *Human Societies*. New York: McGraw-Hill.

Mill, J. S. (1979) *Utilitarianism*. Indianapolis, IN: Hackett Publishing Company.

Nowell-Smith, P. H. (1957) *Ethics*. New York: Philosophical Library.

Parfit, D. (1984) *Reasons and Persons*. Oxford: Oxford University Press.

Rawls, J. (1999/1971) *A Theory of Justice*, 2nd edn. Cambridge, MA: Harvard University Press.

Regan, T. (1983) *The Case for Animal Rights*. Berkeley, CA: University of California Press.

Scheffler, S. (1992) *Human Morality*. Oxford: Oxford University Press.

Singer, P. (1990/1975) *Animal Liberation: A New Ethics for Our Treatment of Animals*, 2nd edn. New York: New York Review, distributed by Random House.

Slote, M. (1964) "An Empirical Basis for Psychological Egoism," *Journal of Philosophy* 61: 530–7.

PART SEVEN

Thinking Ahead

NINETEEN

Moral Speculations

If the arguments in this book are correct, then morality is more demanding than many people suppose. More demanding, but still not terribly demanding. We cannot properly require people to do more than we can reasonably think they are capable of doing, and we cannot reasonably expect most people to be moral saints. That being said, we should not forget that what we can reasonably expect of ourselves and others is not fixed. We can alter social and political institutions so that morality *is* less demanding (since more people carry their share). We can also alter our attitudes (individually and collaboratively) so that we do not experience morality's requirements as especially confining or costly. We can make ourselves people who want to be morally excellent. If we succeed, others will benefit. Given our psychological propensities to be satisfied by doing actions we want to do, then most of us, in most circumstances, can be satisfied living a reasonably demanding moral life.

I want to end with some speculations about ways that our moral responsibilities are more extensive than our strict obligations. Although I am unable to fully defend these claims here, I think each claim is plausible considering the arguments here and throughout the book.

Differential Obligations

There is an important, and generally unrecognized, corollary of the view that we should not require people to do more than we can reasonably expect them to do. Earlier arguments explained why we should not set moral expectations so high that only the most talented can reasonably follow them. At the same time, we should not set them so low that everyone can easily follow them. Instead, we set moral expectations at a level that most people can meet. We can then excuse or mitigate the responsibilities of individuals with special disabilities. For instance, we hold that a preteen has less weighty responsibilities than a normal adult. Why? Because we think the normal adult has more knowledge, skills, and control than the preteen. Although, as I argued earlier, claims about young children's deficiencies are overstated, children do not have the experience, understanding, appreciation, and abilities of a normal adult. If having especially low abilities diminishes responsibilities, then it seems that especially high abilities should increase them. The same considerations of fairness that impel us to hold the impaired less responsible should also lead us to expect more from the very talented. On this view then, morality imposes "differential obligations" based on each agent's ability to "pay": we set moral norms for the vast majority of people, and then can increase or decrease its demands depending on an agent's abilities. Doubtless many of those more talented will find this an unwelcome implication of the previous discussion. Many thinkers believe, or speak as if they believe, that each of us has precisely the same obligations. None of us should kill, steal, or rape. Each of us should do our share to promote the public good. On this view, the only circumstance under which someone could have more stringent obligations is if she voluntarily undertook them. A doctor will have a more stringent obligation than a plumber to help people with a medical emergency. A lifeguard will have a greater obligation than a passerby to rescue a drowning swimmer. They have these more stringent obligations only because they have voluntarily assumed them. I do not find this response plausible. To explain why, let us look more closely at factors that diminish obligations, then I will explain why an abundance of these same factors should heighten responsibility.

The grounds for differential obligations

Factors that alter our moral expectations

Knowledge

Those with (non-culpable) diminished knowledge have diminished obligations. As we noted earlier, if a three-year-old finds a gun, pulls the trigger, and kills her sibling, we do not hold her responsible for what she did. She does not understand or appreciate what a gun is, what death is, and how pulling the trigger might kill him; she does not, to use language introduced earlier, understand the temporal depth of action. What morally distinguishes the child from the standard adult is not her age, but her lack of relevant knowledge. To explain why, suppose an explorer brings a gun into a primitive village. The villagers have no familiarity with or knowledge of guns. If an adult villager accidentally finds the gun and kills a neighbor with it, we should not hold her responsible either. The lack of knowledge likely eliminates, and at least diminishes, her responsibilities.

It seems plausible to think that increased knowledge would increase responsibility. It certainly changes what we expect people to do, even if there is some debate over whether it changes what they are obligated to do. A Dutch mechanical engineer, who oversees all dikes in the Netherlands, is on holiday in Atlanta when Hurricane Katrina hits New Orleans. Barring excusing factors, we would expect her to offer her expertise to Louisiana authorities. We would not expect a Dutch anthropologist on holiday to do the same. We expect the engineer to help, not because she is a government employee, but because she has the relevant knowledge that the ordinary citizen (and the anthropologist) lacks. We doubtless have reasons to not hold her criminally liable if she fails to help. Nonetheless, most people would think badly of her if they thought she could have prevented the breach of several levees, thereby saving many innocent people, without seriously endangering her own life.

Abilities

We hold people with diminished abilities less responsible than those with average abilities. This is most obvious with physical disabilities. We will not expect a frail elderly person to save a drowning child, even if it is a deed that a hardy young man could do easily. If so, then it seems that heightened physical abilities would also increase certain moral responsibilities. We might not expect an average middle-aged man to protect a woman who is being assaulted. However, I suspect we would blame Mr. Universe if he were similarly passive. I have no doubt that were there a Super-man we would fault him if he failed to protect an innocent person from assault because he was too busy ogling Lois Lane.

If differences in physical skills entail different expectations and responsibilities, why not differences in mental or verbal skills? It seems only reasonable to expect an eloquent speaker (rather than a stutterer) to advocate an important policy. During a crisis, we would expect more of someone with extraordinary managerial skills than someone who is horribly shy. We expect more of all these people. Why shouldn't we also think that they have somewhat elevated moral responsibilities? We argued in the last chapter that a central rationale for specifying some limits on morality is to ensure that we do not make unreasonable expectations of people. By this reasoning, we should conclude that expecting the normal person to do the same as a very talented one is unreasonable; after all, the latter one can fulfill the requirements with less effort (they are less confining and costly). Thus, either the more talented person gets off relatively easily or the normal person must meet more demanding requirements. Both options seem unfair. Just as we can expect the normal person to do more than the one with disabilities, we can reasonably expect an exceptionally talented person to do more than the average person.

Ways we already recognize differential expectations

The previous discussion identifies a few ways in which we already recognize differential obligations. There are others.

Taxes

Few governments require each citizen to pay precisely the same tax (say, $1000). Most governments have some flat taxes: they assess taxes as a percentage of the person's income (or wealth or value of their property). They require everyone to pay, say, 10 percent of their incomes (2 percent of their property, etc.). Someone who makes $100,000 dollars pays more taxes than someone making $20,000, especially since most governments exclude some base income (say, the first $10,000) from taxation.

Many governments also have some progressive taxes, that is, they tax the wealthy at a higher *rate* than they tax the poor. Someone making $200,000 a year may pay 25 percent of her income in taxes, while someone making $50,000 may pay 10 percent. The rationale is clear: the rich can afford to pay more. The amount wealthy people are required to pay, although larger, does not diminish their financial well-being any more than – and probably less than – someone less well-off who pays a smaller percentage of her income in taxes. For instance, someone who pays a $100,000 tax on a $1 million annual income will be no more (and probably less) affected than will someone who pays a $1,000 tax on a $20,000 annual income. To use the earlier language, we assess taxes differently because we realize that requiring people to pay exactly the same amount of money is more demanding on the poor than on the wealthy.

Age and education

We also have varying expectations of people depending on their upbringing, age, and education. Contrast the following three people: a six-year-old brought up in a racist home, a relatively uneducated 15-year-old, and a person pursing a master's degree from a highly respected university. All believe that Munich is in Poland. Although the matter is not earth shattering, we will judge the latter person more harshly. Rightly so. We would judge that the latter person's ignorance is less excusable, although the matter is seemingly trivial. Now suppose they all hold the same belief with a decided moral dimension: all three believe the Holocaust never occurred. We might not judge the six-year-old harshly at all; we might simply assume she was repeating what she heard at home. We would expect the 15-year-old to know better, but we might also partly excuse her ignorance because of her age and inexperience, especially if she is from an overtly anti-Semitic home. However, we would not only hold the master's level student culpable for her ignorance – for surely she should know better – we would suspect that the ignorance is selective, born of a deep-seated hatred of Jews.

Time

Finally, our moral judgments about people vary with the time in which they lived. Other things being equal, it is morally worse for someone to be an open racist in 2005 than it was for our grandparents in 1955. Racism is racism; the attitude is heinous and the consequences for African-Americans are profound. Nonetheless, the grandparents' behavior is more understandable given the prevailing tenor of their times; that is why their behavior, although wrong, is less subject to moral censure. For them to have recognized the error of their ways would have taken considerable intelligence, insight, and courage. For them to have acted as they should have would have required moral heroism. In contrast, for us to be overt racists requires extreme moral blindness.

The previous examples are straightforward implications of the doctrine of the "reasonable person." Earlier we used that doctrine to justify limits on morality. However, if diminished abilities and intelligence, as well as changes in circumstances and time, can diminish our moral explanations on others, then increased abilities, etc., can legitimately heighten our moral responsibilities.

Doing More than is Required

Although in certain circumstances our moral obligations may be (or may be experienced as) stringent, overall they are relatively undemanding. To recall an earlier analogy, our moral responsibilities are similar to the expectations employers have of employees. Employers require only that employees do their job competently. They do not require all employees to be stellar – although they would be thrilled if many were. However, even if we may not require an especially talented worker to do more than an ordinarily talented worker, we would expect them to do more, and would be disappointed in them if they didn't. In a similar way, we would certainly not require even the most talented person to spend every waking moment on the moral job. However, we would likely expect that they would do more than required. Indeed, I think it is reasonable to expect others – and especially ourselves – to do more. It is not enough to ask what we morally *must* do. We should also ask: "What can I do to make this a better world?" One way in which we might do so is to cultivate naiveté in our relations with others.

Cultivated Naiveté

Most people decry naiveté; many claim that we should all be realists: that we see the world "as it really is." Children are naive because they do not know any better. That is one reason they are so vulnerable. However, as we become adults, we should, in the words of the Apostle Paul, "put away childish things." Perhaps. However, even if this is prudent advice, we cannot know what we should do until we know what the world is "really like." Many so-called "realists" think – or talk as if – the world is full of mean, selfish people who will stab you in the back if given half a chance. They implore us to be on guard against such people. We must find ways to protect ourselves from them, and, if need be, to return their meanness in kind. To not protect ourselves is imprudent. To assume other people are generally nice, reasonable, considerate, and open-minded is stupid.

To determine the merits of this claim, we must determine (a) if people are as selfish or malicious as this view suggests, and then decide (b) if the realist's proposed defensive stance is morally appropriate. I think both elements of the realist's position are dubious. I think the realist is mistaken about, or least misdescribes and misunderstands, most people's motivations. I also think that she is mistaken about the proper stance to take toward others. Let me explain.

Why "realism" is too pessimistic

Although I understand why people might embrace "realism," I think it is too pessimistic. No doubt some people are cruel. Indeed, we all are cruel sometimes. No doubt some people are inconsiderate. We all are inconsiderate sometimes. It *would* be silly idealism to deny that. Moreover, if we have hard evidence that someone is contemptible and manipulative, then surely the prudent, and perhaps the moral, response is to be on guard against her.

However, this view assumes that most – or at least many – people are intentionally malicious. I have argued throughout the book that that is not true. Immoral behavior is more often a product of inattention than malice. It occurs because people are not as perceptive or responsive as they ought to be. I will say a bit more about this later in the chapter. What is more relevant for the current discussion is: even if people are more malicious than I think they are, I think the realist is wrong about what we ought to do.

Why it is better to act as if realism were false

The realist contends that since many (most?) people are selfish or even malicious, we must take active steps to protect ourselves from them. Minimally we should be leery of anyone whom we have good reason to believe is unscrupulous. Although I do not think this advice is indisputable, it is plausible. That is why, if the realist stopped here, her position would be highly plausible. However, the realist takes a much stronger position. She contends that we should be wary of anyone whom we do not *know* to be decent, altruistic, and trustworthy. Since we do not and could not know enough about most people to know that they are decent, then the realist thinks we should be wary of virtually everyone: we should relate to others as if they were unscrupulous, as if they would take advantage of us if given half a chance.

In the previous section, we briefly saw why these beliefs about the character and motives of other humans are dubious. Here I want to give two further reasons for thinking we should not follow the realist's advice. One, this stance toward others increases the chance that we will systematically misinterpret their behavior in unflattering ways. Two, having done so, we are likely to relate to them in inappropriate ways; we thereby increase the chance that they will become more selfish and manipulative. Let me explain.

In Chapter 13 we saw that our assessment of others is shaped by our background beliefs, including our general background beliefs about what motivates people. If we think that all (or most) people are selfish, we will be far more likely to interpret other people's behavior as selfish, even if it is morally neutral. We are more likely to infer that they are driven by hidden selfish motives even when their action is wholly altruistic ("No one," we say, "is that good!"). And when people act on multiple motives – as most of us do – we will be more likely to ignore the most altruistic elements and interpret their behavior as wholly selfish. Once we interpret other people's behaviors in these unflattering ways, we will naturally relate to them as if they were selfish, unkind, insensitive, and manipulative. We should not be surprised to find that our expectations are often realized.

Especially given the aforementioned difficulties of accurately understanding others' behavior. Even when we try to be as fair as possible when interpreting their behavior, we often err. We always see others' behavior narrowly: we tend to focus on the effects of their actions on us. Far too often our "evidence" about their motives is drawn from a select (and perhaps uncharacteristic) behavior. Too often we do not understand their action since we do not understand the appropriate context. Rarely do we consider the other person's perspective. Together these factors explain why even the most sympathetic people tend to construe others' behaviors in less than flattering ways. The realist's proposal strengthens this tendency. We should, instead, find ways to counterbalance these biases. For when we relate to others as if they were selfish or malicious, we may not only make them *seem* more selfish, we may make them more selfish. After all, they are likely to think they must be guarded around us since, if they are also realists, they will think that we are selfishly motivated. And they, like us, will feel more justified in ignoring ordinary moral considerations when relating to someone they think unscrupulous.

How might we counterbalance these biases? I propose that we cultivate naiveté: that we should choose to "blind" ourselves to the faults of others. More precisely, we need not blind ourselves to their (and they to our) faults – there is no reason to deny the obvious. Rather, we should consciously choose not to focus on their faults but on their more positive traits. To put it differently, we should act as if they were less selfish, more honest, and more trustworthy than we might first think they are. This will help undermine our propensities to negatively construe their behavior. It will likely also affect how those other people behave. If we distrust others, they are likely to become less trustworthy, while if we trust them, we often find that they are more trustworthy (Derlega and Chaiken 1976; LaFollette and Graham 1986: 6). Think about it for a moment. If you meet someone who is friendly and openly trusting, are you likely to take advantage of them? I don't think so. Perhaps some people will. Nonetheless, many people will respond in kind – usually in sufficient numbers to make the person better off. Admittedly this strategy is risky. Others may occasionally hurt us. However, being systematically distrustful is not just risky: it guarantees that others will become people who are unlikely to be caring, sympathetic, and trusting toward us.

Preventing Ourselves from Doing Evil

Although most of us acknowledge that we are guilty of minor "sins," we do not think that we could consciously do anything *seriously* immoral. Therefore, we see no need to actively protect ourselves from that possibility.

This belief is profoundly dangerous. Most evils (serious wrongs) are not consciously chosen. That's not quite right. People may consciously choose to do what they do, and what they do may be evil. However, people rarely choose to do it *because* it is evil. When most people act immorally, they usually have some explanation for their actions – some way to construe their behavior as acceptable, necessary, understandable, or even morally required. They are blind to what they really do and why they do it. Few people realize the myriad ways that ordinary factors – their biases, their tendencies to make exceptions in their own favor, and their unwillingness or inability to understand other people's perspectives – can lead them to do morally outrageous acts. Fewer still take steps to constrain those factors.

For example, most of us excuse our behavior, even if we are outraged at similar behavior in others. When we lie to others we "justify" the lie to ourselves; but we become indignant when others lie to us. We have the same double standard as societies. We excuse our country's behavior even when it is clearly as bad (or worse) than another country's behavior that we roundly condemn. For instance, many Americans excuse war crimes committed by American soldiers (the mass murder of innocent civilians at Mi Lai and No Gun Ri, or the systematic torture of Iraqi prisoners in Abu Ghraib), yet still vilify British soldiers who killed five colonists who were part of a crowd that attacked them (the "Boston Massacre"). We cannot rationally embrace such patent inconsistency. Unfortunately, we often do what is rationally indefensible.

These propensities can usually be traced to our uncritical acceptance of what our parents, peers, teachers, preachers, and governments tell us. We adopt their teachings as if they were indubitably true, and then act upon them reflexively. It never occurs to us that they (and we) might be wrong. It never occurs to us that in our ignorance we may do morally hideous actions. We fail to grasp Arendt's profound insight that the world's worst evils (like those perpetrated by the Nazis) are usually banal, commonplace (1994/1963).

This is not an insight we should forget. Even a cursory glance at history reveals just how much evil is done by basically decent people. These people may not have *been* evil, but they certainly *did* much evil. As Mill notes in *On Liberty*, the people who killed Socrates and Jesus were not the riffraff of their respective ages, but were the religious and political leaders of their time (1985/1885: 23–4). These facts about evil are most obvious in the literature on genocide, torture, and other human rights atrocities. That literature chronicles the ways in which seemingly unimaginable evils are perpetrated by ordinary folk (Arendt 1994/1963; Ortiz 2002; Timerman 1981). The perpetrators of atrocities usually thought of themselves as fulfilling their duty; certainly they did not think of themselves as uniquely evil (Conroy 2002: 244–6). These facts should give us pause. If decent people can torture and kill others – and have little (if any) guilt for what they have done – then we are *all* capable of doing horrible evil under the right circumstances. Our only protection against such evil is diligence, care, education, openness, and self-reflection.

Conclusion

Doubtless when some of you looked at the table of contents you were amused or shocked. It is unlike any ethics book you have ever seen. Many ethics books focus on ethical theories, with perhaps some mention of practical ethical issues; others focus on practical ethical issues, with a bow to theory. A few discuss both, but those that do segregate those discussions. They might open with a few chapters on theory followed by a discussion of some practical issues. This one is different – sufficiently different that unless you understand its overarching aims, as described in the introduction, it would look as if I had written the chapters, tossed them on the floor, and then arranged them in the order in which I picked them up.

There is method in this madness. As I explained from the beginning, I am convinced that normative theory, meta-theory, and practical ethics are not distinct inquiries, but three elements of the practice of ethics. Each informs and is informed by the other. My aim in this book is to show this deep connection. That dictates the order of the chapters. Since I wanted to show that theorizing arises from thinking about practical issues, I had to begin by first discussing a few practical issues and then showing how, in our attempts to reason about them, we are impelled to theorize.

I also wanted to show that – and how – normative and meta-theories are informed by discussion of practical issues. That is why I typically discuss theoretical issues in multiple chapters as they are prompted by practical inquiry. This approach is most obvious in my discussion of the doing/allowing distinction, the discussion of freedom and responsibility, and in my explication and defense of a pragmatist approach to ethics. I first noted the doing/allowing distinction in "Using and Sharpening the Theoretical Tools," and then, having mentioned it in passing in several later chapters, I returned to examine it more carefully in "Is Morality Demanding?"

I explored notions of freedom and responsibility initially in the first chapter, more fully in "Death, Dying, and Physician-assisted Suicide," and then completed the discussion in "Autonomy, Children, and Paternalism." Finally, I first introduced a central feature of pragmatism (the notion of habits) in the first chapter, explained the nature and role of habits more fully in "Racism," and then completed the discussion of a pragmatist approach in "Character, Virtue Ethics, and Pragmatism."

I did this to illustrate one way of tracing the implications of practical issues for normative and meta-theorizing, and also to show the implications of theoretical reflection for practical ethical issues. If I am right, theory and practice are not distinct disciplines but rather interrelated subdisciplines – all part of ethics, broadly speaking. Advance in each will come in concert, not separately.

REFERENCES

Arendt, H. (1994/1963) *Eichmann in Jerusalem: A Report on the Banality of Evil*. New York: Penguin Books.
Conroy, J. (2002) *Unspeakable Acts, Ordinary People: The Dynamics of Torture*. Berkeley, CA: University of California Press.

Derlega, V. J. and Chaiken, A. L. (1976) *Shared Intimacy*. Englewood Cliffs, NJ: Prentice-Hall.

LaFollette, H. and Graham, G. (1986) "Honesty and Intimacy," *Journal of Social and Personal Relationships* 3: 3–18.

Mill, J. S. (1985/1885) *On Liberty*. Indianapolis, IN: Hackett Publishing Company.

Ortiz, S. D. (2002) *The Blindfold's Eyes*. Maryknoll, NY: Orbis Books.

Timerman, J. (1981) *Prisoner without a Name, Cell without a Number*. Madison, WI: University of Wisconsin Press.

Index